LIBRARY OF HEBREW BIBLE/ OLD TESTAMENT STUDIES

506

Formerly Journal for the Study of the Old Testament Supplement Series

THE INTERTEXTUALITY OF ZECHARIAH 1–8

Michael R. Stead

t&t clark

NEW YORK • LONDON

T & T Clark International, 80 Maiden Lane, New York, NY 10038

T & T Clark International, The Tower Building, 11 York Road, London SE1 7NX

T & T Clark International is a Continuum imprint.

Visit the T & T Clark blog at www.tandtclarkblog.com

A catalog record for this book is available from the Library of Congress.

ISBN-13: 978-0-567-29172-1
ISBN-10: 0-567-29172-3

06 07 08 09 10 10 9 8 7 6 5 4 3 2 1

CONTENTS

PREFACE

This book is a revised version of my doctoral thesis, which was submitted to the University of Gloucestershire in 2007. My doctoral research was supervised by Professor Gordon McConville, and I wish to express my gratitude to Gordon for his careful scholarship, wisdom, support and encouragement during this time, and for his ongoing friendship. I also wish to thank Dr Barry Webb, of Moore Theological College in Sydney, Australia, who assisted Gordon in my supervision, and who first stimulated my interest in Zechariah. I could not have wished for a better supervisory team.

I wish to thank my two examiners, Professor Robert Gordon and Dr Janet Tollington, for their helpful comments on my thesis. These comments have enabled me to sharpen and clarify my arguments. Similarly, my thanks go to Professor Carol Meyers for her insightful comments on an earlier version of this manuscript. I am likewise indebted to a number of "Zechariah" scholars who were gracious enough to send me pre-publication versions of their essays, and to read and comment on material that I had been working on—to Mark, Michael, Al and others, I am deeply grateful.

Special thanks go to family members, to friends and to my congregation of St James' Anglican Church, Turramurra, for their support and encouragement, and for the generosity of some anonymous benefactors who made it financially possible for me to complete my research. Thanks also to the staff of Moore College Library, where I was based for most of my research.

My most heartfelt thanks go to my wife, Felicity, who has been a source of ideas, my proof-reader, research assistant and constant companion and for her love, encouragement and support on this long journey.

This book is dedicated to Felicity, and to our three children, Calvin, Verity and Nathaniel.

ABBREVIATIONS

ABR	*Australian Biblical Review*
AJSL	*American Journal of Semitic Languages and Literature*
ANET	*Ancient Near Eastern Texts Relating to the Old Testament*. Edited by J. B. Pritchard. 3d ed. Princeton, 1969
AUSS	*Andrews University Seminary Studies*
BDB	Brown, F., S. R. Driver, and C. A. Briggs. *A Hebrew and English Lexicon of the Old Testament*. Oxford, 1907
BHS	*Biblia Hebraica Stuttgartensia*. Edited by K. Elliger and W. Rudolph. Stuttgart, 1983
Bib	*Biblica*
BibInt	*Biblical Interpretation*
BK	*Bibel und Kirche*
BN	*Biblische Notizen*
BR	*Biblical Research*
BZ	*Biblische Zeitschrift*
BZAW	Beihefte zur Zeitschrift für die alttestamentliche Wissenschaft
CBQ	*Catholic Biblical Quarterly*
CurBS	*Currents in Research: Biblical Studies*
DCH	*Dictionary of Classical Hebrew*. Edited by D. J. A. Clines. Sheffield, 1993–
ESM	European Seminar in Historical Methodology
ESV	English Standard Version of the Bible
EvQ	*Evangelical Quarterly*
ExpTim	*Expository Times*
FOTL	Forms of the Old Testament Literature
GKC	*Gesenius' Hebrew Grammar*. Edited by E. Kautzsch. Translated by A. E. Cowley. 2d. ed. Oxford, 1910
HALOT	Koehler, L., W. Baumgartner, and J. J. Stamm, *The Hebrew and Aramaic Lexicon of the Old Testament*. Translated and edited under the supervision of M. E. J. Richardson. 4 vols. Leiden, 1994–99
HAR	*Hebrew Annual Review*
HeyJ	*Heythrop Journal*
HS	*Hebrew Studies*

HTR	*Harvard Theological Review*
ICC	International Critical Commentary
IEJ	*Israel Exploration Journal*
Int	*Interpretation*
JAOS	*Journal of the American Oriental Society*
JBL	*Journal of Biblical Literature*
JBQ	*Jewish Bible Quarterly*
JETS	*Journal of the Evangelical Theological Society*
JJS	*Journal of Jewish Studies*
JNES	*Journal of Near Eastern Studies*
JNSL	*Journal of Northwest Semitic Languages*
JPS	Jewish Publication Society Tanakh
JQR	*Jewish Quarterly Review*
JSNTSup	Journal for the Study of the New Testament: Supplement Series
JSOT	*Journal for the Study of the Old Testament*
JSOT	*Journal for the Study of the Old Testament*
JSOTSup	Journal for the Study of the Old Testament: Supplement Series
JSPSup	Journal for the Study of the Pseudepigrapha: Supplement Series
JTS	*Journal of Theological Studies*
LBH	Late Biblical Hebrew
LHBOTS	Library of Hebrew Bible/Old Testament Studies
LSTS	Library of Second Temple Studies
LXX	Septuagint
MT	Masoretic Text
NAB	New American Bible
NASB	New American Standard Version of the Bible
NCBC	New Century Bible Commentary
NEB	New English Bible
NIB	*The New Interpreter's Bible*
NIV	New International Version of the Bible
NRSV	New Revised Standard Version
OTE	*Old Testament Essays*
PEQ	*Palestine Exploration Quarterly*
PTR	*Princeton Theological Review*
RB	*Revue biblique*
RSV	Revised Standard Version of the Bible
SJOT	*Scandinavian Journal of the Old Testament*
ST	*Studia Theologica*
TA	*Tel Aviv*
TDOT	*Theological Dictionary of the Old Testament*. Edited by G. J. Botterweck and H. Ringgren. Translated by J. T. Willis, G. W. Bromiley, and D. E. Green. 8 vols. Grand Rapids, 1974–
TynBul	*Tyndale Bulletin*

USQR	*Union Seminary Quarterly Review*
VT	*Vetus Testamentum*
VTSup	Vetus Testamentum Supplements
WBC	Word Biblical Commentary
ZAW	*Zeitschrift für die alttestamentliche Wissenschaft*

Chapter 1

INTRODUCTION

1.1. *Zechariah and "the Former Prophets"*

The books of Haggai, Zechariah and Malachi stand at a peculiar moment in history, one which sets them apart from the works of the classical prophets.[1] This peculiarity is a function both of their historical relationship to the classical prophets, and of their literary relationship to these earlier prophetic works.

In terms of their historical relationship, the most significant feature is that Haggai, Zechariah and Malachi stand on the other side of the return from the exile. That which had been promised by some of the classical prophets—the judgment of exile and the subsequent return from exile—had in fact occurred, which had the effect of validating these earlier prophets in no uncertain terms.[2] However, at the same time, the experience of that post-exilic generation fell far short of the glorious restoration promised by these same prophets.

In terms of their literary relationship, Haggai, Zechariah and Malachi are written at a time when—apparently—the works of the classical prophets are circulating in written (rather than oral) form.[3] This is not

1. I shall use the expression "classical prophets" to refer to the prophets from the eighth century B.C.E. onwards, including those active during the exile (e.g. Ezekiel), but not including any post-exilic prophets.

2. Contra Carroll (1979), who argues that classical prophecy had "failed." However, as noted by Mason (in response to Carroll), "[i]t is strange that, if earlier prophecy were regarded as having proved such a 'failure', the post-exilic period should have been the time when the present prophetic collections were formed and invested with increasing authority" (1982a: 141). For a recent similar critique, see Floyd 2006b.

3. Writing in Israel goes back at least as far as the Iron Age (Millard 1995). Even the Scandinavian school (e.g. Nyberg and Nielsen), which argues that prophecy underwent a long period of oral tradition before reaching a written form, nonetheless views the crisis of exile as a catalyst for the transition into a literary tradition. Thus, even on this model (which I remain sceptical about), the classical prophets had

to prejudge the question as to whether (say) Jeremiah had reached its final form by 520 B.C.E. (a question to which I shall return in Chapter 3), but only to make the point that, by this stage in history, there is a known corpus of written works—in some form—from the classical prophets. This observation as to the literary context of the early post-exilic period is especially significant for our understanding of the book of Zechariah, for it appears that Zechariah in particular is written *with reference to* the works of the classical prophets. To an extent not paralleled in Haggai and Malachi, the book of Zechariah as a whole makes repeated allusion to the classical prophets. This phenomenon has long been the subject of study with respect to Zech 9–14. Beginning with the groundbreaking work of Stade (1881; 1882a; 1882b), there have been a number of studies tracing the connections between Zech 9–14 and words of the prophets, including the works of Delcor (1952), Mason (1973; 1977a; 1982b), Willi-Plein (1974), Person (1993), Schaefer (1993), Larkin (1994), Tai (1996) and Nurmela (1996). However, much less work has been done on investigating this same phenomenon in Zech 1–8. It is the re-use of the classical prophets in Zech 1–8 which will be our particular focus.

As this study will demonstrate, Zech 1–8 engages in an intertextual dialogue with a wide variety of biblical traditions. However, the prophetic tradition is by far the most significant. From its opening paragraph, Zech 1–8 makes explicit that it is to be understood in the context of "the former prophets" (הַנְּבִיאִים הָרִאשֹׁנִים, Zech 1:4). As Floyd (2000: 306) notes, "The introduction in 1:1–6 programmatically defines the capacity of prophecy to outlive the generation to which it was originally addressed."[4] The ongoing currency of these former prophets in Zechariah's day is further underscored by a number of unmistakable allusions in Zech 1–8 to the books of Jeremiah (e.g. the "Branch," "seventy years"), Ezekiel (e.g. the vision of the measuring of the temple) and Isaiah (e.g. the pilgrimage of the nations in Isa 2). The aim of this study is to examine the nature, extent and effect of these allusions in Zech 1–8.

I will argue that Zech 1–8 takes up formerly disparate streams of tradition—especially various streams of the prophetic tradition—and

reached a literary form by the post-exilic period. Furthermore, it is established that, whether or not the general populace was literate in the early post-exilic period, there clearly was a literate subsection of population, and that writing was, by that stage, the preferred medium for preserving prophecy (see further Tollington 1993: 12–19). On the impact of the more recent "revisionist" theories of Davies and others, see further §3.1 below. These theories are well countered by Schniedewind (see esp. 2004: 167–82), who argues that the available evidence challenges the notion that the Persian period was a time of flourishing literary production.

4. So similarly Mason 1976: 234.

creatively combines these traditions in applying them to a post-exilic context. While the phenomenon of one prophet building upon the message of another is hardly unique to Zechariah,[5] what is distinctive about Zech 1–8 is the breadth of the prophetic material which it draws upon. Because it emerges at a later stage in Israel's history, Zech 1–8 has a rich palette of prophetic traditions (and other biblical traditions) to work with. The thing that is new in Zech 1–8 is the reading together of, for example, the Zion tradition of Isa 40–55 with the Davidic hopes of Jer 23 and 33 and the temple-centric restoration program of Ezek 40–48. The kind of reading-together I am suggesting is not some kind of bald conflation which ignores the different emphases. Rather, Zech 1–8 has taken different "melody lines" from the various streams of prophetic tradition and rewritten these into a symphony, with different voices in harmony.

Zechariah 1–8 understands itself to be a genuine revelatory new word from Yahweh, which—paradoxically—comes via a reiteration of (some of) the things that Yahweh has already said through "the former prophets." However, this reiteration occurs in a radically different (i.e. post-exilic) context, and that recontextualization causes various shifts in how those former words were understood to apply.

1.2. *Zechariah and the "Fulfilment" of the Former Prophets*

There is no scholarly consensus on the nature of Zechariah's relationship to the classical prophets. There are three broad approaches: some argue that Zech 1–8 anticipates an imminent fulfilment of the classical prophets, while others argue that it defers these hopes to some future generation, and yet others argue that Zech 1–8 demonstrates the emergence of (proto-)apocalyptic, as the hopes for fulfilment are transferred into an eschatological realm.

1.2.1. *Continuity or Discontinuity with the Prophetic Tradition?*

A number of scholars have examined the extent of continuity (and/or discontinuity) of the message of Zech 1–8 with the classical prophetic tradition.

Christian Jeremias (1977) was one of the first to examine closely the re-use of prophetic traditions in the night-visions of Zech 1–6. Jeremias recognizes Zechariah's links to the prophets spanning from Amos to Deutero-Isaiah and Ezekiel (1977: 228). In my analysis which follows, I am in agreement with many of the conclusions of Jeremias.

5. One thinks, for example, of Hosea's metaphors being developed in the book of Jeremiah, or the re-use of Mic 4 in Isa 2 (or vice versa).

The other main component of Zech 1–8 is its oracles, which were examined comprehensively by Albert Petitjean (1969). Petitjean concludes that Zechariah's programme of restoration in Zech 1–8 comes from the former prophets, principally Jeremiah, Ezekiel and Deutero-Isaiah.[6]

Susan Niditch (1983) traced the development of the "symbolic vision." Niditch argues that Zechariah's night-visions[7] are a development of the classical symbolic vision as exemplified in Amos and Jeremiah, exhibiting an increasing mythologization of symbol objects and symbolism, and a lessening of traditional stylistic elements (Niditch 1983: 74). Niditch's work demonstrates that Zechariah's symbolic visions are firmly rooted in the Israelite prophetic tradition.[8] Niditch's wider thesis on the chronological development of the symbolic vision form is of limited applicability to our present enquiry.[9]

Janet Tollington (1993) examined the extent to which Haggai and Zech 1–8 are a continuation of, or a divergence from, the classical prophetic traditions and ideas.[10] She concludes that oracles, visions and symbolic actions were forms of prophecy which Haggai and Zechariah used in common with their classical predecessors. However, whereas Haggai favoured the traditional style of the proclamation of oracles, Tollington argues that Zechariah marks a transition to "literary" prophecy, in that its message is conveyed by means of a literary composition rather than through an oral ministry alone. She makes a cogent argument for the literary nature of Zechariah's prophecy based on the tight integration and interrelationship between vision and oracle in Zech 1–6. Tollington

6. "Fortement marques par l'influence des prophètes antérieurs, principalement de Jérémie, d'Ézéchiel et du Second Isaïe, les oracles de Zacharie experiment cependant une pensée dense et originale" (Petitjean 1969: 441).

7. Niditch's analysis examines five visions of Zechariah (5:1–4; 4:1–14; 2:1–4; 1:7–17; 6:1–8).

8. Contra, e.g., Collins (1977: 86) who suggests that Zechariah may have borrowed the symbolic vision from the Babylonians.

9. Niditch argues for an evolving development in the form in Zechariah's visions. However, the evolutionary trend which she argues for is based on re-ordering the visions to the sequence 5:1–4; 4:1–14; 2:1–4; 1:7–17; 6:1–8), and the omission of several of the visions. Niditch regards Zech 2:5–9 and 5:5–11 as "experiments" which have "strayed off the mainstream of development" (1983: 10 n. 22), though conceding later in her argument that Zech 5:5–11 "in terms of superficial structure is like visions II, I and VIII" (1983: 165). Niditch does not consider Zech 3 in her analysis.

10. Tollington also traces the points at which Haggai and Zechariah go back to traditions of even earlier times, noting especially the motif "Yahweh of Hosts" and the role of angels.

argues that, although the message of both Haggai and Zechariah obviously differs from their predecessors as a result of the changed social, political and cultural circumstances of the restoration period, Haggai and Zechariah clearly stand in the mainstream of the classical prophetic tradition in many respects, and in particular their expectations regarding the leadership of the community, Yahweh's judgment on his people and the place of the nations. She does, however, detect a degree of "innovation" in Zechariah's divergence from the tradition at points—manifest, for example, in the endorsement of temporary diarchic rule, and in his stance towards universal salvation. There is much to agree with in Tollington's analysis, though at points I will take a divergent path on the reading of the significance of some of the details. Tollington concludes that, while Haggai stood firmly in the classical prophetic tradition, Zechariah was more innovative in both prophetic method and in the theological ideas he proclaimed.

Risto Nurmela (1996) investigates inner-biblical allusion between the book of Zechariah and other Old Testament books. With respect to Zech 1–8, he finds evidence that Zechariah predominantly relies on Jeremiah (with allusions to 15 passages), and also depends on both Isaiah and Ezekiel in roughly equal measure (seven allusions each). With respect to the minor prophets, he detects allusions only to Hosea and Haggai. By examining the dominant theme of the passages being alluded to, Nurmela discerns that Zech 1–8 consistently uses allusions to stress the theme of salvation. He also notes that Zechariah's allusions to Isaiah are limited to Proto-Isaiah.[11] Nurmela uses the evidence of allusion in Zechariah to draw conclusions as to the possible redactional growth of the Isaiah corpus.[12]

Nurmela's work is significant for its methodological approach. He argues for a strict method based on counting the number of textual features in common, which allows him to grade allusions on a scale spanning "sure" to "probable" to "possible." While the mathematical precision of this method has some appeal, it has the effect of creating a very limited field of enquiry. I will return to this issue in the next chapter, to argue that the method which Nurmela advocates is not sensitive to the manner in which texts are re-used in Zechariah.

11. Although it should be noted that this conclusion depends on his assessment that Isa 52:8–9 alludes to Zech 1:16–17, rather than the reverse (as is typically taken to be the case). On this, see further §4.4 below.

12. See also Nurmela 2003.

It is instructive to compare Nurmela's method with that of Holger Delkurt (2000). Delkurt's treatment is both narrower in scope (only examining Zechariah's night-visions) yet at the same time is wider in focus, in that his *traditionsgeschichtlich* approach examines the re-use of the prophetic tradition, and not merely "textual" repetition (as per Nurmela). Delkurt concludes that Zechariah draws in particular on the traditions of Deutero-Isaiah (especially the Zion tradition and the promise of unconditional salvation) in order to give his hearers confidence that Yahweh is able and willing to fulfil all his promises. Delkurt also concludes that, while the thematic connections are strongest with Deutero-Isaiah, the textual connections are strongest with Ezekiel (especially with Ezek 1–3; 8–11; 38–39; 40–48). With respect to Ezek 40–48, Delkurt argues that Zechariah takes up this vision in order to argue critically with it.[13] Delkurt also detects multiple allusions to Proto-Isaiah, Amos, Hosea, Micah, Habakkuk and Jeremiah.[14]

Nurmela and Delkurt come to the opposite conclusion *vis-à-vis* Isa 40–55 because of different methodological presuppositions, reflected in a "textual" versus "thematic" approach. This raises the question as to which is the most appropriate method to apply to Zech 1–8. I shall examine this issue in the following chapter.

1.2.2. *Zechariah 1–8 and the Emergence of Apocalyptic*

A second way of explaining how Zech 1–8 has taken up classical prophecy is to relate it to the emergence of "apocalyptic." It is argued that the dissonance between the promises of the classical prophets and the hard facts of life in the early post-exilic period resulted in a shift away from the expectation of an historical fulfilment and towards an eschatological one. On this line of argument, one might say that Zech 1–8 is prophecy transposed to a different key, resulting in a "proto-apocalyptic" work.

In the early 1970s, a number of scholars argued for a connection between Zech 1–8 and apocalyptic literature. In 1972, Robert North argued that there are elements of apocalyptic in Zech 1–8, but that "[f]irst-Zechariah, like the greatest classic prophets, is completely enmeshed in a concrete moment of history which his oracles depict and interpret and improve" (1972: 70). In the same year (and indeed, at the same Uppsala Colloquium), Samuel Amsler (1972) traced the origin of apocalyptic to Zech 1–8. Similarly, in 1973, Hartmut Gese described the

13. So similarly Petersen 1984b and Bosshard-Nepustil 1997: 387.

14. For details, see Delkurt 2000: 321–24.

night-visions of Zechariah as an apocalypse, and labelled Zechariah as the "ersten Apokalyptiker" (1973: 39), arguing that the night-visions anticipate the transcendental intervention of Yahweh to inaugurate the new age (1973: 37). In reply to Gese, Jeremias found that the distinctive elements of apocalyptic were not present in Zechariah's night-visions, and concluded that Zechariah takes an intermediate position somewhere between classical prophecy and apocalyptic (1977: 227).

Against the position of Gese, Paul Hanson, building on Plöger (1968), argues that Zech 1–8 reflects an opposite worldview to apocalyptic eschatology, even if at points it anticipates some apocalyptic motifs. In Hanson's schema, true "apocalyptic" expects a cosmic redemption by Yahweh alone, unrelated to the particulars of historical events (1979: 244–45). Hanson argues that, in contrast, Zech 1–8 is very much tied to the historical events of the early post-exilic period, and any apparent similarities to apocalyptic were only because "[t]he genre of the vision was used by Zechariah as a literary device in a campaign to win popular support for the hierocratic temple program" (1979: 258).

Stephen Cook (1995) continues Hanson's project of a sociological explanation of the origins of apocalyptic, but arrives at the opposite conclusion to Hanson regarding Zech 1–8. Cook traces the origin of apocalyptic to the second temple Zadokite leadership. He argues (contra Wellhausen and Hanson) that Zech 1–8 is not concerned with the mundane task of restoring Yehud, but implies rather that salvation will only come through the intervention of the transcendent into human history. Cook argues that Zech 1–8 expresses a radical eschatology and a dualism between this age and the age to come. Based on these family resemblances with later apocalyptic literature, Cook affirms that Zech 1–8 is indeed "proto-apocalyptic."[15] More recently still, John Collins (2003) has questioned Cook's assessment of the radical nature of Zechariah's eschatology. Collins finds that the eschatology of Zechariah is not apocalyptic "in any plausible sense of the word" (2003: 82). Instead, he argues that Zechariah anticipated the imminent fulfilment—in history—of the prophetic hopes, particularly the promise of a messiah.

A different approach to the question of Zechariah and apocalyptic is adopted by Eibert Tigchelaar. Tigchelaar describes his work as an "historical approach to the phenomenon of apocalyptic" (1996: 15), in which apocalyptic literature is explained as a literary (rather than, as per Hanson and Cook, a sociological and anthropological) phenomenon. For Tigchelaar, a characteristic mark of apocalyptic is that "revelation stems

15. For another assessment of Zech 1–8 as "apocalyptic," see Knibb 1982.

from the interpretation of tradition" (1996: 260). Tigchelaar argues that Zech 1–8 evinces such a shift towards apocalyptic thinking, in that it is the interpretation of the "prophets of old" which has become a new revelation (1996: 244).[16]

One's assessment of these various "apocalyptic" approaches to Zechariah will depend both on one's definition of apocalyptic,[17] and on the exegesis of particular texts in Zechariah where this apocalyptic shift is argued to have occurred. I shall examine this issue in Chapter 4, and come to the conclusion that Zech 1–8 reflects an imminent eschatology, and does not transfer hopes to an eschatological realm as one might expect in apocalyptic literature.

1.2.3. *Zechariah 1–8 as a Future Expression of the Prophetic Hope*

A third way of understanding the relationship of Zech 1–8 to classical prophecy is in some senses the counter-point of the second. Whereas apocalyptic transposes the prophetic hope into a fulfilment beyond the realm of plain history, this approach affirms the promises of the classical prophets as something still yet to be fulfilled in history, but in a future period. A key issue is the messianic hope (or otherwise) of Zech 1–8.

Walter Rose (2000) argues that Zech 1–8 does promise a messianic figure—"Zemah" (צֶמַח)—who will build the temple and rule, but that this promise is referring to a future figure, and should not be identified with the historical figure of Zerubbabel. Rose also argues (against the typical interpretation of a political diarchy between governor and priest) that there is no promise of a joint rule by king and priest.

The recent dissertation of Anthony Petterson (2006) argues that there is a strong Davidic hope in both Zech 1–8 and 9–14. Petterson's approach differs from Rose's in a number of important respects (most notably in

16. However, it is damaging to Tigchelaar's thesis that, in order to find "apocalyptic" elements in Zech 1–8, he must argue for extensive parallels with "traditional mythic and magical language" (1996: 53) in wider ancient Near Eastern literature, which few will find convincing. For example, the artisans who startle and expel the "four horns" are argued to be picking up a Ugaritic mythic background (1996: 51–54), or the argument that the "flying curse" of Zech 5 is an allusion to an Akkadian myth (1996: 58). As will be argued below, the Israelite prophetic tradition provides closer parallels for these elements, but without the mythical/magical/apocalyptic overtones that Tigchelaar argues for.

17. For my part, I shall follow the definitions proposed by J. J. Collins. For Collins's summary of the features of apocalyptic, see Collins 1979: 21–27, and cf. the definitions in Hanson 1987c: 25–38. However, I note the recent call for new definitions of apocalyptic and its relationship to prophecy by Grabbe (2003), and the strong rejoinder by Collins (2003) in the same volume (Grabbe and Haak 2003).

his recognition of the importance of Jer 22, 23 and 33 for the meaning of צֶמַח in Zech 3 and 6), but is like it in as much that it views the promise of the "Branch" to be pointing forward to a future messianic figure.

Thomas Pola (2003a) does not accept the view (common since Wellhausen) that the text of Zech 1–8 has been redacted because of the "failure" of Zerubbabel to live up to messianic expectations. Rather, he argues that Zerubbabel's role was merely to lay the foundation of the temple, in order for the priesthood and cult to be reinstituted. Pola draws this conclusion from the fact that the cult is the focus of attention in Zech 1–6. The prophet Zechariah does not consider his age to be the moment for the ultimate fulfilment of the messianic hopes. In the interim, it is the cultic realm which is the bearer of the eschatological hopes, as a sign of the expected Messiah. On Pola's reading, Zech 1–6 is thus both hope-deferred and hope-transferred.

While this "future-hope" approach is an attractive solution to the problem of non-fulfilment, it remains to be seen whether the exegesis of the key texts in Zech 3 and 4 can sustain this interpretation. I will examine this in detail in Chapter 5, and conclude that these chapters are depicting events in Zechariah's era, rather than deferring them into an indeterminate future.

That there are these three manifestly different approaches to the question of Zechariah's use of the classical prophets stems in part from the questions of history, regarding both the history of the sixth and fifth centuries B.C.E., and of the history of the text of Zech 1–8. There is still much debate with respect to the history of the period. Was the early post-exilic period (to borrow a phrase from Albertz) "a thwarted restoration"?[18] What actually happened to Zerubbabel? What was the nature of the leadership in Yehud? Speculations about these historical questions have raised other questions related to the textual history of Zech 1–8. For example, do we suppose (with Wellhausen) that Zerubbabel has been removed from key texts because of a failure to meet messianic expectations? Was Zech 3 added to the text to strengthen the monopoly of the priesthood (so Sinclair 1975) and/or was the promise of the "Branch" a later addition of the chapter intended to restore an emphasis on the Davidic monarchy (so Petersen 1984a: 214)? Furthermore, to what extent is Zech 1–8 the product of a redaction in a chronistic milieu (so Beuken 1967)?

18. See further Albertz 2003b.

1.2.4. *Literary Approaches to Zechariah's Intertextuality*

Perhaps in response to these (seemingly intractable) questions of history, in recent times there have been a number of examinations of Zech 1–8 in its literary context alone that seek to bypass these thorny questions of history.

Edgar Conrad (1999) offers a reading of Zechariah in the context of the Book of the Twelve. Conrad subdivides the Book of the Twelve into Hosea–Zephaniah (which he takes to be "the former prophets") and Haggai–Malachi (covering the Persian period). Conrad argues that, in the former era, God spoke to his people through the message of prophets, but in the Persian period, God deals directly with his people via messengers, and that this shift from prophets to messengers is evidenced in the book of Zechariah. In the eight "scenes" in Zech 1–6, the prophet Zechariah is initially one who interacts with messengers, but is drawn into the drama to the point where he himself performs and speaks as a messenger of Yahweh. Conrad argues that Zech 1–6 is not composed of "night-visions" (so most) but of "seeings," in which Zechariah sees real objects in the temple, and understands them to have symbolic significance (e.g. the vision of four horns of Zech 2:1–4 has arisen from seeing the four horns of the altar). The various elements which Zechariah sees all give metaphorical expression to Yahweh's promise "I am with you."

Mark Love (1999) employs various methodologies developed by structuralist and post-structuralist literary theorists in an attempt to penetrate the symbolic logic of Zech 1–8. Initially, he attempts to understand Zech 1–8 as a self-contained literary unit, but concludes that Zech 1–8 alone provides too few clues to explain its symbols. Love then makes a second attempt to understand the symbols, this time with reference to the intertextual links in the wider canon of the Hebrew Bible. However, he finds that this approach again fails to explain the symbols, this time because there are too many possible clues, but none sufficiently determinative. Love concludes that Zech 1–8 frequently appears to suggest sources for discerning its meaning by its phraseology, its quoting and its discussions of other texts, but then fails to provide the promised cessation of the signifying chain when the significance of the suggested key to decipherment is considered. The text is evasive, and this "unreadability" requires us to develop a hermeneutic to read the unreadable as such, rather than accede to the modernist obsession to wrest meaning from texts. Love argues that we must accept that meaning is found as much in its absence as in its content.

Love's conclusion raises sharply the issue as to whether the search for intertexts is going to be a help or a hindrance in our understanding of

Zech 1–8. Furthermore, these kinds of literary approaches to the text raise the question about whether we can legitimately bypass the thorny questions of history. I shall return to these questions in Chapters 5 and 6.

1.3. *Open Questions*

This variety of very different approaches suggests that there are still a number of open questions in regard to the re-use of the prophetic tradition in Zech 1–8:

- To which parts of the prophetic tradition does Zech 1–8 allude? This raises an important subsidiary question about the criteria by which one might determine valid instances of allusions.
- How are the messages of the "former prophets" applied to the early post-exilic context? That is to say, to what extent are the words of the former prophets expected to apply in the immediate context, deferred to a future historical moment, transferred to the eschatological realm and/or rejected as no longer applicable?
- What is the rhetorical effect and theological significance of the re-use of texts in Zech 1–8?

Although the focus of my investigation is on the allusions in Zech 1–8 to "the former prophets," it is necessary to make the Hebrew Bible as a whole the field of enquiry. This is necessary for two reasons. First, because in order to have confidence that a given intertext is the most likely source behind a passage in Zech 1–8, it is necessary to demonstrate that there is not another better intertext elsewhere. If we restrict our enquiry to the "former prophets" alone, there is no way to determine this. Secondly, a broad field of enquiry is also necessary because Zech 1–8 often incorporates material from multiple source texts, combining prophetic and non-prophetic texts into a composite whole. For example, we shall see that the divine council scene in Zech 3 combines elements from both Isa 6 and Job 1–2, and that the depiction of Joshua's reclothing weaves together both Exod 28–29 and Ezek 44. For these reasons, our enquiry will examine the intertextuality of Zech 1–8 as a whole, even though our particular interest is in the re-use of "former prophets."

1.4. *Overview*

Previous research in this field has been hampered by a dichotomy between diachronic and synchronic approaches to the text. In Chapter 2 I will argue for an approach which combines elements of both. Zechariah 1–8 is a work situated in twin contexts—the historical context of the early post-exilic period, and the literary context of "the former prophets" (הַנְּבִיאִים הָרִאשֹׁנִים). I argue that we need to pursue an approach which is sensitive to both contexts, which I dub a *contextual intertextuality*. I demonstrate that this approach falls under the rubric of intertextuality, as classically defined and presently practised. In applying this contextual intertextual approach, I recognize that Zech 1–8 is not a timeless text which could apply equally to any point in history. Rather, it is a text which needs to be read in the context of a specifically identified extra-textual reality ca. 519 B.C.E. The opening verses of Zech 1 suggest that, at this time, the words of "the former prophets" were known by author and audience. Furthermore, Zech 1–8 is a text which has been composed with these former prophets in mind, to such an extent that the text is intelligible only against the symbolic universe that these intertexts help to create. Zechariah is a *gapped text*, where the gaps function as pointers to the textual web created by the former prophets.[19] A synchronic account of how the text of Zech 1–8 operates must be based on a diachronic awareness of the possible intertexts in circulation at the time of composition, since these texts (and not later texts) were relied upon by the author in order to make his text intelligible.

In the second half of Chapter 2 I outline my methodology for detecting the intertexts of Zech 1–8. Previous studies have followed divergent methodologies, with some striking differences in results. For example, as noted above, Delkurt and Nurmela come to the opposite conclusion with regard to whether Zech 1–8 alludes to Isa 40–55. Consistent with my approach, I seek to let Zech 1–8 shape the methodology by which we might determine allusion, rather than impose my own preconceived definition of allusion upon the text. To do this, I examine a series of commonly accepted allusions in Zech 1–8 in order to determine, by a process of induction, how Zech 1–8 typically alludes to other texts, and then from this, to develop a methodology for detecting other instances of allusion in the book.

One clear pattern to emerge is that Zech 1–8 often substitutes cognates and synonyms, and combines multiple passages into one composite allusion. As I pursued my research, it became increasingly clear that existing computer-based concordance programmes were ill-equipped for the kind of searching I required. In order to facilitate my research, I have constructed my own search engine for the Hebrew Bible—*BibleCrawler*—which allows searches based on synonymous words (i.e. words in the same Hebrew semantic domain).

19. I shall explain this notion of Zechariah as a "gapped text" in the next chapter.

Chapter 3 addresses the issue of dating of the relevant texts. In a preliminary way, I seek to establish the possible set of "the former prophets" to which Zech 1–8 refers. To do this, I answer two interrelated questions: When was Zech 1–8 written? And what texts might have been in circulation at this time? In this chapter, I will argue that the substance of Zech 1–8 was written before the completion of the temple in 515 B.C.E. I then turn to the thorny question of the other texts in circulation at this time. Rather than attempting to reconstruct the transmission history of the entire Hebrew Bible, I limit myself to examining those passages where there is an apparent correlation with Zech 1–8, and where there is a live issue as to which direction the dependency might run. I conclude that:

- Zechariah 1–8 alludes to a *book of Jeremiah* which probably contained elements considered by some to be late additions, including Jer 7; 33:14–26 and the expansionist glosses of the MT. It would appear that the author of Zech 1–8 knew a form of the book of Jeremiah that was closer in form to the MT *Vorlage* than to the LXX *Vorlage*.
- Zechariah 1–8 alludes to a *book of Ezekiel* which probably contained sections—like some parts of Ezek 40–48 and Ezek 38–39—which are sometimes argued to be later additions.
- In answer to the redactional theory of Odil Steck, I argue that there is no bar to the view that Zech 1–8 might allude to *Isa 1–55*, and may even allude to parts of Isa 56–66.
- I also conclude that it is likely that *Job 1–2* and *Joel 1–2* predate Zech 1–8.

The next four chapters examine the text of Zech 1–8, two chapters at a time (more or less). In each chapter, I draw two kinds of conclusions. The first set of conclusions has to do with how the intertexts which have been identified in that chapter contribute to our understanding of the message as a whole.

In Chapter 4 I conclude that the intertexts of Zech 1–2 help to answer the "What?" and "When?" questions—What is Yahweh about to do? The answer given is that Yahweh is going to return to a restored Jerusalem and dwell with his people, and that this is now imminent (the when).

In Chapter 5 I conclude that the intertexts of Zech 3–4 (read together with the interpreting oracle in 6:9–15) address the "How?" question—How is Yahweh going to return and dwell with his people? The answer is that Yahweh's return to dwell in Jerusalem will be through the restoration of the priesthood (Zech 3), the temple (Zech 4) and the Davidic line (Zech 6:9–15).

In Chapter 6 I conclude that the intertexts of Zech 5:1–6:8 help to spell out the implication and consequences (the "So what?") of Yahweh's return to dwell in Jerusalem, which is expressed in terms of the removal of sin and the banishment of wickedness.

In Chapter 7 I conclude that the intertexts of Zech 7–8 again spell out the consequences of Yahweh's return, but this time in terms of the restoration of Yahweh's covenant with his people (a theme not stressed in Zech 1–6).

Furthermore, each of these four chapters will also make use of the evidence of textual re-use to draw another set of conclusions, addressing what might be broadly described as the hermeneutics of intertextuality. As the foregoing literature review makes clear, while all scholars recognize that there are parallels between Zech 1–8 and other texts, there are widely divergent conclusions as to the implications of these parallels for our understanding of Zech 1–8. Just what is the literary effect of, say, the allusion to Ezekiel's vision of a man measuring the temple, or to Jeremiah's "Branch"? Is it to affirm, deny, defer or transform these earlier works? Or, perhaps this is to ask the wrong question, and we should instead treat the intertexts of Zech 1–8 as a purely literary phenomenon, and deliberately sideline the questions of historical priority and fulfilment. But, then, if we take a "pure literary" approach, does the plethora of intertexts render Zech 1–8 an unreadable text—a "metaphor stew"?[20] Conversely, if we do not do this, and attempt to relate Zech 1–8 to its extra-textual reality, how do we access this, when our knowledge of this period is so fragmentary? These hermeneutical questions, which are raised by the use of intertexts, will also be addressed in these four chapters.

Chapter 4: Intertexts and "original" meaning—Based on the evidence of Zech 1–2, I conclude that these chapters use "sustained allusions" and "composite metaphors" to affirm the promises of the classical prophets, and apply them to the imminent future of the post-exilic community. However, I also argue that the process of combination of the various literary streams has the effect of nuancing the various "original" messages.

Chapter 5: Intertexts and Context—Based on the evidence of Zech 3–4, I conclude that both the literary context (i.e. the former prophets) and the historical context (i.e. ca. 519 B.C.E.) are essential for our understanding of the intertexts which shape the expectations regarding Joshua and Zerubbabel.

20. This is the argument of Love (1999: 136–37), which will be assessed in Chapter 6, below.

Chapter 6: Intertexts and Indeterminacy—In Zech 5–6, we see three visions which are—on any analysis—somewhat bizarre, and which have spawned a number of suggested interpretations. But, against the claims of "radical intertextuality" that it is the plethora of intertexts which have created this indeterminacy of meaning, I argue that the volume of intertexts in these visions actually has the opposite effect, in that they narrow down the range of possible meanings.

Chapter 7: Intertexts and Intratexts—Zechariah 7–8 contains a number of striking textual links to Zech 1–6. These self-referential allusions—what we might call "intratexts"—have the effect of binding the whole work together and providing important clues as to how Zech 1–8 as a whole is to be understood. At the same time, Zech 7–8 also contains intertexts which draw in themes (especially "covenant" themes) not otherwise explicit in Zech 1–6. This combination of intratexts and intertexts gives an ethical overtone to the message of Zech 1–8 as a whole, and provides the connection between the cultic (e.g. priesthood and temple) and the ethical.

In the final chapter, Chapter 8, I return to the questions with which I began, and offer my conclusions as to the manner in which Zech 1–8 has affirmed and woven together the disparate traditions of "the former prophets." I conclude that there is no evidence in Zech 1–8 of a transferral of these hopes into a (proto-)apocalyptic eschatology (with Collins; contra Cook and Gese), nor is the messianic hope applied to an unknown future figure (contra Rose, Pola and Petterson). Zechariah 1–8 applies the classical prophets with an "imminent" eschatology, rather than a futurist or apocalyptic one.

In doing so, Zech 1–8 anticipates events which, we might say with the benefit of hindsight, only ever found partial fulfilment in the early post-exilic period. I conclude by suggesting that this might give us an explanation for the relationship (both literary and historical) between Zech 9–14 and Zech 1–8. Zechariah 9–14 provides the resolution to the question of "fulfilment" which is left hanging by Zech 1–8. While Zech 9–14 demonstrates a continuity of many of the themes from Zech 1–8, there is also a marked eschatological shift in the time for the fulfilment of these promises. Zechariah 1–8 stresses the imminent (if partial) fulfilment of the classical prophets, whereas Zech 9–14 stresses that the ultimate fulfilment of these prophets still lies in the future.

Chapter 2

APPROACH AND METHODOLOGY

2.1. *Introduction*

In the previous chapter I indicated that my aim is to read Zech 1–8 in light of its intertexts, as it is these texts which made the book of Zechariah intelligible to its original audience. In this chapter, I will explain how I propose to do this. I will argue that the nature of Zech 1–8 suggests that the best hermeneutical approach to the text will be one that is attuned to both synchronic and diachronic issues, a "contextual intertextuality." Based on this approach, I will then examine the existing methods for analyzing connections between texts, and argue that the particularities of Zech 1–8 require a refined methodology to supplement existing techniques.

2.2. *Conflicting Approaches?*

As indicated, my aim is to explore what might broadly be termed "connections between texts." However, there are at least three different—apparently conflicting—methodological approaches to this phenomenon, reflected in the differing terminology of "tradition-historical analysis," "intertextuality" and "inner-biblical allusion."[1] These three different methods are reflected in three recent monographs on Zech 1–8 (or a part thereof). As noted in the introduction, Delkurt (2000) takes a tradition-historical (*traditionsgeschichtlich*) approach to the night-visions in Zech 1–6, following a methodology based on diachronic historico-critical

1. For a description and assessment of the major methodological approaches, see Petersen 2003. Petersen examines "inner-biblical allusions," "inner-biblical exegesis," "intertextuality" and "tradition." Like Petersen, I do not find any instances in Zech 1–8 of true "inner-biblical exegesis" (in the sense defined by Fishbane). As such, I focus only on the three remaining methods. On Fishbane's approach, see further n. 13 below.

analysis.[2] In contrast, Love's examination of Zech 1–8, which he describes as "heavily influenced by theories of intertextuality, reader-response criticism and Bakhtin," explicitly eschews the diachronic questions of historical priority and dependence which are central to Delkurt's approach (see Love 1999: 36, 38–39). Love's methodology is based on a synchronic literary approach to texts, in which the modern reader reads multiple texts together to produce meaning. Different again is Nurmela's approach based on "inner-biblical allusion," which he describes as both "intertextual" and "historico-critical" (Nurmela 1996: 23, 28). There is little dialogue between those sharing different methodological presuppositions.

However, I wish to suggest that there is more methodological common ground between these three approaches than their proponents might be prepared to concede. In this chapter, I will argue that the nature of the text of Zech 1–8 suggests an approach which combines elements of all three. Rather than bringing a predetermined hermeneutical "grid" to the text, my aim is to let the text shape the kind of hermeneutical approach we take.

2.3. *Allowing Zechariah 1–8 to Shape Our Hermeneutical Approach*

One's approach to any text ought to be shaped by some awareness of the kind of text it is. We read newspapers differently from poetry, and phone books differently from history books. If we let Zech 1–8 inform the way in which we approach it, then the text itself suggests two identified contexts which ought to be taken into account. The first context is the historical context of the early post-exilic period. The date-formulae in Zech 1:1; 1:7 and 7:1 locate the "action" of this part of the book in the period 520–518 B.C.E., during the period of the reconstruction of the temple in Jerusalem.[3]

Secondly, Zech 1–8 also indicates that it is to be read in the literary context of "the former prophets" (הַנְּבִיאִים הָרִאשֹׁנִים, Zech 1:4; 7:7, 12).[4] As many have recognized, Zech 1–8 is filled with allusions to and echoes

2. See similarly Tollington 1993, who examines the re-use of tradition in Haggai and Zech 1–8.

3. On these dates, see further the introduction to the next chapter.

4. My usage of the phrase "the former prophets" is not to be confused with the later practice of referring to the historical works of Joshua–2 Kings by the same title. As Childs (1979: 230) notes, this later practice "first emerged in the Middle Ages cf. Sotah 48b."

of earlier works.[5] The explicit references to these "former prophets" flag that the textual web created by these former prophets is going to be an important frame of reference for Zech 1–8.

These twin contexts—the historical and the literary—mean that whichever hermeneutical approach we pursue needs to be sensitive to both diachronic and synchronic issues. I propose that the best way to do this is one form of an intertextual approach, which I have dubbed a "contextual intertextuality."

2.4. *My Approach—a "Contextual" Intertextuality*

There has been an explosion of interest in intertextuality in the discipline of Biblical Studies in the last two decades. There have been a number of edited works on the subject,[6] introductions to the subject,[7] intertextual readings of various biblical books—especially Job,[8] Psalms[9] and Isaiah[10]—and books applying the theory to the whole prophetic corpus.[11] Intertextuality has become such a "vogue" word that it now describes a plethora of approaches, to the point that there is no such thing as a single, unified intertextual approach, but rather a range of intertextualities.[12]

The approach to be followed in this study is an intertextual approach which lies somewhere between the post-structuralist semiotic *intertextualité* of Kristeva and Barthes, and the historically oriented "inner biblical exegesis" (IBE) associated with Michael Fishbane.[13] Many

5. E.g. Beuken 1967; Petitjean 1969; Baldwin 1972; Jeremias 1977; Mason 1977a; Petersen 1984a; Meyers and Meyers 1987; Tollington 1993; Nurmela 1996; Love 1999; Delkurt 2000; Boda 2004.

6. See Draisma 1989; Fewell 1992; Aichele and Phillips 1995; de Moor 1998.

7. See, e.g., Buchanan 1994; Tull 2000a.

8. See, e.g., Mettinger 1993; Pyeon 2003; Newsom 2002; 2003.

9. See, e.g., Tanner 2001.

10. See, e.g., Willey 1997; Klouda 2002; Bergey 2003.

11. See, e.g., Laato 1996.

12. See, e.g., Moyise 2000, who distinguishes between "Intertextual Echo," "Dialogical Intertextuality" and "Postmodern Intertextuality" (see further n. 17 below). See also Sanders 1999: 316 and Fishbane 2000.

13. In his landmark book, *Biblical Interpretation in Ancient Israel* (1985), Fishbane examines the phenomenon of "inner biblical exegesis" (IBE), in which a later biblical (i.e. Old Testament) writer re-uses, reinterprets or reapplies an earlier biblical text. Fishbane argues that the received text (the *traditum*) has been transmitted by human agents, who have incorporated their own exegesis of it in the process of transmission (the *traditio*). Inner-biblical exegesis results from the interplay between two factors—a respect for an authoritative teaching, as well as a concern to "preserve, render contemporary, or otherwise reinterpret these teachings or traditions in explicit ways for new times and circumstances" (Fishbane 1985: 8).

would deny the legitimacy of this kind of approach, arguing that it is invalid to seek a point of intersection between synchronic "intertextuality" and diachronic "inner biblical exegesis" (see, e.g., Eslinger 1992; Snyman 1996). The scholarly literature in this field is a definitional and methodological battleground, with "intertextualists" taking shots across the bows at "inner biblical exegetes" and vice versa.[14] Since I intend to position myself between these two camps, I need to proceed with care, lest I get shot at from both sides.[15]

I intend to show that the term "intertextuality" might legitimately be used to describe an approach (like mine) which encompasses both synchronic and diachronic elements. In the next section, I offer the conceptual underpinnings for this approach, drawing on current literary theory.

2.5. *Defining Intertextuality*

In seeking to define intertextuality, one might begin by considering the origins of the word. There is a delicious double-irony at this point. "Intertextuality" was a word coined by Julia Kristeva to refer to the study of the semiotic matrix within which a text's acts of signification occur: in her words, "tout texte se construit comme mosaïque de citations, tout texte est absorption et transformation d'un autre texte" (Kristeva 1969: 146). This post-structuralist approach (building upon Bakhtin, and further developed by Barthes) specifically refrains from asking questions about historical priority, authorial intent and influence—indeed, Kristeva has since objected to those who use her word "intertextuality" to engage in historical criticism by another name, labelling their work a banal search for sources (see Kristeva and Moi 1986: 59–60). Ironically, those who are arguing for the intense fluidity of meaning in other texts are insisting that *their* definition is the only right definition! But the irony goes deeper, because those who wish to introduce questions of history and authorial intent (where I place myself!) want to use the word "intertextuality" in a way contrary to its original author's intent.

However we resolve that conundrum over the *original* meaning, we must recognize that the word intertextuality, as it is *now* commonly used (particularly in Biblical Studies), refers to a wider phenomenon than that

14. For example, the exchange between Eslinger (1992) and Sommer (1996b) is replete with words such as "confused," "misunderstood" and "flawed." My reference to "shots across the bows" is an intertextual nod to Polzin (1989:1–17).

15. On the interdependency between synchronic and diachronic approaches, see the collected essays in de Moor 1995, especially Barr 1995. In the same volume, Joyce argues in favour of "assign[ing] an equal place to diachronic and synchronic tasks within biblical studies" (1995: 127).

of the semiotics of post-structuralism.[16] While the radical indeterminacy of post-structuralist *intertextualité* is one way in which the term is currently used, it is certainly not the only way (and, I will argue, nor should it be).

Notwithstanding the origins of the term in post-structuralism, intertextuality has now come to be used as an umbrella term, grouping together approaches which share common assumptions.[17] I will suggest below that there are three common features which typify an intertextual approach:

- textual creation—texts are a "mosaic" of quotations of other texts;
- textual meaning—meaning comes from a "dialogue" between texts;
- (textual) hermeneutics—a reader's role in the production of meaning.

However, the diversity of intertextualities comes from the fact that each of these features covers a spectrum of possibilities, which are illustrated in the following diagram:[18]

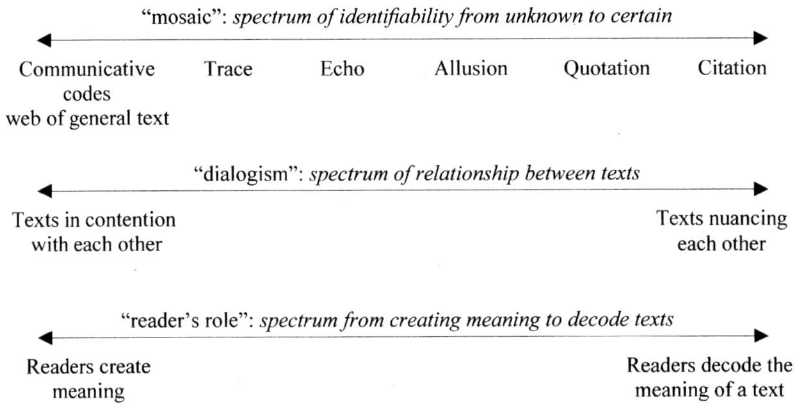

16. It is beyond the scope of the present work to attempt a comprehensive analysis of the phenomenon of intertextuality. The reader is referred to other works on intertextuality in the field of literary studies. See esp. Eagleton 1983; Worton and Still 1990; Clayton and Rothstein 1991; Allen 2000; Culler 2001. See also Thiselton (1992: 499–508) for an analysis of the hermeneutical implications of some intertextual approaches.

17. Moyise (2000: 17–18) similarly describes Intertextuality as an "umbrella" term, for three different approaches: "Intertextual Echo," "Dialogical Intertextuality" and "Postmodern Intertextuality."

18. This particular model of three spectra is my own, but has come about through an "intertextual" melding of three sources. The idea of a continuum of identifiability from "unknown" to "certain" is an adaptation of Patricia Tull (nee Willey; see n. 20 below), and my appropriation of Bakhtin is also similar to hers (Tull 2000b: 76). A

In the following three sub-sections, I will examine each spectrum in turn in order to sketch out the range of possible "intertextualities."

2.5.1. *Text Creation: Texts are a Mosaic of Quotations of Other Texts*

Julia Kristeva classically stated that "any text is constructed of a mosaic of quotations; any text is the absorption and transformation of another" (1980: 66). Roland Barthes further develops this insight:

> Any text is a new tissue of past citations. Bits of code, formulae, rhythmic models, fragments of social languages, etc., pass into the text and are redistributed within it, for there is always language before and around the text. Intertextuality, the condition of any text whatsoever, cannot, of course, be reduced to a problem of sources or influences; the intertext is a general field of anonymous formulae whose origin can scarcely ever be located; of unconscious or automatic quotations, given without quotation marks. (Barthes 1981: 39)

Barthes and deconstructionists such as Derrida are particularly interested in the "general field of anonymous formulae whose origin can scarcely ever be located" because of the implications this has for post-structuralist semiotics.[19] However, while they may validly focus on this feature, this does not nullify the analysis of those parts of the "textual mosaic" where intertexts *can* be identified, albeit with greater or lesser degrees of specificity. I will use the following spectrum of terms to describe this:[20]

"mosaic": *spectrum of identifiability from unknown to certain*

◄————————————————————►

Communicative codes web of general text	Trace	Echo	Allusion	Quotation	Citation

second source is Daniel Boyarin (1990: 14), taking up his three "conceptions" to intertextuality. Thirdly, I have used insights from Sanders's threefold taxonomy of intertextuality (Sanders 1999: 316; cf. 2000: 16).

19. A sign which refers to other signs (which cannot be traced) opens the door to an infinite fluidity of meaning, since a word becomes a sign referring to another sign, which itself refers to another in an infinite regression. Jacques Derrida has taken up this feature of intertextuality, arguing that there is an infinite deferral of meaning for any sign, resulting in a radical indeterminacy of meaning.

20. Patricia Willey similarly describes a continuum, from explicit quotation at one extreme, through to anonymous allusions, untraceable and invisible (to the reader), at the other. Between these two extremes is "the realm of allusion, response, appropriation, recollection, and echo. In this realm the author's sources, while perhaps difficult to trace or even no longer traceable, are hardly anonymous. In fact, for the audience fully to appreciate the richness and resonance of the new text, the precursor must be known" (1997: 61).

- A *citation* is an attributed quotation (i.e. acknowledging source).
- A *quotation* is an identifiable word-for-word repetition.
- An *allusion* is a partial re-use of a sequence of words or ideas.
- An *echo* is similar to an allusion, but where fewer identifiable elements are re-used.[21]
- A *trace* is defined by Derrida as the indications of an absence that define a presence. Any signifier contains "traces" of other signifiers which shape its meaning.

By putting these terms on a spectrum, I am acknowledging that they blend into one another, and that, in practice, it may be difficult to distinguish definitively between (say) an echo and an allusion.[22]

As I am using the terms, the study of allusion and quotation are (potentially) species of the broader field "intertextuality." I recognize that this is a different approach from that of Benjamin Sommer. Sommer argues for a complete dichotomy between "allusion" and "intertextuality." According to Sommer (1998: 6), the former is diachronic in character, "asking how one composition evokes its antecedents, how one author is affected by another, and what sources a text utilizes," whereas the approach of the latter is synchronic in nature, focusing "not on the author of a text but either on the text itself (as part of a larger system) or on the reader…interpret[ing] signs in the text by associating them with related signs in the reader's own mind" (Sommer 1998: 7).[23] Though Sommer's two-category definition is neat, it is an over-simplification of the issues, because not all intertextualists are synchronic reader-response critics![24]

21. The work of Richard Hays (1989) on the "echoes" of Scripture in the letters of Paul has been particularly influential, in both Old Testament and New Testament studies, in opening the field of textual "echoes."

22. As I am using the words, a "quotation" typically involves four or more shared vocabulary features (particularly if that combination is otherwise unattested), an "allusion" involves two or three features, and an echo, one or two. However, there is an inevitable fluidity between these categories, and I recognize that others might use the terminology (or judge the weight of the vocabulary features) differently. On the difficulties surrounding the determination of quotation and allusion, see Nogalski 1996: 103–12.

23. For a similar insistence on the dichotomy between "influence" and "intertextuality," see Hatina 1999.

24. Sommer's categorization relies heavily on the analysis of Clayton and Rothstein (1991), whose work is a normative prescription of how they believe "intertextuality" and "influence" *should* be categorised, rather than a description of how the term is actually used in practice. However, particularly in Biblical Studies, the practice of intertextuality is much wider than this normative categorization

As we shall see, the breadth of usage of the term "intertextuality" means that it can validly encompass a hermeneutical approach which views the author, text and reader as important to the interpretive process, and in which diachronic concerns and synchronic concerns are both addressed to arrive at the meaning of a text.

2.5.2. *Textual Meaning: Meaning Comes from Dialogue Between Texts*
Mikhail Bakhtin described the complex relationship between texts as "dialogism." However, defining what he meant by this is no mean feat, because Bakhtin used the concept of *dialogic* in multiple senses. For our purposes, we should distinguish between:

Dialogical language	*All language* is dialogical, in that it cannot help but assert its meaning in *dialogue* with a complex web of utterances which already exist.[25]
Dialogical discourse	*Some discourses* are dialogical, in that they requires the interaction of multiple voices (i.e. *polyphony*) to produce meaning.[26]
Dialogical truth	*Some truths* are dialogical in nature. In contrast to "monological" truths, which can be reduced to a series of propositions utterable by anyone without affecting their truth value, a dialogical truth is one that cannot be stated as a single proposition or by a single voice. Instead, a dialogical truth can emerge only via the interaction of several unmerged voices (i.e. *multivalency*).

It should be clear from this analysis that while all texts will be *dialogical* in the first sense, only a subset of texts will be dialogical in the second sense, and only some truths will be dialogical in the third sense. The appropriate category (or categories) will vary depending on the text

recognizes. For some recent examples of scholars in the field of Biblical Studies arguing for a definition of intertextuality which explicitly includes the kinds of historical issues excluded by Sommer's definition, see Nogalski 1996; Willey 1997; O'Day 1999: 1:547; Moyise 2000; Schmid 2000; Floyd 2003.

25. On this, see further Claassens 2003. To quote Bakhtin: "Two discourses equally and directly oriented toward a referential object within the limits of a single context cannot exist side by side without intersecting dialogically, regardless of whether they confirm, mutually supplement, or (conversely) contradict one another, or find themselves in some other dialogic relationship (that of question and answer, for example)" (1973: 188–89).

26. Bakhtin distinguishes between dialogical discourses which reproduce the other's words (*active double voiced discourse*), and those that do not (*passive double voice discourse*). See further Bakhtin 1973: 197.

under consideration.[27] One cannot necessarily assume that a "dialogical" text entails "polyphony" or "multivalency" in every case, not withstanding the popularity of these buzz-words in our post-modern milieu.

"Dialogism" recognizes that textual meaning is a function of a dialogue between texts. The dialogue may be friendly or unfriendly—at one extreme, some texts seek to assert their own meaning by overthrowing another, whereas others rely on the other text for their meaning. Moreover, as Floyd (2003) demonstrates, texts relate to other texts with different degrees of dependence.[28]

"dialogism": *spectrum of relationship between texts*

◄——————————————————————►

Texts in contention with each other	Texts nuancing each other

The greater the degree of contention with the existing "voices" in the intertextual web, the greater the potential for multivalency, as multiple meanings compete.[29]

2.5.3. *Hermeneutics: A Reader's Role in the Production of Meaning*

In a post-Gadamer and postmodern world there is a bewildering array of competing hermeneutical approaches. To find meaning, should we be seeking authorial intent? Are we to abandon this, and instead enter the self-contained world of the text? Are these both vain attempts to find objective meaning, and should we instead recognize that each modern

27. For example, see Newsom (2002; 2003) for the application of categories two and three to the book of Job. For an application of Bakhtin's concept of "dialogic truth" to the Bible, see also Newsom 1996.

28. Floyd (2003: 238) describes a continuum with respect to the dependence of the interpreting text on the interpreted text. At one end, the interpreting text is relatively independent, definitely alluding to the interpreted text but capable of being understood without explicit reference to it. At the other end, the interpreting text is completely dependent on the interpreted text, explicitly referring to it at every turn and incomprehensible on any other basis. In between these two poles, there are greater and lesser degrees of dependence.

29. The mechanics of "dialogism" have been analyzed (albeit under different nomenclature) in a diversity of literary studies. At one end of the spectrum above, one might place Harold Bloom's *The Anxiety of Influence* (1973), in which he argues that all literary texts are a strong misreading of those which precede them, stemming from an Oedipal desire of poets to overthrow their poetic "fathers." At the opposite end of the spectrum is a work like Hollander's *The Figure of Echo* (1981), in which he argues that allusion works constructively, by a process of *metalepsis*, whereby a reader is required to bring together old text and new text in order to grasp all the nuances of meaning.

reader is the determiner of his or her own meaning? It is well beyond the scope of the present enquiry to attempt to resolve all these questions. Instead, I will focus much more narrowly on the implications which the form of Zech 1–8 has for our hermeneutical assumptions and approach.

One of the implications of a highly allusive text such as Zech 1–8 is that meaning cannot lie solely within that text alone, because the meaning is only produced by reading that text against its intertexts. With nothing but the bare text of Zechariah, in many places a reader cannot arrive at its sense, because it only makes sense when understood against the background of what (for example) Jeremiah or Ezekiel or Isaiah have already said. These other texts create a symbolic world, or frame of reference, for Zech 1–8. The meaning of Zech 1–8 is thus the product of the combination of the text of Zech 1–8 with those other texts, and this is a process which occurs in the mind of the reader.

Literary theorists have different explanations of the process by which readers are involved in the production of meaning. Writing from the perspective of semantic theory, Umberto Eco describes how "open texts" with "productive codes" are "decoded" by readers (see Eco 1984; 1989). A different description of a similar process can be seen in Michael Riffaterre's concept of an "ungrammaticality"—a word or phrase which, because of its awkwardness in the present context, points to another text which provides the key to its decoding, and so aids readers in the production of meaning:

> ...the dual sign works like a pun. We will see that the pun in poetic discourse grows out of textual "roots." It is first apprehended as a mere ungrammaticality, until the discovery is made that there is another text in which the word is grammatical; the moment the other text is identified, the dual sign becomes significant purely because of its shape, which alone alludes to that other code. (Riffaterre 1978: 82)

From a different perspective again is Iser's description of "indeterminacy" arising from "gapped texts":

> The indeterminate sections or gaps of literary texts are in no way to be regarded as a defect; on the contrary, they are a basic element for the aesthetic response... [T]he reader fills in the remaining gaps. He removes them by a free play of meaning-projection, and thus by himself repairs the unformulated connections between the particular views. (Iser 1971: 12)

> [T]he indeterminate elements of literary prose—perhaps even of all literature—represent the most important link between text and reader. It is the switch that activates the reader in using his own ideas in order to fulfill the intention of the text... The meaning is conditioned by the text itself, but only in a form that allows the reader himself to bring it out. (Iser 1971: 43)

Although I recognize that there are significant differences in approach between Eco, Riffaterre and Iser, a common feature is that they each recognize the role of a reader in the production of meaning. What is significant to note, however, is that granting this role to the reader does not necessarily entail the conclusion that readers "create" meaning. Eco speaks of readers "decoding" a meaning in the text, and Iser speaks of a meaning "conditioned by the text" which is brought out by a reader. That is, reader and text both have an irreducible role to play in the production of meaning for "open" or "gapped" texts.

The hermeneutics of intertextuality suggest that readers have a role to play in arriving at a text's meaning, though (depending on the nature of the text in question) this may range from readers who decode a meaning which has been encoded into a text by an author, to readers who create meaning from texts.

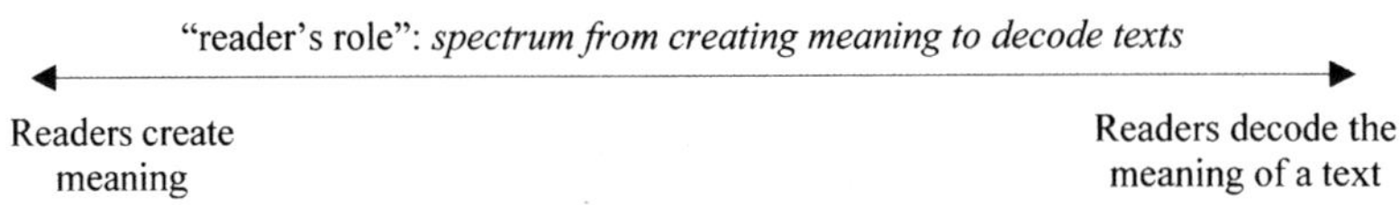

In both semiotic theory and Biblical Studies there is an increasing recognition that both "text" and "reader" have irreducible roles to play in the production of meaning. A fascinating example of this can been seen in the recent work of Conrad (2003). Conrad looks back at his earlier "radical reader response" works (which includes his commentary on Zechariah) and acknowledges that "there was a fundamental tension between my practice and the theory I appealed to" (2003: 6). Instead, Conrad now argues for a hermeneutical approach—based on the semiotics of Eco—which acknowledges that texts have been encoded with an "intention of the work" (*intentio operis*), and that this encoded textual intention places limits on interpretation.[30]

To this point, my aim has been to demonstrate that there is a range of possible approaches which may validly be called "intertextual." I recognize that my approach to intertextuality differs at points with those of some postmodern literary theories. However, I submit that, for those of a post-modern persuasion, their suspicion of all metanarratives ought to make them recoil against any single grand theory which purports to

30. In some respects, Conrad's hermeneutical journey through the 1980s, 1990s and beyond is a parallel to Eco's own journey, first stressing the "role of the reader" (Eco 1979) and then the textual "limits of interpretation" (Eco 1990; 1992; Eco and Collini 1992).

encompass all texts. I am arguing for the validity of a variety of intertextual approaches in which the better approaches will depend on the particularities of the texts at hand.

2.6. *Positioning Zechariah 1–8 in the Field of "Intertextuality"*

The three-spectra schema of intertextuality developed above implies a range of possible intertextual approaches. This begs the question: What does the "shape" of Zech 1–8 suggest as the most appropriate form of intertextual approach? I suggest that certain features of the text position it towards the right-hand side of the each of the three spectra above.

First, Zech 1–8 is made up of a *mosaic* of other texts, and many of these texts are identifiable precursor texts (i.e. texts in circulation before 520 B.C.E.). It goes without saying that Zech 1–8 may well also contain traces of other texts which we cannot identify, but this does not undermine the validity of examining those texts where we can.

Secondly, Zech 1–8 explicitly establishes its meaning in *dialogue* with identifiable dialogue partners ("the former prophets"). Both the general tone of this dialogue and the explicit affirmation of these "words which Yahweh commanded his servants the prophets" (see Zech 1:6) suggest that this is a friendly dialogue, with Zechariah nuancing (rather than seeking to overthrow) the message of his prophetic forebears. The *dialogical* insights of Bakhtin inform my intertextual approach in the following ways:

- Since language is dialogical, the meaning of words and phrases in Zech 1–8 are asserted against the background of the complex web of utterances which already existed. The only access (albeit partial and with degrees of uncertainty) we have to this complex web is the biblical writings which pre-date Zechariah, on the assumption that these writings form the thought-world against which Zech 1–8 was rendered intelligible to its original audience.
- Zechariah 1–8 engages in a *dialogical discourse* with identified dialogue partners—"the former prophets." My aim is to understand Zech 1–8 in the context of this discourse, anticipating that there may be differences in perspective between Zechariah and his dialogue partners, which perhaps arise from his later (i.e. post-exilic) context.
- Zechariah may at times present a truth *dialogically*, by presenting his own voice alongside the voices of the former prophets, where that voice remains unmerged with his dialogue partners.

Thirdly, Zech 1–8 requires the *reader's involvement* in the production of meaning, in a way which does not bypass the text, but rather completes it. Zechariah 1–8 is a good example of a "gapped text" (as per Iser), because at many points the meaning is not exclusively *in* the text of Zechariah alone. With nothing but the bare text of Zechariah, a reader has very few clues to unravel the meaning of, for example, the four horns, the reclothing of Joshua, the lampstand or the woman in the ephah. As I will demonstrate below, it is only when these texts are read together with the conceptual world established by "the former prophets" that it is possible to make sense of them. I will demonstrate that there are sufficient clues in Zech 1–8 to help the reader locate the intended intertexts that make it possible to fill the "gaps."[31]

Not only does Zech 1–8 engage intertextually with the former prophets, but it also engages *intra*-textually with itself, as later chapters (particularly Zech 7–8) use self-referential allusions which pick up the imagery and vocabulary of earlier chapters.[32]

Positioning Zech 1–8 at these points on the three spectra means that questions of history should not be bypassed for this particular text.[33] In order to give a (synchronic) account of how the text of Zech 1–8

31. My use of the word "intended" is deliberate, in that I wish to stress the role of the author of Zech 1–8 in the creation of its meaning. There is a proper place for authorial intention in shaping the meaning of a text. Ever since Beardsley and Wimsatt (1976) decried the "intentional fallacy," the quest for the author's intent has been out of vogue. However, Vanhoozer (2001) helpfully distinguishes between two different uses of the word "intend." It can refer to an inner psychological state ("I intend to be there on time"), and it can also refer to intrinsic component of an act ("He struck with intent to harm"). Vanhoozer suspects that it is the failure to distinguish between these two uses which has led to the death of the author in modern literary studies. Vanhoozer describes the so-called death of the author as the worst form of reductionism, like reducing the "wink" to the "blink." The very thing that makes the wink what it is is the intent behind the act. Likewise, communicative acts are uttered *with intent* (and indeed it is their intent which directs their meaning). Interpretation is the process of inferring authorial intent from what they actually did when they wrote. We are not left guessing what they wanted to do or planned to do (i.e. the other sense of "intent"); rather, we are working with their inscribed actual intent. Authorial intent is inferred from words and phrases, their conventional meanings and their context.

From a different perspective, but arguing to a similar end, see also Eco (1990: 50), who refers to "the intention of the work" (*intentio operis*) as deriving from the message "encoded" for the Model Reader.

32. On this, see further Chapter 7, especially §7.5.

33. The introduction of the historical dimension does not necessarily mean that we are pursuing a "banal search for sources." See further Boyarin 1990: 135 n. 2.

operates, it must be based on a (diachronic) awareness of the possible intertexts which were in circulation at the time of composition, since these texts (and not later texts) constitute the "textual web" and the "dialogue partners" and the "gap-filling texts" for Zech 1–8. We might dub this approach a "contextual intertextuality"—an intertextuality that is conscious of both the literary context of Zech 1–8 (i.e. its relation to "the former prophets") and its historical context ca. 520 B.C.E. In order to pursue an approach of this kind, we must have a suitable methodology for detecting the intertexts of Zech 1–8. It is to the question of methodology that I now turn.

2.7. *A Methodology for Detecting Textual Re-Use?*

It was noted at the outset of this chapter that tradition-historical analysis, intertextuality and inner-biblical allusion have pursued different and competing methodologies. For example, the tradition-historical approach of (say) Jeremias, Mason, Tollington and Delkurt may be prepared to recognize the possibility of the "thematic" allusion, where the themes of a particular tradition are clearly evident even if some of the distinctive vocabulary is not. In contrast, some more recent works have insisted that the only objective evidence of re-use is to be found in "verbal repetition."[34] Nurmela is a vocal proponent of this view, and has been openly critical of the methodology of others (e.g. Mason), arguing that the inclusion of thematic connections and/or tradition influences goes beyond that which can be established on the basis of strict verbal parallels.[35] Nurmela describes his method thus:

> The starting-point of the search for allusions in Zechariah in this study is expressions (i.e., words and phrases) which occur in Zechariah and another book in the Old Testament, but that do not occur as frequently—or at all—in other Old Testament books... Even more common words which are used particularly frequently in Zechariah and another book, or words in a particular form and setting (e.g., a verb in the first person singular with God as subject) are considered. The phrases are indicated by single words, in their turn selected on the basis of these criteria. (Nurmela 1996: 27)

34. See Nurmela 1996: 27. A similar approach is also taken by Schultz. In his contribution to a volume entitled *Thematic Threads in the Book of the Twelve*, Schultz argues (somewhat ironically, given the title of the book) that a method based on thematic allusions is too vague, and that "verbal parallels that offer a more extensive textual basis for positing an intentional interrelationship is a more viable approach" (2003: 28). For a fuller account of Schultz's method, see Schultz 1999: 222–38.

35. See Nurmela 2003: 245–47.

However, this raises the following question: Why should we assume that, when the author of Zech 1–8 wanted to make an allusion, he limited himself to "rare" expressions? It seems to me that much recent work on intertextuality has been shaped by the capabilities (or lack thereof) of our computer-based concordance software. Since our computer concordances are good at searching for words, scholars have pursued methods which rely on this, to the denigration of other approaches. Apparently, the solid objective evidence of our computers is much more reliable than subjective judgments about repeated themes (see Nurmela 1996: 2, 10, 26). This is only true, however, if our computers are looking in the right place. I illustrate with a parable:

> A father enters his son's room, to find the son on his hands and knees under the window. The son explains that he is searching for a coin that he dropped. The father joins in the search, but finds nothing. Eventually, he asks the son "Are you sure it fell here?" The son replies, "No, it rolled under my bed, but the light is better here..."

To be fair to Nurmela, perhaps the better analogy is if the son drops 100 coins; a few roll near the window and the rest roll under the bed. A method based on "rare words and phrases" searches where our computers can give us verifiable answers, rather than searching across a wider base of data, where the results might be less certain. Thus, while a "rare words and phrases" approach can give clear results, it remains an open question whether the selection bias built into the method is distorting the results of the search.

My reason for challenging Nurmela at this point is because the method he proposes sits uncomfortably with my above analysis of intertextuality. Intertextuality recognizes the rich textual web created by the interconnections between multiple texts, including the fact that an author may transform another text in the process of its re-use, and may blend multiple intertexts into one new text. This kind of textual "play" may mean that specific verbal connections are not always there to be found by our computers. These observations led me to the conclusion that it was necessary to develop a methodology which was tailored to the way in which Zech 1–8 actually re-uses other texts, and then to develop a new system of computer-based searching to serve this end.

2.8. *Developing a Methodology Tailored to Zechariah 1–8*

Since intertextuality recognizes a wide range of connections between texts, we need a method which is broad enough to detect this. To date, when the theory of intertextuality has been applied to Biblical Studies, typically it is only a narrow field of connections which have been explored—I suspect this is because of the limits of concordances and computer-based searching software. Without wishing to call into question the suitability of these other methodological approaches *per se*, my argument is that they are ill-suited to Zechariah's intertextuality in particular.

If we allow for the fact that individual authors may have characteristic and distinct ways of re-using other texts, then surely we need to pursue a method which is sensitive to a given author's practice. In order to do this for Zech 1–8, I examined a set of five commonly accepted examples of re-use, systematizing from them some observations as to how Zech 1–8 re-uses texts so that I might develop a method inductively on this basis. I use these accepted examples of intertextuality as a base from which to derive my assumptions about the possible intertexts and patterns of textual re-use, and from this I propose a method for detecting textual re-use in Zech 1–8.

Example 1: Zech 1:4c and Jer 25:5–7

שׁובו־נא אישׁ מדרכו הרעה
ומרע מעלליכם

Turn now, each *from his evil way*
and from the evil of your deeds... (Jer 25:5)

ולא־שׁמעתם
אלי נאם־יהוה

But you did not listen to me,
says Yahweh. (Jer 25:7)

שׁובו נא מדרכיכם הרעים ומעלליכם הרעים
ולא שׁמעו ולא־הקשׁיבו
אלי נאם־יהוה

Turn from your evil ways and your evil deeds
But they did not listẹn or give heed
To me, says Yahweh. (Zech 1:4c)

Zechariah 1:4 reports the message of "the former prophets" using a form of words with closest parallels to Jer 25:5–7. Though there are also some similarities to Ezekiel,[36] it is unlikely that Ezekiel is the primary intertext since Ezekiel never uses the phrase "Yahweh of Hosts"—and yet this

36. For example, Ezek 33:11—noted by Beuken 1967: 97–98; Petersen 1984a: 132–33; Meyers and Meyers 1987: 95.

phrase is included (in Zech 1:4b) as part of the quoted message.[37] The likelihood of a specific connection with Jer 25 is further strengthened by other shared themes in the wider context of the respective chapters—the "seventy years" (Zech 1:12 and Jer 25:11), as well as the theme of Yahweh's instruments of judgment being themselves punished for overstepping the mark (see Zech 1:12–14 and Jer 25:12–14).[38]

Zechariah 1:4 is an abbreviated summary of Jer 25:5–7, which itself is a summary of the message of the prophets of a former generation (see similarly Jer 35:15), the terms of which are echoed in Jeremiah's own preaching (cf. Jer 18:11):

שבו־נא איש מדרכו הרעה
והיטיבו מעלליכם...
ולא הטיתם את־אזנכם
ולא שמעתם אלי

Turn now, each *from his evil way*,
and amend *your deeds*...
But you did not incline your ear
and you did not listen to me. (Jer 35:15)

שובו נא איש מדרכו הרעה
והיטיבו דרכיכם ומעלליכם

Turn now, each *from his evil way* and amend
your ways and your deeds. (Jer 18:11)

By alluding to Jer 25, Zech 1:4 can thus allude to a single prophet (Jeremiah) as an encapsulation of the message of "the former prophets" as a whole.

Note that this purported quotation shows a number of minor differences—person (second person to third) and number (singular to plural), and substituted cognates (the adjective רַע for the noun רֹעַ). The phrase וְלֹא־הִקְשִׁיבוּ in Zech 1:4 does not appear in Jer 25, though it is paralleled elsewhere in the book of Jeremiah, in Jer 6:19.

37. The phrase "Yahweh of Hosts" also occurs immediately after these quoted verses in Jer 25:8 (MT, but not LXX—see further §3.3.1).

38. With respect to Zech 1:4c, Nurmela (1996: 39–40) categorizes Jer 25:4–5 (and 35:15) as a "sure allusion." Tigchelaar says that "the closest analogy is to be found in Jer 25:5" (1996: 77). Cf. Meyers and Meyers 1987: 95 and Hanhart 1998: 24. Tollington argues that the phrase in Zech 1:4 "strongly suggests Jeremianic origin or influence" (1993: 205), listing Jer 18:11b; 25:5 and 35:15 as parallels, and similarly see Petitjean 1969: 39; Baldwin 1972: 90; Boda 2004: 178. Petersen argues that Zech 1:4 is an appropriation of Jer 11:18; 25:5; 35:15 and Ezek 33:11, as the "sort of thing such prophets said" (1984a: 132–33) rather than a single quotation.

Example 2: Zech 6:15 and Deut 28:1[39]

והיה אם־שמוע תשמע בקול יהוה אלהיך

And it will be, if you diligently listen to the voice of Yahweh your God... (Deut 28:1)

והיה אם־שמוע תשמעון בקול יהוה אלהיכם

And this will be, if you diligently listen to the voice of Yahweh your God. (Zech 6:15)

Zechariah 6 has recast Deut 28 in the plural form, and has taken what had been the introduction to a promise of blessing regarding obedience to Yahweh's covenant, and applied it as the conclusion to a specific promise regarding temple rebuilding.

Example 3: Zech 2:14 and Isa 12:6 and/or Zeph 3:14–15

צהלי ורני יושבת ציון
כי־גדול בקרבך קדוש ישראל

Rejoice and sing, O inhabitants of *Zion*,
for great *in your midst* is the Holy One of Israel. (Isa 12:6)

רני בת־ציון הריעו ישראל
שמחי ועלזי בכל־לב
בת ירושלם
...יהוה בקרבך

Sing, O daughter Zion; shout, O Israel!
Rejoice and exult with all your heart,
O daughter Jerusalem!
...Yahweh is *in your midst*. (Zeph 3:14–15)

רני ושמחי בת־ציון
כי הנני־בא ושכנתי בתוכך נאם־יהוה

Sing and rejoice, O daughter Zion!
For behold, I am coming and will dwell *in your midst*, says Yahweh. (Zech 2:14 [ET 2:10])

39. Noted by, e.g., Beuken 1967: 117; Petitjean 1969: 301; Mason 1977a: 64; Meyers and Meyers 1987: 365–66; Tollington 1993: 46–47; Nurmela 1996: 189–90; Hanhart 1998: 473.

Zechariah 2 bears clear thematic parallels to Isa 12:6 and/or Zeph 3:14 (a call to female-personified inhabitants of Zion to sing and rejoice because Yahweh is in the midst of his people).[40]

The actual direct lexical links with Isa 12:6 are surprisingly sparse, and the intertextual parallels depend on two sets of synonyms—"Rejoice" (צַהֲלִי / שִׂמְחִי) and "in your midst" (בְּתוֹכֵךְ / בְּקִרְבֵּךְ), and parallel phrases which identify the inhabitants of Zion (יוֹשֶׁבֶת צִיּוֹן / בַּת־צִיּוֹן) and their God (יְהוָה / קְדוֹשׁ יִשְׂרָאֵל).

There are slightly more connections with Zeph 3:14–15, which shares the phrase "daughter of Zion" and the same word for "rejoice" (שִׂמְחִי), though the causal כִּי is absent in Zeph 3:15. However, it does not matter whether Isa 12 or Zeph 3 (or, as I think, both) are the textual background for Zech 2:14, since in either case we would come to similar conclusions about the kinds of transformations which Zech 2 has wrought in its process of textual re-use. Zechariah 2:14 has substituted at least one word for its synonym (בְּתוֹכֵךְ / בְּקִרְבֵּךְ) and has substantially shifted the sense of the passage, from being about Yahweh presently "in the midst" (as per Isa 12 and Zeph 3) to a promise that Yahweh is to come in the (near?) future, and shifted from words spoken about Yahweh to words spoken by Yahweh.

Example 4: Zech 8:21–22 and Isa 2:3[41]

והלכו עמים רבים ואמרו לכו ונעלה אל־הר־יהוה אל־בית אלהי יעקב

Many peoples shall come and say, "Come, let us go up to the *mountain of Yahweh*, to the house of the *God of Jacob.* (Isa 2:3)

40. Nurmela says Zech 2:14 is a "sure allusion" (1996: 56–58) to Isa 12:6, and regards Zeph 3:14–15 as a later adaptation of Zech 2:14. See also Petitjean 1969: 132. Tollington 1993: 232 notes possible connections with both Isa 12:6 and Zeph 3:14, as do Petersen (1984a: 179) and Baldwin (1972: 110). Meyers and Meyers (1987: 167) note parallels with Zeph 3:14, but not Isa 12:6.

41. For simplicity's sake, I have focussed on Isa 2:3 rather than the parallel passage in Mic 4:2. On the relative merits of Isa 2 *vis-à-vis* Mic 4 as the intertext of Zech 8, see Rudman 2001. However, it does not substantially change the outcome of this analysis if Mic 4 were the prior passage.

Nurmela lists Zech 8/Isa 2 as a "sure allusion" (1996: 89–90). See also Baldwin 1972: 155, Mason 1977a: 72; Petersen 1984a: 317; Boda 2004: 397 (citing Isa 2// Mic 4). For those who link Zech 8:21–22 to the wider "pilgrimage to Zion" tradition (of which Isa 2 is a part), see Mitchell (1912: 216), who also notes connections to Isa 45:14ff.; also Beuken (1967: 179) and Petitjean (1969: 429–31). Cf. Tollington (1993: 236–37) who identifies the possible connections with Isa 2:3 and Mic 4:2, but leaves open the question of dependency/influence.

והלכו ישבי אחת אל־אחת לאמר נלכה הלוך לחלות את־פני יהוה ולבקש
את־יהוה צבאות אלכה גם־אני

The inhabitants of one [city] shall come to another, saying "Come, let us go to entreat the favour of Yahweh and to seek *Yahweh of Hosts*; I myself am going." (Zech 8:21)

ובאו עמים רבים וגוים עצומים לבקש את־יהוה צבאות בירושלם ולחלות
את־פני יהוה

Many peoples and strong nations shall come to seek Yahweh of Hosts in *Jerusalem*, and to entreat the favour of Yahweh. (Zech 8:22)

Again, the direct lexical links are somewhat sparse ("many peoples," עַמִּים רַבִּים, and the construction "come…and say 'come, let us'"). However, there are unmistakeable conceptual parallels between both passages—"Jerusalem" is the location of the "mountain of Yahweh," the "God of Jacob" is the same person as "Yahweh of Hosts," and the "inhabitants" in Zech 8:21 are the same group as the "many peoples" of the nations in Isa 2:3 (shown by the parallelism of Zech 8:22). Both passages share the (relatively rare) theme of the nations making pilgrimage to Zion.

Example 5: Zech 2:5–6 and Ezek 40:3[42] *(and Zech 1:16 and Jer 31:3)*

ויביא אותי שמה והנה־איש מראהו כמראה נחשת
ופתיל־פשתים בידו וקנה המדה

And he brought me there, *and behold, a man*, whose appearance shone like bronze,
and in his hand was a linen cord and *a measuring reed*. (Ezek 40:3)

ואשא עיני וארא והנה־איש ובידו חבל מדה

I lifted my eyes and saw and *behold, a man, and in his hand was a measuring line*. (Zech 2:5 [ET 2:1])

In addition to the connections highlighted above, it should also be noted that in the immediate context there is another set of connections— the man in Ezekiel also proceeds to measure width (רֹחַב, 40:6) and length

42. This connection is noted by, e.g., Beuken 1967: 247; Jeremias 1977: 164; Nurmela 1996: 51–52; Hanhart 1998: 125; Delkurt 2000: 105–7. Meyers and Meyers (1987: 151) refer generally to Ezek 40–42 rather than specifically to Ezek 40:3. Petersen (1984a: 169–72; 1984b) notes the connection with Ezek 40–48, but argues that Zechariah's version "appears to challenge notions of restoration in Ezek 40–48." Petersen's view is contra Tollington (1993: 104–5), who argues that there is no direct dependency on Ezek 40.

(אֹרֶךְ, 40:7), which is the same vocabulary used to describe the task of the man in Zech 2:6. However, there are also some key differences between the two passages. The man in Ezekiel is measuring the temple, while the man in Zechariah is measuring Jerusalem. This difference suggests that an adaptation of Ezekiel is taking place.[43] Seven verses earlier, Zechariah has used another construction/measuring metaphor, in that case drawing on the language of Jeremiah.

נבנתה העיר ליהוה ממגדל חננאל שער הפנה
ויצא עוד קוה המדה

> *the city* shall be rebuilt for Yahweh from the tower of Hananel to the Corner Gate.
> And the *measuring* line shall go out. (Jer 31:38–39)

ביתי יבנה בה נאם יהוה צבאות
וקוה ינטה על־ירושלם

> *my house* shall be built in it, says Yahweh of Hosts, and the line shall be stretched out over *Jerusalem*. (Zech 1:16)

Zechariah 1:16 duplicates Jeremiah's unusual spelling of קוה (instead of the usual קו)[44] and uses the same metaphor to describe the extended limits of the city of Jerusalem. However, Zech 1:16 adds the phrase "my house (בֵּיתִי) shall be built in it." Temple rebuilding is not mentioned in the Jeremiah passage, though it *is* the subject of the vision of Ezek 40–48 Taken together, Zech 1:16 and 2:7 are a composite metaphor, combining the imagery and concerns of both Jeremiah and Ezekiel into a single image.

2.8.1. *Zechariah 1–8 and the Re-use of Texts*

From these examples we may make three observations regarding how Zech 1–8 uses other texts.[45]

43. See Petersen (1984a: 116–19) for the argument that Zechariah presents an "alternative vision of restoration" to Ezekiel. Similarly, Delkurt (2000: 138–40) argues that it represents a correction to the expectations of Ezek 40–48. I shall return to this issue in §4.6.1.

44. Note that the Ketib/Qere are also the same in both places. The typical spelling is reflected in 2 Chr 4:2; 2 Kgs 21:13; Ezek 47:3; Isa 28:17; 34:11, 17; 44:13; Job 38:5; Lam 2:8; Ps 19:5. The only other instance of the defective spelling is 1 Kgs 7:23.

45. Though they were derived independently, it is interesting to note that my conclusions are very similar to Willey's observations on the "recollection of the former things" in Isaiah; see Willey 1997: 141–42.

Loose Quotation: Zechariah rarely quotes clause-for-clause, nor even word-for-word, but instead freely adapts a source text. Not only does Zechariah adapt tense and person (singular/plural), but he also substitutes *cognate forms* (e.g. Zech 1:4—adjective רַע for noun רֹעַ) and *synonyms* (see Example 3).

Multiple Sources: Zechariah interweaves multiple source texts into one new composite picture—for example, the measuring of Jerusalem in Zech 1–2 is a combination of Ezek 40 and Jer 31. To use a musical analogy, while one dominant intertext might provide the "melody line," this is often nuanced by "overtones" from other intertexts.

A Variation on a Theme (Reworking and Extending a Metaphor Across a Passage): To use another musical analogy, Zechariah does not copy a source text word-for-word, but instead takes enough of its words/themes/metaphors to ensure that the reader will hear echoes of the original, then creatively works these elements into a new composition, in the same way that a composer creates a variation on a theme. An instance of this is the reworking of Isa 2:3 in Zech 8:20–23 (see Example 4).

2.9. *A Refined Methodology*

These observations regarding the re-use of texts in Zech 1–8 suggest that a method based on a strict word-search methodology is too narrow an approach for assessing intertextuality in Zech 1–8, not least because it is unable to detect where synonyms or cognates have been used, or where multiple texts have been interwoven.

Instead, what is needed is a method able to detect "thematic allusions," particularly where the same theme is expressed using different vocabulary. Even after some recent significant advances in computer software,[46] existing software was not able to perform this kind of searching.

Thus, in order to facilitate my research, I developed a new computer search engine (*BibleCrawler*). *BibleCrawler* is able to perform "semantic searches" on the Hebrew Bible by searching for synonyms, using data drawn from the Semantic Dictionary of Biblical Hebrew (SDBH).[47] I also

46. The two most significant recent products for students of the Hebrew Bible are the Hebrew Morphology prepared by the Workgroep Informatica of Vrije Universiteit (WIVA) under the direction of Professor Eep Talstra and the Andersen–Forbes Analysed Hebrew Bible. Versions of these databases are available for the Logos Bible Software system. For a description of the respective approaches of these two databases, see Talstra 1991; 1992; 1995, and Andersen and Forbes 1992.

47. An earlier (prototype) version of *BibleCrawler* was based on data from *A Dictionary of Biblical Languages with Semantic Domains: Hebrew (OT)* by James

created my own database of word families to facilitate cognate searching. In addition, I created a new search technique (modelled on internet searching) whereby the results are returned "scored and ranked" based on the frequency of search hits and their proximity to each other. This is particularly helpful for detecting possible echoes of multiple sources.

I wish, however, to stress that there is more to my methodology than a clever new computer tool. As I have suggested above, a weakness of other studies has been their over-reliance on computer tools, at the expense of human analysis. The proper use of computer tools is merely to identify patterns of word and theme usage which might aid human readers to identify intertexts. Recognizing intertextuality requires a *human* process of interpretation. Thus, my methodological approach to Zech 1–8 will use established critical tools and methods, integrating data from computer searches where appropriate.

My starting point is to seek to understand each subunit of Zech 1–8 in its immediate context, and in the context of Zech 1–8 as a whole. To interpret difficult words and phrases, I use all the normal tools of exegesis, including standard lexica and grammars. However, where I find that there are still "gaps" in the interpretation of the passage after these steps have been taken, I will look for possible allusions to other parts of the (then extant) corpus of the Hebrew Bible, and ask the question whether the first audience of Zech 1–8 might reasonably have used these other texts to make sense of the "gaps." I will use what is clear from the passage as the control to evaluate which, of the many possible intertexts, are likely intertexts for this passage.[48]

At this point, the computer tools described above assist in the identification of intertexts. In most cases, I am using the computer to confirm what I have found through an ordinary process of reading. In successive readings of the Hebrew Bible, I noted passages where I heard "echoes" of Zech 1–8 and vice versa, and in many cases I register the same "thematic allusions" that others have long identified in the book. However, the

Swanton, published as an electronic resource by Logos Research Systems ca. 1997. However, I moved to using the SDBH data when this became available, since SDBH provides a better conceptual model for the semantic analysis for Biblical Hebrew, rather than relying on semantic model developed by Louw and Nida for Koine Greek.

48. I note that this approach is similar to Rex Mason's approach to Zech 9–14. As Floyd (2003: 228) notes, Mason turns to "inner-biblical" investigation "where there seems to be ambiguity in the relationship between the main sections of the text. He then uses these parallels to explicate this ambiguity, so that readers can better understand the text's line of thought… Mason showed that there are often illuminative parallels with earlier prophetic texts at such points of rhetorical ambiguity."

chief benefit of the methodology I propose is that it can give a verifiable control to the concept of the "thematic allusion" as a basis for intertextuality. This provides a way to respond to Nurmela's claim that "other methods are less objective and less verifiable" (2003: 246–47). That two passages might share a theme is not in itself remarkable should that theme be a common one in the Hebrew Bible. The benefit of my computer search technique is that it can help to establish the rarity (or otherwise) of a theme, which in turn gives better grounds for arguing that Zech 1–8 is intended to be read in light of a specific intertext.

Where Zech 1–8 is reusing a rare theme or combination of themes and words, I will argue for a "specific text" form of intertextuality—for example, that Zech 1–8 has re-used a particular text from (say) Jer 25. However, this is not the only type of intertextuality I shall register. There are instances where Zech 1–8 clearly alludes to a common theme from the "general text" of the Hebrew Bible, even though the particular source cannot be identified with precision. For example, the paradisiacal image of "each man under his own vine and fig tree" is clearly alluded to in Zech 3:10, but is the source 1 Kgs 4:25; Mic 4:4; Isa 36:16 (parallel 2 Kgs 18:31) or some other text? This is an example of "general text" intertextuality. Those pursuing a "search for sources" approach have typically excluded these kinds of intertexts from their enquiries, whereas they are obviously relevant to the focus of my enquiry, since they are part of the textual background which makes Zech 1–8 intelligible. My computer tools also help to give grounds for distinguishing between examples of "specific text" and "general text" intertextuality.

Having established the likely intertexts which provide the textual web for understanding Zechariah, the final stage in my analysis is to read the relevant passage in Zechariah against the "background" of the identified intertext, to explore the additional depth of meaning which these intertexts provide to our understanding of Zech 1–8.

This refined methodology draws together elements from the three different approaches mentioned at the outset of this chapter: like *tradition history* approaches, it goes beyond the word-search in order to recognize "thematic allusions"; like *intertextual* approaches, it seeks to be sensitive to the literary effect of textual re-use in its various forms; like recent *inner-biblical* approaches, it focuses on "objective" results that can be quantified and analyzed.

Chapter 3

DATING ZECHARIAH 1–8 AND ITS INTERTEXTS

3.1. *Twin Context—Historical and Literary*

In the previous chapter I outlined the ways in which "connections between texts" have been analyzed in Biblical Studies generally, and positioned my approach in this field. My aim in this chapter is to lay the foundations for the application of my approach to one particular text, namely, Zech 1–8.

Zechariah 1–8 is commonly recognized as a discrete unit in the book.[1] The date-formulae in Zech 1:1; 1:7 and 7:1 function as structural markers, and locate the "action" of this part of the book in the period October 520 B.C.E.–December 518 B.C.E.[2] This historical context is of great significance. Although the first returnees from the exile had arrived some time after their liberation by Cyrus in 539 B.C.E., the temple still lay (more or less) in ruins in 520 B.C.E.[3] It was at this time that renewed activity under the leadership of Zerubbabel and Joshua finally led to the

1. An alternate (minority) view is that Zech 1–6 is a literary unit, and that Zech 7–8 is cataphoric, introducing the two oracles of Zech 9–14 (see Kline 1991; Sweeney 2000: 573–74; Webb 2003: 30–31).

2. The dates in Zechariah (and Haggai and Ezra 4–6) are expressed with reference to the reign of Darius. Darius's accession, after the assassination of a rival claimant to the throne, was in late 522 B.C.E.—perhaps December 22, though see Edelman (2005: 99–103) for other options. The Julian calendar equivalents for key dates are:

Zech 1:1	2nd year of Darius, 8th month, (no day)	October 27+, 520 B.C.E.
Zech 1:7	2nd year, 11th month (Shebat), 24th day	February 15, 519 B.C.E.
Zech 7:1	4th year, 9th month (Kislev), 4th day	December 7, 518 B.C.E.
Ezra 6:15	6th year, 12th month (Adar), 3rd day	March 10, 515 B.C.E.

3. Ezra 5:15–16 refers to an earlier refounding of the temple under Sheshbazzar under the aegis of Cyrus, but this had clearly not progressed very far since Hag 1:4 can say in 520 B.C.E. that the house of Yahweh is still a "desolation."

restoration of the temple in 515 B.C.E.[4] Zechariah 1–8 situates itself in the midst of this tumultuous period.

Furthermore, Zech 1–8 indicates that it is to be read in another context—the literary context of "the former prophets" (הַנְּבִאִים הָרִאשֹׁנִים). The importance of this group is signalled both by the explicit references to them in 1:4 and 7:7, 12, as well as by the plethora of echoes of the words of these earlier prophets in Zech 1–8 (which will be analyzed in the chapters which follow). Clearly, for these references and echoes to have any meaning, there must be some set of prophetic works in "circulation"—that is, known to both author and audience—at the time Zech 1–8 is written.

Thus, in order to examine Zech 1–8 in these twin contexts, we must make some initial assumptions about dating by asking the following questions: When was Zech 1–8 written? And what texts might have been in circulation at this time? The aim of this chapter is to provide some *prima facie* answers to these questions. I stress that I am *not* attempting to prove definitively what (say) the book of Ezekiel must have contained around 520 B.C.E., but seeking only to establish that there are reasonable grounds to proceed on some initial assumptions about what the book of Ezekiel contained at that point in time. For the most part, this *prima facie* case will be established by undercutting those arguments which *necessitate* a late date for particular material. This will allow us to consider the hypothesis that Zech 1–8 has alluded to other passages.

My reason for beginning with *prima facie* assumptions about dating is that to reach any conclusions about dating requires an iterative process. One relevant piece of evidence about dating is whether one passage alludes to another. However, to test for allusion requires some initial assumptions about the origins of passages. For example, later in this chapter I will argue that it is reasonable to begin with the assumption that Ezek 38–39 was an exilic (rather than post-exilic) composition. Then, in the following chapter, I will demonstrate a number of textual parallels between Zech 1–2 and Ezek 38–39, and make the argument that Zech 1–2 is making a sustained allusion to Ezek 38–39 (and not vice versa). The evidence of these allusions (should it be convincing to my reader) is an important piece of evidence confirming our *prima facie* assumption, since it shows that by 519 B.C.E. (which is when I take Zech 1–2 to have been written), those parts of Ezek 38–39 being alluded to must have been

4. Contra Edelman (2005: 92), who argues the temple was completed in 518 B.C.E. on the basis of Zech 7:1–4. However, the cessation of fasting in these verses does not necessarily imply that the temple reconstruction is finished, but only that there is not longer a need to continue to fast over its destruction.

extant. Thus, the evidence of allusion feeds back into the question of dating, to either confirm or nullify our starting assumption.

In this chapter, I argue that it is reasonable to proceed on the assumption that the substance of Zech 1–8 was written in the last part of the sixth century B.C.E. I also seek to establish what writings might have constituted "the former prophets" to which Zech 1–8 refers at this point in history.

I realize that the quest of this chapter is likely to raise eyebrows among historical "revisionists." Philip Davies and others[5] have argued for a thoroughgoing revision of the dating of biblical literature, to such an extent that all biblical texts would post-date the putative ministry of the prophet Zechariah. Davies argues that all biblical texts are the product of scribal schools working in the Persian Period (fifth century B.C.E. and beyond). In these texts, the scribes have created an *apparent* history of the kingdoms of Judah and Israel, but this "history" is nothing more than a literary construct. According to Davies, this "history" is an ideological projection of the social elite in Persian-period Yehud, who were aware that they were an alien culture who had been transplanted there by the Persians, and so had assembled a fictional history of "exodus" and "united monarchy" and "exile" and thence "return" in order to give themselves indigenous roots and legitimization. "This new society generated its own identity, via literature, through the production of a history," according to Davies (1992: 118). While Davies's interest is primarily in the "history" of Israel, his conclusion must necessarily extend to prophetic works as well, since the historical markers woven into a book such as Jeremiah endorse the same apparent history of Israel. And so, according to Davies, prophecy too is a post-exilic product; the social critique of (say) an Amos or Jeremiah are merely words put on the lips of these prophets by scribes in the fifth century "criticizing their own régime" (1992: 107; cf. 24); and the poems of Deutero-Isaiah were written in Jerusalem in the fifth century (1992: 118).[6]

I am not persuaded by the argument for revisionism, because (in part) of the evidence of Zech 1–8. As I demonstrate in the chapters which follow, Zech 1–8 is composed of numerous allusions to, and echoes of,

5. See Davies 1992. Other important figures in the "revisionist" camp are Niels Peter Lemche (1991; 1998) and Thomas Thompson (1999). Similarly, Robert Carroll (1986; 1996) takes the book of Jeremiah to be a product of Persian-period ideology.

6. Davies concedes that "the prophetic books of the Bible may well have a basis in collections of archived materials remaining from the Iron Age" (1992: 111). However, in Davies's view, these collections are fragments of generic prophecy, and not "scrolls of collected oracles assigned to individual prophets" (1992: 112).

"the former prophets," which I take to be *prima facie* evidence that there was a body of prophetic works that predated Zech 1–8, since any appeal to non-extant prophetic works would have been nonsensical to Zechariah's first hearers.[7]

3.2. *When Was Zechariah 1–8 Written?*

Many scholars would accept that (most of) the "night-visions," which comprise the core of Zech 1–6, come from the time—and perhaps even the pen—of Zechariah himself. But there the consensus ends. There are four key issues which impact on the question of the dating of various sections of Zech 1–8.

1. The "Joshua" vision—Is Zech 3 original to the sequence of night-visions or a later addition?
2. "Messiah Zerubbabel"—Has the book been adjusted to remove original "messianic" promises concerning Zerubbabel in light of the "failure" of Zerubbabel to ascend to the throne?
3. The Oracles—Are the oracles which now follow many of the night-visions original, or later additions which alter the theological thrust of the original visions?
4. An "editorial framework"—To what extent is the present shape and content of Zech 1–8 the result of a later editorial framework, perhaps as part of a "Chronistic" redaction?

Since my aim at this point is merely to establish a *terminus ad quem* (to help delineate the date range for "the former prophets"), I can simplify these issues somewhat. It would not substantially change the data set under consideration should the book have been written by the prophet Zechariah in its entirety before 515 B.C.E., as against the addition of an editorial framework (or even a more thoroughgoing redaction) sometime within a decade or two of this date. For the sake of convenience, I will bracket these and similar positions together, where the common feature is the view that Zech 1–8 is a product of the "Zecharian milieu." By this I mean that the substance of the book was written in the period of the prophet Zechariah (late sixth century B.C.E.), reflecting the theological outlook of that era.

7. In answer to this argument, a revisionist could no doubt reply that these "allusions" are also only a literary construct, artfully woven into Zech 1–8 in order to give the prophetic corpus an apparent pre-history. As a matter of logic, the revisionist argument is technically irrefutable, since any contrary evidence can be explained as a literary artifice. However, while I concede the revisionist case is possible, I am not at all convinced that it is likely.

This position is to be contrasted with the view that Zech 1–8, as we now have it, is a product of a later generation, which I shall dub the "Priestly milieu."[8] I use this phrase to refer to the view that Zech 1–8 has been edited in an era subsequent to the prophet Zechariah, at a time (say the mid-fifth century B.C.E.) when—it is supposed—the effective rulers of Yehud are now the priests, and that the book has been edited in such a way as to reinforce/legitimate their hierocracy.

A third alternative is that Zech 1–8 as we now have it is later still—a product of the "Chronistic milieu." Beuken argues that Haggai and Zech 1–8 share with the Chronicler both a common interest in the rituals of the temple and the Davidic line, as well as common forms like the "Levitical" sermon. Beuken (1967: 331–36) argues that these commonalities stem from a redaction of Haggai and Zechariah in the time of the Chronicler (fourth century B.C.E.?), perhaps even from the hand of the Chronicler himself.

There is a deliberate elasticity in the use of the terms "Zecharian milieu," "Priestly milieu" and "Chronistic milieu." My aim in using these terms is not the precise delineation of dates (because the paucity of historical data makes this impossible), but rather to suggest successive stages of historical development, which is of direct relevance to the questions at issue. If Zech 1–8 in substance reached its present form in the "Zecharian milieu," then the texts to which it alludes are in circulation in the last decades of the sixth century. At the other extreme, if it reaches its final form in "Chronistic milieu," then the set of antecedent texts might include another two centuries of literary development.

3.2.1. *Arguing for a Zecharian Milieu*

Having outlined these three alternatives, I now argue the case that the best approach is to view Zech 1–8 as a product of the last decades of the sixth century—a "Zecharian milieu."

To make this case, I will examine those features which some have argued date from a later milieu (i.e. Zech 3, the oracular material, and "Chronistic" features in the editorial framework), in order to demonstrate that there are no compelling reasons to date these features subsequent to the Zecharian milieu.

8. This is my version of Mason's "theocratic tradents." Mason distinguishes his position from that of Beuken, arguing that "we need not limit them [i.e. theocratic tradents] as closely as Beuken does to circles akin to the Chronicler" (Mason 1982a: 145).

3.2.2. *The Originality of the "Joshua" Vision (Zechariah 3)*

Commentators are divided as to whether Zech 3:1–10 (or some part thereof) is original or not.[9] The argument that Zech 3 is a secondary addition is based on its divergences in form from the other visions. In the following table of the introductory formulae of the eight night-visions, the fourth vision differs from the others in a number of ways:

- the absence of the phrase "and I lifted my eyes…and behold,"
- the inclusion of the direct object marker,
- the single instance of the Hiphil form of the verb.

1:8		ראיתי הלילה והנה־איש רכב	
2:1 (= ET 1:18)	והנה ארבע קרנות	ואשא את־עיני וארא	
2:5 (= ET 2:1)	והנה־איש ובידו חבל מדה	ואשא עיני וארא	
3:1	את־יהושע הכהן הגדול	ויראני	
4:1–2	הנה מנורת	ראיתי	ויאמר ואמר
5:1	והנה מגלה עפה	עיני ואראה	ואשוב ואשא
5:5	מה היוצאת הזאת	עינך וראה	שא נא
6:1	והנה ארבע מרכבות	עיני ואראה	ואשב ואשא

It should, however, be noted that no two introductions are identical—even the four formulae which are closest (underlined references in the list above) differ in minor ways from each other. In addition, Zech 3:1 is not the only introduction which has a divergent form. Zechariah 5:5 also diverges significantly from the pattern, in that instead of the narration "I lifted my eyes and saw," it contains the command "lift up your eyes and see." However, most commentators do not consider the seventh vision to be secondary for this reason. It should also be noted the Hiphil form in Zech 3:1 (וַיַּרְאֵנִי, "and he caused me to see") has already been used in Zech 2:3 in exactly the same form, so the phraseology is clearly not foreign to the prophet.

While I agree that Zech 3:1 is formally different, I will argue presently that this has been done intentionally by the original author, rather than being a sign of a (clumsy) redaction. The vision sequence in Zech 1–6 has inherited its form from multiple sources. I agree with Tollington (1993: 99) that there are formal connections with Gen 31:10–12 which are striking.[10] The phrase וָאֶשָּׂא עֵינַי וָאֵרֶא בַּחֲלוֹם וְהִנֵּה in Gen 31:10

9. The following scholars argue that Zech 3 is non-original/disruptive to the sequence: Elliger 1963: 112, 118–22; Jepsen 1948: 96–97; Chary 1969: 73; Horst 1964: 210; van der Woude 1988: 237–38; Tigchelaar 1996: 16–19. In contrast, the following scholars are examples of those who argue that it is integral to the original sequence: Bič 1964; Baldwin 1972; Rudolph 1976; Rose 2000: 37–41.

10. On the role of this dream in Gen 31, see Lipton 1999: esp. 115–44.

provides the formal template for the majority of the visions,[11] and the otherwise curious departure from form in the seventh vision follows the pattern of Gen 31:12 (וַיֹּאמֶר שָׂא־נָא עֵינֶיךָ וּרְאֵה).

However, Gen 31 explains only some of the elements of Zechariah's visions. In Gen 31, the objects of the dream (multi-coloured goats) corresponds to real-world objects, whereas in Zech 1–6, the visionary objects are symbolic (e.g. horns = nations, olive trees = two men). As Niditch (1983) has convincingly demonstrated, Zech 1–6 has also drawn on the tradition of the symbolic vision from both Amos and Jeremiah.[12]

Furthermore, Zechariah's angelic interpreter would appear to be a development of the interpreter in the book of Ezekiel.[13] A further formal connection between the night-visions and Ezekiel is evident in the phrase אֶרְאֶ(ה) וְהִנֵּה. First-person vision reports in Ezekiel are typically introduced by אֶרְאֶה וְהִנֵּה,[14] and this same phrase is used to introduce five of Zechariah's visions.

Having established the (hardly controversial) point that the night-visions in Zech 1–6 have inherited their form from multiple sources, my argument on Zech 3 requires only one more step—that is to say, Zech 3:1 is formally different because the author is consciously imitating a different form at this point. In particular, Zech 3 bears striking similarities with other examples of the divine council scene,[15] especially Isa 6, which likewise describes a cleansing from sin of an identified historical person. I suggest that the differences in form between Zech 3 and the other night-visions are because of a deliberate patterning after Isa 6 and other "divine council" scenes. For example, as noted by Jeremias (1977: 204 n. 1) there are parallels in structure between Zech 3:1 and Isa 6:1, in that what the prophet "sees" (ראה) is marked by אֵת and a participial construction.[16] Conversely, the phrase "and I lifted my eyes...and behold"

11. This form is also imitated in Dan 8:3 and 10:5, which replicate the phrase וָאֶשָּׂא (אֶת־)עֵינַי וָאֵרֶא.

12. E.g. Amos 7:7–9 (plumb line); 8:1–3 (ripe fruit); Jer 1:11–12 (almond bud); 1:13–19 (boiling pot); 24:3 (fig baskets). As discussed above at §1.2.1, Niditch (1983) argues that Zechariah's symbolic visions are a development of the "symbolic vision" form in Amos and Jeremiah.

13. E.g. Ezek 8:2, 5; 40:2–4; 47:6–12 where an interpreter explains the meaning and significance of the heavenly vision. This imagery appears to have been combined with the form of "explanatory dialogue" (e.g. Ezek 37).

14. E.g. Ezek 1:4; 2:9; 8:2, 7, 10; 10:1, 9; 44:4.

15. Examples of the "divine council scene" are 1 Kgs 22; Isa 6; 40; Job 1; 2; Zech 3. See §5.3.1 for a further analysis of this.

16. While this is not unique to Isa 6 and Zech 3, it is rare, appearing elsewhere only at Amos 9:1 and Eccl 4:1. Given the other thematic connections between Isa 6 and Zech 3, it seems very likely that Zechariah has imitated the form of Isa 6.

(וָאֶשָּׂא עֵינַי...וְהִנֵּה), which is absent from Zech 3:1, is also not present in Isa 6:1. This patterning after Isa 6 also explains other formal divergences between Zech 3 and the remaining night-visions, because Zech 3 (like Isa 6) is not merely a *symbolic vision*, but a *symbolic act* involving the prophet.

In summary, considerations of form and content do not provide sufficient reasons to conclude that Zech 3 is secondary when it is understood that the unique features of Zech 3 stem from a patterning after Isa 6 and other divine council scenes.[17]

The final objection which has been raised against the originality of Zech 3 is an argument from literary and/or theological context. Jeremias argues that the "original" vision sequence involved a sequence of seven units, with the "lampstand" vision the focal point, and that the insertion of Zech 3 has disrupted the symmetry (1977: 201–3). A theological variation on this argument is that Zech 3 was inserted in a later era to shift the focus away from a (failed) revival of the Davidic monarchy through Zerubbabel and onto the high priestly office (e.g. Sinclair 1975: 45). But there is a much stronger argument to the contrary, an argument also based on context. As Meyers and Meyers have noted, "the messages of the two central visions are...complementary, with the meaning of the one being incomplete and incomprehensible without the meaning of the other" (1987: lviii). The vision in Zech 4 involves two olive trees. I will argue in Chapter 5 that these two trees represent Joshua and Zerubbabel. While Zerubbabel is explicitly named in Zech 4, Joshua is not. Without Zech 3, there are no clues as to the identity of the second "olive tree." Either one must accept some form of Zech 3 as original, or else follow the lead of Redditt, who argues that *all* the passages which mention Joshua and Zerubbabel must be secondary additions. Redditt argues that:

> the original series of visions numbered seven, none of which made any reference to Joshua or Zerubbabel... The night visions were composed for Jews still in Babylon to urge them to return home and participate in God's new order. (Redditt 1992: 255)

Redditt's argument is similar to that of Galling (1964a), who argued that the first three night-visions originated in the exilic period, on the basis that their emphasis was on renewal and restoration. In the next chapter, I shall evaluate this claim, and demonstrate that the emphasis on restoration and reversal after "seventy years" most reasonably situates these visions in the historical context given in Zech 1:7 (i.e. ca. 519 B.C.E.). However, for the sake of the argument, let us suppose (with Redditt) that

17. I shall consider the reasons why Zech 3 should allude to Isa 6 below at §5.3.

there might have been an early "edition" of the night-visions. If this was so, then the addition of Joshua and Zerubbabel to the night-visions cannot have been much later than 519 B.C.E. As Redditt acknowledges,

> The addition of the Joshua/Zerubbabel materials (4:6b–10a; 6:11b–13; 3:1–10) provided the visions with new contents and directed them to a new audience. The new focus was the events of 520BC and the future those events were inaugurating... The addition of 4:6b–10a, 6:11b–13, and 3:1–7,9 resulted in a "revised, enlarged" edition of the night visions, now aimed at the community in Jerusalem in the flush of the building of the temple under Zerubbabel and promising them a new day. It advocated carrying forward two of the basic institutions of preexilic Judah: the priesthood, under the high priest Joshua, and the Davidic monarchy, under Zerubbabel. (Redditt 1992: 255, 257)

As Redditt notes, the "Joshua/Zerubbabel materials" presuppose a very particular historical and political situation. It can hardly be supposed that Zech 4:6b–10a—which promises that Zerubbabel *will* complete the temple—was written later than 515 B.C.E. Thus, by 515 B.C.E. there must have been a version of Zech 4 in which Zerubbabel is identified by name, in the context of a vision of a lampstand and two olive trees. However, this then also requires that there must also have been a Zech 3, in order to give us the identity of the other "olive tree." Thus, we come in the end to the same position, that all eight night-visions were present in Zech 1–8 as it stood in (say) 518 B.C.E. Furthermore, as we shall see when we look at the details of Zech 3 (see §5.3.2 and 5.3.3), there is no compelling reason to view these verses as reflecting anything other than the historical/political/theological outlook of that era.

3.2.3. *The Originality of the Oracular Materials*

A number of the night-visions are followed by oracles which report the word of Yahweh (typically marked by כֹּה אָמַר יְהוָה or נְאֻם־יְהוָה). Though there is a variation between scholars on the precise number and demarcation of these oracles, a typical list of the oracular materials would include 1:14–17; 2:8b–17; 3:8–10; 4:6aβ–10a; 5:4 and 6:9–14.[18]

Recognizing the formal distinction between vision and oracle is helpful for interpretation. However, some scholars not only distinguish between vision and oracle, but divide them completely. For example, in

18. Following the identification of Meyers and Meyers (1987: 132). Petitjean's list is similar, though it includes Zech 1:1–6 and excludes Zech 5:4. For another slightly different delineation, see Petersen 1984a: 121. See Clark 1994 for an analysis of the structural characteristics and placement of the oracular material.

seeking to undercut the argument that Zechariah's visions are about the reconstruction of the temple, Petersen argues

> Most of the direct references to the reconstruction of the temple in Zech i-viii occur in the oracular material not in the visions themselves... This distinction is critical since, as many scholars maintain, the visions comprise a quite distinct body of material from the oracles. (Petersen 1984b: 196–97)

In discussing the oracular materials, it is helpful to contrast the positions of Beuken and Petitjean, who have both contributed magisterial studies on the Zecharian oracles.

Beuken (1967) argues that the book has undergone a redaction in a Chronistic milieu. He argues that, although parts of the oracles were composed by Zechariah ca. 520 B.C.E., some of the oracles now reflect a much later theological viewpoint, which has been added in a chronistic-era redaction. For example, Beuken detects the hand of this redactor at several points in Zech 3 in the exalted role given to the priesthood (1967: 296–97) and similarly argues that Zech 6 (with its depiction of an enthroned priest apparently on par with a Davidic king) is likewise a product of a later theological era (1967: 281). Mason's work continues (in a measure) the trajectory of Beuken's work.[19]

Petitjean (1969) argues that the oracles were composed as independent literary units, rather than as interpretations of the night-visions. According to Petitjean, the oracles were prompted by three historical phases, as shown in the following table (summarized from Petitjean 1969: 440–43):

The return from exile	*Temple commencement*	*Temple completion*
1:14b–17		1:1–6
2:10–13		
	3:8–10	
	4:6b–7	4:9–10a
	6:(9)10–12	6:13–15
7:4–14		
8:1–8		8:9–13 8:14–17, 18–23

Accordingly, Petitjean argues that almost all the oracles are authentically "Zecharian":

19. Mason writes, "there are signs that Zech 1–8 were also edited in similar [Priestly/Chronistic] circles. Traces of such editing are found mainly in the passages before and after the visions" (1977a: 10).

> Il nous a paru qu'on ne peut dénier l'authenticité zacharienne d'aucune partie importante de l'ensemble formé par les oracles. Les retouches rédactionnelles sont rares; elles portent particulièrement sur les formules d'introduction. Le rédacteur a remanié le texte originel de *Zach.* I, 1 ; le verset IV, 8 a été déplacé et VII, 8 provient d'une interpolation. En outre, la finale de la péricope I, 1–6 résulte vraisemblablement du travail rédactionnel. (1969: 440)

This comparison between Beuken and Petitjean highlights the intrinsic difficulties in dating the oracles. Petitjean, who thoroughly interacts with Beuken's views and is working with the same body of evidence, has come to very different conclusions about the dating of the oracles. In particular, he sees nothing inconsistent with what is promised to the high priest in the context of the theological viewpoint of the late sixth century B.C.E. (This view shall be confirmed in the detailed exegesis of Zech 3 below—see §5.3.3.) Though it is difficult to speak of a consensus, it is fair to say that the majority of work on Zechariah since Beuken has not been convinced by his argument that the theological viewpoint of the oracles necessarily reflects the era of the Chronicler. For example, Petersen takes the opposite position to Beuken in arguing that the oracles in Zech 1–6 seem to be "designed to soften the proposals for high-priestly authority that are expressed in the visions" (Petersen 1984a: 125). Different again are Meyers and Meyers, who take the view that the oracles complement (rather than ameliorate) the message of the visions (1987: lxxi). This lack of consensus suggests that the evidence is far from unambiguous, and hinges on the exegetical decisions regarding what precisely is being promised to Joshua and Zerubbabel in the visions and oracles (on which, see Chapter 5 below).

There is an increasing stress in recent scholarship that the oracles must be understood in both the literary context of the night-visions and the historical context of the era of the temple's reconstruction (whether or not any elements of the oracles may have had an earlier independent existence), because of the thematic connections between vision and oracle. For example, while Petersen argues that the oracles offer *reactions to* the visions,[20] and Meyers and Meyers view the oracles as *explanations of* the visions,[21] they alike recognize that vision and oracle must now be understood in the context of the other.[22]

20. See esp. Petersen 1984a: 120–22; 1984b.

21. See, for example, Meyers and Meyers 1987: 172.

22. See also the analysis of Tollington (1993: 37–47), who demonstrates that the oracles are best understood as coming from the hand of Zechariah before the temple was complete. It should be noted that Tollington assigns Zech 3:8 and the final form of Zech 6:9–15 to a later era. See the analysis of this below in Chapter 5.

Furthermore, as noted above, Zech 1–8 draws on the tradition of the symbolic vision from both Amos and Jeremiah. These parallels establish the precedent that an explanatory "word of Yahweh" is an integral part of the symbolic vision from the outset.[23] For many of Zechariah's visions, the oracles provide that "word," without which the vision would not make sense. For example, if we remove the oracle (1:14–17) from the first vision (1:8–13) then we are left with an incomplete message: the plea of "How long, O Yahweh?" in 1:12 results in kind and comforting words (1:13), but the content of these comforting words is nowhere given, except in the "oracle" which follows in 1:14–17.[24] I agree with the conclusion of Meyers and Meyers:

> the ideas contained within the oracles amplify themes found in the visions and at the same time are based upon features of these associated visions. In other words, vision and oracle complement and supplement each other. They are alternative modes of prophetic communication, used in tandem by the prophet. Each is particularly suited to an aspect of his message, and so the message is communicated in two modes. But the message is incomplete without the mutuality of these two forms of prophetic language. (1987: lix)

In reaching this conclusion, I must necessarily anticipate the exegesis of particular passages (especially Zech 3, 4 and 6) and I beg my reader's patience until then for the substantiation of my view that there is nothing in these chapters which prohibits a dating in Zechariah's time, because vision and oracle present complementary (rather than alternate) visions of the restoration.

3.2.4. *A "Chronistic" Editorial Framework?*

There are undeniable thematic connections between Zech 1:1–6 and Zech 7–8.[25] These two units seem to act as a frame around the "night-visions." In 1952, Ackroyd made the suggestion that these two units of material had been added to the book to provide an editorial framework to the vision and oracles of Zechariah in order to adapt their message to a later generation. This editing was part of a larger project which involved adding a similar framework to the book of Haggai:

> We can perhaps picture someone in a period not far removed from the 'Chronicler' setting out the evidence which would provide encouragement to his own generation... The theory here propounded that the two

23. So also Floyd (2000: 328): "[t]he vision report genre typically contains some explication of the symbolic figures that are visualized by prophetic recipients of visions, and this explication frequently takes the form of oracular speech."
24. A point similarly made by Tollington 1993: 38.
25. These will be taken up in the discussion of Zech 7–8 in Chapter 8.

> collections of Haggai and Zechariah i–viii were brought out together, with a concluding exhortation and promise in Zech viii.9–23, would explain the special character of the two books and in particular their similarities of style and content. (1952: 155)

Since Ackroyd's work, the idea of some kind of editorial framework has come to be generally accepted,[26] though its timing and extent are greatly debated. At one extreme, Meyers and Meyers argue that the editorial framework was added to Haggai and Zech 1–8 in order to create a single composite work some time prior to the rededication of the temple in 515 B.C.E. (1987: 98).[27] At the other extreme, Beuken has argued that the editorial framework, which transformed prophetic oracles into a "chronicle," was added in the "chronistic milieu," perhaps even by the Chronicler himself (1967: 331–36).

Beuken's argument regarding dating is based on his identification of some ideology and phraseology in Zech 1–8 which is distinctively "Chronistic." With respect to ideology, it is undeniable that the Chronicler and Zech 1–8 have a shared interest in the temple cultus and the continuity of the Davidic line, though these issues would surely have been high on the agenda from the moment of return from exile, and so it is hardly possible to establish that they are unique to a Chronistic milieu. With respect to the alleged "Chronistic" phraseology in Zech 1–8, it must be noted that serious questions have been raised about the nature and extent of these parallels.[28]

26. Though, in my opinion, the case for an editorial framework in Haggai (see, e.g., Mason 1977b; Tollington 1993: 19–23) is more persuasive than it is for Zech 1–8. Furthermore, if the editorial frameworks of both Haggai and Zech 1–8 are the product of a common redaction, then why are there different titles for Zerubbabel? In Hag 1:1, 12, 14, Zerubbabel is explicitly identified as "son of Shealtiel, governor of Judah," acknowledging both his Davidic descent and his leadership role within the community. There is no corresponding description in Zech 1–8 (either in the "framework" or otherwise) of the genealogy or role of Zerubbabel, though both are clearly presupposed. One would have thought that a common redactional hand would have replicated the same titles. On the differences between the date formulae in the "frameworks" of Haggai and Zech 1–8, see further Kessler 2002a.

27. Similarly Baldwin 1972: 30.

28. For a strong rebuttal of Beuken's argument for Chronistic phraseology in Zech 1:1–6, see Tigchelaar 1996: 75. Mason (1977b: 415–16) notes that the phrase וַיְהִי דְבַר־יְהוָה בְּיַד—which Beuken characterized as Chronistic—"accords more with deuteronomistic usage." See also Petersen (1984a: 37–38) and Meyers and Meyers (1987: 94) for a similar critique of Beuken's position.

While not denying the parallels between Haggai/Zech 1–8 and the Chronicler, it is more likely that the former influenced the latter, rather than that the latter edited the

Not only is Beuken's evidence for explicitly "Chronistic" phraseology found wanting, but his thesis is also significantly undercut by more recent investigations into the linguistic features of Late Biblical Hebrew (LBH).[29] The distinctive features of LBH which are present in the work of the Chronicler are *not* present in Zech 1–8 as a whole, and in particular are also *not* present in those parts of Zech 1–8 which Beuken assigns to a Chronistic redaction, as shown in the following table:

LBH Features[30]	*Features of Zech 1–8*
1. Collectives are construed as plurals	Singular collectives (2:8, 17; 7:2; 8:3)
2. Preference for plural forms of words and phrases which the earlier language used in the singular	no instances of Polzin's examples of "pluralized singulars"
3. Increased use of את before noun in the nominative case	Only one instance of את before noun in the nominative case (see Zech 7:7)
4. אני for אנכי	
5. Repetition of a singular word to express a distributive.	No repetition of singular word to express a distributive
6. Substantive occurs before the numeral and plural	Substantive after number: e.g. Zech 5:3; 1 Chr 3:3
7. Order of material weighed or measured + its weight or measure	n/a
8. Radically reduced use of את with pronominal suffix	Frequent use of את with pronominal suffix: Zech 2:4, 10, 12; 3:4; 5:8; 6:8; 8:8, 13–14

former. Beuken concedes that the Chronicler often inherited deuteronomistic language (1967: 28, 35), and so, by extension, I take it as likely that it should not also have been influenced by other works (like Zechariah) which have a deuteronomistic "flavour" (see also the comments below at §3.2.1).

29. A decade or so after Beuken's work on Zech 1–8, Robert Polzin (1976) analyzed the language of the Chronicler, and isolated 19 grammatical/syntactic features which were distinctive of Late Biblical Hebrew. On this, see further the summary in Hill 1982 and the analysis in Naudé 2003: 190–94. Since that time, Avi Hurvitz has been a leading exponent of the distinctive features of LBH as a criterion for the dating for biblical texts (see, e.g., Hurvitz 1982; 1988; 1997; 2000). While I am not arguing that we can date biblical texts on linguistic grounds—on which, see the debates in Young 2003—the absence of the stylistic traits of the Chronicler in Zech 1–8 is a telling indictment against the claim that Zech 1–8 bears the marks of Chronistic editing.

30. List based on Rooker 2003: 57.

9. Less frequent use of the infinitive absolute in immediate connection with a finite verb of the same stem.	Moderate use of the infinitive-absolute + finite verb in Zech 6:15; 7:5; 8:21
10. More frequent use of the infinitive construct with כ and ב not preceded by ויהי	Infrequent use (Zech 7:7; 8:14) of infinitive construct + ב
11. Avoids *waw* consecutive	Frequent use of *waw* consecutive perfect ×47, imperfect ×97
12. Participle with היה	Very infrequent use of participle with היה (participle ×54, once with היה)
13. ל often the mark of the accusative	ל only twice marks the accusative (Zech 1:15; 8:14)
14. אשר for כי	n/a

The only distinctive feature of LBH which does occur in Zech 1–8 is the use of אֲנִי, rather than אָנֹכִי (Zech 2:9; 5:2; 7:5; 8:8, 11, 21). However, this can hardly be significant in and of itself, since the book of Jeremiah uses אֲנִי more than אָנֹכִי, and the book of Ezekiel uses אֲנִי almost exclusively, and Zechariah often follows the phraseology of both. On the basis of this evidence, I conclude that Zech 1–8 is not characterized by the LBH which characterizes Chronicles.[31]

This undercuts Beuken's suggestion that Zech 1–8 was edited in a Chronistic milieu, since there are no traces of the distinctive marks that we might have expected to see in the Chronicler's writings. The best explanation for similarities between the Zech 1–8 and the work of the Chronicler is that the language of Zech 1–8 has influenced a later generation of authors.[32]

3.2.5. *Conclusion to this Section*

Zechariah 1–8 purports to be have been written in a "Zecharian" milieu (i.e. sixth century B.C.E.). The burden of proof lies on those who would argue for a later dating to establish their case. We have examined the arguments typically advanced for a later dating, and have found that none is sufficiently compelling to displace the presumption for dating established by the text. Accordingly, we shall proceed on the basis that Zech 1–8 was a product of the last decades of the sixth century.[33]

31. See also the analysis of Ehrensvärd (2003: 175–85), which demonstrates that Zech 1–8 is classical Biblical Hebrew (BH).

32. So similarly Meyers and Meyers 1987: 95 and Baldwin 1972: 30.

33. See similarly Floyd 2000: 311–13 and Meyers and Meyers 1987: 95.

3.3. *Texts in Circulation when Zechariah 1–8 was Written*

Having made the case that Zech 1–8 is a product of the last decades of the sixth century B.C.E., it is now necessary to establish what texts might have been in circulation at this time, since this will help to delineate "the former prophets" to whom Zechariah refers.

The dating of prophetic texts is no easy matter. Outside the "revisionist" camp, few scholars would object to the assumption that *some form* of Isaiah, Jeremiah and Ezekiel had been written by 520–500 B.C.E. However, there is still much debate on particular sections (e.g. Jer 33:14–26, the suggested "priestly additions" to Ezek 40–48; Isa 56–66 etc.).

Since it is well beyond the scope of this present work to attempt to reconstruct the transmission history of the entire Hebrew Bible, I will simplify matters by focussing only on those passages which might be alluded to by Zech 1–8, and analyze only those passages where there is a significant debate about whether their composition may have post-dated the composition of Zech 1–8.

3.3.1. *The Book of Jeremiah in 520 B.C.E.*

In 1914 Sigmund Mowinckel partitioned the book of Jeremiah into oracles (source A), Baruch's biographical material (source B), deuteronomistic additions (source C) and the oracles of hope in Jer 30–31 (source D). Since that time, scholarship has sought to account for this variety in the book—and for the "Oracles against the Nations" (OAN) which Mowinckel had dismissed as a late secondary addition (1914: 65–66)—by proposing a variety of redactional theories. For the present purposes, these theories can be grouped into three sets:

1. Those where the book of Jeremiah as we now have it is the product of a short redactional process, perhaps completed in the lifetime of Jeremiah, or subsequently by Baruch. Exponents of this view include Holladay 1986; 1989; Unterman 1987; McConville 1993.
2. Those where the book of Jeremiah has emerged through a deuteronomistic redaction (or multiple redactions) during the exilic period. Exponents of this view include Nicholson 1970; Thiel 1973; 1981.
3. Those where the book of Jeremiah was produced by an ongoing redactional process extending well into the post-exilic period. Exponents of this view include Carroll 1986; McKane 1986.[34]

34. Carroll argues that Jeremiah is a collection of polyphonic voices reflecting the reconstruction of the Palestinian communities in the Second Temple period.

Since my focus is on the book as it stood around 520 B.C.E., either of the first two sets of theories resolves to the same position (i.e. that the book of Jeremiah would have been substantively in its present form by the time of the prophet Zechariah). But the third set of theories opens up the possibility that some parts of the book of Jeremiah post-date Zech 1–8. There are three matters in particular which may have an impact on our present enquiry: (1) the extent of any ongoing (i.e. Persian period) deuteronomistic redaction of Jeremiah; (2) the version of the book (MT*Vorlage* or the LXX*Vorlage*) to which Zech 1–8 alludes; and (3) the relationship to some specific passages (esp. Jer 33) which are sometimes argued to be late additions to the book of Jeremiah.

3.3.1.1. *Zechariah and Jeremiah's Deuteronomistic Redaction(s).* There are two passages in Zech 1–8 which explicitly purport to be echoing the words of "the former prophets" (הַנְּבִיאִים הָרִאשֹׁנִים)—1:4 and 7:7–14.

The first of these instances is a clear allusion to Jer 25:5–7 (as argued above, see §2.8, example 1). The verses in Jer 25 to which Zech 1:4 alludes are commonly recognized to have a deuteronomistic flavour.[35] Thus, to whatever extent these verses are the product of a later deuteronomistic redaction, this must have occurred before the time of the writing of Zech 1:4.[36]

With reference to the second explicit reference to "the former prophets," I must anticipate my later argument somewhat. I will demonstrate in §7.5 that Zech 7:7–14 alludes to Jer 7. It is commonly held that Jer 7

35. Thiel describes them as a "freie D Komposition" (1973: 272). As Aejmelaeus demonstrates with respect to Jer 25:3b–7, "the passage contains no single phrase that does not occur elsewhere in the book" (see especially the table in Aejmelaeus 2002: 468). Aejmelaeus concludes that "[t]he greatest concentration of dtr language is found in the dtr speech in vv.3–7" (2002: 481).

36. Contra Aejmelaeus, who argues that Jer 25 is a late Dtr composition which post-dates the completion of the temple, and that "vv.3–7 is a purely literary product, put together on the basis of other passages, above all Jer xxxv(xlii) 14–15" (2002: 476). However, this explanation accounts poorly for the putative quote in Zech 1:4. If Aejmelaeus were to be correct, then Zech 1:4 must presumably be alluding to Jer 35:15. However, at precisely the point at which Zech 1:4 differs from Jer 35, it agrees with Jer 25. The essence of the exhortation in Jer 35:15 is "Turn from evil ways and *make good* (וְהֵיטִיבוּ) your deeds," whereas in both Zech 1:4 and Jer 25:5, the sense is "Turn from evil ways *and evil deeds*." While is it not beyond the bounds of possibility that the author of Zech 1:4 and a late redactor of Jeremiah should have happened to have independently recast the sense of Jer 35 in exactly the same way, this is hardly likely. By far the easier explanation is that Zech 1:4 has alluded to Jer 25:5. This conclusion is further strengthened by other allusions to Jer 25 in Zech 1, especially to the "seventy years" (Jer 25:12; Zech 1:12).

consists of a core which comes from the prophet Jeremiah (typically identified as most of vv. 4, 9a, 10, 11, 12, 14), to which deuteronomistic material has subsequently been added. (See, e.g., Thiel 1973: 114–16; Holt 1986; Kang 1996.) While I must leave until later a consideration of the details of the allusion between Zech 7 and Jer 7, for present purposes it should be noted that the most striking allusions are to the deuteronomistic verses of Jer 7 (esp. Jer 7:5–6 // Zech 7:9–10; Jer 7:13 // Zech 7:13). Given that these allusions in Zech 7:9–14 are introduced by the claim that Zechariah is repeating the words of "the former prophets" (see Zech 7:7), the most reasonable inference is that these deuteronomistic elements were present in the text of Jeremiah in circulation in Zechariah's day. Otherwise, we should have to suppose that Zech 7 has purported to cite a former prophet, but in fact has invented a quotation which has then been subsequently "retrofitted" (by others? by Zechariah himself?) into Jer 7 in order to put these words onto the lips of the prophet Jeremiah. While not impossible, this alternative is hardly the most likely. Thus, from the evidence of the two explicit references to the former prophets in Zech 1–8, we might reasonably conclude that the version of Jeremiah in circulation in Palestine in the era of Zechariah already (in substance) had its deuteronomistic flavour.[37]

3.3.1.2. *Does Zechariah Allude to MT^{Vorlage} or LXX^{Vorlage}?* LXX Jeremiah is shorter than MT Jeremiah by one eighth, and with a different arrangement of some material (Lundbom 1999: 57–62). Various theories have been offered to explain this phenomenon, with the three main possibilities being that:

1. the LXX represents the original, and the MT is the result of expansionistic glosses.[38]
2. the MT represents the original, and the LXX arose through translation/adaptation.[39]
3. the MT and the LXX reflect two different editions of the book.[40]

While not directly addressing the question of the original text, the evidence of allusion in Zech 1–8 suggests that the form of text of Jeremiah known to the prophet Zechariah was closer to the MT^{Vorlage} rather than the

37. Jer 25 and Jer 7 are often held to be the products of later redactions—see, e.g., Aejmelaeus 2002: 476 and Carroll 1986: 490–91. Thus, if these two passages predate Zech 1–8, then there is strong evidence that the work of the deuteronomistic redactor(s) must have been substantially complete by this time.

38. E.g. Janzen 1973.

39. E.g. Soderlund 1985; Fischer 1991; Lundbom 1999; 2004a; 2004b.

40. E.g. Tov 1981; 1985; 1997; Shead 2002.

LXX[Vorlage]. If we consider again the allusion to Jer 25:4–7 in Zech 1:4, the following table demonstrates that Zech 1:4 is closer to the MT than the LXX:

Jer 25 (from MT)	*Jer 25 (from LXX)*	*Zech 1:4*
Yahweh sent his servants the prophets… saying, "Turn, each of you, from his evil ways and from your evil deeds" But you have not listened to me, *says Yahweh.*	*I sent my servants* the prophets…saying, "Turn, each of you from his evil ways and from your wicked doings" But you have not listened to me.	Do not be like your fathers, to whom *the former prophets cried out*, "Thus says the Yahweh of Hosts, 'Turn from your evil ways and from your evil deeds'." But they did not listen or give heed to me, *says Yahweh.*

The striking difference between MT and LXX is that the MT refers to Yahweh in the third person, whereas in the LXX, Yahweh speaks directly in the 1st person. Zechariah 1:4, like the MT of Jer 25, records the former prophets speaking Yahweh's words in the third person. I grant that this in and of itself is not conclusive, since the author of Zech 1:4 may well have recast a 1st person original into the third person in order to fit the present context. However, what makes this argument persuasive is the last phrase—"says Yahweh." Zechariah 1:4 ends with this phrase (נְאֻם־יְהוָה), which is present in the MT of Jer 25, but without an equivalent in the LXX.[41] This phrase in Zech 1:4 is unlikely to be Zechariah's own "expansion" on Jer 25, as the phrase is superfluous in its context in Zech 1, given that the quote has already begun with the phrase "Thus says Yahweh of Hosts," כֹּה אָמַר יְהוָה צְבָאוֹת). It only makes sense to have included the phrase נְאֻם־יְהוָה should this have been part of the original message being quoted from "the former prophets." On the basis of this evidence, I conclude that Zech 1 is alluding to a form of text of Jeremiah closer to the MT[Vorlage] than the LXX[Vorlage].

41. That Zech 1:4 ends with a third person references to Yahweh in Zech 1:4 is all the more surprising, since Yahweh has been speaking in the 1st person in Zech 1:3. Yahweh quotes his own word through the former prophets in Zech 1:4. If (as I argue) the last clause נְאֻם־יְהוָה is part of the quote from the former prophet, then the third person reference makes sense in the context. However, the equivalent clause to נְאֻם־יְהוָה is not part of the quote in the LXX, which again suggests that the MT is the text being quoted.

3.3.1.3. *Does Jeremiah 33:14–26 Pre-date or Post-date Zechariah?* Jeremiah 33:14–26 is present in the MT but absent in the LXX. It has just been concluded that Zechariah alludes to the MT*Vorlage* of Jeremiah rather than the LXX, and so the omission of Jer 33:14–26 from the LXX does not answer the question as to whether it was present in the version of Jeremiah with which Zechariah was familiar. If we assume, for the sake of the argument, that Jer 33:14–26 was indeed a later addition to the MT, then the question becomes "How late?"

It is my contention that the view of the "levitical priesthood" in Jer 33 suggests that it comes from an earlier historical period than Zech 3. As Nurmela (1998) demonstrates, there is a dramatic shift in the role of the Levites by the time of the post-exilic period. In Deuteronomy and Joshua–2 Kings, the priests are simply described as "the levitical priests" (הַכֹּהֲנִים הַלְוִיִּם). However, in Ezekiel, the Priestly Code and the Chronistic History, there is a demarcation between "priests" and "Levites" in which the Levites are clearly a "second-class priesthood" (to use Nurmela's phrase). Where the "levitical priesthood" is referred to in this later era, it is further qualified to make clear that only a subset of Levites is intended. For example, Ezek 44:15 refers to "the Levitical Priests, *the sons of Zadok*" (וְהַכֹּהֲנִים הַלְוִיִּם בְּנֵי צָדוֹק).[42] We see this same "narrowing" of the priesthood in Zech 3:8, where the priesthood encompasses Joshua the high priest and his "associates."[43]

In contrast to this narrowing of the priesthood, Jer 33:18 reflects the standard deuteronomistic description of the priesthood, in that it refers to the "levitical priests" (וְלַכֹּהֲנִים הַלְוִיִּם) without further qualification.[44] If we were to suppose that Jer 33:14–26 was a later post-exilic addition to the book, we might reasonably expect to see the same limiting of the priesthood seen in Ezek 44:15 and Zech 3:8, and which continues into the later post-exilic period. The fact that we do *not* see this suggests that Jer 33:14–26 is earlier than Zech 3:8.[45]

42. 1 Chr 16:39; Ezra 3:2 and Neh 3:1 all follow the pattern "XXX the priest and his brothers the priests." See also the greater demarcation in roles between the priests and Levites (Neh 10:38–39; Ezra 3:9–10).

43. רֵעַ is literally "neighbour," but in this context is understood by most commentators to refer to the Zadokite priesthood. See §5.3.4 below.

44. For example, see Deut 17:9, 18; 18:1; 24:8; 27:9; Josh 3:3; 8:33, where the phrase הַכֹּהֲנִים הַלְוִיִּם or equivalent occurs without further distinction or qualification. So also Nurmela 1998: 143.

45. So also Boda 2001: n. 31, and cf. VanderKam 2004: 39–40 who argues that the writer of Zech 6 is "leaning heavily on Jer 33, from which he seems to borrow his most important terms and ideas." Contra (in part) Goldman 1992: 225–37, who

3.3.1.4. *Conclusion on the Dating of Jeremiah.* There are reasonable grounds for proceeding on the basis that the book of Jeremiah to which Zech 1–8 alludes already has its deuteronomistic flavour, was closer in form to the MT^{Vorlage} than the LXX^{Vorlage} and probably also contained Jer 33:14–26.

3.3.2. *The Book of Ezekiel in 520 B.C.E.*

Ezekiel Studies have travelled something of a full-circle in a little over 100 years. In 1891, S. R. Driver could write:

> No critical question arises in connection with the authorship of the book, the whole from beginning to end bearing unmistakably the stamp of a single mind.[46]

However, within half a century a considerable body of scholarship had swung to the opposite extreme—that sizable portions of the book were not original to the prophet Ezekiel, and were instead added later, perhaps centuries after the exile (e.g. Hölscher 1924; Torrey 1930).

In the last 50 years, the pendulum has swung back, stemming in part from the realization that the earlier paradigm shift on Ezekiel had been driven more by negative presuppositions about "priestly religion" and theories about the evolutionary development of religion than from careful analysis of the text.[47] Now, many would agree with the conclusion of Clements, that the substance of the book of Ezekiel was completed by the end of the sixth century B.C.E. (Clements 1996b: 169).[48]

argues that Jer 33:14–26 was added by a "Restoration Redactor (RR)" in the same period as Zerubbabel. See also Pomykala 1995: 42–45.

46. Here cited from the ninth edition of Driver's *Introduction* (1913: 279).

47. For a more detailed account of the swinging pendulum of Ezekiel Studies, see Ahroni 1977: 2–4 and Joyce 1995.

48. For some scholars, the text is a product of the exile, because it is in essence the work of the prophet Ezekiel (see, e.g., Greenberg 1983; Kohn 2002; Renz 2002). Other scholars argue for a substantial Ezekielian core, to which additional layer(s) have been added in the later exilic period (see, e.g., Gese 1957; Zimmerli 1979; 1983). For example, Zimmerli argues for three layers of additions to Ezek 40–48, as a result of the "near approach of the hour of a return to the land, and the necessity that thereby arose for the realistic planning of the reconstruction" (1979: 70). Contra Tuell, who argues that the bulk of Ezek 43–47—the "law of the temple"—was inserted into a pre-existing literary frame in the Persian Period, in order to enact the "religious polity of the Judean Restoration" (1992: 14). However, damaging for Tuell's thesis (and for all those who posit a late date for this material) is the disparity between the idealism of Ezek 43–47 and the harsh reality of the post-exilic situation, which became increasingly divergent the more history unfolded. The later one posits the completion date of Ezek 40–48, the more difficult it becomes to explain the

One passage where there is a measure of disagreement over dating is Ezek 38–39 (the Gog pericope). A number of scholars have regarded Ezek 38–39 as a very late addition to the book, either because of the "apocalyptic" overtones,[49] and/or because it is argued to be a later explanation of why the prophet's promises of salvation remain unfulfilled.[50] As to the issue of apocalyptic, it is reasonable to say (notwithstanding the ongoing debate regarding the definitions of "apocalyptic")[51] that most of the constituent elements of the apocalyptic genre are absent from Ezek 38–39,[52] and that whatever elements are present are not of a type to necessitate a post-exilic date.[53] As for the suggestion that Ezek 38–39 is a much later *apologia* for non-fulfilment, it should be noted that this turns on a particular interpretation of Ezek 38:17, and that more recent examinations of this verse have proposed other (and, I think, better) interpretations of it that suggest an exilic *Sitz im Leben*.[54]

focus on matters which seem so disconnected with the putative context. See further Levenson 1976: 116. The book of Ezekiel reflects exilic (rather than post-exilic) realities—see further Wevers 1969: 29; Greenberg 1984: 208; Mein 2001: 218.

49. See, e.g., Cooke 1936: 408; Ahroni 1977. See further Astour 1976.

50. See, e.g., Eichrodt 1970: 520; Clements 1996a: 171.

51. See the exchange between Collins (2003) and Grabbe (2003) in Grabbe and Haak (2003), and see further §1.2.2 above.

52. As to the marks of the genre, see Collins 1998: 2–9.

53. Cook argues that Ezek 38–39 exhibits both a radical eschatology and dualism, and on this basis concludes that Ezek 38–39 is "proto-apocalyptic" (1995: 88–94). However, Cook also details the very close correspondences between these chapters and the rest of the book of Ezekiel, demonstrating that "Ezekiel 38–39 clearly belongs to the mainstream of the Ezekiel priestly tradition" (Cook 1995: 103).

54. In Ezek 38:17, Yahweh asks Gog: "Are you he of whom I spoke in former days by the hand of my servants the prophets of Israel prophesying in these days (and) years to bring you against them?"

Current interpretation of this verse turns on whether the answer to this rhetorical question is "Yes" or "No." Most interpreters have taken the answer to be "Yes." If this is the case, then it implies that there should be some earlier prophecies about "Gog" elsewhere in the former prophets. However, there are no such prophecies. This has led to the conclusion that "Gog" must therefore be a cipher for another nation, with the obvious candidate being Babylon (cf. Ezek 21; Jer 25). As McKeating notes, "nowhere in the book of Ezekiel, in all the oracles against foreign nations, is there any oracle against Babylon. This seems remarkable in view of all that Judah suffered at Babylonian hands over the period which the book of Ezekiel covers. It is not remarkable, however, if Ezekiel is prophesying in Babylonia, where such oracles, if they had come to public notice, would doubtless have involved the prophet in immediate and serious trouble. What is more likely, then, than that the land of Gog is a cypher for Babylon itself, and the prophecies of Gog's destruction a

The most reasonable context for the Gog pericope as a whole is the exilic period, since the picture it paints of life after the exile does not correspond to reality after the exile.[55] As Zimmerli argues:

> One would prefer to locate the Gog pericope before the conquest of Babylon by Cyrus also because the situation of an Israel gathered from among the nations and dwelling securely in her land is painted in 38:8 in colors to which the reality of the situation after the dispensation of the edict of Cyrus and the incipient return corresponds but little (cf. Haggai and Zechariah 1–8). (Zimmerli 1983: 303)[56]

For these reasons, I will proceed on the *prima facie* assumption that the substance of the book of Ezekiel was complete by 520 B.C.E.

3.3.3. *The Book of Isaiah in 520 B.C.E.*

It is commonplace in Isaiah scholarship to divide the book of Isaiah into those parts written by Isaiah of Jerusalem, those parts composed during

heavily coded message predicting the demise of the Babylonian power?" (1993: 121–22; cf. Odell 2005: 470).

The view that "Gog" is a coded reference to Babylon dates back to the nineteenth century (Ewald 1875: 4:180–82; Boehmer 1897, cited from Zimmerli 1983: 304). On this view, the prophecy presupposes an exilic context, since the use of the cipher presumes that Babylon was still a world power, suggesting a pre-539 B.C.E. dating of the passage. This is not inconsistent with the position of both Zimmerli (1983: 304) and Wevers (1969: 284), through they hesitate about the specific identification of "Gog" as Babylon, and instead view it as reference to an indeterminate foe from the north.

More recently, Daniel Block (1992) and Margaret Odell (2005: 473–74) have both (independently) argued that the correct answer to the rhetorical question of Ezek 38:17 is "No"—that is, that Gog is *not* the nation whom Yahweh spoken of through his prophets as an instrument of his wrath on Israel. Block argues "This oracle…is not about unfulfilled prophecy… Contrary to the delusion of Gog himself, the misunderstanding of 2300 years of interpretative tradition, and the misreading of all the modern translations, the answer is a firm 'No!'" (1992: 172). On this view, there is no longer an issue of "unfulfilled prophecy," which obviates the need to date Ezek 38–39 to a period later than that of the prophet Ezekiel.

Thus, on either of these two interpretations, Ezek 38:17 does not necessitate a post-exilic dating.

55. Ezek 39:25–29 also clearly posits an exilic context. Those who argue that Ezek 38–39 are post-exilic argue that these verses have been composed as a "bridge" to link Ezek 38–39 to Ezek 40–48, and dismiss the exilic context of 39:25–29 as a "literary artifice" (Ahroni 1977: 24).

56. Consistent with this conclusion, Zimmerli argues that, while the "original" prophecy of Ezek 38–39 contained only 38:1–9; 39:1–5, 17–20, "the basic text of chapters 38f should not be removed too far from Ezekiel, even that a derivation from the prophet himself is not impossible" (Zimmerli 1983: 302).

the Babylonian exile by a "Deutero-Isaiah" (DI)[57] and those parts written after the return from exile. For the purposes of determining the contents of Isaiah in 520 B.C.E., it is the third body of material that is most at issue.

The redaction-critical approach taken by Claus Westermann in his 1966 commentary on Isa 40–66 has shaped much of the subsequent study of Isa 56–66. Westermann identified a nucleus of material—which he attributed to a post-exilic prophet, "Trito-Isaiah"—to which layers of additional material have been subsequently added. According to Westermann:

> The nucleus was formed by chs. 60–62, the proclamation of salvation made by the prophet Trito-Isaiah. This was set within the framework of the two community laments, chs. 59 and 63/64… Together with this block were transmitted a few unconnected utterances of Trito-Isaiah's [*sic*] (57.14–20; 65.16b–25; 66.6–16; and perhaps 58.1–12)…
>
> A second strand is made up of a number of independent utterances and additions, in all of which the main feature of the situation in face of which they were uttered is the rise of a cleavage between the devout and the transgressors (56.9–57.13; 57.21; 59.2–8; 65:1–16a; 66.3f.; 66.5, 17). A third strand…seeks to amend Trito-Isaiah's friendly and open disposition towards foreign nations by proclaiming judgment upon them (60.12; 63.1–6; 66.6, 15f.; 66.20, 22ff.). Similar to it is a series of apocalyptic additions to the oracles of salvation; again, these are found only in chs. 60–66 (60.19f., 65.17, 25; 66.20, 22ff.). A fourth strand consists of additions at the beginning and the end of the book (56.1f., 3–8; 66.18f., 21). (Westermann 1969: 307)

A sizeable body of scholarship has adopted this "nucleus-plus-accretions" model of Isa 56–66, though with considerable variation among scholars on the delineations and sequence of the accretion layers. Significant for the present purposes is the difference of opinion regarding the time scale over which this growth has occurred. For example, at the "short" end of the scale, Smith argues that (apart from Isa 59:21 and 66:18–24) "Isa 56–66 should be dated between 538 and 515BC" (Smith 1995: 205).[58] Smith's model of the growth of Isa 56–66 can be represented by the following diagram:

57. Though for the argument that the first edition of Deutero-Isaiah is post-exilic, see Albertz 2003a.

58. See similarly Hanson (1979), on whose model most of Isa 56–66 is complete by 510 B.C.E., with a final redaction (which added 56:1–8 and 66:7–24), taking place around 475 B.C.E. See also Tiemeyer 2006b: 74–80.

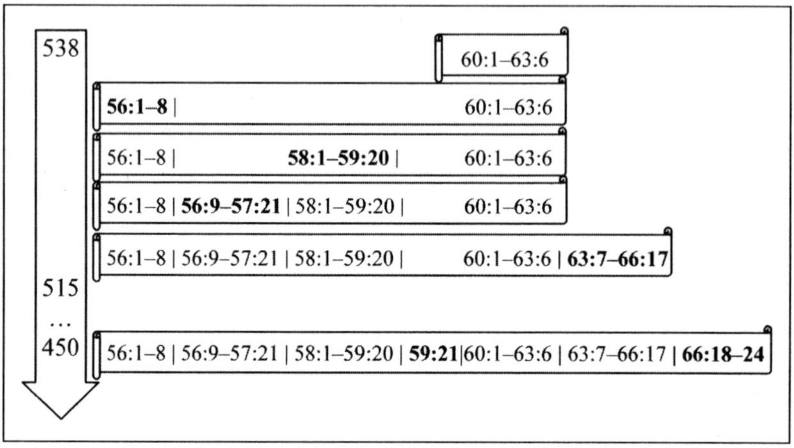

The Growth of Isaiah 56–66 (adapted from Smith 1995: 204–5)

At the opposite end of the time-scale, Odil Steck argues that Isa 56–66 emerged via a process of additions to the book of Isaiah as a whole which extended well into the Greek period.[59] Because an extended-redaction view (*à la* Steck) has significant implications for our enquiry in terms of dating and the direction of dependency, it is necessary to consider the theoretical underpinnings of this approach.

3.3.3.1. *Odil Steck and Trito-Isaiah in the Book of Isaiah*

Steck's theory has implications, not merely for Isa 56–66, but for the growth of the book of Isaiah as a whole. Steck argues that Isa 56–66 emerged as the result of amplifications, first of Isa 40–55, and then of the

59. It should also be noted that there is a growing body of scholarship which applies the insights of modern literary criticism to the book of Isaiah, and comes to conclusions which question the traditional tri-partite partitioning of the book. In particular, some scholars account for the variation in tone within Isa 56–66 on the basis of rhetorical rather than redactional grounds. For example, the difference between the unconditional salvation offered in Isa 60–62 and the conditional salvation in Isa 57–59 is not due to the differing viewpoints of multiple authors (*à la* Westermann), but rather because Isa 60–62 is addressed to just a subset within Israel. Seitz argues that Isa 59:21 is an important transition which serves to contextualize the promises of Isa 60–62 (Seitz 1994: 505). Isa 59 ends on the note of a promise of a redeemer and a covenant for those who repent, and Isa 60–62 then follows, as a word addressed to those who have repented. Thus it is literary flow of the book which accounts for Isa 60–62's tone of "salvation and nothing but salvation." On Seitz's view there is no necessary time gap between Deutero- and Trito-Isaiah (Seitz 1994: 474).

book as whole.[60] Steck argues for four main stages of development, where each stage prompted further redactional additions to earlier parts of the book (see Steck 1991a). Steck argues that the process of redaction occurred from the Persian period down to the early third century:

Stage	*Timing*	*Key Growth in Book*
Persian Period Redaction	515–445 B.C.E.	Addition of *Isa 60–62 to *Isa 40–55, in stages
Homecoming Redaction	After 323 B.C.E.	Joining *Isa 1–39 and *40–62 to form one book, focussing on salvation for the people of God and the return to Zion (Isa 62:10–12 created in the redaction)
Penultimate Redaction	After 320 B.C.E. Context: fighting between Alexander's *diadochi* (successors)	Addition of *Isa 56–59 and 63:1–6 and editing to reflect the insight that the promised salvation has been stopped by ungodly behaviour, particularly in Jerusalem (1991a: 33)
Concluding Redaction	After 302/301, up to 270 B.C.E.(?)	Addition of Isa 63:7–64:11, followed by 56:1–8 and 65:1–66:24

Steck's Four Stages in the Growth of Isaiah
(adapted from Steck 1991b: 278–79)

Steck's theory on Trito-Isaiah is too complex for it to be given a thoroughgoing analysis here. However, for the present purposes, we need only focus on the means by which Steck gives absolute dates to the various layers. There are two important planks in Steck's argument for establishing his chronology. The first plank concerns the dating of the Homecoming Redaction (*Heimkehrredaktion*) to the Greek Period. Steck argues that the nations of Egypt and Assyria have been stressed in this Homecoming Redaction (e.g. the promise of another return of a remnant from Egypt and Assyria in Isa 11:11–16), and that this reflects the historical context after the death of Alexander the Great:

60. Steck argues that Isa 1–39 and Isa 40–55 had once circulated independently, and that the core of Isa 60–62 came about as the result of a redactional expansion of Isa 40–55 (before it had been joined to Isa 1–39). Steck bases this conclusion on the observation that Isa 60–62 exhibits a substantial number of cross-connections with Deutero-Isaiah, but not with Proto-Isaiah. However, it should be noted that this "pattern" for connections with Deutero-Isaiah alone only appears once Steck has removed (on the hypothesis that they are a later addition) those passages which do show cross-connections with Proto-Isaiah (60:12, 17–22; 62:8–9, 10–12); see Steck 1991a: 14–15. There would appear to be a circularity in Steck's argument at this point.

> Zusätzlich aber fällt auf, daß angesichts des Weltgerichts an Heimkehrgebieten in Eigenformulierungen Assyrien und Ägypten betont hervorgehoben werden; dies hat mich mit einem Seitenblick auf Sach 10,3–12 dazu bewogen, als zeitgeschichtlichen Hintergrund dieser Ersten und Zweiten Jesaja erstmals vereinigenden Redaktion den Zusammenbruch des persischen Weltreiches und nach dem Tode Alexanders die ersten Auseinandersetzungen der Diadochen im Vorderen Orient und Ägypten um Palästina anzunehmen... (Steck 1991a: 25)

That is, Steck argues that the references to "Egypt" and "Assyria" refer to the empires of Ptolemy and Seleucus respectively, and that the redaction anticipates a return of diaspora Jews from these places.[61]

The second plank in Steck's chronology argument depends upon historical reconstructions of the various contexts and attitudes of the post-exilic community. For example, he regards Isa 60:10–11 and 62:1–7 as later additions within the first layer, because they reflect the issues of the building of the wall and the *Heilsverzögerung* (delay of salvation) which, according to Steck (1991b: 15), are issues of the mid-fifth century B.C.E. Where this same theme is detected in other parts of the book of Isaiah (e.g. Isa 54:2–3 and 54:11–17a), this is taken as evidence that these verses were added to the book in the same redaction which created Isa 60:10–11 and/or 62:1–7. Steck similarly stratifies passages based on their views of Israel and the nations,[62] the temple and the mountain of Yahweh,[63] and the identity of the "enemies,"[64] and how these views might have emerged in history of the second temple community up to the third century B.C.E.[65] Steck likens these various views to fossilized remains which allow different geographic strata to be dated (Steck 1991b: 13).[66] Steck's chronology is thus the combination of the fixed date of 323 B.C.E. (the death of Alexander the Great), together with a relative chronology established by evolving views about salvation/nation/temple and so on.

61. For Steck's defence of this position, see Steck 1991a: 25–26 n. 63.

62. E.g. Steck stratifies layers with Isaiah based on whether the focus is on "salvation for all-Israel" vs. "salvation for some part within Israel" vs. "salvation for foreigners" (Steck 1991b: 13, 25, 30).

63. According to Steck (1991b: 35–36), Isa 66:1–6 (in the context of Isa 66) depicts a picture of a "radicalized" temple that could not have even been dreamt of in the time of Darius. Beuken (1989) takes the opposite view to Steck on this.

64. Steck offers three possibilities for the hostilities apparently being alluded to in Isa 63/64, concluding that it is most likely to refer to the incursion of Ptolemy I into Jerusalem in 302/301 (1991b: 38–39).

65. For a summary of the thirteen steps in the development of the restoration hope, see Steck 2000: 65–81.

66. For more details on Steck's chronology, see Schmid and Steck 2001.

In assessing Steck's position, the first point to be made is that few scholars are as confident as Steck in the necessary identification of Isaiah's "Egypt" and "Assyria" with the empires of Ptolemy and Seleucus.[67] Without this, the theory loses its critical fixed date.

Secondly, the evidence of Zech 1–8 makes some telling points against Steck's relative chronology of evolving views and issues. The rebuilding, re-establishment and repopulation of Jerusalem is clearly the issue at the heart of Zech 1:16–17 and 2:8—passages which are now typically dated *prior to* the completion of the temple in 515 B.C.E. This undercuts Steck's argument that this concern only emerged significantly later (when the hoped-for new age had failed to materialize). Similarly, Zech 1–8 also reflects a view of the nations (both for and against) and of the temple,[68] which demonstrates that these views (which Steck defers until much later) are very much at home in the sixth century B.C.E. If Steck were correct, and "true fasting" (Isa 58) and "foreigners joined to Yahweh" (Isa 56:1–8) are issues of the fourth/third centuries B.C.E., then what do we make of the fact that Zech 2:11 ("nations joined to Yahweh") and Zech 7 ("true fasting") address these same issues in the context of the sixth century B.C.E.?

If all of these views did in fact co-exist in the sixth century B.C.E., then Steck's hypothesis also loses the criterion by which the separate strata can be identified and sequenced. The evidence of the book of Zechariah undercuts the argument that Isaiah *necessarily* reached its present form via a development over four centuries, at least in terms of the themes that it raises. Based on the evidence of Zech 1–8 and other literature of the period, there is no compelling reason to view any of the themes raised in Isa 56–66 as anachronistic to the situation of the last decades of the sixth century B.C.E.

A secondary reason for not following the redactional schema proposed by Steck is because it necessitates positing wide-ranging redactions to the rest of the book of Isaiah in order to support the theory. However, the evidence of allusion in Zechariah counts against these late additions. For example, Steck's theory means that Isa 54 was written over three centuries, straddling the composition of Zech 1–8.

67. See, e.g., Childs 2001: 104–5 and Sweeney 1996: 201. For equivocal views on whether Isa 11:16 indicates an early Hellenistic era, see Kaiser 1983: 268 and Blenkinsopp 2000: 267–68.

68. The views of Zech 1–8 on the nations and the temple will be discussed in the analysis of the exegetical chapters below, and be summarized in my conclusion (Chapter 8).

Time

Isa 54:1, 4–8	Original Layer
→ Composition of Zech 1–8	
Isa 54:2–3	"enlarge your tent, stretch out to right and left"
Isa 54:9–10	The end of wrath
Isa 54:11–17	"O afflicted city, lashed by storms and not comforted"

The Stages of Development of Isaiah 54, according to Odil Steck

I will argue in the next chapter (for a summary, see §4.7) that there are a substantial number of textual connections between Isa 54 and Zech 1–2. The textual connections between Zech 1–2 and Isa 54 run across at least three of the layers that Steck has identified. Should Steck's theory be valid, then this means that the author of Zech 1 first alluded to Isa 54:4–8 (picking up the language of the end of the time of wrath and Yahweh's return in mercy), but then subsequent redactors of Isa 54 have returned the compliment, and alluded to Zechariah in the material they have added (especially the theme of the expansion of Jerusalem and the unusual "wrathed wrath"), and then a yet later redactor has picked up Zechariah's language of "storm tossed," "comfort" and the "reconstruction of Jerusalem" imagery. The sheer complexity of this explanation contrasts sharply to the simplicity of the alternative theory—that Isa 54 was written first, and that the prophet Zechariah made a *sustained allusion* to it (consistent with the practice of sustained allusion elsewhere in Zech 1–8).[69] For these reasons, I remain unpersuaded of the need for a redactional theory which necessitates the composition of the book of Isaiah in the manner (and timeframe) which Steck suggests.

3.3.4. *The Book of Joel in 520 B.C.E.*

An unexpected conclusion that I have reached was that there probably *was* a book of Joel in 520 B.C.E. It is fair to say that, while the date of Joel is still an open question, the majority of recent scholarship would date Joel after Zechariah.[70] From this starting point, it had seemed

69. I will develop this point in the next chapter.

70. On the dating of Joel, see further Fowler 1897; Treves 1957; Myers 1962; Stephenson 1969; Thompson 1974: 453–64; Allen 1976: 19–25; Crenshaw 1995: 23–28; Barton 2001. Some suggested dates include: seventh century (e.g. Koch 1982: 159–61); sixth–fifth century (e.g. Hubbard 1989); fourth century or later (e.g. Wolff 1977; Soggin 1989; Cook 1995; Barton 2001. Duhm argued that Joel 2:28–3:21 was a Maccabean addition). Mason (1994: 116) best sums up the situation when he concludes that the date of Joel remains a mystery.

reasonable to explain the intertextual parallels between Zechariah and Joel (on which, see the next chapter) as having arisen from a reuse of Zechariah by the author of Joel. Since the intertextuality of Joel is commonly recognized, this was a defensible hypothesis.[71]

However, as I looked more closely at the textual parallels and sought to explain them in the light of the historical context and rhetorical strategies of each book, this explanation was ultimately unsatisfying.[72] This forced me to re-examine the arguments for the later dating of Joel, and to see whether it was possible that Joel 1–2 (at least)[73] was the prior work.

I accept the argument of Cook that a strong case can be made for a post-exilic dating of the book of Joel:

> A postexilic dating is indicated by probable references to the fall of Jerusalem and the exile in Joel 4:1, 17 (Eng. 3:1, 17); the lack of mention of a king; and Joel's dependence on earlier written prophets (e.g. Isaiah 13; Ezekiel 38–39; Obadiah 7). Late vocabulary in Joel provides general support for this dating. (Cook 1995: 167)

However, Cook then suggests that Joel is not only post-exilic, but that it can be dated well into the Persian period.[74] Cook argues that

> the picture of an operational central cult in the book (Joel 1:14; 2:17) indicates a date for Joel after 515 B.C.E. A more specific late Persian-period dating may be indicated by such evidence as the possible quotation of Mal 3:2 by Joel 2:11, and the possible reference to the walls of Jerusalem (post-433 B.C.E.) in Joel 2:7–9. (Cook 1995: 167)

However, the evidence which Cook cites for this later dating is open to question. Let us consider Cook's three points in reverse order. First, few would be convinced that a reference to invaders scaling and running on

71. On the nature and extent of Joel's intertextuality, and the implications this has for its dating, see further Day 1995: 240–41 and Coggins 1996; 2000.

72. As to the reasons why I think Joel 2 predates Zech 1–2, see §4.4 below.

73. It is increasingly argued that Joel consisted of an original core (most of Joel 1–2), to which the so-called "apocalyptic" material was later added. Wellhausen (1911: 184–88) divided the book into two, arguing that Joel 1:1–2:17 came from an early post-exilic prophet, and the remainder was added to the book at a much later time, perhaps during the Maccabean era. Duhm's position is evaluated by Sweeney (2003). Barton takes a variation on Duhm's position, dividing the book into 1:1–2:27, the work of the cultic prophet Joel, and 2:28–3:21, a later apocalyptic addition (see Barton 2001: 13–16).

74. Cf. Redditt (1986: 235) who argues that Joel, in its current form, probably originated between 515 and 445 B.C.E., because it presupposes a functioning, post-exilic temple as well as the existence of the Sabeans, who went into decline around 450 B.C.E.

walls necessarily implies that the full reconstruction of the walls under Nehemiah must have occurred.[75] Secondly, the parallels between Mal 3:2 and Joel 2:11 might just as reasonably be explained as Malachi's allusion to Joel. Lastly, and most crucially, Joel 1:14 and 2:17 do *not* require a dating after the reconstruction of the temple (contra also Crenshaw 1995: 23–28 on this issue).

Joel 1:14 summons the people to "the house of Yahweh" (בֵּית יְהוָה). However, this does not necessarily mean that the temple has been rebuilt. This same phrase is used in Ezra 2:68 to describe the temple in its ruined state. Similarly, Hag 1:2, 4, 8 and 14 speak of "Yahweh's house" with reference to the building in its partially constructed state. Evidently, whatever structure remained on the temple mount at Jerusalem was regarded as the "house of Yahweh" during the early post-exilic period, not just post 515 B.C.E.[76]

Joel 2:17 says "let [the priests] weep between porch and altar." It is important to recognize that Joel 2:17 is an ironic intertextual reversal of Ezek 8:16. In place of the detestable sun worship which had gone on in Ezekiel's day "between porch and altar," Joel calls the priests of his day to true worship. Thus, the reference to "porch" and "altar" may not be making any necessary reference to objects actually present in Joel's era, but to the memory of these objects in Ezekiel's day. However, even if Joel 2:17 is referring to actual objects in Joel's day, then this still does not imply a fully constructed temple, because, according to Ezra 3:1–6, the altar was rebuilt prior to the reconstruction of the temple, and the "porch" may refer merely to the area at the front of the temple, rather than any structure as such (cf. Ezek 8:16).

Joel 1:14 and 2:17 do not give sufficient evidence to compel a post-515 B.C.E. dating of the first part of the book.[77] All that the evidence thus

75. See further Myers 1962: 191; Redditt 1986: 234; Barton 2001: 15–16.

76. Similarly, Japhet (1991b: 224–25) notes that Jer 41:5 describes men who come with offerings "to present at the house of Yahweh" at a time when the temple had been destroyed, which suggests that "some kind of worship continued to exist within the temple's precincts" (1991b: 225).

77. The dating of the so-called "apocalyptic" chapters (Joel 3–4 = ET 2:28–32; 3:1–21) is a more difficult issue, since is depends on wider decisions about the emergence of apocalyptic and Joel's place within this phenomenon. Though I recognize that my approach is at variance with the common consensus, I position Joel 3–4 in the same milieu as Joel 1–2. With regard to the argument for a later dating based on the apocalyptic elements, I submit that the *apocalyptic-esque* elements need not be particularly late, as they can be explained on the basis of intertextual echoes of prophecy which was extant before the end of the exile, especially Isa 13–14; Ezek 38–39; Obadiah and Zeph 3. Isa 13 predicts the destruction of Babylon, and so

far examined allows us to conclude is that Joel 1–2 was written in the early post-exilic period.[78] However, this does not tell us about the relative priority between Joel 1–2 and Zech 1–8.

The intertextual parallels between Joel 1–2 and Zech 1–8 give us a vital clue to resolve this question. The nature of the parallels, and the fact that both works are highly intertextual, suggests that one work has used the other. By assessing which pattern of re-use is more consistent with the historical context and rhetorical strategies of each book, we can make a judgment about the directionality of re-use. This argument can only be made once we have an opportunity to consider the evidence of the intertextual parallels. For that reason, I will return to this question in §4.4, once I have been able to establish the nature of Zechariah's intertextuality and the particular connections with Joel 2.

3.3.5. *The Book of Job in 520* B.C.E.

Both Zech 3 and the prologue of Job share the (otherwise rare) image of "the Satan" as a member of the divine council. While there is little doubt that one derives from the other, commentators are divided as to which came first. Many take Job to be the earlier work, although Tollington argues for the opposite, based on the trajectory of character development:

> The Satan is portrayed in Zechariah as a prosecuting counsel who fulfils a necessary role in the council, whose own character and motivation are regarded as inconsequential and who remains nothing more than a shadowy functionary. This contrasts with the developed personality attributed to the Satan in Job. (1993: 116)

There is no consensus as to the date of authorship of the book of Job, with suggestions ranging from pre-Mosaic times to the second century B.C.E.[79] However, recent linguistic examination of the book of Job has narrowed the range somewhat by suggesting the exile as the *terminus a quo*. Lévêque notes the close connections between Job 3 and Jer 20:14–18, and the shared vocabulary between Job 19 and Lam 2–3, and argues

predates 539 B.C.E. Similarly, as I have argued above (see §3.2.2), Ezek 38–39 is a (coded) prophecy against Babylon, and so must predate its overthrow. Obadiah and Zephaniah are, by common consensus, earlier than the post-exilic period.

78. Cf. Barton, who treats the book "as coming from the Judean community of the early second temple period, while being alert to the possibility that the second half may be substantially later than the first, since it represents a secondary addition to the words of Joel himself" (2001: 18).

79. For proponents of the various dates, see Lévêque 1981: 209 n. 13. Tollington argues (1993: 116 n. 2) that the prologue (with its characterization of the Satan) was not added to the book until the third century B.C.E.

that Job must therefore post-date these works (1981: 210–11). Hurvitz argues that, at points, Job reflects some of the vocabulary and phraseology of Late Biblical Hebrew.[80] For both Lévêque and Hurvitz, the presence of "the Satan" gives a vital clue for the question of dating. As Hurvitz notes, the word שׂטן is found in earlier texts, but in all the early instances, it still carries the general meaning of "stumble":

> However, the emergence of the figure of The Satan in the Bible—which is linguistically associated with a semantic development שׂטן 'Stumble' > שׂטן 'The Satan'—is an exclusive feature of post-exilic literature. (1974: 20)

Similarly, Lévêque argues

> ...la légende, telle que le poète l'a reprise, comprenait déjà les deux interventions du Satan comme membre de la cour céleste; or le Satan n'apparaît avec cette fonction qu'au niveau du Proto-Zacharie. Le poète de Job a donc réalisé son oeuvre au plus tôt pendant le ministère de ce prophète, ce qui nous amène vers la fin du VIe siècle. (1981: 210)

While both Lévêque and Hurvitz believe that Job has taken his imagery of "the Satan" from Zechariah, there is nothing in the logic of their linguistic arguments which dictates this conclusion. (Indeed, one suspects that they have chosen Zechariah as the earlier work because this gives a fixed point of reference ca. 520 B.C.E. in the otherwise fluid debates about the dating of Job). However, the most that one can say based on their linguistic arguments is that *one author* in the early post-exilic period was responsible for the emergence of the figure of "the Satan" through the semantic development from "stumble" to "the Satan." The linguistic arguments advanced by Lévêque and Hurvitz do not help us to decide the priority between two works apparently authored in the same milieu.

However, the recent work of Strauss provides a way to resolve the impasse. Strauss argues that the word שׂטן in Job 1–2 comes from a folk-etymological allusion to the root שׁוט, stemming from that heavenly being's assigned role to "rove about" (שׁוט, Job 1:7), and that the negative connotations typically associated with שׂטן (e.g. "to accuse" or "to oppose") only arose out of the specific divine commission in Job 1–2 (Strauss 1999: 256–57). As such, the book of Job must be the cause of

80. For example, the word לקבל in Job 2:10, meaning "to receive, take" is widely used in post-exilic (and post-Biblical) Hebrew, but never occurs in any of the biblical compositions which are undoubtedly pre-exilic. Similarly, Job 42:8 has the unusual להתפלל על (instead of the typical להתפלל בעד), which otherwise occurs only in Nehemiah and Chronicles (Hurvitz 1974: 20–23). I will demonstrate below (§5.4.4) that Zech 1–8 is similarly "atypical" in its use of על.

the semantic development of the word שָׂטָן, since the Satan of Zech 3 is not described using the root שׂוט.

This conclusion as to the temporal priority of Job is further reinforced by the observation of Tidwell (1975: 347) that other elements of Job's divine council scene are reflected in the role of the heavenly attendants in Zechariah's first and last night-visions,[81] since this suggests that Zech 1–6 is an expansion and development of an image created by another work.

For these reasons, I conclude that it is reasonable to proceed on the basis that Job 1–2 predates the composition of Zechariah's night-visions.[82]

Having established these broad conclusions with respect to the dating of the relevant texts, we can now begin the examination of the intertexts of Zech 1–8.

81. In Zech 1:10–11; 6:7, the horses/chariots go "to patrol the earth" (לְהִתְהַלֵּךְ בָּאָרֶץ). The same (rare) terminology describes the Satan's role in Job 1:7; 2:2. Similarly, in Zech 6:5, the spirits "present themselves before" (מֵהִתְיַצֵּב עַל) Yahweh, which is only otherwise found in Job 1:6; 2:1 (×2).

82. For further analysis of the development of "satan" imagery, see Day 1988.

Chapter 4

ZECHARIAH 1–2

4.1. *Introduction*

My aim in this chapter is to analyze the effect of the intertexts in Zech 1–2. I will argue that the function of the allusions (particularly allusions to the "former prophets") is to signal the answers to three vital questions—*What?*, *When?* and *Who?*

1. *What is Yahweh about to do?* Zechariah 1–2 utilizes the imagery of Ezekiel, Isaiah and Lamentations (*inter alia*) to reveal that Yahweh is about to "return" to his people, by returning to dwell in the temple in Jerusalem, which will reverse the devastation of the exile and usher in a time of paradisiacal blessing.
2. *When will this happen?* The promises of Jeremiah (especially the "seventy years") are re-activated to show that the time for Yahweh's return is imminent. Furthermore, those things which the former prophets had identified as necessary preconditions to Yahweh's return are now depicted as having occurred.
3. *Who will benefit from this?* The intertexts signal that a generational shift has occurred. The current generation is not the generation of the "fathers," whose sins caused the exile, nor the "sons" of that sinful generation who endured the consequences of exile, but the sons of sons, for whom the consequences of exile are about to be undone, and who are about to experience the dawning of the day of salvation.

In this chapter I will demonstrate that two features of these chapters are *sustained allusion* (i.e. the repeated references to another "background" passage, which stretch across multiple passages in Zechariah) and *composite metaphors* (the simultaneous allusion to imagery from multiple source passages).

4.2. *The Intertexts of Zechariah 1:1–6*

Zechariah 1:1 begins with a dating formula (בַּחֹדֶשׁ הַשְּׁמִינִי בִּשְׁנַת שְׁתַּיִם לְדָרְיָוֶשׁ, “In the eighth month, in the second year of Darius”). As already noted (see Chapter 3), the threefold repetition of this pattern provides chronological structural markers for Zech 1–8. However, might there also be an intertextual significance to the form of this phrase?[1]

There is merit in the argument of Curtis that the book of Jeremiah (especially in the historical appendix—e.g. Jer 52:12–13) provides the model for the date formula in Zech 1–8. Curtis argues that

> the Book of Jeremiah’s year+month+day formulae, which are synchronised with pagan regnal years, [and] memorialize temple destruction provided the specific model for those of Haggai–Zechariah 1–8, which are year+month+day in form, keyed to pagan regnal years, and point towards temple completion. (1991: 12)

There is also merit in his suggestion that the literary function of the date formulae in Zechariah is to stress the impending conclusion of the “seventy year” chastisement promised by Jeremiah, which had been understood by the returned exiles as “seventy years of temple-desolation” (1991: 16).[2] Zechariah 1–8 begins with a dating formula because the issue of timing—the “When?” question—is a vital part of its message about the impending return of Yahweh.

After its dating formula, Zech 1:1 continues with another formulaic expression הָיָה דְבַר־יְהוָה אֶל (“The word of Yahweh came to…”), which

1. Some commentators, noting that the book of Haggai also uses dating formulae after this pattern (5 times), have argued that this common dating formula is evidence that Haggai and Zech 1–8 have been redacted together into a “composite work” (Meyers and Meyers 1987: xliv–xlviii). Sykes takes this analysis one step further, and argues that the dating formula is a chronological construct that renders Haggai–Zech 1–8 a “single utterance” (1997: 103). Sykes argues that this dating formula in Haggai–Zech 1–8 is part of a wider prophetic parody of the ancient Near Eastern genre of the “chronicle.” Whereas the typical Babylonian chronicle is king-and-palace-centric, Haggai–Zech 1–8 has parodied this with a chronicle which is Yahweh-and-temple-centric (1997: 111–24). Damaging to Sykes’s thesis, however, is the reference to Darius in the dating formula. It is difficult to see how a dating formula calculated with reference the regnal years of the pagan king Darius helps to create this parody. In my opinion, it is more likely that the commonalities in form between Haggai and Zech 1–8 are due to the fact that the two prophets shared an overlapping ministry in post-exilic Jerusalem, rather than having necessarily arisen from a single editorial hand attempting to create a “composite work.”

2. On the motif of “seventy years,” see further §4.4 below.

is different from the form used in Haggai.[3] The message reception formula in Zechariah has numerous parallels across a range of prophetic literature (particularly Jeremiah and Ezekiel), which serve to highlight Zechariah's continuity with the prophetic tradition.[4]

Zechariah 1:2–3 also invokes echoes of Jeremiah and Ezekiel, though in a different manner to Zech 1:1. These verses are both grammatically odd. Zechariah 1:2 announces "Yahweh wrathed wrath[5] upon your fathers" (קָצַף יְהוָה עַל־אֲבוֹתֵיכֶם קָצֶף), but without providing an explicit audience in this verse—who are the "you" denoted by "*your* fathers"? This awkwardness is compounded by v. 3, in which the addressees shift from second person to third person (from "you" to "them"), but still leaves the audience unidentified. Moreover, Zech 1:3 is also curious for another reason. The verse is almost invariably translated with imperatival force—"*You say* to them...," even though the rules of grammar

3. Haggai uses the expression "by the hand of" (בְּיַד) instead of "to," as, for example, in דְּבַר־יְהוָה בְּיַד־חַגַּי הָיָה (see Hag 1:1; cf. 1:3; 2:1). This difference between the formulae in Zechariah and Haggai is another piece of evidence against the proposition that the "editorial framework" of both books come from a common hand.

The expression בְּיַד is used later in Zech 7:7 and 7:12 to refer to the message which came through the former prophets. The form "by the hand of" appears in later prophecy (cf. Dan 9:10; Mal 1:1), and it has earlier precedents in 2 Sam 12:25; 2 Kgs 17:13; 24:2 (cf. Hos 12:11), and probably reflects a metaphoric adaptation of the common imagery of "a message sent by the hand of..." (1 Sam 11:7; 16:20; 2 Sam 10:2; 11:14; 2 Chr 36:15 etc.). On this, see the helpful summary in Conrad (1999: 141–43), though I remain unconvinced by Conrad's wider argument that the prophet Zechariah marks a point of transition between the role of a "prophet" and a "messenger" (see esp. Conrad 1999: 19–20, 27–42, 145–47).

Given that there are uses of the phrase בְּיַד which both predate and postdate Zech 1–8, it is hard to argue that the absence of this phrase in Zech 1–8 is anything more than a stylistic variation, perhaps based on a preference for alluding to the typical forms used in Jeremiah and Ezekiel.

4. The closest parallel is with the foundational word to Ezekiel (Ezek 1:3), but variations on the phrase occur 30 times in Jeremiah (see, e.g., Jer 14:1; 46:1; 47:1; 49:34) and 50 times in Ezekiel—for details, see Meyers and Meyers 1987: 91. See also similar forms in Hos 1:3; Jon 1:1; Hag 2:1.

The combination of "dating formula + message reception formula" (which occurs three times in Zechariah, each time as a structural marker—Zech 1:1, 7; 7:1) is a construction typical of Ezekiel. See, e.g., Ezek 1:2–3; 20:2; 24:1; 26:1; 29:1, 17; 30:20; 31:1; 32:1, 17. In contrast, it occurs only at the beginning of Jeremiah (Jer 1:2).

5. On the pairing of the verb קָצַף with its cognate accusative קֶצֶף, see the comments below on Zech 1:15.

seemingly dictate that it should be translated as a simple past-tense—"And *you said* to them 'Thus says Yahweh of Hosts…'" (וְאָמַרְתָּ אֲלֵהֶם כֹּה אָמַר יְהוָה צְבָאוֹת).[6]

I wish to suggest that there is an intertextual basis for these grammatical peculiarities. Clearly, parts of Zech 1:2–3 are grammatically awkward. But perhaps this is deliberately so, because the phrases in question are allusions to other texts. At this point, we can make profitable use of Riffaterre's conception of an *ungrammaticality*. As noted above (§2.5.3), Riffaterre defines an ungrammaticality as an awkward grammatical construction in one text which points the reader to another text to resolve the apparently "ungrammaticality."

The fact that Zech 1:3 sits awkwardly in its context functions to prompts the reader to consider whether this phrase has come from an original context where it does fit more naturally—that is, Zech 1:3 is "ungrammatical" because it is a quote.[7] The phrase in Zech 1:3—וְאָמַרְתָּ אֲלֵהֶם כֹּה אָמַר יְהוָה צְבָאוֹת—also occurs in Jeremiah and, with stylistic variations, in Ezekiel.[8] In the present context of Yahweh's "wrath against the fathers," the closest semantic parallel to Zech 1:3 occurs in Ezek

6. Almost all translations render v. 3 with an imperatival force—"Say to them…" However, as a matter of strict grammar, it is difficult to see how this can be justified. Verse 3 is a Qal perfect, coordinated with a preceding Qal perfect in v. 2 (קָצַף), which typically denotes an ongoing past action (GKC §112h)—that is, "Yahweh was angry…and you said to them." Van der Woude (1980: 164) argues that Zech 1:3 should be construed as a consecutive perfect which stands in loose connection with the preceding verb, and cites GKC §112x,aa in support. However, as Floyd demonstrates, the other examples which van der Woude gives are explicable because there are imperfect verbs in the context which give the perfect verb its imperatival force, which is not the case in Zech 1:3. Floyd is one of the few commentators to follow the grammar strictly, and argues for an interpretation in which 1:3 is a continuing report of past events—that is, "Yahweh was angry with your fathers, and you [i.e. Zechariah] said to them…" (2000: 318–19). This view requires that the prophet Zechariah is old enough to have had an (earlier) prophetic ministry to the generation of the fathers. According to Floyd (2000: 322), "[t]he unit narrates just one action, the prophet's reception of a revelation. The revelation is quoted directly as a speech of Yahweh, and this speech takes the form of a story… In effect, Zechariah's audience is allowed to overhear Yahweh telling him a story that is also intended for them."

7. Cf. the comments of Petersen on this verse: "one senses something drawn out of its original context and placed in a new setting" (1984a: 129).

8. Exact parallels in Jer 19:11; 25:28; 43:10. Otherwise, Jeremiah typically uses the title "Yahweh" alone. Ezekiel uses "Lord Yahweh" instead of "Yahweh of Hosts." The full list of similar phrases is Ezek 2:4; 3:11, 27; 14:4; 20:3, 5, 27; 24:3; 37:12; Jer 8:4; 11:3; 13:3; 19:11; 25:27, 28; 26:4; 43:10.

2:3–4, which is addressed to "they and their fathers," and in which the prophet is told "You say to them, thus says Lord Yahweh" (וְאָמַרְתָּ אֲלֵיהֶם כֹּה אָמַר אֲדֹנָי יְהוִה). In Ezek 2:4, this phrase fits grammatically—the antecedent of אֲלֵיהֶם is defined, and the perfect וְאָמַרְתָּ, which follows a participle, has imperatival force. I submit that Zech 1:3 is grammatically odd because it is a quotation of Ezek 2:4.

We might make a similar observation about Zech 1:2. As noted above, the phrase "your fathers" (אֲבוֹתֵיכֶם) in Zech 1:2 hangs in midair, grammatically speaking, because there is no antecedent for the pronominal suffix.[9] However, this exact construction (אֲבוֹתֵיכֶם) occurs frequently in Jeremiah (22 times) and Ezekiel (8 times)—and only otherwise in a handful of prophetic texts[10]—typically as part of a prophetic critique of the sins of the fathers. I suggest that the grammatically awkward reference to "your fathers" in Zech 1:2 functions as an intertextual pointer to the wider prophetic critique of a former generation, particularly as expressed in Jeremiah and Ezekiel.[11] Zechariah's hearers are thus being reminded of the prophetic critique of sins of their fathers.[12]

Thus, in both Zech 1:2 and 1:3, the use of peculiar phraseology points the reader to the condemnation of the fathers which came through the former prophets, especially Ezekiel and Jeremiah. The grammatical peculiarities of Zech 1:2–3 are an intertextual pointer to the wider prophetic critique of the sins of the father.

The remainder of Zech 1:3 gives the content of Yahweh's message which Zechariah is to proclaim to his present generation:

שׁובו אלי נאם יהוה צבאות
ואשׁוב אליכם אמר יהוה צבאות

"Return to me, declares Yahweh of Hosts,
and I will return to you, says Yahweh of Hosts"

9. As Petitjean (1969: 28) has shown, this construction in v. 2 is not without precedent. Petitjean argues that the "your" in "your fathers" (אֲבוֹתֵיכֶם) implicitly denotes the audience, that is, Zechariah's contemporaries living in the second year of Darius. I come to the same conclusion on Petitjean, though on different grounds.

10. Only otherwise in the prophets in Isa 65:7; Hos 9:10; Joel 1:2; Mal 3:7.

11. In Jeremiah, the phrase "your fathers" sometimes simply refers to an earlier generation, with no negative overtones. However, in the later chapters, "your fathers" takes on clearly negative overtones (e.g. Jer 44:9). In Ezek 20, the negative critique is maintained throughout.

12. Indeed, in Zech 1:4 this allusion to the prophetic critique of the fathers will be made explicit.

שׁוּב is the key word in this section, occurring five times in four verses. In Biblical Hebrew, the word has a semantic range of meaning which spans "turn/return/relent/repent." The call to "return to Yahweh" occurs in a variety of prophetic contexts, though nothing precisely matches Zech 1:3 in form. Jeremiah 24:7 anticipates the day when "they shall return to me" (יָשֻׁבוּ אֵלַי), but this is not an imperative form (שׁוּבוּ).[13] In Jeremiah (and Ezekiel too, for that matter), the imperative always has the sense of "Turn *from*" rather than "Return *to*." In Joel and Hosea, the imperative occurs with the sense of "Return *to*,"[14] but with a different preposition (עַד not אֶל).[15] The closest parallel to Zech 1:3 occurs in Isa 44:22b (שׁוּבָה אֵלַי).[16] However, given the variety of possible intertextual connections, perhaps the most that we can say is that Zech 1:3 echoes a common prophetic call to return to Yahweh.

What is not common is for this prophetic call to be paired with a promise by Yahweh that "I will return to you." This pairing does occur in Mal 3:7 and 2 Chr 30:6, but these texts postdate Zechariah and are perhaps dependent on it.[17] Even the promise of Yahweh—"I will return"—is quite rare. The idea of Yahweh's spatial return (שׁוּב)—as implied by "Return *to*"—only occurs in one text that predates Zechariah, namely, Isa 52:8. This intertextual connection between Zechariah and Isa 52:8 has also been noted by Petitjean and Hanhart.[18] The other suggestive intertext

13. And see also Jer 3:1, 7, 10 for the criticism of the people's failure to return, and Jer 4:1 for the promise of blessing should the people return to Yahweh.

14. "Turn, O faithless Israel/children" (Jer 3:12, 14, 22); "Turn from your evil ways" (Jer 18:11; 25:5; 35:15); "Turn from your [*various evil acts*]" (Ezek 14:6; 18:30; 33:11). We should note, however, the non-imperative use of שׁוּב in Jer 4:1 and 24:7, and see also Jer 15:19 for the sense "repent…restore."

15. Hos 14:2: "Return O Israel to (עַד) Yahweh your God"; Joel 2:12: "Return to me (עָדַי) with all your heart." Conrad (1999: 49–54) notes this intertextual parallel with Joel. Amos 4:6–11 has this שׁוּב + עַד construction five times in six verses, though not in imperatival form. I note that Zech 3 alludes to Amos 4:11 (the "burning stick snatched from the fire"), which shows that the prophet Zechariah was aware of Amos 4. For other similar constructions, see also Deut 4:30; 30:2; Job 22:23; Isa 10:21; 31:6; Lam 3:40; 2 Chr 30:6, 9 and Neh 1:9.

16. The case for allusion to Isa 44 is strengthened by a subsequent allusion to Isa 44:28 in Zech 1:16 (see §4.4).

17. Rather than (as per Beuken) evidence that these words have been added to Zechariah in a chronistic milieu. See §3.2.4 above for my critique of Beuken.

18. See, especially, Petitjean 1969: 58–61. Petitjean (speaking about the parallel phrase in Zech 1:16) draws a connection with both Isa 52:7–10 and Ezek 43:1–9 (which describes Yahweh's return to the temple, though without using שׁוּב vocabulary). Petitjean concludes, "On perçoit, en Zach., i, 16, un écho de la prédication

for this verse is Joel 2:13–14, which combines the call to return to Yahweh with the hope that Yahweh might return to his people.[19] The usage of שׁוב elsewhere in Zech 1–8 helps to clarify exactly what is being promised when Yahweh says "I will return to you" (אֲלֵיכֶם וְאָשׁוּב) in Zech 1:3, especially:

Zech 1:16	I *am returning* (שבתי)[20] to Jerusalem in mercy.
	My house *will be built* (יבנה) in it.
Zech 8:3	I *am returning* (שבתי) to Zion.
	and *I will dwell* (ושכנתי) in the midst of Jerusalem.

In Zech 1:3, the promised "return" is still future (i.e. imperfect verb), but thereafter (subsequent to the people's response in v. 6) the process of "return" has begun, though this process will not be complete until Yahweh is dwelling with his people again, which is connected with the rebuilding of his "house." In Zech 2:5–17, the imagery of "Yahweh dwelling" with his people is further explained (after the manner of Ezekiel) in terms of God's glory dwelling in the midst of Jerusalem. That is to say, the promise of Yahweh's return in Zech 1–8 clearly has "spatial" overtones. As Petersen says in the context of Yahweh's promise to return to dwell in Zech 8:3, "There can be little doubt about the "temple" focus of such language" (1984a: 298–99).

d'Ézéchiel et du Second Isaïe" (1969: 61). See also Hanhart 1998: 36. If we widen the parameters of our search to include synonyms of שׁוּב, then we might also note parallels with Ezek 36:9: "I will turn to you" (וּפָנִיתִי אֲלֵיכֶם).

19. See further Conrad 1999: 51–54.

20. שַׁבְתִּי is a Qal perfect, which might legitimately be translated either in a past completed sense (i.e. "I have returned") or in a present continuous sense—"I am returning." See GKC §106g for perfects used to describe past action which continues into the present. The present-continuous rendering in this instance was chosen in order to be consistent with the translation of the same phrase in Zech 8:3. Zech 8:3 clearly describes an ongoing process of return, both because it stands in parallel to the word קִנֵּאתִי in Zech 8:2 (also a perfect, with the present-continuous sense "I am jealous"), and because the next clause in Zech 8:3 ("and I *will* dwell"—וְשָׁכַנְתִּי—following the Masoretic accenting) indicates that the "dwelling" of Yahweh in Jerusalem is still in the future. For the counter view, see Edelman (2005: 128). The present and future mix of "returning" and "dwelling" is paralleled for Yahweh's people in Zech 8:7–8—Yahweh is rescuing (ישׁע Hiphil participle, present continuous) his people, and they (like Yahweh) *will* "dwell in the midst of Jerusalem" (וְשָׁכְנוּ בְּתוֹךְ יְרוּשָׁלָם, 8:8; cf. 8:3).

Petersen (1984a: 298) also translates שַׁבְתִּי in 8:3 as "I am returning." Meyers and Meyers translate it as "I have returned," but then comment "The use of the perfect tense indicates that Yahweh's return has already begun" (1987: 413). The meaning of שַׁבְתִּי is thus much the same on either approach.

The confluence of these themes only occurs elsewhere in Ezekiel.[21] Ezekiel 10–11 describes the stages of the departure of the glory of Yahweh from the temple in Jerusalem (see Ezek 10:3, 18–19; 11:23).[22] Ezekiel 37:26–7 promises a reversal, one in which Yahweh's sanctuary and dwelling will again be with his people. The prophet Ezekiel foresees this reversal unfold in Ezek 43. Reversing the stages of departure, Yahweh will re-enter the temple and declare "I will dwell there in the midst of the sons of Israel forever" (Ezek 43:7). As we shall see later in this chapter, there are a number of striking allusions to Ezek 40–48 in Zech 1–2. On the basis of these verbal and thematic parallels, we may conclude that Yahweh's promise "to return" in Zech 1–8 combines imagery from Isa 52 and Ezekiel (esp. Ezek 43). These allusions, which begin at Zech 1:3, thus "hook" Zech 1–8 into the prophetic thought-world which understood the exile as Yahweh's withdrawal of his presence from Jerusalem. Zechariah 1 holds out the promise of Yahweh's return to dwell with his people in Jerusalem.

In Zech 1:4, Zechariah's generation is to be told "Do not be like your fathers" (אַל־תִּהְיוּ כַאֲבֹתֵיכֶם). As Tigchelaar notes, the "implicit and explicit warnings not to be like 'your fathers' are commonplace in Jeremiah, Ezekiel and Deuteronomy" (1996: 75).[23] The specific action which Zech 1:4 warns against is ignoring the proclamation of "the former prophets." Zechariah 1:4 reports both the message of these prophets and the response of the former generation, and, as argued above (see §2.8, example 1), does so by means of a clear allusion to Jer 25:5–7. Although there are also some similarities to Ezekiel,[24] it is unlikely that Ezekiel is the prime intertext, since Zech 1:4 uses the phrase "Yahweh of Hosts" as part of the message of "the former prophets," and this phraseology is not found in Ezekiel.[25] The case for a specific allusion to

21. Cf. Deuteronomy and Jeremiah, which use the language of "a dwelling for his name" (e.g. Deut 12:11; Jer 7:12). There are partial thematic similarities (though none as compelling as the links to Ezekiel) with: "Yahweh who dwells among his people" (e.g. Exod 29:46; Num 35:34); "Yahweh who dwells on Sinai" (Exod 24:16); "Yahweh who dwells on Zion/Jerusalem" (e.g. Isa 8:18; Joel 4:17; Ps 135:21).

22. On this theme of divine presence and absence in Ezekiel, see further Kutsko (1997: 139–40, 52–62).

23. The only exact match to this phrase is 2 Chr 30:7 (which is later), but thematic parallels occur in Jer 16:12; 34:14; 44:9, and Ezek 20:18, 30.

24. E.g. Ezek 33:11, as noted by Beuken (1967: 97–98), Petersen (1984a: 133) and Meyers and Meyers (1987: 95).

25. The exact phrase "Yahweh of Hosts" (יְהוָה צְבָאוֹת) occurs 260 times—not at all in Ezekiel, but frequently in Isaiah (60 times) and Jeremiah (76 times), and then

Jer 25 is further strengthened by the fact that another part of Jer 25—the "seventy years" of Jer 25:11–12—is also alluded to later in this same chapter (Zech 1:12; see §4.4 below).

Zechariah 1:5 warns his generation why they should not "be like their fathers" by means of two rhetorical questions:

אבותיכם איה־הם והנבאים הלעולם יחיו

> Your fathers, where are they?
> And the prophets, do they live forever? (Zech 1:5)

There are two intertextual connections which help to explain this verse. The answer to the first rhetorical question—"Your fathers, where are they?"—is clear from Lam 5:7: "Our fathers sinned, and they are no more."[26]

However, the second question—"the prophets, do they live forever?"—is not as easy. There are three references to prophets in the space of three verses: "the former prophets" (הַנְּבִיאִים הָרִאשֹׁנִים) in Zech 1:4; "the prophets" (הַנְּבִאִים) in Zech 1:5; and "my servants the prophets" (עֲבָדַי הַנְּבִיאִים) in Zech 1:6. I follow the lead of the many commentators who take "the prophets" in 1:5 to be referring to *false* prophets, since they are paralleled with "the fathers" in the first clause, and a negative connotation for the phrase would seem to be required by the immediate context.[27]

Tigchelaar objects to this approach, arguing that "it is not very likely that the 'prophets' in Zech 1:4, 6 and 1:5 refer to two different groups" (1996: 83). Tigchelaar and others who seek to maintain a single (positive) referent for "the prophets" in all three verses argue that the second clause of v. 5 is setting up a point of comparison with their words in the

dominantly in post-exilic prophecy (Haggai, ×12; Zechariah, ×46 times; Malachi, ×24). For the connections between this title and "Zion Theology," see below on Zech 1:16.

26. See Van der Woude (1980: 167) for examples of rhetorical questions in the form "Where are they?" He lists (in this order) 2 Kgs 18:34; Jer 17:15; Pss 42:4, 11; 79:10; Deut 32:37; Jer 37:19; Nah 2:12 (ET 2:11); 3:18 (though this should be 3:17); Jer 13:20, and Ezek 13:12.

27. See, e.g., Beuken (1967: 100) and Rudolph (1976: 69). Van der Woude (1980: 168–69) comes to the same conclusion, though via an emendation to the MT from וְהַנְּבִאִים הַלְעוֹלָם to וְהַנְּבִאִים הַלָּעוּ לָמוֹ, producing "And {where are} the prophets who spoke unreasonably (לעע) to them." This change also requires relocating the consonants חיו to the beginning of v. 6. Van der Woude's suggested emendation has not convinced many.

next verse—that is, "The prophets don't live forever...but the word of Yahweh spoken through them does."[28]

The intertexts of this verse provide us with a way to resolve this question, in that there is an intertextual precedent in the book of Jeremiah. Jeremiah also uses the phrases "the prophets" and "my servants the prophets." Each of the six instances of the phrase "my servants the prophets" has a positive connotation,[29] whereas each of the 43 instances of "(the) prophets" has a negative connotation.[30] Thus, a person familiar with Jeremiah, who heard the (unqualified) phrase "the prophets," would almost certainly have thought of the false prophets whom Jeremiah had decried, rather than "Yahweh's servants the prophets." I take it that the form of Zech 1:5 has also been influenced in particular by Jer 37:19: "Where are your prophets who prophesied to you?"[31]

The fate of the "fathers" is made explicit in Zech 1:6a: "Surely my words and statutes, which I commanded my servants the prophets—did they not overtake your fathers?" This clause contains an allusion to Deut 28 (esp. v. 15), which is the only other place we find the combination of "statutes" (חק) which "overtake" (נשׂג).[32] As noted by Meyers and Meyers, this allusion serves to remind Zechariah's hearers that the cause of the exile was the curses embedded within the deuteronomic covenant (1987: 101).[33] As in Jeremiah, here also the qualified description "*my servants* the prophets" differentiates between this group and the "the

28. E.g. Elliger (1963: 101) "[M]ögen die Väter, das Objekt der Verkündigung, und die Propheten, das Subjekt der Verkündigung, nicht mehr vorhanden sein, so ist doch der Inhalt der Verkündigung noch da, das prophetische Wort Gottes." See also Mason 1977a: 33; Petersen 1984a: 133–34; Meyers and Meyers 1987: 95; Tigchelaar 1996: 86; Floyd 2000: 322.

29. The phrase "my servants the prophets" occurs in Jer 7:25; 26:5; 29:19; 35:15; 44:4, and in the LXX of Jer 25:4. The MT of Jer 25:4 has "his servants the prophets." See further §3.3.1.2 above.

30. Jer 2:8, 26, 30; 4:9; 5:13, 31; 6:13; 8:1, 10; 13:13; 14:13, 14, 15 (×2); 18:18; 23:9, 10, 13, 14, 15 (×2), 16, 21, 25, 26, 30, 31; 26:7, 8, 11, 16; 27:9, 14, 15, 16, 18; 28:8; 29:1, 8, 15; 32:32; 37:19; 50:36.

31. Though I note the similar rhetorical construction in Isa 19:12, "Where are your sages now?" See n. 26 for further references to the rhetorical construction "Where is...?."

32. Petitjean (1969: 46) also notes a connection with Deut 17:19, in the combination of "my words" and "statutes."

33. See similarly Petitjean (1969: 46): "Se heurtant à la négligence ou à la rébellion, les «paroles» divines se sont transformées en malédictions frappant la communauté. La pensée de Zacharie rejoint un thème majeur du *Deutéronome* et de la théologie deutéronomique de l'histoire."

prophets" of Zech 1:5. I take it that "my servants the prophets" are the same group as "the former prophets" in Zech 1:4.[34] It is interesting to note that these "words and statutes" which "overtake" are not those which have come through Moses (as per Deut 28:15), but those which Yahweh had "commanded [his] servants the prophets." That is, there is a perceived commonality between the message of the deuteronomic covenant and the message of the "former prophets," especially the book of Jeremiah, which has just been alluded to in Zech 1:4.

Apart from one retrospective reference in Zech 8:14, Zech 1:5 is the last explicit reference to "the fathers." It is important to note the significance both of this early concentration on the sins of the fathers (four times in five verses), and the effect of the cessation of this language. Although Zech 1:1–6 clearly draws on its prophetic forebears (particularly Jeremiah and Ezekiel) in framing this language, there is also an important difference, signalling a "generational shift." The former prophets had condemned "you and your fathers,"[35] but in Zech 1 the present generation are not included in the condemnation. It was the fathers (alone) who did not listen to the prophets. It was the fathers with whom Yahweh was angry. It was the fathers who were "overtaken" by Yahweh's judgment (i.e. exile). Zechariah 1–8 is not addressed to "the fathers," nor indeed their sons, who (as in Lam 5:7 above) suffered in exile for the sins of the fathers. Rather, it is addressed to the "sons of the sons," to the sons of the restoration. It is this generation to whom the prophet Zechariah now declares "Do not be like your fathers" and who must instead "return to Yahweh" (Zech 1:3).

We must now turn our attention to the remainder of Zech 1:6—"and they turned and said, 'Just as Yahweh of Hosts purposed to do to us according to our ways and deeds, thus he has done to us.'" There is some debate about whether the word "they" in this verse refers to the "fathers" of 1:6a, or to Zechariah's audience (i.e. the "them" to whom the prophet speaks in 1:3–5). If "they" refers to the fathers, then this verse records

34. The language used in Zech 1:4 to describe God's people failing to listen to "the former prophets" is elsewhere paralleled by Israel's failure to listen to "my servants the prophets" (see 2 Kgs 9:7; 17:13; Jer 7:25; 26:5; 29:19; 35:15; 44:4). See also Ezek 38:17, in which Yahweh spoke in former days "by the hand of my servants the prophets of Israel" (בְּיַד עֲבָדַי נְבִיאֵי יִשְׂרָאֵל). For the third person form of this phrase (i.e. "his servants the prophets"), see 2 Kgs 21:10; 24:2; Jer 25:4; Amos 3:7; Dan 9:6, 10. The second person form "Your servants the prophets" occurs in Ezra 9:10.

35, See, e.g., Jer 7:25–26; 35:12–16; 44:2–3; Ezek 2:3.

the repentance of a former generation.[36] Otherwise, it records the repentance of Zechariah's generation, and reads as a kind of historical postscript to Zechariah's words in Zech 1:1–6a (i.e. the prophet Zechariah preached "Return to Yahweh"...and his first hearers did just that).[37] A factor that counts heavily against the first interpretation is that it creates the logical difficulty of exhorting Zechariah's generation to be *not like* their fathers (1:4) while at the same time exhorting them to repent, which is what the fathers had eventually done.[38] For this reason, I am inclined to the view that 1:6b describes the response of Zechariah's first audience.

However, on either view—whether it is the repentance of Zechariah's generation or a repentance of those in exile—the important point is that 1:6b regards the "return" of the people as a completed event. In Zech 1:3, Yahweh had promised "Return to me and I will return to you." The people's "return" in 1:6 means that the precondition for the "return" of Yahweh has been met. This observation is important because it undercuts the suggestion that Zech 1:2–6 adds a call to repentance (and with it a conditionality) which is absent from the rest of the book, which some have taken to be evidence that parts of Zech 1:2–6 were a later addition to the book.[39] However, if we take seriously the fact that the repentance of Zechariah's generation (or the generation prior) is described as a completed act at the outset of the book, then this removes the expectation that we should expect further calls to repentance in the remainder of the

36. See, e.g., Mitchell 1912: 113; Petersen 1984a: 134; Tigchelaar 1996: 85–86; Floyd 2000: 322. For a careful weighing up of evidence for each position, see van der Woude 1980: 171–73.

37. See, e.g., Beuken 1967: 103–4; Petitjean 1969: 50; Mason 1977a: 33, Meyers and Meyers 1987: 96–97; Boda 2004: 176.

38. Tigchelaar counters this argument regarding the inconsistency created by "repenting fathers," concluding that "No real contradiction exists between Zech 1:4b and Zech 1:6b, since the former describes the disobedience before the punishment, the latter the acknowledgment of Yahweh's plan afterwards" (1996: 85).

39. For example, Ollenburger argues that Zechariah's editors have composed the initial sermon (including 1:3) on the basis of Zech 7–8, but from a different theological perspective, by adding a note of conditionality which is absent from the visions. As such (he argues), Zechariah has been edited in the direction of Haggai—Yahweh's saving acts in the remainder of the book are now predicated on the people's return (1996: 736). Similarly, Mason (1984: 229) argues that Zech 1:2–6 "seems to be to impose a conditional note at the outset of the book. It certainly strikes a different note from the visions and their accompanying oracles with their promises of divine action."

book. Zechariah 1:2–6 establishes that the people have already "returned to Yahweh," raising the expectation that the time is ripe for Yahweh to "return to them."

There is a final intertextual echo in this verse in the reference to a judgment "according to our ways and deeds" (כִּדְרָכֵינוּ וּכְמַעֲלָלֵינוּ). Hosea 12:3 is the only place where כִּדְרָכָיו and כְּמַעֲלָל occur in the same verse, but Ezekiel and Jeremiah both have minor variations on this phrase, and so this phrase may be an echo of any or all of these.[40]

4.2.1. *Conclusions on Zechariah 1:1–6*

The opening verses of Zechariah indicate an awareness (and appropriation) of passages from Jeremiah, Ezekiel, Lamentations, Isa 52 and 54 and Deuteronomy, elements of which have been woven together to form one composite whole. However, Zech 1:1–6 is more than just a "pastiche…[of] the kind of thing a prophet would have been expected to say" (Petersen 1984a: 133), or an indication that Zechariah has "quoted Jeremiah freely" (Tigchelaar 1996: 87).[41] Rather, these opening verses of Zechariah are programmatic for the chapters which follow, signalling the manner in which "the former prophets" are to be read together and reapplied to a new generation.

These opening verses establish important matters of timing. Though recalling the exile as the purposeful outpouring of Yahweh's wrath because of the disobedience of the "fathers," Zech 1:1–6 indicates that there has been a generational shift. Zechariah's generation is called to return to Yahweh, that he might return to them. That generation responded to this call (cf. Hag 1:12), and so the way is now clear for Yahweh to return. Zechariah 1:1–6 thus creates an expectation of Yahweh's imminent return.

4.3. *The Intertexts of Zechariah 1:7–11*

This section begins with another dating and message reception formula, one which dates the night-vision sequence to 24th of Shebat in the second year of Darius (i.e. 15 February 519 B.C.E.).

40. The phrase in Ezekiel uses a cognate noun for "deeds" (עֲלִילָה instead of מַעֲלָל) (see Ezek 20:44; 24:14; 36:19). Jer 17:10 and 32:19 use an additional word—"fruit of"—that is, כִּדְרָכָיו כִּפְרִי מַעֲלָלָיו.

41. Cf. Mason's analysis of these verses as a "tissue of quotations and allusions" (1990: 199–205).

In Zech 1:8–11, the prophet recounts his first night-vision, which involves a man riding a red horse amid the myrtle trees, surrounded by other coloured horses.

There is much in this vision that is bizarre. Commentators typically posit a variety of intertexts to make sense of "the myrtles in the deep" and the colours of the horses and so forth. However, the fact that there are almost as many interpretations of these verses as there are commentators would suggest that the alleged intertexts are not particularly compelling. Rather than offer my own intertextual speculations on this, I propose focussing on those elements of the vision which are taken up in the interpretation, and for which there are clear intertexts.

4.3.1. *Horses which "Patrol the Earth"*

The function of the horses is explained in vv. 10–11: "Yahweh sent them to patrol the earth" (שָׁלַח יְהוָה לְהִתְהַלֵּךְ בָּאָרֶץ). There are two sets of intertexts which have combined to shape this image. First, there is an allusion to Job 1–2. In Zech 1:10–11, the role of the horses is "to patrol in the earth" (לְהִתְהַלֵּךְ בָּאָרֶץ), which parallels the description in Job 1:7 and 2:2 of one who comes from roving "in the earth" (בָּאָרֶץ) "and from patrolling in it" (וּמֵהִתְהַלֵּךְ בָּהּ).[42] The likelihood of a deliberate allusion in Zechariah to Job 1–2 is strengthened by the continuation of this allusion in the final night-vision in Zech 6:7,[43] together with further parallels between the roles of the horses/heavenly attendants. In Job, the heavenly attendants come "to present themselves before Yahweh" (לְהִתְיַצֵּב עַל־יְהוָה, Job 1:6 and 2:1), which parallels the figures in Zech 6:5 who go out "from presenting themselves before the Lord" (מֵהִתְיַצֵּב עַל־אֲדוֹן).[44] This repeated imagery in Zech 1 (and 6) constitutes an unmistakable allusion to Job 1–2.

The second set of intertextual connections relates to the equine imagery, and in particular to horses in Yahweh's service. There are only three other places outside Zechariah where we see horses used by Yahweh—Hab 3:8; Joel 2:4–5[45] and Isa 66:15.[46] While the data are too

42. The Hithpael infinitive construct of the verb הלך occurs in Job (1:7; 2:2), Zech (1:10; 6:7 [×3]) and only otherwise in Prov 6:22 and Ps 56:14. Only in Job and Zechariah does this construction occur in the context of a "divine council" scene.

43. In Zech 6:7 the chariots go out to patrol the earth (לְהִתְהַלֵּךְ בָּאָרֶץ).

44. Job and Zechariah have the only instances of יצב (Hithpael) + עַל.

45. The parallels with Joel are particularly evident in relation to Zechariah's other "horse" vision. Both Joel 2:4–10 and Zech 6:1–8 share the common elements of horses (סוּס) and war chariots (מֶרְכָּבָה) coming from mountains (הַר) and travelling (הלך) in formation upon the earth.

sparse to be able to claim that any one of these three is a *specific* intertext of Zechariah, we may make an important observation about the *general* intertexts of "Yahweh's horses." It should be noted that in all three other instances of this equine imagery the horses are agents of Yahweh in bringing judgment and destruction.[47] This bellicose imagery continues in Zech 6:1–8 (see my analysis below in Chapter 6), which makes it all the more surprising that Yahweh's horses in Zech 1:7–17 do not have these expected overtones of violence.[48] My suggestion is that these overtones have been omitted for rhetorical effect, to create a jarring dissonance. That is, the general intertextual background of equine imagery creates the expectation that "Yahweh's horsemen" should be going to go out to trounce the nations, and so their discordant role here contributes to the shock of v. 11 (see below) that the messengers come back with the message that the world is at peace.

4.3.2. *The Divine Council Scene*

It is important to recognize that Yahweh's horses are a part of a "divine council" (or "heavenly assembly") scene, one which would seem to derive from other similar scenes in the Hebrew Bible.[49] In particular, 1 Kgs 22:19–22; Isa 6; Ezek 3 and Job 1:6–12; 2:1–7 all share the imagery of creatures around the throne of Yahweh, who are sent out

46. I take it that the imagery in Jer 4:13 refers to the chariots of the destroyer from the north, not Yahweh. It may be however, that the ultimate source for the imagery of the chariots of Yahweh is the deliberate reversal of this imagery of the chariots of the foe from the north.

47. See also Hahlen 2000: 253.

48. Instead of a destructive role, the role of the horse(men) in Zech 1:7–17 is much closer to those in Isa 21:9, who have a "messenger" role. Isa 21:9 describes "riders, horsemen in pairs" (רֶכֶב אִישׁ צֶמֶד פָּרָשִׁים) who come to announce the fall of Babylon. However, even given some points of verbal connection between these two passages, there is a jarring dissonance between the messages of the respective horsemen. Whereas Isaiah's horsemen come back with the message of the fall of Israel's enemy, Zechariah's horsemen return to say that the world is at peace.

49. I take a slightly different view on this to Tollington, who argues "[a]lthough I accept that the prophetic traditions determined Zechariah's concept of a divine council, I believe that his depiction of it displays no evidence of classical or pre-classical prophetic dependence" (1993: 111). Tollington argues instead that Zechariah's depiction of this scene is based on the background of the Psalms (1993: 114–15). However, based on the evidence (discussed above at §3.2.2) of the parallels between Isa 6 and Zech 3, I conclude (contra Tollington) that we can trace specific elements of Zechariah's divine council scene to the classical prophetic tradition.

to do his bidding. As Jeremias notes, Zechariah's usage differs in one important respect, in that, in the first vision, the heavenly assembly has already occurred, and the prophet Zechariah only witnesses its after-effects, and does not see Yahweh or his throne directly (1977: 117–21). However, we should not read too much significance into the apparent absence of Yahweh from the scene, given the presence of the "angel of Yahweh." I take it that the "man standing amidst the myrtles" in 1:8 is to be identified with the "angel of Yahweh" in 1:11, as he is likewise "standing amidst the myrtles."[50] Tollington argues that "the angel of Yahweh" in Zechariah is a revival of an old concept which existed before classical prophetism (1993: 96). In that older tradition there is a blurring between Yahweh and the angel of Yahweh, and this same blurring occurs in Zech 1–8.[51] I shall comment more on the significance of the angel of Yahweh when I discuss the fourth vision (see Chapter 5 below), though for the present purposes we may safely conclude that this scene in Zech 1 bears a number of similarities to other divine council scenes.

The other key figure in this scene is the "The angel who was talking to me," usually described as the "interpreting angel."[52] I agree with the suggestion of Tollington (1993: 98–99) that Jacob's dialogue with the "angel of God" in Gen 31:10–13 has influenced Zechariah's depiction of the angel of Yahweh.[53] In addition, I also detect the influence of several passages from Ezekiel in which an intermediary explains a heavenly vision.[54] Zechariah 1–8 has combined this "interpreting angel" motif with

50. So also Baldwin 1972: 93, Clark 1982: 213–18; Smith 1984: 189; Meyers and Meyers 1987: 110, 115; Merrill 1994: 103; Delkurt 1999a; Boda 2004: 196. Contra Petersen 1984a: 144–45, who takes the "man standing among the myrtles" to be a different figure to "the messenger of Yahweh." Contra also Conrad 1999: 64, who identifies the prophet Haggai as the "messenger of the LORD" being referred to in these verses.

51. See, for example, Gen 22:15–16, where the angel of Yahweh speaks as Yahweh. See also Exod 3:2–5; Judg 2:1; 6:11–14, 22–24; 13:21–22; 2 Sam 24:16–17. The blurring of roles also occurs in Zech 1:12, where the angel of Yahweh speaks to Yahweh, and Zech 3:1–2, 5–6, where he speaks as Yahweh.

52. Though there is some force to Love's comment (1999: 151) that this is perhaps a less than satisfactory title for a figure who leaves so much unexplained, leaving both Zechariah—and us—scratching our heads in bewilderment.

53. Common elements include:

Gen 31:10	וָאֶשָּׂא עֵינַי וָאֵרֶא...וְהִנֵּה	Zech 2:1	וָאֶשָּׂא אֶת־עֵינַי וָאֵרֶא וְהִנֵּה
Gen 31:11	מַלְאַךְ הָאֱלֹהִים	Zech 1:11	מַלְאַךְ יְהוָה
Gen 31:12	וַיֹּאמֶר שָׂא־נָא עֵינֶיךָ וּרְאֵה	Zech 5:5	וַיֹּאמֶר אֵלַי שָׂא נָא עֵינֶיךָ וּרְאֵה

54. See esp. Ezek 8:2–5; 40:3–4; 47:1–12. This imagery appears to have been combined with the form of "explanatory dialogue" (e.g. Ezek 37). The likelihood of

another strand of tradition—the question-and-answer dialogue. In Jer 1:11–13; 24:3–5 and Amos 7:7–8; 8:1–2 we have examples of a question-and-answer dialogue being used to explain the significance of a vision, a vision that has obvious parallels in Zech 1–8.[55] However, there is also an interesting reversal of roles. In the passages in Jeremiah and Amos the question is typically initiated by Yahweh, who asks the prophet "What do you see?" (מָה־אַתָּה רֹאֶה). In Zech 1–8, the directionality is reversed, in that it is typically the prophet who asks "What are these things?" (מָה־אֵלֶּה). I say "typically" because at two points (Zech 4:2 and 5:2) the prophet reverts to the "What do you see?" form, exactly paralleling the usage in Amos and Jeremiah. Again, we are seeing a combination of streams of tradition, a *composite metaphor*.

4.3.3. *The Message of the Heavenly Scouts*

The message which the heavenly scouts bring back is "Behold, the whole earth is inhabited and at rest" (וְהִנֵּה כָל־הָאָרֶץ יֹשֶׁבֶת וְשֹׁקָטֶת).[56] From the

Ezekiel's influence here is strengthened by the presence of other clear allusions/ echoes of Ezekiel elsewhere in Zech 1–8—see §4.6.1 on the connections between Ezek 40 and 47 and Zechariah's man with a measuring rod, and §6.3.2 on textual connections between Ezek 8 and Zech 5. Contra Tollington, who considers the first two of these passages, and, while recognizing Zechariah's possible dependence on Ezekiel for the visionary language, concludes that Ezekiel is not a source for Zechariah's "interpreting angel" (1993: 97–98).

55. On the various elements which have contributed to the form of Zechariah's visions, see further §3.2.2.

56. The RSV, NRSV and ESV translate the clause יֹשֶׁבֶת וְשֹׁקָטֶת as "remains at peace." The NIV translates it as "at rest and in peace." However, these translations do not correctly reflect the sense of יֹשֶׁבֶת. They are apparently rendering this as though it were analogous to the phrase יֹשֶׁבֶת־לָבֶטַח, "dwelling securely" (attested in various forms in Lev 25:18–19; 26:5; Judg 18:7; 1 Kgs 5:5; Ezek 28:26; 34:25, 28; 38:8, 11, 14; 39:6, 26; Isa 47:8; Jer 32:27; 49:31; Prov 3:29; Ps 4:9; Zeph 2:15; Zech 14:11. See also 1 Sam 12:11; Deut 12:10 (וִישַׁבְתֶּם־בֶּטַח). However, it is doubtful that יֹשֶׁבֶת standing alone can have this sense.

The meaning of the clause יֹשֶׁבֶת וְשֹׁקָטֶת in Zech 1:11 is best determined by analogy with the only similar phrase in the Hebrew Bible, which occurs in Zech 7:7. In Zech 7:7, the construction יֹשֶׁבֶת + ו occurs in the phrase "Jerusalem was inhabited and at ease" (יְרוּשָׁלַם יֹשֶׁבֶת וּשְׁלֵוָה). That "inhabited" is the correct translation here for יֹשֶׁבֶת is indicated by second instance of the same verb in the last clause of Zech 7:7, which describes how the Negeb and Shephelah were also "inhabited" (יֹשֵׁב). BDB (ישׁב §6) and *HALOT* (ישׁב §6) both list "be inhabited" as a meaning of ישׁב in the Qal, when applied to a city/territory, and include Zech 7:7 in the listed examples. Other examples include לֹא תֵשֵׁב, meaning "not inhabited" (Isa 13:20; Jer 17:6; 50:13, 39; cf. Ezek 29:11; Zech 9:5), and תֵּשֵׁב, meaning "[Jerusalem] is inhabited" (see Zech 2:8; cf. 12:6; Jer 17:25). For response of the angel of Yahweh which follows in v. 12 it is clear that this message of weal for "all the earth" is in fact a lamentable situation as far as Jerusalem and Judah are concerned. In the historical context of the "second year of Darius," the political tumult of recent years in the Persian Empire had recently subsided, and is now "at rest."[57] However, the expectation raised by the former prophets would have led one to expect the opposite situation for the post-exilic period. After their punishment, it should be Yahweh's people who enjoy peace and security,[58] and the nations should have been overthrown.[59] The exile is apparently over, but the promised age of peace and security has not materialized for God's people—in fact, it is still "all the earth" which enjoys this peace instead. This allusion to the promises of weal of the former prophets (like Jeremiah) serves to stress the fact that the time for reversal is long overdue.

In addition to a general allusion to the prophetic expectation of reversal, there may be a specific allusion to Ezek 38:11–12 (which is the only other passage to use the words שקט and ישב in this sense). In Ezek 38, Gog's destructive plan was against an unsuspecting people "at rest" (הַשֹּׁקְטִים, 38:11), and against the places now "inhabited" (נוֹשָׁבֹת).[60] The likelihood of a specific allusion to Ezek 38 in this verse is strengthened by the occurrence of other allusions in Zech 1–2 to Ezek 38, in particular

these reasons, I conclude that the phrase יֹשֶׁבֶת וְשֹׁקָטֶת should be translated "inhabited and at rest."

57. See Meyers and Meyers (1987: xxxvii–xxxix) for an account of the comparative instability under Cambyses (530–522) and for the first 2 years of Darius' reign. However, Wolters raises questions about whether "all the world" was indeed at peace in February 519 B.C.E. Wolters notes that two addenda to the Behistun inscription indicate continuing conflict for this period. "Zechariah's visions are dated in the middle of the great upheavals which were threatening the Persian Empire during the first few years of Darius's reign. It seems very paradoxical that the horsemen of the first vision should report at that time that the whole world was 'at rest and in peace'" (Wolters 2009: 130).

58. See Jer 30:3–11 (esp. vv. 10–11) and Jer 46:27–28. See also Isa 32:18.

59. Jer 25:12 promises that, after the "seventy years," Babylon will be punished and made desolate forever—see further below on Zech 1:12 for Zechariah's appropriation of this passage. For this theme elsewhere, see generally Isa 10:5–19 (esp. 10:12–13); 13–14; 21:1–10; 41:15–16; 47:6; 54:7. The depiction in Isa 14 is particularly interesting, for both Isa 14:7 and Zech 1:11 describe peace (שקט) over all the earth (כָּל־הָאָרֶץ), but to the opposite effect. In Isa 14, it brings joy; in Zech 1, lament (see 1:12).

60. In addition, Ezek 38:14 also uses the same verb with the sense of "in security" (בְּשֶׁבֶת).

to the "open regions" (פְּרָזוֹת, Ezek 38:11 = Zech 2:8) and Yahweh "rousing himself" (עוּר, Zech 2:17; cf. Ezek 38:14).[61]

In Zechariah, this metaphor from Ezek 38 (which is apparently itself a working-over of Jer 49:31–32) is reversed and reapplied.[62] Clearly, one rhetorical effect of this allusion would be to remind the hearer that the time is ripe for the judgment on "Gog"—but perhaps we can go further and see in this allusion a reversal of situations. In Ezek 38, Gog's plan was to attack Israel when they were "inhabited and at rest." In Zech 1:7–11, Yahweh's scouts have come back with the message that it is now all the earth which is "inhabited and at rest." In a great reversal, it is now Yahweh who will rouse himself and attack, and do to "Gog" what "Gog" had done to Israel.[63]

4.4. *Zechariah 1:12–17*

In response to the report received from the heavenly scouts, the angel of Yahweh laments the ongoing anger of Yahweh for "these seventy years" (1:12). In response, Yahweh speaks words of comfort to the interpreting angel (1:13), who then speaks to Zechariah, presumably passing on the same message of comfort from Yahweh (1:14–17).

The cry "O Yahweh of Hosts, how long…?" (יְהוָה צְבָאוֹת עַד־מָתַי) takes up the lament form.[64] The lament "how long?" (עַד־מָתַי) occurs in several places in the Hebrew Bible.[65] Delkurt (2000: 83) claims that Zech 1:12 obviously alludes ("anspielt offenbar") to Isa 6:11. While there are other clear allusions to Isa 6 elsewhere in Zechariah,[66] there is a much

61. I follow (with many) the proposal in *BHS* on Ezek 38:14 to read תֵּעֹר instead of תֵּדָע (with LXX, ηόσηθρεγέ, "you will be roused," and several manuscripts in the Latin tradition with forms of *exsurgo*, "to rise, stand up"). See Zimmerli 1983: 288.

62. See Zimmerli (1983: 310) for further discussion on the links between Ezek 38 and Jer 49:30–31. There would appear to be overlapping "layers" of allusion in Zech 1–8 to both Ezek 38–39 and Jer 49. As noted above (n. 56), Zech 7:7 describes "Jerusalem at ease." At this point, Zech 7:7 echoes Jer 49:31—an attack on a city "at ease" (שְׁלֵיו). If indeed Ezek 38–39 is a "working over" of Jer 49, then Zech 1–8 alludes to both source and derivative.

63. For a further development of this "reversal," see my comments on Zech 2:10–13 in §4.6.2 below.

64. As recognized by, for example, Beuken (1967: 240–41), Niditch (1983: 137) and Petersen (1984a: 146).

65. In the prophets only in Isa 6:11, but more frequently in the Psalms (see Pss 6:4; 74:10; 80:5; 90:13; 94:3). For עַד־מָה, see also Pss 79:5 and 89:47.

66. As I have argued above at §3.2.2, the cleansing of Joshua in Zech 3 is patterned after Isa 6.

higher degree of formal correlation between Zech 1:12 and Ps 80:5, and both Ps 80:5 and Zech 1:12 (but not Isa 6) use this form to plead for a (post-exilic) restoration after judgment.

The angel's complaint is that Yahweh has "not shown mercy" (לֹא־תְרַחֵם)[67] to Jerusalem with whom he been "angry" (זָעַמְתָּה). This particular vocabulary is a further clear allusion to Lam 2, which again serves to recall the depravities of the exile.[68]

The angel describes the time of Yahweh's anger as "these seventy years" (זֶה שִׁבְעִים שָׁנָה). The motif of "seventy years" is pivotal in Jer 25 and Jer 29. Though some past commentators have argued that the "seventy year motif" in Jeremiah was a late addition to Jeremiah, under the influence of Zechariah,[69] the consensus position now is that the direction of influence goes the other way around—that is, Zech 1:12 is an allusion to Jer 25:11–12 and/or Jer 29:10,[70] or that Jeremiah and

67. Yahweh not showing mercy (רחם + לֹא) towards his people (or a subset thereof) is elsewhere only attested in the pre-exilic prophets. In Hos 1–2, this theme is a *leitmotif*, in association with the name of Gomer's first daughter (לֹא־רֻחָמָה) (see Hos 1:6, 7, 8; 2:3, 6, 21, 25). Otherwise (apart from Zech 1:12), the combination of רחם + לֹא with Yahweh as the subject only occurs in Isa 9:16 (ET 9:17); 27:11 and Jer 13:14; 21:7, describing Yahweh's withdrawal from his people in response to their sin. The imagery of Yahweh "showing no mercy" is so powerful because it inverts the normal expectation that Yahweh is the God who "shows mercy" (see, e.g., Isa 49:15; 54:10; Ezek 39:25).

68. When one considers the 34 instances of זעם and its cognates, and especially the six times that this word is used of Yahweh's anger towards his people (Ezek 22:31; Isa 10:25; Lam 2:6; Pss 38:4; 78:49; 102:11), only Lam 2:6 refers to God's ongoing anger with the (post)exilic generation. Similarly, the description of Yahweh "showing no mercy" is a recurring theme in Lam 2 (לֹא חָמַל in Lam 2:2, 17 and לֹא חָמָלְתָּ in Lam 2:21 are synonymous with Zech 1:12 לֹא תְרַחֵם). This is another intertextual connection with Lam 2, which is further evidence of sustained allusion (see below in the conclusion to this chapter).

69. For example, Whitely argues that, contrary to appearances, Jeremiah cannot be the primary source of the seventy years. His argument is that the events in Jeremiah do not span an exact seventy years and he rejects the "round number" approach (i.e. 66 years is close enough). Whitely instead argues that the primary referent of the seventy years is the period from 586–516 B.C.E., which is the period of the desecration of the house of God (as in the book of Zechariah). Whitely argues that the references in the book of Jeremiah to the seventy years are post-exilic additions (Whitley 1954: 72).

70. The word "these" in the phrase "*these* seventy years" (זֶה שִׁבְעִים שָׁנָה, Zech 1:12) suggests a recognized motif to which Zech 1:12 alludes. See further Nurmela 1996: 42–44 and Meyers and Meyers 1987: 117.

Zechariah both depend on an even earlier ancient Near Eastern tradition.[71] When we compare the theme of the seventy years in Jeremiah and Zechariah, there is an important shift in the metaphor in Zechariah. Whereas Jeremiah describes the seventy years of Babylon's supremacy, Zechariah describes the seventy years of Israel's desolation. Furthermore, whether or not Jeremiah's seventy years was meant to be understood as an exact span of seventy years,[72] in Zechariah the metaphor is being used with that chronological emphasis.[73] In Zech 1–8, the period of seventy years refers to the period of the desolation of the temple (which in fact spanned a literal seventy years: 586–515 B.C.E.).[74] While the

71. For the argument of an ancient Near Eastern tradition of "seventy years" punishment for a city, see, e.g., Lipiński 1970: 38; Petersen 1984a: 149–50; Avalos 1998. This argument is based on the inscription on the Black Stone of Esarhaddon, which records that Marduk had decreed seventy years as the period for Babylon's desolation: [70] *šanâte^pl mi-nu-ut ni-du-ti-šú iš-ṭur-ma* ("Seventy years as the period of its desolation he wrote down," cited from Luckenbill 1925: 167). However, this text goes on to say that Marduk, in his mercy, had reduced this period to only eleven years. I note that this single anecdote (in two similar versions) of "Marduk's seventy years" hardly proves an ancient Near Eastern tradition, especially since in the only instance in which Marduk has decreed this, he had also shortened the duration to just eleven years. It is by no means certain that this hypothesized ancient Near Eastern "seventy year" tradition is also reflected in Isa 23:15. On this, see similarly Leuchter 2006.

72. Jer 25:9–12 makes clear that the seventy years *of Babylon* runs from the first year of Nebuchadnezzar (= 605 B.C.E.). Orr argues that "the period 605–539 is sufficiently close to seventy years" (1956: 305–6). Winkle (1987: 289–299) further extends this approach by arguing that the effective rise of Babylon as a world power (as far as Israel is concerned) is 609 B.C.E., and that the seventy-year period in the book of Jeremiah is thus an exact seventy years, referring to the ascendancy of Babylon (609–539 B.C.E.). See similarly Gurney 1981: 31.

73. It may also be that Jeremiah's "seventy years" lies in the background of Hag 1:2. Bedford (1995) argues that the reason why the people say "The time has not yet come for Yahweh's house to be built" is because the time of judgment (as implied by Jeremiah's prophecy) has not yet run its course, and Yahweh has not yet sanctioned a rebuilding. However, Kessler (2002b) questions whether this interpretation can stand, in light of the fact that "the editor of Haggai is concerned to present the people's reticence to reconstruct the temple as culpable neglect" (2002b: 250), rather than a pious waiting for the "seventy years" to run their course.

74. On my basis for these dates, see the introduction to Chapter 3, and footnotes thereto. According to Ezra 6:15, the temple was completed on the third day of the month of Adar, in the sixth year of the reign of King Darius (= March 515 B.C.E.). On the assumption that Jerusalem was destroyed in July 586, the temple was thus in ruins for a full seventy years, and rededicated during the seventy-first year. The promise of Jer 25:12/29:10 is that the seventy years are to be "completed" (כִּמְלֹאות),

emphasis on Israel's desolation is already a theme in Jer 25:11,[75] Zechariah's innovation is to see these two seventy-year periods as not necessarily co-terminus. The differences are a question of perspective.[76]

Zechariah's re-use of the "seventy year motif," together with the wider allusions to Lam 2 and Ps 80, suggest that—theologically speaking—the time of Jerusalem's "desolation" is still continuing, notwithstanding the fact that the "return" from exile had begun almost two decades before. This stress on timing is further reinforced by the chronological markers in the book, which, as noted by Curtis (1991), follow Jeremiah's pattern of date formulae which memorialize the destruction of the temple.[77] The implication for Zechariah's generation is that the desolation has continued while "Yahweh's house" remains in ruins. (Indeed, this implication will be made explicit in Zech 1:16.) However, for Zechariah's hearers, the "seventy year motif" sounds a hopeful note. The rhetorical effect of the mention of seventy years has the opposite effect to that which it has in the book of Jeremiah. In Jeremiah, "seventy years" meant a long wait, whereas for Zechariah's generation, standing on the cusp of the end of the seventy years, the re-use of this motif raises the hope of an imminent reversal of fortunes.

In response to the lament by the angel of Yahweh in v. 12, Yahweh speaks "gracious and comforting words" (דְּבָרִים טוֹבִים דְּבָרִים נִחֻמִים) to the interpreting angel in Zech 1:13. The motif of Yahweh's comfort (נחם) occurs only in prophetic texts—principally Isa 40–66.[78] Isaiah 40:1 establishes the programmatic place of the word נחם in the chapters which follow.[79] I agree with Delkurt that Zech 1:13–14 has taken up the message (and messenger) of Isa 40–55:

which, strictly speaking, requires that a reversal not occur until the seventy-first year. See also Jeremias 1977: 131 and Applegate 1997: 102–6.

75. Applegate (1997: 92) argues that each of the three references to the seventy years in Jeremiah has a different emphasis—Judah's servitude (25:11), Babylon's punishment (25:12), and the promised restoration (29:10).

76. See similarly Jeremias 1977: 134.

77. See also my comments above in §4.2 on Zech 1:1 above. In Jeremiah, the switch from dating with respect to the kings of Judah to dating with respect to the (pagan) king Nebuchadnezzar stresses the function of Nebuchadnezzar as the temple-destroyer. This can be seen from the fact that the only dating formulae in this form in Jeremiah (see Jer 52:12; cf. 25:1; 32:1) either refer to or anticipate the destruction of Jerusalem.

78. Apart from a single reference in Jer 31:13, the image of Yahweh speaking words of comfort occurs only elsewhere in Isa 40–66. The imagery is used in reverse in Lam 1 (i.e. "no one to comfort").

79. Isa 49:13; 51:3, 12; 52:9; 61:2; 66:13.

> In seiner Verkündigung nimmt Sacharja die Botschaft von Jes 40ff mit den Stichworten »erbarmen« (Sach 1,12; vgl. v.a. Jes 49,10.13; 54,7f) und »trösten« (Sach 1,13; vgl v.a. Jes 40,1–8) auf und führt sie fort (2000: 82).[80]

If, for example, we look at all the references to נחם in Isa 40–55 there are striking thematic parallels with Zech 1:14–17. The messenger in Isa 40–55 proclaims a message of comfort (נחם) to those still experiencing "exile" and who think that "Yahweh has forgotten me" (49:13). Their comfort shall come through restoration (51:3), freedom from oppressors (51:12) and Yahweh's return to his people (52:8–9). By this intertextual connection to Isa 40–55, Zech 1 has re-activated the Isaianic promises.[81]

These words of "comfort" spoken *to* the interpreting angel in Zech 1:13 are presumably the same as the message spoken *by* the interpreting angel in Zech 1:14–17,[82] which the prophet Zechariah is commissioned to proclaim (קרא).[83] Niditch (1983: 137) argues that the imagery of prophetic commissioning in these verses "must bring to mind the initiation form exemplified by Isaiah 6 and Ezekiel 1." While I would agree that there are some parallels with the prophetic commissioning in Isa 6 and Ezek 1, I suggest that there is an even clearer intertextual parallel with Isa 40:1–8. Not only does Isa 40 have a dominant message of "comfort" (as noted above), but it also shares the same imperatival command to proclaim (קְרָא)—"a voice says 'Proclaim'"—Isa 40:6.[84]

The prophet Zechariah is to proclaim that Yahweh is jealous with a "great jealousy"[85] for "Jerusalem and Zion."[86] The theme of Yahweh's

80. On this theme, see also Seitz 1990: 233, who argues that Zech 1:7–17 is a divine council scene which parallels Isa 40.

81. On this, see further Sweeney 2000: 579.

82. This seems a reasonable assumption, since the message ends with "comfort" (נִחַם, see Zech 1:17).

83. This message of comfort is a dual message—Zechariah is told to proclaim both Yahweh's anger at the nations (1:14–15) as well as the restoration of Jerusalem resulting from his return (1:16–17). I will argue below (§4.6.3) that the prophet does in fact proclaim exactly these themes in Zech 2:10–17 (ET 2:6–13).

84. Delkurt (2000: 82) also argues for a connection between this verse and Isa 40:1–8, on similar grounds.

85. The phrase "great jealousy" (קִנְאָה גְדוֹלָה) is unattested outside the book of Zechariah, but is likely a rhetorical construction to counter-balance the "great wrath" (קֶצֶף גָּדוֹל) of the next verse (see comments below). "Great jealousy" and "great wrath" (חֵמָה גְדוֹלָה) are paired in Zech 8:2.

86. The pairing of Jerusalem and Zion is typical in Isaiah, Psalms, Zeph 3, Mic 3–4, Joel 3 and Zechariah (five times). Thus, while a specific source cannot be identified, it is clear that Zech 1–8 incorporates this theme from the Zion tradition.

"jealousy" (קנא) is a frequent theme across the Hebrew Bible.[87] Nurmela (1996: 46) argues for a "probable" connection between Zechariah's usage (here, and also in Zech 8:2) and Ezek 39:25, on the grounds that only here does God speak (first person) of his jealousy. However, I suggest that this argument places too much stress on morphological form alone. Upon closer examination of the passages, it is clear that the object of the jealousy is different. In Ezekiel, the object is "my holy name," compared to "Zion/Jerusalem" in Zech 1:14 and 8:2. Instead, a better approach is to look for the same kind of construction (קנא + ל = "jealous for") with a similar object. On this basis, the only relevant match is with Joel 2:18,[88] where Yahweh is jealous for his "land" and "people." We have already had cause to highlight two other parallels between Zech 1 and Joel 2. The instance of another allusion to Joel 2 in this verse suggests that there might be good cause to look for evidence of a sustained allusion. I note the following points of connection between the two passages:

Zech 1–2	*Joel 1–2*
1:3 Return to me (שׁוּבוּ אֵלַי) and I will return to you	2:12–14 Return to me (שֻׁבוּ עָדַי)... Who knows if [God] will return.
1:10 horses patrolling the earth. Cf. Zech 6:1–8 Horses (סוּס) and war chariots (מֶרְכָּבָה) going out from between mountains (הַר) to patrol (הלך) the earth.	2:4–10 Yahweh's army, like horses (סוּס) and war chariots (מֶרְכָּבָה) leaping on mountains (הַר), travelling (הלך) in formation.
1:14 I am jealous (קנא) for Jerusalem	2:18 Yahweh was jealous (קנא) for his land
1:13 Yahweh responded (וַיַּעַן יְהוָה)	2:19 Yahweh responded (וַיַּעַן יְהוָה)
1:13, 17 Comfort (נִחֻמִים, נחם)	2:14 Comfort (נחם)
2:12 The Holy Land. Cf. 8:3 the holy mountain (הַר הַקֹּדֶשׁ)	2:1 In Zion ... in my holy mountain (בְּהַר קָדְשִׁי)
2:14 Shout and be glad (רָנִּי וְשִׂמְחִי), O Daughter of Zion (בַּת־צִיּוֹן). For I am coming, and I will live in your midst (בְתוֹכֵךְ).	2:23 O sons of Zion (וּבְנֵי צִיּוֹן), be glad and rejoice (גִּילוּ וְשִׂמְחוּ) 2:27 You will know that I am in the midst (בְקֶרֶב) of Israel

87. The word and its cognates occur 87 times (קִנְאָה, ×43; קנא, ×36; קַנָּא, ×6; and קַנּוֹא, ×2). Typically, it describes Yahweh's character—that is, "Yahweh is a קַנָּא God." See, e.g., Exod 34:14 (×2); Deut 4:24; 5:9; 6:15; 20:5 (cf. קַנּוֹא, Josh 24:19; Nah 1:2). However, both here and in Zech 8:2 (קִנֵּאתִי לְצִיּוֹן), the construction focuses on the object of Yahweh's jealousy, which is not as frequently attested (see below).

88. Though it should be noted that elsewhere in Ezekiel (e.g. Ezek 16:42; 23:23) the cognate noun קִנְאָה is used to refer to Yahweh's "jealousy," which burns against his people for their sins.

The extent of the parallels between these chapters suggests that Zech 1–2 contains a sustained allusion to Joel 2.[89] I shall discuss the rhetorical effect of this sustained allusion in the conclusion to this chapter.

Zechariah 1:15 announces the counterpart to Yahweh's jealousy for Jerusalem—his "great wrath" (קֶצֶף גָּדוֹל) directed at the nations. Everywhere else in the Hebrew Bible, Yahweh's "great wrath" is directed at his people for their covenant malfeasance.[90] Earlier in this chapter, Zech 1:2 described Yahweh's "exceeding wrath" (קָצַף...קֶצֶף) against the forefathers, but now there has been a *reversal of wrath*. The "great wrath" formerly directed against God's people has ended (as anticipated by Jer 32:37–38), and is now directed against the nations. Zechariah 1 reiterates the message of "wrath reversal" of Isaiah, drawing in particular on the language and themes of Isa 54:7–8.[91]

The objects of Yahweh's wrath are the nations "at ease" (הַשַּׁאֲנַנִּים). Though using a different vocabulary, this links thematically with the picture of a world "at rest" in Zech 1:11. Elsewhere, this word[92] recalls

89. My working assumption in §3.3.4 was that Zech 1–2 and Joel 2 come from the same early post-exilic milieu. Now, with the evidence of these parallels before us, we are able to draw some conclusion about the relative priority of these two texts. The fact that the there is a sustained allusion to Joel 2 that fits the patterns of the other sustained allusions in Zech 1–2 suggests that Zech 1–2 is the later work. This conclusion is borne out by a comparison of the context and tone of each book. On the whole, Joel appears to be more reserved and uncertain about the future, whereas Zech 1–2 is more confident about the future. Joel asks "Who knows if Yahweh will return?," against which Zech 1:16 declares "Yahweh is returning" (or "has returned"). Similarly, Joel 1:12 describes a negative "before" picture, against which Hag 2:19 gives a much brighter prognosis for the future. In Joel 2:17–19, the nation is still an "object of scorn," which corresponds to the situation to which Zech 1:13 speaks. For these reasons, I come to the conclusion that Joel 2 is an intertext used by Zech 1–2. Conrad (1999: 51–54) also lists Joel 2 as a significant intertext of Zech 1.

90. For other instances of קֶצֶף גָּדוֹל, see Deut 29:27; Jer 21:5; 32:37–38; Zech 7:12; 8:2. Seybold (1974a: 83–84) argues that Zechariah's "großer Zorn" follows Ezekiel's usage, though the verses he cites (Ezek 5:13; 23:25; 36:5–6; 38:19) are based on a thematic rather than verbal connections. For other possible intertexts, see Petitjean 1969: 73–78.

91. Zech 1:15 combines the verb קצף with its cognate accusative קֶצֶף. The combination of this verb and noun also occurs in Zech 1:2, but otherwise occurs nowhere else except in Isa 54:8–9. Isa 54:8–9 also shares with Zech 1:15 the same theme of "wrath reversal."

92. The word is attested both as an adjective (שַׁאֲנָן, ×10) and a verb (שׁאן, ×5) though noting that the verbal form—Pilpel third masculine singular—is שַׁאֲנַן, which is exactly the same as the adjectival form.

the complacency of Assyria (Isa 37:29 // 2 Kgs 19:28) and Moab (Jer 48:11),[93] and also serves as a tantalizing reminder of the promise of "ease" for God's people (Jer 30:10; 46:27) which is still being enjoyed by her enemies instead (cf. Zech 1:11).

Zechariah 1:15 goes on to say that Yahweh had only been a "little angry" (אֲנִי קָצַפְתִּי מְּעָט) with these nations, but his wrath has been made great because "they are helpers of evil" (וְהֵמָּה עָזְרוּ לְרָעָה).[94] This imagery builds on Isaiah's critique of Assyria (Isa 10:5–15) and Babylon (Isa 47:6; 54:7–8) who were tools of Yahweh who have overstepped the mark.[95]

We should note that, in Zechariah, Yahweh's wrath is directed against "the nations" generally, rather than against specified nations such as Assyria (as in Isa 10) and Babylon (as in Isa 47). However, the message of these intertexts from Isaiah is the same—because "the nations" have gone too far in executing Yahweh's judgment, they themselves will experience that judgment. We shall return to the question of who "the nations" might be later in this chapter.

In Zech 1:16 Yahweh declares "I am returning to Jerusalem with mercy" (שַׁבְתִּי לִירוּשָׁלַםִ בְּרַחֲמִים). I have already discussed this phrase above, in connection with Zech 1:3, and we have seen that the promise of Yahweh's return to Jerusalem is an appropriation of the promises of Isa 40–55, especially Isa 52:8–9 (Yahweh's return to Zion)[96] and Isa 54:7 (בְּרַחֲמִים, "in mercy"), combined with the Ezekielian imagery of Yahweh's return to "dwell" with his people.[97]

The notion of Yahweh dwelling in Jerusalem is further developed in Zech 1:16b, where it is promised that "my house will be built in it" (בֵּיתִי יִבָּנֶה בָּהּ). I shall return to this theme of "temple building" in the next

93. On this, see Niditch 1983: 145.

94. This phrase is closest to Isa 31:2, "the helpers of the doers of iniquity" (עֶזְרַת פֹּעֲלֵי אָוֶן), which recalls Yahweh's promise to rise up against the wicked.

95. So also Delkurt 2000: 82–83. Seybold (1974a: 84) argues that the parallel between Isa 54:7 and 47:6 and Zech 1:15 is "provable." Nurmela (1996: 47–48) categorizes the parallels between Zech 1:15 and Isa 47:6 (Yahweh's wrath at Babylon not showing mercy) as a "probable allusion."

96. Nurmela (1996: 49) lists this as a "sure" allusion. The evidence from Qumran suggests a further connection. The version of Isa 52:8 in 1QIs[a] contains an additional word (ברחמים, "with compassion"), which is not present in the MT. If original, this offers a further point of correlation with Zech 1:16. However, Koenig (1982: 269–74) argues that 1QIs[a] arose under the influence of Zech 1:16.

97. See further below, in relation to Zech 2:15–16. Nurmela (1996: 60) argues for a "sure" allusion from Zech 2 to Ezek 43:7, 9. See similarly Mason 1977a: 38, 42.

chapter (see especially §5.2). However, for the present purposes (given the extent of Isaianic allusions already identified), we should note that the promise of a rebuilt temple particularly echoes Isa 44:26–28. Whereas the theme of a "rebuilt city" is frequent elsewhere (especially in Jeremiah),[98] there are few explicit promises of a rebuilt temple, with Isa 44:28 (וְלֵאמֹר לִירוּשָׁלַםִ תִּבָּנֶה וְהֵיכָל תִּוָּסֵד) providing the closest parallel to Zechariah.[99]

Zechariah 1:16 promises that "the measuring line will be stretched over Jerusalem." Most commentators find an allusion to Jer 31:38–39 and/or Ezek 40–42 in the reference to the "measuring line." However, in terms of textual parallels, by far the closest parallels are 2 Kgs 21:14 and Lam 2, read together, as shown in the following:[100]

2 Kgs 21:13:	And I will stretch (וְנָטִיתִי) over Jerusalem (עַל־יְרוּשָׁלַםִ) the measuring line (קָו) of Samaria
Lam 2:8:	He stretched (נָטָה) the measuring line (קָו) over the walls of Daughter Zion
Zech 1:16:	And the measuring line (קוה) will be stretched (יִנָּטֶה) over Jerusalem (עַל־יְרוּשָׁלִָם)

Presumably, commentators are reluctant to find an allusion in Zech 1:16 to 2 Kgs 21 and/or Lam 2, on the grounds that the metaphor is working in opposite directions—the context in Zech 1:16 demands a positive connotation, whereas 2 Kgs 21:4 and Lam 2:8 are unmistakably negative. However, this is to miss the very point that Zechariah is making. As elsewhere in this section, Zechariah is announcing a great reversal—Yahweh is about to undo the destruction of 586 B.C.E. I suggest that

98. Jer 30:18; 31:4, 28, 38–40. See also Pss 69:36; 102:16; Isa 45:13; 54:11; 60:10; 61:4; Ezek 36:33–36; Amos 9.

99. I shall discuss further the significance of Isa 44:26–45:1 as an intertext of Zech 1–8 below in §5.2 (noting that Cyrus is designated a "messiah" for his role in temple rebuilding). There are few other passages which promise a rebuilt temple. Ps 102:16 (ET 102:16) anticipates the time when "Yahweh will (re)build Zion" (בָנָה יְהוָה צִיּוֹן). There is also an implicit promise of this in Ezek 37:27–28: "my dwelling place shall be with them…my sanctuary among them" (cf. Zech 2:15). Similarly, there is reconstruction implied in the movement from Mic 3:12, when Jerusalem is a heap, to Mic 4:2, where the nations will go up to the temple.

100. The wider context of 2 Kgs 21 also has other connections with Zech 1–2. 2 Kgs 21 is a message of Yahweh by "his servants the prophets" (cf. Zech 1:4), describing Yahweh casting off the "remnant of his heritage" (שְׁאֵרִית נַחֲלָתִי) (reversed in Zech 2:16). Elsewhere in this chapter, I have noted the wider connections between Zech 1–2 and Lam 2.

Zech 1:16 has taken up the negative image of the measuring line from 2 Kgs 21:4 and Lam 2:8, inverting it through further allusion to Jer 31:38–9 and Ezek 40–2.[101]

The use of the title "Yahweh of Hosts" (יְהוָה צְבָאוֹת) in Zech 1:16 is especially significant in the present context of a promise of temple rebuilding because of its connections to the Zion Tradition.[102] As Mettinger has convincingly argued, "the mainstream of the Jerusalem cultic tradition [is] a 'Zion–Sabaoth theology,' whose main theme was the notion of God enthroned in the temple" (1982a: 15; cf. 1982b: 117).[103] To whatever extent there was a "dethronement of Sabaoth" (to echo Mettinger) in the exilic period, Zech 1:16 reactivates the themes of this Zion–Sabaoth theology, announcing the return of "Yahweh Sabaoth" (i.e. Yahweh of Hosts) and the rebuilding of his temple—a re-enthronement of Sabaoth.[104]

In Zech 1:17, Zechariah is given a further word to proclaim (קְרָא). Yahweh declares that "My cities shall again spread out[105] *from the good* (i.e. because of good blessings)." The imagery of a city which "spreads out" is further explained in Zech 2:8, where the city overflows into the

101. The case for the specific allusion to the "measuring line" of Jer 31:39 is strengthened by the observation that Zech 1:16 and Jer 31:39 use the unusual (Ketib) form קוה (which is in both cases replaced by Qere קָו). This form only otherwise occurs in 1 Kgs 7:23. For more on the "measuring line" see §4.6.1 below.

102. This title has already been discussed above in n. 25. It is the dominant title for Yahweh in Zech 1–8, and in the post-exilic period more generally.

103. On the theme of the temple in Jerusalem as the royal "palace" for King Yahweh, see further Clements 1965; Clifford 1972; Mettinger 1982a: 19–37; Ollenburger 1987; Bedford 2001: 66–70. On the centrality of the Jerusalem/Zion tradition in Zech 1–8, see further Meyers and Meyers 1992.

104. Although I differ from Tollington over the provenance of title "Yahweh of Hosts" in Jeremiah (see §3.2.1.2 above), we come to similar conclusions about the significance of this title in Zech 1–8. I agree with her suggestion that this title reflects "the importance that [Haggai and Zechariah] attached to the temple and the re-establishment of the cult… By reintroducing the name applied to Yahweh in the cult of Solomon's temple, they were legitimating the new temple…as being the place where Yahweh still chose to make his dwelling" (1993: 69–70).

105. This is an unusual sense of פוץ ("scattered"). The word typically has negative connotations (e.g. Jer 13:24; 18:17). The only other usage similar to this one is in Prov 5:16. See Petitjean (1969: 68–69) for the suggestion (following Houbigant) that the consonantal text תפוצנה is a corruption of תפרצנה (i.e. third person feminine plural of פרץ), which would then have the same sense as Isa 54:3. Alternatively, the verb פוץ might be used here in an ironic sense, deliberately reversing the negative connotations elsewhere (see, e.g., Jer 18:17).

open country because of the prosperity within. These verses undoubtedly pick up the general theme from the former prophets of a time of prosperity beyond the exile.[106] However, we may trace a specific intertextual source for this theme in both Zech 1:17 and 2:8 to Isa 54:2–3, "Enlarge the place of your tent...for you will spread out to the right and to the left."[107] This thematic allusion is more likely in the light of the fact that we have already identified Isa 54 as an intertextual source for the awkward "wrathed wrath" (noun קֶצֶף and verb קָצַף) in Zech 1:2 and 1:15, and highlighted a number of other thematic connections in the near context of the respective passages, including the end of the time of wrath (Isa 54:7–8 // Zech 1:15) and Yahweh's return "in mercy" (Isa 54:7 // Zech 1:16).

This further word concludes with the promise that "Yahweh will again comfort Zion and again choose Jerusalem." The language of "comfort for Zion" (וְנִחַם...אֶת־צִיּוֹן) occurs only in two other places—Isa 51:3 and Lam 2:13. Given the sustained allusions throughout these sections to both Isa 40–55 and Lam 2, we should perhaps read this promise as a double allusion.[108] The language of Yahweh's "choice" (בחר) of Jerusalem has particular connotations in Deuteronomy and deuteronomistic texts regarding the place of the temple—Jerusalem is the place where Yahweh has chosen to put his name.[109] Thus, for Zechariah to proclaim that Yahweh will again choose Jerusalem is an implicit promise of a rebuilt temple (reiterating the promise of Zech 1:16–17, "my house will be built in it").

4.4.1. *Conclusions on Zechariah 1:7–17*

In this section we have seen a particular concentration of allusions to Isaiah, particularly Isa 40–55. I reassert the conclusions of Delkurt:

106. E.g. Jer 31:34.

107. If Petitjean is correct (see n. 105), and תפוצנה in Zech 1:17 is corruption of תפרצנה, then this verse would be a verbal allusion to Isa 54:3 (based on the verb פרץ), and not merely a thematic allusion.

108. Also significant in this regard are the conclusions of Willey (1997), who demonstrates that Deutero-Isaiah is a sustained recollection and reapplication of the book of Lamentations. As such, Zech 1:17 may not be so much a "double allusion" as a "chain allusion"—Zech 1 alluding to Lam 2 alluding to Isa 54.

109. Deut 12:5 (plus 20 other instances in Deuteronomy); 1 Kgs 11:13, 32, 36; 14:21; 2 Kgs 21:7; 23:27; cf. Jer 7:12. See also Ps 132:13 for the language of Yahweh "choosing Zion" (בָּחַר...בְּצִיּוֹן) for his "dwelling" (מוֹשָׁב). I note that Isaiah can use the language of "choice" of Israel without this "temple" focus (see Isa 14:1), but the "choice" of Jerusalem always does have this focus on the temple.

> Sach 1,12–15 verbindet die Aussagen Deuterojesajas. So wird die Zeit des Gerichts als Ausdruck des Zorns Jahwes verstanden (Jes 47,6; 54,8; Sach 1,15). Das Gericht war jedoch begrenzt (Jes 54,7f; Sach 1,15) und unerheblich gegenüber dem, was jetzt folgt (Jes 54,7b.8b; Sach 1,14.15). Die Babylonier werden als Gehilfen Jahwes gedeutet, die allerdings zu weit gegangen sind und darum nun Strafe verdienen (Jes 47,6; Sach 1,15). Die Babylonier haben kein Erbarmen gezeigt (Jes 47,6; vgl. Sach 1,15); demgegenüber ist Jahwe derjenige, von dem Erbarmen zu erhoffen ist (Jes 54,7f; vgl. Sach 1,12.14). (2000: 77)

In addition to these allusions to Isa 47 and Isa 54 (as highlighted by Delkurt), I also note the allusions to Isa 52 (Yahweh's "return to Zion"), and to the words of comfort (נחם) (Isa 40–55; cf. Zech 1:13). However, over and above these allusions to Isa 40–55, there are also sustained allusions to Joel 2 (as tabulated above) and Lam 2 (which will be discussed in more detail below). Furthermore, Jeremiah's motif of "seventy years" provides an important chronological positioning for the book. The divine council scene, particularly in its form in Job 1–2, provides the background for the role of the heavenly horsemen, which is further nuanced by allusion to Isa 6.

The allusions in Zech 1:1–17 combine to stress the imminence of the end of the exile. Even though some from Zechariah's generation had returned from exile in Babylon, the period of Jerusalem's "desolation" still continues, because Yahweh's house has not yet been rebuilt in Jerusalem. Since the time of the "exile" is still running (so to speak), the language of exilic laments (like Ps 80) can be "recycled," as can the promises of Isa 40–55 to the returning generation. The vision of vv. 7–13 and the interpreting oracle of vv. 14–17 combine to make this point. The theme could be summed up in the phrase "imminent reversal."

4.5. *Zechariah 2:1–4 (*ET *1:18–21)*

Zechariah's second night-vision concerns "four horns." Though this same phrase is present in the description of the "four horns" of the altar,[110] this is unlikely to be related to the subject matter of Zechariah's vision.[111] Instead, we should note that the "horn" (קֶרֶן) is often used in a

110. See, e.g., Exod 27:2; 38:2; Ezek 43:15, 20; cf. Amos 3:14.

111. Contra Amsler 1972: 228; Halpern 1978: 177–78; Petersen 1984a: 165–66; Love 1999: 183; Conrad 1999: 77; Sweeney 2000: 582. As indicated in my discussion of methodology (Chapter 3), my approach is to let the context shape the possible intertextual domains in order to limit the possibilities of spurious word-matches to unrelated semantic domains. In this case, Zech 2:4 makes clear that the horns are "the horns of the nations" (אֶת־קַרְנוֹת הַגּוֹיִם), which have scattered God's people.

metaphorical sense as a symbol of strength and/or courage, and this is the one meaning of קֶרֶן which co-inheres with the wider imagery of this passage.[112] From this we may conclude that the "horns of the nations" (אֶת־קַרְנוֹת הַגּוֹיִם, Zech 2:4) symbolize mighty nations who have "scattered" God's people.[113] This then raises the question: Which nations are (or, perhaps, which nation is) being represented by these horns? In the patristic era, the fact that there were "four" horns was taken literally as implying four specific nations.[114] A more recent variation on this approach is taken by Lurie (1988/89).[115] However, most interpreters understand the "four" as a symbol of universality, in line with the way that "four" is used symbolically elsewhere in Zech 1–8 (e.g. four winds of heaven, four chariots).[116] But, before we draw any conclusions about whether particular nations are on view, we should consider the other imagery in the passage.

In Zech 2:4 these four horns "scatter" (זרה) the people of God. This is an unusual use of this biblical metaphor of "scattering." Elsewhere, it is typically Yahweh—not the nations—who "scatters" his people.[117] If we

112. The dominant metaphorical use of קֶרֶן denotes a symbol of strength and/or courage (25 instances out of a total of 89). On the semantic range of the word, see further Süring 1980; 1985.

113. So also Rignell 1950: 61; Bič 1964: 61; Baldwin 1972: 104; Jeremias 1977: 156–58; Meyers and Meyers 1987: 136; Boda 2005. Contra Niditch, who endorses Othmar Keel's view of the horns "as magically, divinely potent instruments of victory. The horns are no mere metaphor for strength" (1983: 123).

The "four horns" in Dan 8 have a similar metaphorical function to the horns in Zech 2. However, there are important differences between the two. The four horns in Dan 8:8–9 represent four concurrent rulers of one nation (I take these to be the four successors to Alexander the Great), whereas the four horns in Zech 2:1–4 represent the nations (plural). I agree with Jeremias (1977: 162–63) that the metaphor in Zech 2 moves in a very different direction to the metaphor in Daniel.

114. For example, Assyrians, Babylonians, Medes and Persians. This example is cited by Chary 1969: 64.

115. Lurie (1988/89) argues that the four horns represent the four nations which had expanded as the result of the fall of Israel and Judah—Edom, Ammon, Moab, and Philistia.

116. See Zech 2:10; 6:1, 5. For examples of interpreters who take the "four" as a symbolism of universality, see Baldwin 1972: 104; Petersen 1984a: 163; Meyers and Meyers 1987: 136; Tollington 1993: 226–26.

117. Contra Nurmela (1996: 49–51), who suggests an allusion to Ezekiel, on the basis of multiple references there to Yahweh "scattering" (זָרָה) Israel. However, this does not give sufficient weight to the fact that it is the nations who are the ones "scattering" Israel in Zech 2. Apart from Zech 2, the verb זָרָה ("to scatter") always has God as the subject when Israel is the object. That is, elsewhere it is God who

seek intertextual parallels to this usage, we discover that the only places where the theme of "nations scattering God's people" otherwise appears are in Jer 50:17–18 and Joel 4:1–2. In Jer 50:17–18, the nations of Assyria and Babylon are "lions" who have scattered Israel. In Joel 4:1–2, it is "all nations" who have scattered God's people. In both passages, judgment is announced against the nations who scattered God's people. It seems likely that both Zech 2 and Joel 4 are alluding to Jer 50.[118] Logically, there are three possible explanations of the relationship between these three texts:

1. Jeremiah *influenced* Joel *which influenced* Zechariah;
2. Jeremiah *influenced* Zechariah *which influenced* Joel; or
3. Jeremiah *influenced* both Joel and Zechariah independently.

Counting against the third option is the very curious combination "Judah, Israel and Jerusalem"[119] in Zech 2:2, and which (in two components) also occurs in Joel 4:1–2, but not in Jer 50. It would seem that the best explanation is that Zech 2:2 is an "intertextual concatenation" of Joel 4:1 (Judah and Jerusalem) and Joel 4:2 (Israel), rather than that Joel 4:1–2 is an "intertextual expansion" of Zech 2:2.[120]

scatters (זָרָה) Israel, not (as in Zech 2) the nations who do the scattering. My semantic search of "nations scattering Israel," was based on the following synonym set for word זָרָה, "scatter": פזר, פוץ, פרד, פרץ, פלג, נסח, נפץ, נטשׁ, מתח, בזר, שׁטח, זרה, זרע, סער.

118. Zech 1–2 elsewhere alludes to Jer 48–51 (see the summary below at §4.7), which increases the likelihood of an allusion here. Joel 4:1–2 also clearly demonstrates an awareness and re-use of the book of Jeremiah, since Joel 4:1 is a virtual concatena of Jeremian phraseology, especially "in those days and at that time" (see Jer 33:15; 50:4) and "when I restore the fortunes" (see Jer 30:18; 33:11). This, together with the verbal echo of פזר ("scatter"), makes it highly likely that Joel is alluding to Jer 50. Thus, we have two texts (Zech 2:4 and Joel 4:1–2) which both allude to Jer 50.

119. As Meyers and Meyers (1987: 138) note, various LXX manuscripts omit either "Israel" or "Jerusalem," presumably to avoid the apparent redundancy in the phrase "Judah, Israel, and Jerusalem." However, the Naḥal Ḥever minor prophets scroll has a (partial) witness to this verse (see Tov 1990: 70–71), and the gaps between the extant text indicates that all three place names were probably present—Tov reconstructs the text as λυκμήσαντα τόν Ιουδαν τόν Ισραηλ και τὴν ιερουσαλημ. Thus, we should regard the MT as the original (and more difficult) text, and the various LXX versions as attempts to "smooth" this text.

120. I regard it is more likely that Zech 2 is a further development of the imagery of Joel 4 (and Jer 50), because Zech 2:4 adds a "symbolic" layer (e.g. the "horn" and "craftsman" imagery) which is not present in the other passages. Should Joel 4 have been the last in the sequence, then we have to suppose that the author of Joel appropriated the "Judah, Jerusalem and Israel" of Zech 2, but deliberately

Given the correspondences to other parts of Jeremiah and Joel already noted, it is not unreasonable to conclude that both of these passages lie in the background of the metaphor in Zech 2:1–4.

The importance of recognizing either or both of these texts from Jer 50 and Joel 4 as intertexts of Zech 2:1–4 is that these texts make two matters explicit which are only implicit in Zech 2:1–4. First, the intertexts make clear that Yahweh's action in overthrowing the nations is for the benefit of his people. We may well have inferred this from the fact that the craftsmen apparently act to reverse Israel's degradation by the horns, where "no man was able to raise his head" (Zech 2:4). However, Mark Love (pursuing a very different intertextual method to my own) has argued that this phrase (and most of Zech 1–8) is hopelessly ambiguous.[121] Whether or not we find Love's line of argumentation persuasive, my argument is that the intertexts of Zech 2:1–4 clarify this issue. In Jer 50:19, God acts in order to "bring Israel back to his own pasture," and in Joel 4:1, it is to "restore the fortunes of Judah and Jerusalem." When we read Zech 2:1–4 against the background of these intertexts, it is clear that the reason why the "horns" are being cast down is to enable Yahweh's scattered people to return.

The second matter in Zech 2:1–4 which is made explicit by its intertexts is that the fate of these nations is to be themselves overthrown. This matter is not completely resolved by Zech 2:1–4 because of a degree of uncertainty about whether destruction is implied by the words "to make afraid" (חרד Hiphil)[122] and "to cast down" (ידה Piel).[123] However, Jer 50

stripped it of its other symbolic elements. For this reason, I conclude that Zech 2:2 contains an intertextual trace of Joel 4:1 (Judah and Jerusalem) and Joel 4:2 (Israel), which further reworks the "scattered by the nations" imagery of Jer 50.

121. Love's method involves letting any instance of a word potentially bear all possible connotations in its semantic range. A consequence of this is that Love is often overwhelmed by a plethora of possible meanings, with no way to determine the "proper" one. In contrast to Love's method, I seek to let the immediate context of a passage determine which of the possible semantic values for a word are likely in each particular instance.

122. חרד (Hiphil) occurs 16 times, most frequently as אֵין מַחֲרִיד ("there is no-one to make afraid," Lev 26:6; Deut 28:26; Job 11:19; Isa 17:2; Jer 7:33; 30:10; 46:27; Ezek 34:28; 39:26; Mic 4:4; Nah 2:12; Zeph 3:13). If we consider the three remaining (i.e. apart from Zech 2:4) instances (Judg 8:12; 2 Sam 17:2; Ezek 30:9), the word describes the panic arising from being overthrown in battle, but does not necessarily imply destruction. However, it is worth noting that Ezek 30:9, which is the only instance which has exactly the same form as Zech 2:4 (לְהַחֲרִיד Hiphil infinitive construct), does imply the destruction of those who have been "terrified." I take it that Zech 2:4 is probably echoing Ezek 30:9 at this point.

and Joel 4 make explicit that "punishment/judgment" is the fate of the nations who scatter Israel. By recognizing these texts as the intertextual background to Zech 2:1–4, we are also provided with the conceptual framework for the interpretation of the imagery of the "four craftsmen." The intertexts suggest that these "craftsmen" (חָרָשִׁים) are acting as Yahweh's instruments of judgment. As such, the best intertext to explain this strange image is the "craftsmen of destruction"[124] (חָרָשֵׁי מַשְׁחִית) in Ezek 21:36 (ET 21:31),[125] perhaps further nuanced by the "craftsman" (חָרָשׁ) and "destroyer" (מַשְׁחִית) of Isa 54:16.

But who do the "horns" and the "craftsmen" signify? Are the horns symbolic of all nations who seek to oppress and scatter God's people, and the craftsmen thus symbolic of any instruments which Yahweh uses to repay them?[126] Or, as Boda has recently argued, are the horns symbolic of Babylon, only recently overthrown by the "craftsmen" (Persia)?[127]

123. ידה in the Piel only otherwise occurs in Lam 3:53, where it means "throw," referring to stones cast upon someone in a pit. ידה also occurs (once) in the Qal in Jer 50:14, where it means "shoot," referring to arrows from a bow. Otherwise, the word occurs frequently in Hiphil/Hithpael, where it means "praise/confess," but this meaning is unlikely to shed much light on Zech 2:4. On the basis of the parallels with Lam 3:53 and Jer 50:14, we may say that the word in Zech 2:4 probably means "cast down" or "cast out," but it is not clear whether this necessarily implies the destruction of the horns, or merely their removal.

124. Contra Good (1982: 56–59), who gives the vision a much more "bucolic" meaning. Good claims that the word חָרָשׁ cannot carry the "destructive" meaning required by typical interpretations of Zech 2, and instead that it refers to "ploughmen," who have come to subdue the plough animals (the possessors of the "horns"). However, in my view, his argument on the limits to the semantic range of חָרָשׁ is unsustainable in the light of the use of the word elsewhere in the Hebrew Bible (esp. Ezek 21:31; Isa 54:16), and the Hebrew Bible should be our prime semantic field for determining meaning, rather than the Ugaritic parallels Good relies on.

125. See similarly Jeremias 1977: 159–61. Seybold (1974b: 104) registers a connection to the "blacksmiths" of Isa 54:16 as well as Ezek 21:36. Delkurt (2000: 101) also list these two passages as the possible source of Zechariah's imagery. For others who recognize a parallel between Ezek 21:36 and Zech 2:3, see Mitchell 1912: 133; Tollington 1993: 226; Meyers and Meyers 1987: 139.

126. So, e.g., Seybold 1974b: 110; Jeremias 1977: 161.

127. Boda (2005: 40) notes that the expectation created by the former prophets was for a violent destruction of Babylon, and that the conquest of Babylon by Cyrus in 539 B.C.E was far from the gruesome demise predicted by Israel's prophets. Boda argues that it is only as Darius battles to secure his kingdom in the years 522–520 B.C.E. that Babylon finally begins to receive its promised punishment, and that this is behind the imagery of Zech 2:1–4.

Again, I must beg my reader's patience on this question, as the oracles in Zech 2:10–17 also have a bearing on this question. It is only once we have all this material before us that we should seek to resolve the question of the identity of the nations in Zech 1–2.

For the present purposes, it is sufficient to note that the intertextual precursors we have located make the broad contour of Zech 2:1–4 intelligible, and so we need not turn to alleged parallels with ancient Near Eastern mythology for "clarification."[128] Nor do we need to treat Zech 2:1–4 as a completely indeterminate text whose readers must make of it what they can.[129] Instead, the "former prophets" provide a sufficient context for unpacking its metaphors.[130]

4.5.1. *Conclusions on Zechariah 2:1–4*

Zechariah 2:1–4 depicts "horns" which represent the nations who have scattered Judah, Israel and Jerusalem, and these horns are to be destroyed for what they have done. Jeremiah 50:17–18 and Joel 4:1–2 (ET 3:1–2) provide the conceptual background, one which reminds Zechariah's audience that the promised overthrow of the "nations who scatter Israel" is not a new promise. Rhetorically, this gives the basis for an increased confidence in the fulfilment of the promise in Zech 2:1–4. The logic of Jer 50 was "What God *has done* to the Assyrians, so he *will do* to the Babylonians." That which was still future tense for Jeremiah's readers is now past tense for an audience in 519 B.C.E. Zechariah's first hearers are being reminded that what Yahweh has done before, Yahweh will do again.

Another set of background texts helps to explain *what* is going to happen to the nations—they are going to be destroyed. Ezekiel 21:36 (ET 21:31) reveals that the significance of the four craftsmen is that they are those "skilled in destruction." They come as God's agents to terrify (חרד Hiphil infinitive construct), like Yahweh's servants in Ezek 30:9.

128. Contra, for example, Tigchelaar, who turns to Ugaritic passages to find the background and imagery of the artisans who startle and expel the horns (1996: 51–54). He concludes that the horns "signify demons in charge of and representing the nations" (1996: 54), and that the language in Zech 2 "is not symbolic, but describes a world standing between Yahweh and men" (1996: 55).

129. Cf. Mark Love's views—see comments above in n. 121.

130. I shall return to the hermeneutical implications of an intertextual approach in Chapter 6 (see esp. §6.1).

4.6. *Zechariah 2:5–17*

In the third night-vision Zechariah sees a man with a measuring line, about to measure Jerusalem. An angel is told to tell this man that Jerusalem will be an overflowing city, and that Yahweh himself will be a wall of fire around her (2:5–9). This vision is complemented by the oracle in 2:10–17, which exhorts a scattered people to return to Jerusalem (vv. 10–13), because Yahweh himself is returning to dwell with his people (vv. 14–17).

4.6.1. *Zechariah 2:5–9 (ET 2:1–5)—The Man with the Measuring Line*

The vision of the man with the measuring line (חֶבֶל מִדָּה) in Zech 2:5–6 is an unmistakable allusion to Ezek 40–48.[131] "Measure" (מִדָּה) is a *leitmotif* in Ezek 40–48. More particularly, Ezek 40:3 is, like Zech 2, a prophetic vision of a man who is measuring. In both Ezek 40:3 and Zech 2:5, the report begins "And, behold, a man" (וְהִנֵּה־אִישׁ) and each report draws attention to the fact that the man holds a measuring instrument "in his hand" (בְּיָדוֹ). The intertextual parallels are clear, notwithstanding the difference in terminology for the measuring instrument—Ezekiel's man holds a linen cord (פְּתִיל־פִּשְׁתִּים) and a measuring reed (וּקְנֵה הַמִּדָּה) whereas Zechariah's man holds a measuring line (חֶבֶל מִדָּה).[132]

The prophet Zechariah questions the man in Zech 2:6, and the man's reply—"To measure Jerusalem, to see what is its width (רֹחַב) and what is its length (אֹרֶךְ)"—again echoes Ezek 40, where the man measures "width" and "length" of various parts of the temple.[133] However, an important point of difference between the two visions is that Zechariah's man is measuring Jerusalem, rather than the temple precincts. The motif of "measuring Jerusalem" recalls Zech 1:16, which describes the "measuring line being stretched out over Jerusalem." As was concluded above on Zech 1:16, one of the intertexts which explains this motif is Jer 31:38–39.[134] In Jeremiah, the function of the "measuring line" is to

131. Thirty of the 55 instances of this word occur in these eight chapters.

132. In Ezek 47:3, the man measuring the river from the temple uses a קָו.

133. See Ezek 40:7, 11, 18 etc. "Width" and "length" (in that order) is a common combination (×26) to describe the sanctuary (earthly or heavenly) or its contents, especially in Exod 25–39; 1 Kgs 6–7; Ezek 40–48 // 2 Chr 3–4. However, the terminology is not exclusively cultic, in that King Og's bed (?) is also measured this way (Deut 3:11). Cf. also the flying scroll in Zech 5:2.

134. The measuring instrument in Jer 31:39 is the קוה, which is the same unusual spelling of the "measuring line" in Zech 1:16 (in both places, the Ketib קוה is replaced by Qere קָו).

symbolize the extent of the rebuilding of Jerusalem after its destruction, a meaning which the book of Zechariah now "builds upon."[135]

That Zech 2:5–9 alludes to the vision of Ezek 40–48 is not in dispute—the principal point of disagreement among scholars is whether Zechariah is a *restatement of* or a *correction to* that vision.

Delkurt, while acknowledging the "majority" opinion (citing Rignell, MacKay, Jeremias, Hanhart, Elliger and Hanson) that Zechariah is a reapplication of the vision of Ezekiel, argues that his investigations lead to another conclusion: that Zech 2:5–9 represents a *correction* to the expectations of Ezek 40–48 (2000: 138–40).[136] Similarly, Petersen argues that Zech 1–8 presents an "alternative vision of restoration" to Ezek 40–48, and argues for eight major points of contrast (1984a: 116–19), and that the divine response to the intended measurement of the city "appears to challenge the notions of restoration in Ezek 40–48" (1984a: 169).

In answer to the view that Zech 2 is repudiating Ezekiel (e.g. Delkurt and Petersen), it has to be noted that, strictly speaking, Ezek 40–48 and Zech 2 are describing different things—Ezekiel describes the rebuilt temple, whereas Zech 2 describes the rebuilt city.[137] There is no inconsistency (logical or theological) between a walled temple in Ezekiel (where the literary function of this wall is not to stress exclusion—contra Delkurt—but to stress the sheer size of the sacred zone at the heart of Jerusalem) and an unwalled city in Zech 2 (where this image is being used to a different rhetorical effect, stressing abundant blessing—see the discussion below). Exactly the same comment (in reverse) needs to be

135. As likewise argued by Jeremias 1977: 166.

136. Delkurt notes that: (1) v. 5 refers clearly to Ezek 40, but the cultic terminology of Ezekiel has been replaced by common terminology; (2) the measuring of the city is found only in Ezek 48:15; 45:6 and Zech 2:6. In Ezekiel, this activity is to separate the city into sacred and common areas, and it is (according to Delkurt) this activity which the man in Zechariah's vision is about to do, but then is forbidden to do; (3) Ezekiel describes a heavily partitioned city, Zechariah describes an unwalled city; (4) Yahweh's announcement that he will be a wall of fire is a corrective to Ezek 42:20, and its conception of a city with the sacred areas partitioned from the common; (5) in Ezek 40–48, Yahweh's glory lives in the holy-of-holies, shielded from the common parts of the city—in contrast, in Zechariah, Yahweh's glory dwells in the city itself. Delkurt argues that the closest conceptual links that Zechariah has are not with Ezekiel, but with Zion theology, and particularly with Deutero-Isaiah, though without replicating its wording (see Delkurt 2000: 140).

137. Cf. Jeremias (1977: 164): "In Ez 40ff geht es bis in alle Einzelheiten um das himmlische Modell des Tempels, der bemerkenswerterweise im Unterschied zu früher ganz von der Stadt getrennt ist, dagegen ist bei Sacharja der Blick auf die gesamte wiederaufzubauende Stadt Jerusalem und ihr Areal gerichtet."

made in answer to the "majority position"—Zech 2 is not a "restatement" or even a "reapplication" of Ezekiel vision *per se*. The allusion picks up the imagery of Ezekiel, but transforms it in its application to the post-exilic context.[138]

Thus far in our analysis of Zech 2 we have found allusions to both Ezek 40 and Jer 31, woven into a composite metaphor. Zechariah 2 is not the slavish repetition of either, but a new metaphor created from both. As we see elsewhere in Zech 1–8, the imagery of Zech 2 is produced by a *reading together* of Jeremiah and Ezekiel (and, as we shall see in a moment, Isaiah and Lamentations as well) rather than a repudiation of one stream of tradition or another.

In this night-vision, the prophet Zechariah begins to take an active role in the visionary process, by questioning "the man" directly. The shift in roles continues in vv. 6–7, with the "interpreting angel" himself participating in the vision, being directed by another angel to run with a message to "that lad." The text is ambiguous as to whether "that lad" to whom he is to deliver the message is the man with the measuring line, or the prophet Zechariah,[139] though this matters little, since either way the message (Zech 2:8b–9) is (over)heard by the prophet Zechariah.

The angel's message is that Jerusalem will dwell (in) open country (פְּרָזוֹת, i.e., unwalled villages). The only prior usage of this word is in Ezek 38:11.[140] As noted above with reference to Zech 1:11, Zech 1–2 contains an extended allusion to Ezek 38–39,[141] stressing a reversal of roles between Israel and its aggressors. Whereas in Ezek 38 dwelling in open country had been a sign of vulnerability, this same imagery is now re-used as a symbol of the overflowing blessings of Yahweh.

The extent of these blessings is described in Zech 2:8b in terms of the multiplication of humans and beast (מֵרֹב אָדָם וּבְהֵמָה). This imagery may be traced back to God's original purposes for creation, for the multiplication of beasts (Gen 8:17) and humankind (Gen 9:1). That blessing is unwound in judgment, such that Jerusalem becomes "without humans or

138. That is, Zech 2 is a verbal "play" on the imagery of Ezekiel, but making a different point.

139. Perhaps this phrase is imitative of Jer 1:6, where the prophet Jeremiah is only a "lad" (נַעַר).

140. Jeremias (1977: 170) also makes this connection.

141. The outcome for Israel's enemies is the same in both Ezek 38–39 and Zech 2. In Ezek 38–39, Gog says "I will invade a land of *unwalled villages*," but the Lord says in reply "I will fight for Israel" (vv. 18–23), bringing *fire* against her enemies (38:22; 39:6; cf. Zech 2:9 "*wall of fire*"). The end result (as in Zech 2:13) is "they will *plunder* (בזז) those who plundered them" (39:10).

beast" (Jer 33:10–11), but with the promise of future reversal (cf. Jer 31:27; Ezek 36:10–11). By the re-use of this common theme, Zechariah declares the promised reversal to be at hand.[142]

This vision reiterates the promises in Zech 1:16–17. I have already mentioned the re-use of the "measuring line" (1:16) and its connection to the rebuilding of Jerusalem. There is a further parallel with Zech 1:16–17 in Zech 2:8, in the image of the city unable to be contained by walls because of the multiplied population. This parallels Zech 1:17a ("towns overflowing with prosperity"). As argued above, the use of this theme in Zech 1–2 is best understood as an intertextual appropriation of Isa 54:1–3.[143]

Furthermore, to counter the vulnerability of spreading out into "open country," Zech 2:9 declares that Yahweh himself will provide the protection for his people—he will be a "wall of fire surrounding" (חוֹמַת אֵשׁ סָבִיב) Jerusalem. There are no direct intertextual parallels for this phrase.[144] However, Jeremias is surely right to see in this metaphor a reference to the general intertextual theme of protection through fire. Jeremias argues (1977: 174–76) that multiple lines of tradition converge to produce this metaphor:

1. the flaming sword guarding the Garden of Eden (Gen 3:24);
2. Priestly tradition: God's theophanic appearance in fire and light;
3. Zion tradition: A weapon for the protection of Zion (Pss 46; 48).

While I affirm these conclusions, I also wish to extend them somewhat. In this list we should also include a number of other passages with a similar "protecting fire" theme:

1. the pillar of fire which protected Israel (Exod 14:19–20, 24);
2. the chariots of fire which protected Elisha (2 Kgs 6:17).

Furthermore, the fire at the giving of the Law at Sinai (Deut 5:23–24), like Zech 2:9, associates fire with Yahweh's glory (כְּבוֹדוֹ). Finally, in light of observations elsewhere in this chapter about the sustained allusions to Lam 2 we should also see in these verses a reversal of Lam 2:3b. Whereas in Lam 2:3b Yahweh had burned "like a flaming fire consuming all around" (כְּאֵשׁ לֶהָבָה אָכְלָה סָבִיב), in Zech 2 this image is

142. Delkurt 2000: 138 draws a connection between this verse and Jer 33:10–11. Jeremias 1977: 171 draws a connection with Ezek 36:11 and Jer 31:27.

143. Jeremias (1977: 172–73) notes this connection, and also lists Isa 49:18–22.

144. There are no other instances of the phrase "wall of fire" (חוֹמַת אֵשׁ). The phrase "fire surrounding" (אֵשׁ סָבִיב) only otherwise occurs in 2 Kgs 6:17 where it describes the "chariotry of fire surrounding Elisha." See also Ps 34:8, for the imagery of the angel of Yahweh surrounding (סָבִיב) his people to protect them.

reversed—Yahweh is a fire (אֵשׁ) of protection all around (סָבִיב). Also, whereas in Lam 2:8 Yahweh had determined to destroy the walls (חוֹמַת) of Zion and to stretch out the measuring line (קָו) in judgment, now in Zech 2 Yahweh himself will be the walls, and Jerusalem will be rebuilt, not destroyed. We cannot identify a single intertext for Zech 2:9, because all the intertexts just listed (and perhaps more) contributed to the fund of imagery in circulation in Zechariah's day which made this particular metaphor of "a wall of fire surrounding" intelligible to its first hearers (and likewise to us). I conclude that this diversity of imagery and tradition elements lie in the background of Zech 2:9.

The last phrase in v. 9—"and for glory I will be in her midst" (וּלְכָבוֹד אֶהְיֶה בְתוֹכָהּ)—echoes Ezekiel's emphasis on "glory" (Ezek 43:1–5) and "dwelling in the midst" (Ezek 43:7, and see below on Zech 2:15),[145] perhaps also nuanced by Isa 4:2.[146]

4.6.2. *Zechariah 2:10–13 (ET 2:6–9)*

The promise of prosperity and protection in Zech 2:8–9 provides the grounds for the imperative of vv. 10–11, exhorting those still "scattered" to "flee" (נֻסוּ) and "escape" (מלט) from Babylon (בָּבֶל) to Zion because Yahweh is about to turn the tables on the oppressors of old. The phraseology of these verses bears many striking similarities to Jeremiah.

The imperative to flee (נֻסוּ) occurs otherwise only in Jer 48:6; 49:8, 30 and 51:6. Furthermore, Jer 51:6 also combines this with a call to escape (מלט) from Babylon (בָּבֶל),[147] suggesting that Zech 2:10–11 is making specific reference to this verse.

145. See likewise Mitchell 1912: 139; Baldwin 1972: 107; Jeremias 1977:174–76; Meyers and Meyers 1987: 157; Hurowitz 2003: 585.

146. The construction לְכָבוֹד in Zech 2:9 is unusual, occurring only seven times: Exod 28:2, 40; Isa 4:2; 43:7; Zech 2:9; 1 Chr 17:18; 2 Chr 26:18. Of these, Isa 4:2 provides the closest conceptual parallel to Zech 2:9. When Isa 4:2 is read in its wider context (esp. Isa 4:5) there are striking parallels between the imagery of Isa 4 and Zech 2: "On that day the *branch* (צֶמַח; cf. Zech 3:6; 6:12) of Yahweh shall be for beauty and *for glory* (וּלְכָבוֹד)" (Isa 4:2); "Then the LORD will create over the whole site of Mount Zion and over its places of assembly a cloud by day and smoke and the *shining of a flaming fire* by night. Indeed over *all the glory there will be a canopy*" (Isa 4:5). In addition, some have argued that the double use of אֶהְיֶה in Zech 2:9 echoes the "I AM" of Exod 3:14 (see, e.g., Chary 1969: 67; cf. Meyers and Meyers 1987: 156). I find this suggestive, but not conclusive.

147, In the wider context (Jer 50:42; 51:33), the full phrase "*Daughter of* Babylon" (as in Zech 2:11) is used. However, this construction is not unique to Jeremiah (see, e.g., Isa 47:1; Ps 137:8).

The return from the land of the north is a typical theme of Jeremiah (Jer 3:18; 16:15; 23:8; 31:8), as is the general theme of "the foe from the north."

The concept of "the four winds of heaven" occurs only five times in the Hebrew Bible, and Jer 49:36 is best understood as the source of the remaining four.[148]

On this basis, I conclude that this section is a clear allusion to the book of Jeremiah. The significance of this re-use of Jeremiah (at a time when Jeremiah's "foe from the North"—Babylon—had been defeated) is a topic to which I shall return.

The reason (כִּי) that they should "flee" and "escape" is given in vv. 12–13 (ET vv. 8–9). In these verses, someone is being sent "to the nations which have plundered you" (אֶל־הַגּוֹיִם הַשֹּׁלְלִים אֶתְכֶם) because "the one touching you touches the apple of his eye" (בְּבָבַת עֵינוֹ), and for this reason Yahweh declares "Behold I am stretching out my hand against them (הִנְנִי מֵנִיף אֶת־יָדִי עֲלֵיהֶם), and they will become spoil to their servants (וְהָיוּ שָׁלָל לְעַבְדֵיהֶם)."

Zechariah 2:12–13 are difficult to interpret because of uncertainty over a number of issues:

1. Who is the subject and object of the verb שׁלח—who is sent, and who sends?
2. Should we read עֵינוֹ ("his eye") with MT, or עֵינִי ("my eye")?[149]
3. What should we make of the unusual phrase אַחַר כָּבוֹד?[150]
4. What in vv. 12–13 is the direct speech introduced by כֹּה אָמַר יְהוָה צְבָאוֹת?

148. The other instances are Zech 2:10 and 6:5, and Dan 8:8 and 11:4.

149. Barthélemy (1963) has argued that the original reading was "my eye" as indicated by the logia recording a *tiqqun* on Zech 2:12, which was changed to "his eye" early in the first century C.E. This argument is followed by McCarthy (1981: 61–70). Fuller (1990) has re-evaluated this argument, arguing that the *tiqqun* on Zech 2:12 may in fact indicate euphemism, not emendation. Furthermore, Fuller (who was the editor of Qumran Scroll 4Q12[e]) argues that the reading in 4Q12[e] on Zech 2:12 supports the MT reading עֵינוֹ (1990: 26). The majority of Greek and Latin versions support the MT reading.

150. The combination only occurs elsewhere in Ps 73:24. There are a number of different interpretations of the phrase אַחַר כָּבוֹד. For example, Mitchell (1912: 141) takes אַחַר in a temporal sense—that is, "*after* the glorious manifestation of Yahweh…" Scott (1949) argues for a locative sense—that is, "with glory…" Kloos (1975: 736) argues that אַחַר in this construction can denote purpose; thus, the purpose of the "sending" was "for the sake of Yahweh's glory" (אַחַר כָּבוֹד). On this issue, I follow Kloos in my translation below.

5. To whom does the authentication formula ("then you will know Yahweh sent me") refer? Does שְׁלָחַנִי in both 2:12 and 2:13 refer to the same person?[151]

I confess to having no settled conclusion on some of these matters, but I outline arguments from two other scholars which I find the most persuasive of the myriad interpretations which this verse has spawned. Kloos (1975) argues that, in the phrase "after glory" (אַחַר כָּבוֹד), the word אַחַר denotes purpose—that is, "for the sake of [glory]." Yahweh has sent the prophet for the sake of his glory (i.e. honour) "among the nations" (אֶל־הַגּוֹיִם).[152] On Kloos's interpretation, these verses could be translated (words of the prophet in *italics*, words of Yahweh underlined)

> *Because thus says Yahweh of Hosts—For the sake of [his] honour, Yahweh sent me among the nations who are spoiling you, for whoever touches you touches the apple of his eye—*"Behold I am stretching out my hand against them, and they will become spoil to their servants"*— and you will know that Yahweh of Hosts has sent me.*

In contrast, Tiemeyer (2004) argues that the most natural grammatical construction is that God is the speaker (and therefore the "me" of 2:12), which leaves כָּבוֹד as the subject of the verb שׁלח. In Tiemeyer's interpretation, Yahweh's "honour" will[153] send him against the nations. The preceding אַחַר is taken as an adverb of time, that is, "afterwards." Tiemeyer understands God to be speaking most of vv. 12–13 (requiring the emendation to "my eye"), and the final clause must be regarded as an unrelated interjection by the prophet. Following Tiemeyer's approach (2004: 371–72), we might translate:

> *Because thus says Yahweh of Hosts:* "Afterwards, [my] honour will send me against the nations who are spoiling you, because whoever touches you touches the pupil of my eye. And behold I am stretching out my arm against them, and they will become spoil to their servants" *[and you will know that Yahweh of Hosts has sent me].*

151. Typically, the prophet Zechariah is understood as the "me" who is sent in one or both of these verses. However, see van der Woude (1988: 239), for the argument that the "sent one" is the angel of Yahweh, and that the validation formulae in Zech 2:13 and 2:15 refer to him.

152. Kloos (1975: 735) recognizes that this as an unusual translation for אֶל־הַגּוֹיִם and cites BDB (אֶל #8) in support. However, I agree with the assessment of Tiemeyer (2004: 362–63) that this usage cannot be sustained in Zech 2, since BDB establishes only (at best) that the word can mean "by" as in "nearby," but not "among." In my translation below, I follow Tiemeyer in translating אֶל־הַגּוֹיִם as "against the nations."

153. Tiemeyer's interpretation interprets שְׁלָחַנִי as a "prophetic perfect."

While these two approaches imply very different answers to the five questions listed above, it must be noted that they are alike to the extent that it is Yahweh's honour which compels this response against the nations. Further, both draw connections between this passage and Ezekiel. Kloos concludes: "for the thought (Jhwh's honour among the nations) a striking parallel is to be found in Ezekiel xxxix 21" (1975: 736). Similarly, Tiemeyer concludes

> This reading is reminiscent of the message of Ezekiel, another priestly prophet, who often declared that God saved Israel, not due to any of her good deeds but rather due to His own name, i.e. His honour. (2004: 372)[154]

I agree with Kloos that Ezek 39:21 is a striking conceptual parallel to Zech 2, particularly in the phase "I will put my glory among the nations" (וְנָתַתִּי אֶת־כְּבוֹדִי בַּגּוֹיִם).

Though not convinced about which of these two exegetical roads to take (and, indeed, below I shall offer my own small variation as a third alternative), I agree with their shared conclusion that Yahweh's honour motivates this action against the nations, and that Ezekiel is the source of this concept. This conclusion was confirmed by computer searches for passages which share similar vocabulary and themes to Zech 2:12–13. Ezekiel 38–39 was highlighted several times. Ezekiel 38:12 describes a nation who plunders (שׁלל) Israel. One of the closest parallels to "plunder for their own slaves" (Zech 2:13) is Ezek 39:10: "they will plunder those who plundered them" (וְשָׁלְלוּ אֶת־שֹׁלְלֵיהֶם).[155] Yahweh's outstretched "hand" (יָדִי) as a metaphor for judgment occurs frequently in Ezekiel, including Ezek 39:21, and in the same verse also occurs the imagery of Yahweh's glory (כְּבוֹדִי) being set among the nations (הַגּוֹיִם), where that display of glory is related to Yahweh's judgment being executed. From this I conclude that Ezekiel's concept of Yahweh's honour (and in particular Ezek 38–39) lies in the background to these verses. I shall return to the significance of this allusion to the Gog pericope in the conclusion to this chapter.

The phrase הַנֹּגֵעַ בָּכֶם נֹגֵעַ בְּבָבַת עֵינוֹ ("the one touching you is striking the pupil[?] of my eye") is also unusual. The "pupil" (בָּבָה) is a *hapax legomenon*. Its meaning would seem to be best explained as an allusion

154. Tiemeyer cites Ezek 20:44 as an example and does not refer to Ezek 39:21, though presumably her conclusion is even stronger *vis-à-vis* Ezek 39:21.

155. If we extend the search to include thematic parallels, there is also a strong connection to the theme of "plundering (נצל rather than שׁלל) the Egyptians" in Exod 3:22; 12:36. As recompense for Israel's treatment as slaves at Egypt's hand, she plundered Egypt at the time of her exodus.

to the phrase "apple of his eye" used in Deut 32:10 and Ps 7:2 (כְּאִישׁוֹן עָיִנוֹ; cf. Ps 17:8, כְּאִישׁוֹן בַּת־עָיִן).

Zechariah 2:13 concludes with the formula "And then you will know that Yahweh of Hosts sent me" (וִידַעְתֶּם כִּי־יְהוָה צְבָאוֹת שְׁלָחָנִי). Since Zech 2:15 uses exactly the same phrase (with the additional phrase "to you," אֵלָיִךְ), I shall defer for a moment both my discussion of the meaning of this phrase, and my analysis of how the repetition of this phrase helps to structure the oracle as a whole.

4.6.3. *Zechariah 2:14–15*

As noted above, the oracle in 2:10–17 can be divided into two parts—vv. 10–13 are directed against the nations, encouraging Yahweh's scattered people to return to Jerusalem, and vv. 14–17 are about Yahweh himself returning to dwell with his people.

Zechariah 2:14 (ET v. 10) calls upon Zion to rejoice because Yahweh is coming to dwell in the midst of the city. As noted above in §2.8 (example 3), there are striking parallels between this verse and Isa 12:6 and/or Zeph 3:14. Many commentators recognize the parallels between Zech 2:14 and Isa 12:6 and/or Zeph 3:14 (a call to female-personified inhabitants of Zion to sing and rejoice because Yahweh is in the midst of his people),[156] notwithstanding the fact that most of the links are based on synonyms rather than verbal parallels.[157] In my opinion, the form of Zech 2:14 is best explained by seeing it as a combination and reworking of both Isa 12 and Zeph 3.[158]

However, the points of difference between Zech 2:14 and these intertexts are just as significant as the points of similarity. Both Isa 12 and Zeph 3 declare Yahweh to be (presently) in the midst of his people, whereas Zech 2:14 presupposes that Yahweh is not presently "in the midst of his people," and furthermore it introduces the language of "dwelling" which is absent from both Isa 12 and Zeph 3.

156. For a list of scholars who have recognized this connection, see §2.7 (example 3) and the footnotes thereto.

157. To reiterate part of my argument from §2.8, the actual direct lexical links between Zech 2 and Isa 12:6 are surprisingly sparse. In addition, there are two sets of synonyms—"rejoice" and "in your midst," and parallel phrases which identify the inhabitants of Zion and their God. There are slightly more connections with Zeph 3:14–15 in the phrase "daughter of Zion" and the same word for "rejoice" (שִׂמְחִי), though the causal כִּי is not present in Zeph 3:15.

158. Contra Nurmela (1996: 56–58), who argues that Zeph 3 is a later development, dependent on Zechariah.

There are two lines of intertextual enquiry which may help to explain the points of difference between Zechariah and Isa 12/Zeph 3. First, we should recognize that there is another text that calls on a female-personified Zion to rejoice (Joel 2:23, 27), one which also has significant verbal and conceptual parallels to Zech 2:14:

ובני ציון גילו ושמחו
וידעתם כי בקרב ישראל אני

O sons of Zion, *be glad* and rejoice in Yahweh your God...
And then you will know that *I am in the midst of Israel* (Joel 2:23, 27)

רני ושמחי בת־ציון
כי הנני־בא ושכנתי בתוכך

Sing and rejoice, *O daughter* Zion!
For behold, I am coming and will *dwell in your midst*, says Yahweh.
(Zech 2:14 [ET 2:10])

It has already been argued that Zech 1–2 makes a sustained allusion to Joel 2 (see §4.4), and this further connection strengthens the evidence for this. It should be noted that in the wider context of Joel 2, the promise of "Yahweh in the midst" looks forward to a future, rather than present, reality.[159] This means that both Joel 2 and Zech 2 share a perception that Yahweh is not presently "in the midst" (in contrast to Isa 12:6 and Zeph 3:14–15, where Yahweh is "in the midst"). I argue that Zech 2 has taken over from Joel 2 the idea that Yahweh's being "in the midst" of his people is a future expectation.

However, the intertextual background of Joel 2 alone does not explain the language of "dwelling" (שכן) in Zech 2:14.[160] To explain this, we must turn to a second line of enquiry. The language of "Yahweh dwelling in the midst of his people" typically has specific reference to God's presence in the tabernacle and/or temple (e.g. Exod 25:8; 29:44–45; Lev 26:11; 1 Kgs 6:12–13), which describes Yahweh's dwelling as a

159. In the context, the phrase "you will know that" (כִּי וִידַעְתֶּם) points to the future state of "knowledge." Cf. exactly the same phrase in Zech 2:13: "and then you will know (כִּי וִידַעְתֶּם) that Yahweh of Hosts sent me." Similarly, Joel 4:17–18 looks forward to the *future* day of Yahweh's "dwelling in Zion."

160. Though an alternate explanation is that the language of dwelling has come in through association with Joel 4:17—Yahweh "dwelling in Zion, my holy mountain" (שֹׁכֵן בְּצִיּוֹן הַר־קָדְשִׁי). However, since Joel's language reflects Ezekiel in any case, the outcome is much the same. Either way, the ultimate source of this tradition is Ezek 37:26–27 and 43:1–9.

present-tense reality. In contrast, the book of Ezekiel describes Yahweh's return to dwell as a *future* reality. As already noted, Ezek 11:23 describes the departure of the glory of Yahweh from the midst of Jerusalem, signalling that the time of the exile is understood as the absence of his presence from Zion. Ezekiel 37:26–27 anticipates the return of Yahweh to dwelling in the sanctuary—note "I will set my sanctuary *in their midst* (בְּתוֹכָם)" and "*my dwelling* (מִשְׁכָּנִי) will be upon them." The vision in Ezek 43:1–9 foresees the day of this promised return of the glory of Yahweh to his dwelling—note especially the promise of 43:7: "I will dwell there in the midst" (אֶשְׁכָּן־שָׁם בְּתוֹךְ). Yahweh's promise in Zech 2:14, that "I will dwell in your midst" (וְשָׁכַנְתִּי בְתוֹכֵךְ), echoes Ezek 37:26–27 and 43:7, both in the use of the verb "to dwell" (שׁכן) and also in the use of בְּתוֹךְ for the phrase "in the midst" (in contrast to בְּקֶרֶב, which is the consistent vocabulary in Isa 12:6; Zeph 3:15; Joel 2:27). Thus, in Zech 2:14, we have a composite metaphor which draws together elements from Isa 12:6 (and later developments in Zeph 3:14–15 and Joel 2:23, 27); Ezek 37:26–27 and Ezek 43:1–9.

Zechariah 2:15 continues this theme, repeating "I will dwell in your midst," while at the same time introducing a new element, promising that "many nations (גּוֹיִם רַבִּים) shall join themselves (לוה) to Yahweh on that day, and shall be my people (וְהָיוּ לִי לְעָם)." There are several intertextual echoes which combine in this verse.

First, the motif of nations "*joining to Yahweh*" echoes Isa 56 and Isa 14. Of the 12 instances of the verb לוה ("to be joined"), only the usage in the book of Isaiah can be understood as providing the conceptual background to this verse.[161] The closest (textual) parallel is with Isa 56:3–7, which mention the "son of a foreign [place]" (בֶּן־הַנֵּכָר) who is "*joined to Yahweh*" (הַנִּלְוָה אֶל־יְהוָה). However, Isa 56 is addressed to individuals. What then is the source of Zechariah's "many nations"? The other instance of the verb לוה in Isaiah occurs in Isa 14:1, which describes the aliens who are "joined" to God's people, and in context, this is clearly a collective image (cf. Isa 14:2) and so perhaps it is the conflation of Isa 56 and Isa 14 that has created the imagery in Zech 2:15. The other possibility is that the phrase "many nations" here is an echo of Isa 2:3 (the pilgrimage of גּוֹיִם רַבִּים, "many nations," to Zion). While the repetition of these two words alone from Isa 2:3 is hardly conclusive, the subsequent re-use

161. The twelve instances are Gen 29:34; Num 18:2, 4; Isa 14:1; 56:3, 6; Jer 50:5; Dan 11:34; Eccl 8:15; Esth 9:27; Ps 83:9; Zech 2:15. Jer 50:5 has the people of Israel and Judah (rather than "the nations") joining themselves to the Lord.

of Isa 2:3 in Zech 8:21–22 (as discussed above in §2.8, example 4) significantly increases the likelihood of explicit allusion. I conclude that Zech 2:15 is a composite allusion to Isa 14, Isa 56 and Isa 2:3.

The covenant formula—"and they shall be for me for a people" (וְהָיוּ לִי לְעָם)—in this verse also occurs frequently in Ezekiel and Jeremiah.[162] However, it is significant to note that only here in Zechariah is the covenant blessing explicitly extended to people from "many nations." Otherwise, the nearest parallel comes from Isa 19:23–25, where, in the eschatological day, Egypt and Assyria are incorporated into "my people," along with "Israel my inheritance" (cf. Zech 2:16 below). As we have seen elsewhere, Zech 1–8 is not just a mere repeater of the prophetic tradition, but offers its own unique development of the "prophetic trajectory"—that is, Zech 1–8 combines elements of its prophetic forebears to make explicit what is only implicit in those earlier works.

In Zech 2:15 we find both the "covenant formula" and the promise of God's dwelling in the midst of his people. This combination only otherwise occurs in Ezek 37:26–28 and Lev 26:11–12. In Zech 2, the promise is expressed using a verbal form, וְשָׁכַנְתִּי ("and I will dwell"), whereas in both Lev 26 and Ezek 37, the promise involves the nominal form מִשְׁכָּנִי ("my dwelling"). The verbal form of God's promised dwelling does not occur at all in Leviticus, but does occur in the wider context of Ezekiel's restoration promises (Ezek 43:7, 9). Thus, the combination in Zech 2:15 of the covenant formula and the promise "I will dwell in their midst" is best understood as deriving from Ezek 37 and Ezek 43, read together.

Zechariah 2:15 concludes with the phrase "And then you will know that Yahweh of Hosts sent me to you." This phrase (with minor variations) occurs just four times, and all instances are in the book of Zechariah (Zech 2:13, 15; 4:9; 6:15). Elsewhere, the more common formula is the divine authentication formula "And then you will know that I am Yahweh."[163] However, the difference between this form and the present instance is that, here, Yahweh validates his servants, rather than being himself authenticated. The possible precursors to this idea are shown in the following:

162. See Ezek 11:20; 14:11; 36:28; 37:23, 27 and Jer 7:23; 11:4; 13:11; 24:7; 30:22; 32:38. The formula only otherwise occurs in Exod 6:7; Lev 26:12 and Zech 8:8.

163. E.g. 1 Kgs 20:13; Isa 49:23; 60:16; Ezek 16:62; 22:16; 25:7; 35:4 etc.

Jer 28:9: then it will be known (יִוָּדַע)...that Yahweh sent (שְׁלָחוֹ יְהוָה) [that prophet]

Num 16:28: You will know that Yahweh sent me (תֵּדְעוּן כִּי־יְהוָה שְׁלָחַנִי)

Ezek 2:5: And they will know that a prophet was in their midst (וְיָדְעוּ כִּי נָבִיא הָיָה בְתוֹכָם). (Cf. Ezek 33:33.)

Deut 21:18: When a prophet speaks in the name of Yahweh, and this matter does not come to be, this is not the word that Yahweh has spoken

I take it that Zechariah has created his own "prophetic validation formula" through a creative combination of some or all of these passages. The formula in Zech 1–8 reflects the thought of Deut 21:18 expressed in the vocabulary of Ezekiel and Jeremiah.[164]

We must now turn our attention to the function of the repetition of this formula (with small variation) in the space of three verses. In Zech 2:15, as in 2:13, the formula, which speaks of Yahweh in the third person, follows directly on from words spoken in the first person by Yahweh. Clearly, it would make nonsense of the verse to suggest that the validation formula is spoken by Yahweh about himself. It is clear that, in both Zech 2:13 and 2:15, there must be an oscillation between Yahweh's words and the words of another (which in the context of the oracle must be the "one who has been sent"). But who exactly is this sent one? As noted above, some have argued that the "sent one" is the angel of Yahweh (e.g. van der Woude) or Yahweh himself (e.g. Tiemeyer), but if we take our clues from the intertextual connections (especially the "prophetic validation" formula of Jer 28:9), and from the usage of the same phrase in Zech 4:9 and 6:15, then the most reasonable conclusion is that the "sent one" is the prophet Zechariah.

Thus in this passage we have both Yahweh's "voice" and Zechariah's "voice," and this reflect the cross-over between Yahweh and his prophet. In Zech 2:10–17, it is the prophet who actually speaks all of the words, with *some* of his words reporting the direct speech of Yahweh. The content of these prophetic words is especially significant in the light of the role given to the prophet Zechariah in Zech 1–2. It should be recalled that, in Zech 1, the prophet was commissioned to proclaim a double message—Yahweh's anger at the nations (1:14–15) and Yahweh's return to Jerusalem (1:16–17). In Zech 2:10–17, the oracle is likewise a double message—first, the prophet speaks *against the nations*, exhorting the

164. On this, see further Tollington 1993: 71–75.

people to flee from Babylon, and then, secondly, he speaks of Yahweh's return *to Jerusalem*. I suggest that, in the oracle in Zech 2:10–17, we are seeing the prophet find voice to proclaim the twofold message he was commissioned to proclaim in 1:14–17—namely, Yahweh's anger at the nations (1:13; cf. 2:13) and Yahweh's return to Jerusalem (1:17; cf. 2:14). It is the outworking of each of these messages which will provide a validation of Yahweh's messenger, which is why each part of the oracle in Zech 2 ends with a validation formula. Based on this approach, I suggest that Zech 2:12–16 should be read as follows (prophet's words in *italics*, Yahweh's reported direct speech underlined):

> *For thus says Yahweh of Hosts, (after [or the sake of] his honour sent me against the nations who plundered you, for one who touches you touches the apple of his eye.)* "Behold, I am going to raise my hand against them, and they shall become plunder for their own slaves." *Then you will know that Yahweh of Hosts has sent me.* (Zech 2:12–13)

> "Sing and rejoice, O daughter Zion! For behold, I will come and dwell in your midst, says Yahweh. Many nations shall be joined to Yahweh on that day, and shall be my people; and I will dwell in your midst." *Then you will know that Yahweh of Hosts has sent me to you.* (Zech 2:14–15)

The prophet validation formula in 2:13 is different to the other three instances of the formula in Zechariah (see Zech 2:15; 4:9; 6:15) in that it does not end with the phrase "to you." This phrase is omitted in vv. 12–13 because the one who is "sent" in these verses is sent to a different destination. In vv. 12–13, the prophet is sent "to the nations" (in the sense of "against the nations," in declaring God's judgment on them), whereas the other three instances refer to the prophet being sent to the people of God. Yahweh's prophet will be validated both when the judgment that he prophesied falls on the nations, and when the Yahweh returns, as prophesied, to dwell with his people.

Furthermore, we should also note that the words of Yahweh in Zech 2:13–15 (underlined above) bear striking parallels to Isa 12–14:[165]

165. The likelihood of allusion here is strengthened by three further connections between Isa 13–14 and Zech 1–2. The language of Yahweh's compassion (רחם) on Jacob and choosing (בחר) of Israel is reflected in both Isa 14:1 and Zech 1:16–17. Isa 14:7 says that all the earth is "at rest and at peace (נָחָה שָׁקְטָה)," which is similar to Zech 1:11: the earth is "inhabited and at peace (יֹשֶׁבֶת וְשֹׁקָטֶת)." Finally, both Zech 1:12 and Isa 13:5 refer to Yahweh's anger (זעם).

Zech 2:13–15	*Isa 13–14*
Behold, I am going to raise my hand against them	Isa 13:2: raising the hand, to beckon the destroyers of Babylon.
and they shall become plunder for their own slaves	Isa 14:2: They will take captive those who were their captors, and rule over those who oppressed them.
Sing and rejoice, O daughter Zion! For behold, I will come and dwell in your midst, says Yahweh.	Isa 12:6: Rejoice and sing, O inhabitants of Zion, for great in your midst is the Holy One of Israel.
Many nations shall be joined (לוה) to Yahweh and shall be my people	Isa 14:1: Foreigners joined (לוה) to Israel

To put it another way, when the prophet speaks the words of Yahweh in Zech 2:12–15, it comes in the form of an adaptation of the message of Isa 12–14, and at the same time (as we have seen above), the adaptation has been nuanced with overtones from Ezek 38–39. Isaiah 13 is an oracle against Babylon, and likewise (as argued above at §3.3.2), Ezek 38–39 uses a mythical "Gog" as a cipher for Babylon. This recurrence of intertextual references to Babylon raises again the question of the identity of "the nations" in Zech 1–8.

We are now in a position to consider the question of the identity of "the nations" more fully. Mark Boda has argued that Babylon is the continuing object of the "anti-nations" polemic in Zech 1–8. Boda points in particular to the use of the motif of "seventy years" (which was to come to an end when Babylon was punished), to the emphasis in the second night-vision on the "horns" which scattered Judah (which he argues refers to Babylon) and to the explicit focus on Babylon in the intertexts of 2:10–17 (see Boda 2005 esp. pp. 23–28). Furthermore, in a very recent analysis, Boda has identified several key intertexts of Zech 2:10–17, namely, Jer 25, 50–51; Ezek 38–39; Isa 13–14; Zeph 3 and Hab 2. Boda convincingly demonstrates that these passages "are part of an enduring anti-Babylonian tradition in the Hebrew Bible."[166]

My analysis of the intertexts in Zech 1–2 (above) supports Boda's conclusions *to the extent that* Babylon was the *original* referent of these intertexts. However, we should also note that, alongside these allusions to passages with an explicit "anti-Babylon" thrust, there are also intertextual echoes of passages making a strong critique of "Assyria."[167]

166. Boda 2009: 189.

167. E.g. Yahweh's wrath at the "complacent" (שַׁאֲנָן) nations in Zech 1:15 echoes the condemnation of Assyria in Isa 37:29; Yahweh's anger at the nations who have overstepped their role as punishers of Israel resonates with the critique of both

When Zech 1:15, for example, picks up the condemnation of "complacent" (שַׁאֲנַן) Assyria, this is *not* because Assyria still needed to receive her due punishment. Rather, Zech 1:15 uses the past example of Assyria to encapsulate the Assyria-like attitudes of "the nations." Yet, once we grant that a level of abstraction has occurred in these allusions to Assyria, it becomes a live possibility that the same process has occurred with respect to prophecies originally given against Babylon. There are some indications from the intertexts of Zech 1–2 that this may in fact be the case. In my discussion of the intertexts of Zech 2:1–4, it was noted above that Joel 4:1–2 itself echoes Jer 50 (which names the nations who scattered as "Babylon" and "Assyria") but has taken the imagery and applied it in a universal direction (against "all nations"). I suggest that it is reasonable to see Zech 2:1–4 as a continuation of this same universalization of Jer 50,[168] and to interpret the "four horns" of Zech 2:1–4 as "all nations."

What then should we make of the "recycling" of prophecies against Babylon? Is it because the oracles in Zech 1–2 were in fact written pre-539 B.C.E., when Babylon was still a world superpower?[169] Or (per Boda) is the historical nation of Babylon still the referent of these oracles, because, at the time Zechariah is prophesying, Babylon has not yet received its promised destruction? Or is it because "Babylon" has by this stage become a cipher for any or all enemy peoples (as it does in the later Christian tradition; cf. Rev 18:1)?[170] Are "the four horns" of Zech 1–2 a representation of all of Israel's enemies?[171]

Assyria (Isa 10:5–7) and Babylon (Isa 47:6; Ezek 38:17); and Jer 50:17–18 (one of the intertexts for Zech 2:1–4) focuses on both Assyria and Babylon.

168. I recognize that my argument that Zech 2 alludes to Joel 4 will not have convinced all my readers because the consensus position is that Joel 3–4 is a later post-exilic composition. However, even if we suppose, for the sake of argument, that Joel 4 post-dates Zech 2, then this is still evidence that, in the early Second Temple period, a prophet could allude to Jer 50, but replace the specific nations of "Babylon" and "Assyria" with a universalized reference to "all nations."

169. So Galling 1964a. Redditt (1995: 42) takes a variation on this position. He argues that the visions and oracles were written some time after 539 B.C.E., but were addressed to those still in exile in Babylon. This "original edition" of the book was augmented by the addition of the passages concerning Joshua, Zerubbabel and the temple rebuilding in response to the events of 520 B.C.E.

170. This possibility is canvassed by Tollington 1993: 220.

171. See, e.g., Delkurt 2000: 76, Cf. Lurie 1988/89. Cf. Meyers and Meyers (1987: 147–48) who argue that the four horns represent Babylon, who have been "cut down" by the four craftsmen (Persia). However, this past conquest is indicative of the kind of treatment which Persia will meet, should they turn against Yehud.

On the basis of the intertexts identified above, I conclude that "the nations" in Zech 1–2 represent all the nations of the world, even including the apparently benevolent Persia. While Persia's treatment of the people of God had been favourable, the fact remains that the prophets had promised a reversal in situation for Israel and "the nations," and this had not yet materialized. Zechariah 1–2 is an affirmation that Yahweh is still going to deliver on this promise. I suggest that the imagery and metaphors in Zech 1–2 are deliberately cryptic at this point in order to conceal this message from Judah's Persian overlords. Zechariah's intended audience, being familiar with the prophetic critique of Babylon/Gog in Isa 13–14; Jer 48–50 and Ezek 38–39, would have understood the implication of this message for "all the nations" (including Persia), whereas this same message would have remained cryptic to their Persian masters. Zechariah 1–2 uses intertexts to encode a message for a select audience.

4.6.4. *Zechariah 2:16–17*

The final two verses of this oracle (Zech 2:16–17) continue the theme of Yahweh's return to dwell, but using intertexts drawn from a wide cross-section of the Hebrew Bible. Zechariah 2:16 begins with the promise that "Yahweh will inherit (וְנָחַל) Judah as his portion (חֶלְקוֹ) in the holy land." The theme of "God's people as his inheritance"[172] finds an expression in a range of literature. The closest parallel is Deut 32:9, "Yahweh's portion (חֵלֶק) and…his inheritance (נַחֲלָה)," but see also Isa 19:25, "Israel my inheritance (נַחֲלָה)," noting also the possible connection between Isa 19:23–25 and Zech 2:15 discussed above.[173] However, it would be to go beyond the evidence to argue for a specific connection to any of these passages. We can be more specific with the phrase עַל אַדְמַת הַקֹּדֶשׁ ("on the holy ground"). This phrase occurs elsewhere only in Exod 3:5, where Moses stands עָלָיו אַדְמַת־קֹדֶשׁ while Yahweh speaks with him from the burning bush.[174]

Zechariah 2:16 promises that Yahweh "will again choose Jerusalem" (וּבָחַר עוֹד בִּירוּשָׁלָםִ), repeating verbatim this clause from Zech 1:17. As

172. It is unusual to have God as the subject of the verb נחל—this otherwise occurs only in Ps 82:8

173. And for more examples of נַחֲלָתִי, see 2 Kgs 21:14; Isa 47:6; Jer 2:7; 12:7–9; 16:18; 50:11; Joel 4:2. A related theme is Israel as Yahweh's "treasured possession" (סְגֻלָּה) (see Exod 19:5; Deut 7:6; 14:2; 26:18; Ps 135:4; Mal 3:17).

174. There may also be some influence from the phrase "holy portion of the land" in Ezek 48:12–14.

argued above, Yahweh's "choice" of Jerusalem has connotations which stem from its significance as the place of the temple. Thus, in Zech 2:16, we have a confluence of themes—the "choice of Jerusalem" (i.e. temple site), "holy ground" (i.e. the place where God speaks) and (in the wider context of Zech 2:14–15) the promise of God again "dwelling in their midst." The effect of the combination of these themes is to stress again the significance of the reconstruction of the temple in the fulfilment of these promises.

In Zech 2:17 this oracle concludes with an unmistakable inverted allusion to Hab 2:20:[175]

הס כל־בשׂר מפני יהוה
כי נעור ממעון קדשׁו

Be silent, all flesh, before Yahweh
for he rouses from his holy habitation. (Hab 2:20)

ויהוה בהיכל קדשׁו
הס מפניו כל־הארץ

Yahweh is in his holy temple
be silent, all the earth, before him. (Zech 2:17)

It is commonly accepted that Hab 2 is the prior text. In re-utilizing Hab 2:20, Zech 2:17 has replaced the static picture in Habakkuk ("Yahweh is in his holy temple") with an active image ("Yahweh rouses himself")[176] which draws on imagery from Isa 42:13; 51:9 and several psalms[177] (and perhaps also from an ironic reversal of Ezek 38:14)[178] to describe Yahweh rousing himself (עור) on behalf of his people, and acting for the sake of their restoration. Zechariah 2 also replaces Habakkuk's "holy temple" (הֵיכַל קָדְשׁוֹ) with the phrase "holy habitation" (מְעוֹן קָדְשׁוֹ).[179]

175. For other commentators who note this connection, see, e.g., Mitchell 1912: 144 and Tollington 1993: 39. Some commentators note parallels with both Hab 2:20 and Zeph 1:7 (see, e.g., Baldwin 1972: 113; Meyers and Meyers 1987: 171).

176. Interestingly, the verb עור in Zech 2:17 also occurs in the verse in Habakkuk which immediately precedes the verses quoted above (i.e. Hab 2:19). Perhaps there is an ironic reversal intended between the lifeless idols who cannot be roused (עור), and Yahweh, who rouses himself.

177. See, e.g., Ps 80:3 (significant in light of other parallels to Ps 80). See also Pss 7:7; 35:23; 44:24; 59:5.

178. As noted above (see n. 61), this assumes the emendation in Ezek 38:14 of תֵּדָע to תֵּעֹר (on the basis of LXX's ησηθρεγ́ε, "you will be roused," and manuscripts in the Latin tradition with forms of *exsurgo*, "to rise, stand up").

179. The same phrase is found in Deut 26:15; Jer 25:30; Ps 68:6; 2 Chr 30:27. The book of Zechariah is apparently reflecting the thinking of Deuteronomy at this

This is done in order to make clear that it is the heavenly dwelling from which Yahweh has roused himself. This variation in terminology is necessary in Zech 2 because the earthly temple is still in the process of reconstruction. The imagery of the wider section suggests that Yahweh has roused himself from his holy habitation to return to dwell with his people in Jerusalem, and that this process will be complete once the temple is rebuilt.

4.7. *Conclusions*

We have seen that in Zech 2 the two visions and oracle combine to stress the point already made in the vision of Zech 1—Yahweh is about to return to his people in Jerusalem by again "dwelling" in the temple at Jerusalem. In the historical context of 519 B.C.E. (with a temple still only partially complete), these promises anticipate the completion of the temple a few years hence (cf. 1:16, "my house shall be built in it"). Zechariah 2 adopts a variety of ways of describing this from different streams of tradition (e.g. Ezekielian: "dwelling in the midst"; Isaian: "Rejoice and Sing O inhabitants of Zion"; Jeremian: "measuring line stretched out," etc.) and weaves these distinct traditions into *composite metaphors*.

A second feature which we have observed in Zech 1–2 is the *sustained allusions* to other texts. These sustained allusions are like threads in a tapestry. In a well-worked tapestry, the eye is not drawn to a thread of any particular colour, but rather to the picture as a whole. And yet, at the same time, each coloured thread is important in creating the picture as a whole. In the same way, the sustained allusions in Zech 1–2 are so deftly woven that it is possible to miss the fact that the same particular threads (i.e. background passages) are being woven in and out. In this chapter I have already had occasion to call attention to some of the sustained allusions, but it is now appropriate to draw the threads together (so to speak) and consider the impact of some key sustained allusions.

Lamentations 2 has so much shared (rare) vocabulary and themes with Zech 1–2 that the parallels cannot be accidental. Some of the key allusions noted above include:

point, which distinguishes between the earthly temple ("the place which Yahweh will choose as a dwelling for his name," Deut 26:2) and Yahweh's heavenly habitation (Deut 26:14).

- stretching the measuring line (קו + נטה): Lam 2:8 = Zech 1:16.
- Daughter Zion (בת־ציון): Lam 2:1 = Zech 2:14.
- raising up/casting down (ידה / גדע) horns (קרן): Lam 2:3, 17; cf. Zech 2:1–4.
- Yahweh's anger (זעם) at his people: Lam 2:6 = Zech 1:12.
- Yahweh showing no mercy: Lam 2:21 (לא חמלה); cf. Zech 1:12 (לא תרחם).
- concern for the wall (חומה) of Jerusalem: Lam 2:8; cf. Zech 2:8–9.
- Yahweh a fire (אש) consuming its surroundings (סביב): Lam 2:3; cf. Zech 2:9.
- Yahweh has done what he purposed (זמם) to do: Lam 2:17 = Zech 1:6.
- Yahweh comforting (נחם) Zion: Lam 2:13; cf. Zech 1:17.

These connections demonstrate that Zech 1–2 makes a sustained allusion to Lam 2. These allusions have the effect of both calling to the reader's mind the devastations of exile, and also providing the metaphors which will be systematically reversed when Yahweh acts to restore his people (the "measuring line" is used to rebuild rather than to judge, the "horns of the nations" are now the ones being cast down, Yahweh himself will be their "wall" of fire surrounding, etc.)

Joel 2 also shares a significant number of parallels with Zech 1–2:

- Return (שוב) to me + God's return to Israel: Joel 2:12–14; cf. Zech 1:3.
- Yahweh's jealousy for (ל + קנא) Jerusalem: Joel 2:18; cf. Zech 1:14.
- Yahweh's horses (סוס) and chariots (מרכבה): Joel 2:4–10; cf. Zech 1:10; 6:8.
- "Yahweh responded" (ויען יהוה): Joel 2:19 = Zech 1:13.
- the theme of "comfort" (נחם): Joel 2:14; cf. Zech 1:13, 17.
- Zion the "Holy Mountain" (הר קדשי): Joel 2:1; cf. Zech 2:12; 8:3.
- sons/daughters of Zion, be glad and rejoice: Joel 2:23; cf. Zech 2:14.
- Yahweh's promise to be "in the midst": Joel 2:27; Zech 2:14.

Joel 2 would appear to be from a similar milieu as Zech 1–2, echoing a number of the same intertextual themes and "activating" many of the same promises of classical prophets. However, the tone of Joel 2 is more muted, in contrast to the hopeful tone in Zech 1–2. For example, Joel 2 says "Return to Yahweh…and who knows, he *may* return to you," while Zech 1:4 declares absolutely—"Return to me and I *will* return to you." Zechariah 1–2 are the words of the prophet Joel "made more certain."

Jeremiah's Oracles Against the Nations (esp. Jer 48–51) shares a significant number of parallels with Zech 1–2, including:

- The nations scattering God's people: Jer 50:17–18 = Zech 2:2.
- Flee! (נוס) Escape! (מלט) from Babylon (בבל): Jer 51:6 = Zech 2:10–11.
- Scattering the nations in judgment: Jer 49:36 = Zech 2:4.

- Nations at ease (השאננים, Zech 1:15) = complacency of Moab (Jer 48:11).
- The four winds of heaven: Jer 49:36 = Zech 2:10.
- Judgment on a nation from the north: Jer 50:2–3; cf. Zech 2:13; 6:8.

(See also the comments on Jer 49:31–32 in the next section on Ezek 38–39.)

Zechariah's sustained allusions to Jer 48–51 provide the imagery for comprehending Yahweh's impending judgment on the nations, who are now to face a time of reversal.[180]

Ezekiel 38–39 also shares a significant number of parallels with Zech 1–2, including:

- the land inhabited and at rest (שקט and ישב): Ezek 38:11–12; cf. Zech 1:11.
- the "open regions" (פרזות): Ezek 38:11 = Zech 2:8, no other instances.
- Yahweh rousing himself (עור): Zech 2:17; cf. Ezek 38:14.
- Yahweh's fire (אש) against Israel's enemies: Ezek 38:22; 39:6; cf. Zech 2:9.
- "plundering (בזז) those who plundered them": Ezek 39:10; cf. Zech 2:13.
- Yahweh's glory (כבודי) among the nations (הגוים): Ezek 39:21; cf. Zech 2:12, and in the same context, Yahweh's "hand" (ידי) as a metaphor for judgment).

Zechariah 1–2 contains an extended allusion to Ezek 38–39, stressing a reversal of roles between Israel and her aggressors. Dwelling in open country is now not a sign of vulnerability, but of the overflowing blessings of Yahweh. Conversely, in Ezek 38 Gog's plan was to attack Israel when they were "inhabited and at rest," but in Zechariah Yahweh's scouts have come back with the message that now it is all the earth which is "inhabited and at rest," and so (implicitly) now is the time for Yahweh to rouse himself and attack, and do to "Gog" what Gog had done to Israel. In Zechariah, this metaphor from Ezekiel (which is apparently itself a working-over of Jer 49:31–32) is reversed and reapplied.[181]

180. This conclusion about Jer 48–51, and similarly with regard to Ezek 38–39, is contra Nurmela (1996: 96), who says that there are no allusions in Zech 1–8 to the oracles against the nations.

181. As noted by Sauer (1967: 202), there is also a parallel between the "holy war" imagery in Hag 2:21–23 and Ezek 38:20–22. On this basis, I suggest that Zech 1–2 and Hag 2 both allude to Ezek 38–39. Hag 2:21 reads: "I am about to shake (מַרְעִישׁ) the heavens and the earth"; Ezek 38:20: "all that are on the face of the earth shall shake (רעשׁ) before me"; Hag 2:22: אִישׁ בְּחֶרֶב אָחִיו ("Each [slain] by the sword of his brother"); Ezek 38:21: חֶרֶב אִישׁ בְּאָחִיו ("And the sword of each will be against his brother").

Ezekiel 40–48 provides Zech 1–2 with the background to explain the connection between the temple and Yahweh returning to dwell in the midst of his people, including:

- measuring (והנה־איש...בידו וקנה המדה): Ezek 40:2–3 = Zech 2:5–6.
- a man who measures "width" and "length": Ezek 40:7, 11, 18 = Zech 2:6.
- Yahweh dwelling in the midst: Ezek 43:7, 9 = Zech 2:14.
- Yahweh returning to dwell: Ezekiel *passim* = Zech 1:16.

The language of "Yahweh dwelling in the midst of his people" is a programmatic theme in the book of Ezekiel. In Ezek 11:23, the glory of Yahweh departs from the midst of Jerusalem. Theologically, the exile is understood as Yahweh's absence from Zion. Ezekiel 37:26–27 anticipates the return of Yahweh to his dwelling place at the sanctuary, and this promised return of the glory of Yahweh to his dwelling unfolds in the vision of the new temple (Ezek 40–48, especially in Ezek 43:1–9). Zechariah develops a sustained allusion to these themes from Ezekiel, and applies this understanding to stress the imminent return of Yahweh to dwell in Jerusalem.

Isaiah 12–14 celebrates Yahweh turning aside his anger and comforting his people, in parallel with the judgment of Babylon. Zechariah 1–2 appropriates these themes for its own historical context. Notable parallels include:[182]

- Yahweh's anger gives way to "comfort" (נחם): Isa 12:1; cf. Zech 1:12–13.
- rejoice and sing + Zion + God in your midst: Isa 12:6; cf. Zech 2:14.
- Yahweh's compassion (רחם), choosing (בחר): Isa 14:1; cf. Zech 1:16–17.
- all the earth (כל־הארץ) at rest and at peace (שקט): Isa 14:1; cf. Zech 1:14.
- raise the hand (הניפו יד): Isa 13:2; cf. Zech 2:13.
- nations as the instruments of Yahweh's anger (זעם): Isa 13:5; cf. Zech 1:12.
- take captive their captors: Isa 14:2; cf. Zech 2:13 (plunder for their slaves).
- foreigners joined (לוה) to Israel: Isa 14:1; cf. Zech 2:15.

Isaiah 13–14, like Jer 40–48 and Ezek 38–39, describe the outworking of Yahweh's judgment on the nations (esp. Babylon). Zechariah 1–2 reapplies this imagery in his own day to assure his generation that the promised reversal will soon be at hand.

182. My analysis of Isa 13–14 has been enhanced by the opportunity to read essays by Mark Boda and Al Wolters which appeared in the recently published *Tradition in Transition* (Boda and Floyd 2009). I wish to acknowledge my indebtedness to both Boda and Wolters for drawing to my attention some intertextual connections between Isa 13–14 and Zech 1–2 which I had overlooked.

Isaiah 40–55 (especially Isa 54) provides the promises of restoration which the book of Zechariah activates for its own generation—a message of comfort proclaimed through a messenger (Isa 40; cf. Zech 1:13), announced to those experiencing "exile," and to those in Zion who say "Yahweh has forgotten me" (49:13; cf. Zech 1:12). They are promised a rebuilt temple (44:26–28; cf. Zech 1:16) and the comfort which comes through restoration (51:3), freedom from oppressors (51:12; cf. Zech 2:1–4) and Yahweh's return to his people (52:8–9; cf. Zech 2:5–17). There are particularly close correspondences (almost verse-by-verse) between Isa 54 and Zech 1:15–17, particularly:

- the expansion of Jerusalem: Isa 54:1–3; cf. Zech 1:17; 2:8.
- "wrathed wrath" (קֶצֶף + קָצַף): Isa 54:8–9 = Zech 1:15 (cf. 1:2).
- the end of the time of wrath: Isa 54:7–8; cf. Zech 1:15.
- Yahweh's return "in mercy": Isa 54:7 = Zech 1:16.
- the rebuilding of the city: Isa 54:11; cf. Zech 1:16.
- Yahweh as sovereign over the "craftsmen": Isa 54:16; cf. Zech 2:3–4.

This sustained allusion in Zech 1–2 to the return and rebuilding depicted in Isa 40–55 suggests that this programme of restoration forms Zechariah's conceptual framework for the future of Zion.

What difference should recognizing these sustained allusions make to our reading of Zechariah? If, as argued by Ben-Porat (1976: 107), an allusion is the "simultaneous activation of two texts," then the sustained allusions give warrant for reading Zech 1–8 against the entire context of the passages being alluded to (and not just against the specific verses where we can identify an allusion). These texts—in their wider context—create a backdrop which makes the text of Zech 1–8 intelligible.

I conclude this chapter by standing back from the close detail of the "threads," and returning again to the significance of the "textual tapestry" as a whole. The combined effect of these allusions to Lam 2; Joel 2; Jer 48–51; Isa 12–14; 40–55; Ezek 38–39; 40–48 and a host of other passages, is to position the message of Zech 1–8 in the context of the words of the "former prophets," and in particular to function as a reminder that the long-awaited return of Yahweh to dwell with his people is imminent. These intertexts clarify what Yahweh is about to do, when he is about to do it and for whom he shall do it.

At one level, this is hardly a controversial conclusion, in that many other commentators have understood Zech 1–2 to be a promise of imminent salvation. However, it is important to stress this point, because it means that these chapters were addressed to a very particular situation (ca. 519 B.C.E.). The intertexts have been used throughout to focus on a particular historical situation (i.e. the end of Jeremiah's seventy years). Recognizing this fact has important implications for how we should understand the material which follows, in that it creates the *prima facie* expectation that this same historical period is the focus throughout Zech 1–8. This counts against the suggestion (made by some) that other parts of Zechariah's prophecy (especially concerning the coming "Branch") are directed towards a future and/or eschatological figure.[183] I am suggesting that Zech 1–2 establishes the time references by which we should understand the focus of the night-vision sequence as a whole.

However, this particularization of the timing raises the issue of the apparent gap between promise and fulfilment. If Zech 1–2 describes what was to happen at the completion of the temple and Yahweh's return to dwell with his people, what are we to make of the apparent discrepancy between this promise and what actually transpired in the post-exilic community after 515 B.C.E.? This issue is made even more pronounced by the double "prophetic authentication formula" in 2:13 and 2:15. If Zechariah's words were thought to have "failed," then Zechariah is not the "one whom Yahweh has sent," and it is hard to understand why Zechariah's words were preserved.[184] At this stage, I shall simply note the apparent gap between "promise" and "fulfilment," and return to offer a solution to this issue in my conclusion.

In this chapter we have seen that Yahweh's return to dwell in Jerusalem is inextricably connected with the restoration of the temple in Jerusalem. The restoration of the temple raises issues of the *temple*-priesthood and *temple*-builder, which are taken up in visions 4 and 5 respectively. This is the subject matter of the next chapter.

183. So also Floyd (2000: 340), who argues that Zech 1–8 should not be identified as apocalyptic because Zech 1:7–6:15 is "not eschatological in the root sense of the word," but rather focused on a "divinely initiated turning point in world history."

184. See Coggins (1993) for the argument that, in Second Temple Judaism, prophets and prophecy are increasingly understood in terms of predictions about the future which could be either "true" or "false." Also see further Barton 1986. On the problems created by the "failure" of prophecy, see further Carroll 1979.

Chapter 5

ZECHARIAH 3–4 AND 6:9–15

5.1. *Introduction and Rationale*

In this chapter we shall see the importance of interpreting a text in the light of both its intertextual context and its historical context. I begin this chapter by recalling my earlier conclusion (see §3.3.1) that the promises in Zech 3–4 regarding the priesthood and the temple builder must have arisen in the particular historical context of the late sixth century B.C.E. Whether or not Zech 4:6–10b (with its promise to Zerubbabel regarding temple building) was a redactional insertion, clearly these verses must have been written prior to the completion of the temple in 515 B.C.E. Furthermore, since Zech 4:6–10b—which identifies Zerubbabel by name—occurs in the context of a vision involving two "olive trees" (= Zerubbabel *and Joshua* [see below]), then there must have also been some form of Zech 3 in existence at this time, in order to explain the identity of the second olive tree.[1] Zechariah 3–4 (as well as Zech 6:9–15) are therefore to be understood in the historical context between 519 B.C.E. and 515 B.C.E.

As I begin, it is necessary to explain my rationale for treating Zech 6:9–15 together with Zech 3–4. Zechariah 6:9–15 stands apart from the "oracles" which precede it in Zech 1–6. The prior oracles have, in some way, related to the vision(s) which they immediately follow.[2] However, the oracular material in Zech 6:9–15 does not relate to the material in night-visions six, seven or eight. Zechariah 6:9–15 also stands apart because it is the only instance of a "sign-act" in Zech 1–8.[3] The points at

1. Of course, this argument does not settle the issue as to whether the entirety of Zech 3 was in its present form at this time. On this, see §5.3.4 below.

2. For example, the oracle in 1:14–17 explains the vision in 1:7–13, the oracles in 2:8b–17 relate to the second and third vision, and so on.

3. The reclothing of Joshua in Zech 3 comes close to a symbolic act, especially if, as I take it, the prophet issues the instruction in Zech 3:5 ("Put a clean turban on his head"). On the genre of the sign-act, see Friebel 2001.

which Zech 6:9–15 connects with the night-vision sequence is to material in Zech 3–4. The following table shows some of the interlocking themes in Zech 3–4 and 6:9–15:

Theme	*Zech 3*	*Zech 4*	*Zech 6:9–15*
symbolic action involving Joshua	He showed me Joshua the high priest standing before the angel of Yahweh (3:1, cf. 3:8) → "put a turban on his head"		Set [the crown] on the head of the high priest, Joshua (6:11)
Priesthood promised authority	You will govern my house and have charge of my courts (3:7)		And there will be a priest on his throne (6:13c)
"Branch" (צמח)	Joshua and his associates are a sign that "I am going to bring my servant the Branch" (3:8)		Behold, a man whose name is Branch: for he shall branch out in his place… (6:13a)
Temple Building		The hands of Zerubbabel have laid the foundation of this house; his hands shall also complete it (4:9a)	… and he [the Branch] shall build the temple of Yahweh (6:13b)
Two Figures	Joshua + "my servant the Branch" (3:8)	*Two* olive trees (4:3); These are the *two* sons of oil who stand before the Lord of all the earth (4:14)	There shall be a counsel of peace between the *two* of them. (Branch + Priest) (6:13d)
Prophetic Authentication Formula Tied to Temple Building		The hands of Zerubbabel will complete the house of Yahweh… And you shall know that Yahweh of Hosts has sent me to you (4:9b)	Those who are far off shall come and build the temple of the Yahweh; and you shall know that Yahweh of Hosts has sent me to you (6:15)

These parallels suggest that the sign-act in Zech 6:9–15 is of a promissory nature, in some way symbolically guaranteeing the promises about the priesthood, the branch and the rebuilt temple made in Zech 3–4 (see esp. 6:12–15). This sign comes directly upon the return of some exiles from Babylon, whose return is something of a "firstfruits"—an indication that the fulfilment of the promises of the night-visions has begun.[4] It is for these reasons that I regard Zech 6:9–15 as an important interpretive key in unlocking the meaning of Zech 3–4. As such, I will begin this chapter with an analysis of Zech 6:9–15, focusing in particular on the intertexts which best explain these interlocking themes in Zech 3–4 and 6:9–15.

5.2. *Zechariah 6:9–15 in the Light of Its Intertexts*

In order to understand Zech 6:9–15 correctly it is critical that we recognize that it depicts a "symbolic" crowning. That is, although Joshua is the one physically crowned in Zech 6:11, it cannot be that he is merely being crowned in his own right, since (at least one) crown does not remain with him, but rather is given to others, to be a memorial in the temple (6:14). Moreover, the promises spoken in Zech 6:12 are not addressed to him, but rather are spoken in regard to a different individual.[5] Zechariah 6:12 reads: "And you say to him [*Joshua*] 'Thus says Yahweh of Hosts 'Behold, a man, his name is Branch'."

As Boda (2001: §4.3.1) has observed, the direct speech which begins הִנֵּה־אִישׁ ("Behold, a man") is not addressed to Joshua himself:

> When this phrase appears in direct speech elsewhere in the Hebrew Bible, it does not refer to the one addressed, but rather to a third party who may be approaching from a distance (2 Sam 18:26), may be present in the scene (1 Sam 9:17), may be absent but accessible (1 Sam 9:6), or may have been encountered at an earlier point (1 Kgs 20:39). Thus, צמח (Zemah) cannot be Joshua to whom the speech is addressed.

This conclusion is reinforced by the fact that a close parallel to the phrase "Behold, a man, 'Branch' is his name" occurs in 1 Kgs 13:1.

4. We should note that Zech 2:11 (ET 2:7) has called upon God's people to flee from Babylon, and that Zech 6:9–15 is the first reference to events which are an outworking of that call. It is these returnees from Babylon who trigger, on the same day, a sign-act guaranteeing the key promises of the central night-visions.

5. This difference between addressee and subject is paralleled in the other "Branch" oracle, in Zech 3:8, where the oracle is also spoken to Joshua, but concerns a different figure (the "coming" Branch).

In 1 Kgs 13:1, this phrase occurs in the context of prophecy about a Davidic scion who will act in the future to restore right worship at God's altar. Similarly, the prophecy in Zech 6 is addressed to a Davidic "Branch" describing *his* (not Joshua's) future actions in rebuilding the temple.

A further indication that Joshua is not to be understood to be "the Branch" is the promise in Zech 6:13 that there shall be a "counsel of peace between the two of them" (וַעֲצַת שָׁלוֹם תִּהְיֶה בֵּין שְׁנֵיהֶם), in that this anticipates that the "Priest" and "Branch" are separate figures.[6] As Petersen has noted, the language of "counsel" (עֲצַת) suggests an element of subordination in the role of the priest.[7] Zechariah 6:12–13 is addressed to two different parties, as follows:[8]

Branch (Zech 6:12–13a)	*Priest (Zech 6:13b–c)*
הנה־איש צמח שמו ומתחתיו יצמח ובנה את־היכל יהוה והוא יבנה את־היכל יהוה והוא־ישא הוד וישב ומשל על־כסאו	והיה כהן על־כסאו ועצת שלום תהיה בין שניהם
Behold, a man, his name is Branch, and he shall branch out from his place, and he shall build the temple of Yahweh. It is he who shall build the temple of Yahweh and shall bear royal honour, and shall sit and rule on his throne.	and a priest shall be on his throne,[9] and a counsel of peace shall be between the two of them.

6. Contra MacKay (1968: 208) who identifies Joshua as the Branch, and sees the "two" as the combination of the kingly and priestly roles of the Messiah. See similarly Barker 1977. The only other instances of the phrase בֵּין שְׁנֵיהֶם ("between [the] two of them") describes a relationship between two individuals, rather than two abstract entities or roles (see Exod 22:10; 2 Kgs 2:11).

7. See Petersen 1984a: 278.

8. For some examples of commentators who construe 6:12–13 as addressed to two individuals, see Rignell 1950: 231–32; Petitjean 1969: 293; Petersen 1984a: 277–78; Smith 1984: 218.

9. My translation treats the two instances of the phrase עַל־כִּסְאוֹ ("upon his throne") alike. So also, e.g., VanderKam 2004: 40. Some commentators, in trying to avoid the implications of an "enthroned" high priest, have suggested that the second instance of this phrase should be translated "by his throne," with the Branch sitting on the throne, with the priest standing nearby. This interpretation finds some support in the LXX translation (ἐκ δεξιῶν αὐτοῦ), though as Mastin (1976) has shown, the LXX is unlikely to reflect a different *Vorlage*, but rather be an instance of the LXX exegeting the MT, perhaps under the influence of 1 Kgs 2:19, where Solomon sits "upon his throne" (עַל־כִּסְאוֹ) and sets up a "throne" (כִּסֵּא) for the Queen Mother, who "sits at his right hand" (וַתֵּשֶׁב לִימִינוֹ).

On this reading, there are two individuals,[10] each on his own "throne."[11] The English word "throne" is a less than ideal translation, because "throne" in English typically denotes royal authority. While כִּסֵּא *can* mean this in Hebrew (and, indeed, does denote this with respect to the throne of the "Branch"), it does not necessarily denote this in every case. For example, Eli the Priest sits on a "seat" (כִּסֵּא).[12] I submit that the "seat" (כִּסֵּא) which the priest is promised in Zech 6:13 is not a king's "throne," but rather his seat of authority[13] (like Eli's seat, and perhaps akin to "Moses' seat").[14] I shall return to the question of what this imagery might imply for the relationship between civil and religious authorities below.[15]

The intertexts to Zech 6:12–13 provide the key to unlocking the riddle of the "Branch." My argument is that there are two sets of intertexts which combine to explain these verses.

The first set of intertexts arises in connection with the Jeremianic צֶמַח ("Branch"). Almost all commentators recognize an allusion in Zech 6:12 to Jer 23:5 (the promise of a Davidic צֶמַח). What is not as often recognized, however, is that the allusion is not merely to Jer 23 alone, but rather to a complex of ideas which develop across Jer 22, 23 and 33.

In Zech 6:9–15 there is an unmistakeable allusion to the "Jehoiachin" prophecy in Jer 22:24–30. Zechariah 6:13 says that the Branch "shall sit and rule upon his throne" (וְיָשַׁב וּמָשַׁל עַל־כִּסְאוֹ). Jeremiah 22:30 is the

10. So also Mastin 1976. Contra Bič 1964: 85 and Petterson 2006: 104, who take all of Zech 6:13 to refer to a future (messianic) Branch. Petterson argues that כֹּהֵן is the complement, rather than the subject, of the verb in Zech 6:13b (i.e. "And he [*the Branch*] shall be a priest," rather than "And a priest shall be…"), and that the "two" figures sharing the "counsel of peace" in Zech 6:13c are Yahweh and the Branch. However, this construction is forced, requiring Yahweh to switch to speak of himself in the third person in Zech 6:13c. Contra also Snaith, who argues that these verses in their entirety refer to Joshua: "Joshua the high-priest is the new ruler, the successor of David for it is of him that the messianic term 'Branch' is used" (1967: 246).

11. Contra Tiemeyer 2006b: 255, who assumes that there is only one throne.

12. 1 Sam 1:9 records that Eli the Priest was sitting "upon the seat" (עַל־הַכִּסֵּא) by the doorpost of the temple. See similarly 1 Sam 4:13, 18.

13. So also Meyers and Meyers 1987: 361 and Tollington 1993: 174–75.

14. Exod 18:13 records how "Moses sat to judge the people." From this seems to have developed an authoritative "seat" (perhaps the place from which the law of Moses was read). In the remains of synagogues at Hamath-Tiberias, Chorazin, En-Gedi and Delos, archaeologists have discovered a great stone chair adjacent to where the law was kept. This "seat" is presumed to be what Matt 23:2 refers to as "Moses' seat." See further Sukenik 1934: 57–61; Roth 1949; Newport 1990; Powell 1995.

15. See §5.5.

only prior instance of a verse with these same three words (כִּסֵּא, מֹשֵׁל and יֹשֵׁב). In the context of the passage in Jer 22:30, these words describe a stripping of royal rule from Jehoiachin's offspring—"There shall not be a successor from his seed, a man who sits on the throne (יֹשֵׁב עַל־כִּסֵּא) of David and rules (וּמֹשֵׁל) over Judah."

Zechariah 6:13 alludes to Jer 22:30 in order to reverse it. The likelihood of a direct allusion is strengthened by another "reversing" allusion in Zech 6:13 to an adjacent passage in Jer 22. Zechariah 6:13 also says that the Branch will bear "honour" (הוֹד), which is a reversal of Jehoiakim's loss of honour—"They will not say 'Alas, his honour'" (הוֹי הֹדֹה, Jer 22:18). This combination of vocabulary used in this way is without parallel outside these two passages,[16] which makes a compelling case for allusion, notwithstanding the fact that most commentators have not made the connection.[17]

The allusions in Zech 6:9–15 are not limited to Jer 22:18–30. It is widely accepted that Zechariah's figure of the "Branch" (צֶמַח) derives from Jer 23.[18] In the literary flow of the book of Jeremiah, the promise of the Righteous "Branch" in Jer 23 is the answer to the unrighteous King Jehoiachin (Jer 22:24–30). Though Jehoiachin was the Davidic King, he is clearly a paradigmatic example of the "evil shepherds" whom Yahweh will "visit" (Jer 23:2), and in whose place Yahweh will raise up true "shepherds" (רֹעִים) who will shepherd his people faithfully (Jer 23:4). This provides the context for the promise in Jer 23:5 of a "righteous Branch for David." This is a promise that the Davidic line will endure, notwithstanding the fact that Jehoiachin and his children will be excluded from it. The "activation" of this promise in Zech 6:9–15 must, at the very least, be understood as indicating that the negative consequences of Jehoiachin are about to be reversed.

In addition to these allusions to Jer 22:18–30 and Jer 23, Zech 6:9–15 also has strong connections with Jer 33.[19] There are three notable points

16. The only other chapter where יֹשֵׁב, מֹשֵׁל, כִּסֵּא, and הוֹד appear is 1 Chr 29 (see vv. 12, 23, 25), but in that passage, the "rule" (מֹשֵׁל) applies to Yahweh, whereas the other words apply to Solomon.

17. The allusion is noted by Boda (2001: §4.3.2.4). Jer 22:30 is *not* mentioned in connection with Zech 6:13 by Baldwin 1972; Meyers and Meyers 1987; Tollington 1993; Nurmela 1996; Love 1999.

18. On the emergence of צֶמַח as a technical term in the prophets, see further Baldwin 1964.

19. Some scholars would dismiss Jer 33 from consideration as a source for Zech 6 on the grounds that Jer 33:14–26 is a late addition to the book of Jeremiah. However, as argued above (see §3.3.1.3), there are good grounds for saying that Jer 33:14–26 pre-dates the book of Zechariah.

of contact. First, both Jer 33 and Zech 6 use the otherwise unattested (and slightly awkward) combination of "a Branch branching out" (+ צֶמַח צמח).

Jer 33:15	*Zech 6:12*
אצמיח לדוד צמח צדקה I will cause a righteous *Branch* to *branch out* for David	צמח שמו ומתחתיו יצמח *Branch* is his name, and from his place he shall *branch out*

Secondly, both Jer 33 and Zech 6 refer to "the Branch" and the priesthood working in parallel.

Jer 33:17–18	*Zech 6:13*
David shall never lack a man to *sit on the throne* of the house of Israel (Jer 33:17)	And he ["Branch"] will bear royal honour and he will *sit and rule upon his throne* (6:13a)
and the *levitical priests* shall never lack a man in my presence… (Jer 33:18)	And a priest shall be upon his *throne*, and there shall be a compact of peace between the two of them (Zech 6:13c)

Thirdly, the "Branch" passage in Jer 23 makes no favourable references to the priesthood,[20] suggesting that Zech 6 has derived its "Branch" (with its concomitant priesthood) from both Jer 23 and 33, rather than from Jer 23 alone.[21] For these reasons, we should recognize an allusion to Jer 33 in Zech 6:9–15 as part of a complex allusion to Jer 22, 23 and 33.

Before I offer my observations on the implications of this complex allusion, it is important to recognize that there is a second allusion in this passage, overlaying the first. This allusion occurs in the last phrase of Zech 6:12—"And he shall build the temple of Yahweh" (וּבָנָה אֶת־הֵיכַל יְהוָה). This phrase is repeated almost verbatim in the very next verse (וְהוּא יִבְנֶה אֶת־הֵיכַל יְהוָה, Zech 6:13), further highlighting the activity of "temple-building" as the defining role of "the Branch." We have already noted the importance of the theme of temple building in Zech 1–2.[22] This "thematic allusion" reoccurs across Zech 1–8, and has the effect of drawing in the wider "temple builder" tradition.

20. In Jer 23, the priests are condemned (together with the prophets) for their wickedness (see 23:11).

21. I also note that both Jer 33 and Zech 6 use the language of building (בנה, Jer 33:7; Zech 6:12) which is likewise absent from Jer 23. This is similarly noted by Boda 2001: §4.3.2.3.

22. See especially the comments on Zech 1:16–17 in §4.4, and comments in §4.6.3 on implications of "dwelling" language in Zech 2:14–15.

Without doubt, the divine promises in 2 Sam 7 are at the heart of the biblical motif of “temple building.” Yahweh promises to David that his son “will build a house for my name” (הוּא יִבְנֶה־בַּיִת לִשְׁמִי). We should note the similarity in form between this promise and Zech 6:13 (הוּא יִבְנֶה אֶת־הֵיכַל יְהוָה). The parallel is striking, notwithstanding the fact that the language of “house” (בַּיִת) of Yahweh in 2 Sam 7 has been replaced by the language of “temple” (הֵיכָל) in Zech 6:13.[23]

This promise of a temple builder in 2 Sam 7 is intrinsic to the wider promise which establishes the Davidic dynasty:

> When your days are fulfilled and you lie down with your fathers, I will raise up your seed after you, who shall come forth from your body, and I will establish his kingdom. He shall build a house for my name, and I will establish the throne of his kingdom forever. (2 Sam 7:12–13)

The three important elements in this “messianic” promise are Davidic descent, an everlasting kingdom (dynastic succession?) and temple building. I place the word “messianic” in quotes to give me an opportunity to define how I am using this word.[24] Though various individuals were “anointed” (משׁח), the biblical concept of a “messiah” (מָשִׁיחַ) stems from the fact that the king was Yahweh’s anointed (e.g. Saul, 1 Sam 15:1; David, 1 Sam 16:3; Solomon, 1 Kgs 1:34 etc.). Each successive king in Judah was “Yahweh’s anointed.” That is, each king was “an anointed one,” or “a messiah.” For the present purposes, the significance of the promises in 2 Sam 7 is that they establish that the temple building role was intrinsic to the promises which inaugurated the Davidic line. This observation is very important for our present enquiry, since the tendency among interpreters has been to downplay the significance of the temple builder, by referring to Zerubbabel as “merely” the temple builder. However, if we are sensitive to the intertextual echoes of 2 Sam 7, we should expect “temple building” to be a highly significant role.

By using the “temple builder” theme, Zech 6 alludes not only to the specific promises of 2 Sam 7, but also incorporates the subsequent wider biblical development of this theme. For example, I take it that this elevated significance of the temple-building role is also reflected in what Yahweh says to Cyrus in Isa 44:28–45:1:

23. Nurmela (1996: 188–89) lists 2 Sam 7 as a “sure allusion.”

24. I am following a thematic definition of “messianism,” rather than limiting myself to passages which use the word “Messiah” (מָשִׁיחַ). This seems entirely appropriate in the present context, given that neither Zech 1–6 nor 2 Sam 7 (which is regarded by many as the *locus classicus* for messianism) uses the words משׁח/מָשִׁיחַ.

> He is my shepherd and will accomplish all that I please; he will say of Jerusalem, "Let it be rebuilt" (בנה), and of the temple (היכל), "Let its foundations be laid." This is what Yahweh says to his anointed (משיח), to Cyrus.

Cyrus is described as the Yahweh's "anointed" (מָשִׁיחַ) precisely because of his role as a restorer of Jerusalem and a rebuilder of the temple.

Furthermore, the same correlation between Yahweh's anointed and temple-building can be seen in both the DtrH and the work of the Chronicler. For example, in 2 Chronicles there are five kings who are given an unqualified "good" assessment. In each case, a key part of their characterization as "good" kings is that they rebuild or restore the temple (or part thereof).[25] This wider development of the connection between king and temple reinforces the conclusion that temple building is a role undertaken by God's chosen ruler (i.e. temple building is a "messianic" role).

25. This is demonstrated in the following table:

Asa	Removed idols and rebuilt the altar in the temple (2 Chr 15:8)
Joash	Restored the temple and collected money for repairs to it (2 Chr 24:4–14)
Jotham	Rebuilt the upper gate of the temple (2 Chr 27:1–4)
Hezekiah	Purifies the temple and priesthood for the worship of Yahweh (2 Chr 29:1–11, 35–36)
Josiah	Repairs the temple and tore down idols (2 Chr 34:1–8)

For three of those kings (Joash, Jotham and Josiah), the parallel passage in 2 Kings already records their rebuilding works, but in each case the Chronicler adds to the earlier account to make explicit the "good" motives of the kings. For the other two kings (Asa and Hezekiah), the Chronicler records temple repairs for which there is no parallel in 2 Kings. Their temple-repairing exploits are integral to their characterization as good kings. Conversely, "bad" kings are characterized as such because they set up rival places of worship, or their worship of other deities in Yahweh's temple. For example, for Manasseh, see 2 Chr 33:2–4a, and see also Stravrakopoulou 2005.

Ben Zvi (1997: 140 n. 14) notes (with respect to building activity in general in Chronicles): "As widely recognized in Chronicles, only kings who behave piously may build." On the importance of the temple in the Chronicler's account, see Van Seters (1997). On the role of the Davidic line in temple construction, see Ackroyd (1967: 512–13). See also Pomykala (1995: 109), who comments that the Chronicler "may have been instrumental in handing on—or creating—the image of David and patron of the Jerusalem cult… In the same way, the portrait of David and the davidic kings as devotees of the cult and its ceremonies is prominent in early Judaism." While I accept Pomykala's view regarding the king's temple-centric role in Chronicles, I would not follow him in divorcing this role from the messianic expectations attached to the Davidic dynasty.

Given the historical context ca. 518 B.C.E. (i.e. post-exile, but with no temple), surely any reference in Zech 1–8 to "temple building" would have been pregnant with expectation. I take it that use of this motif in Zech 6:13 would have called directly to mind a stream of tradition which associated temple building with God's chosen ruler from the line of David.

Thus, in Zech 6:12–13, there is a double allusion—both to the Davidic "Branch" (Jer 22, 23 and 33) and to the temple-building-Son-of-David (2 Sam 7 and beyond). This conclusion is hardly controversial in and of itself,[26] but I acknowledge that the implications which I am about to draw from this do "branch out" from the majority (and perhaps some would even say, "go out on a limb"). In particular, the issue is how this double allusion should be understood with reference to its sixth-century B.C.E. context.

Broadly speaking, there are two main positions on interpreting Zech 6:12–13 with regard to "the Zerubbabel problem."[27] The first position is that the prophet Zechariah had originally identified Zerubbabel as the messianic "Branch," but that the evident failure of this messianic expectation led to a redaction of Zech 6 which recast these expectations in terms of an anonymous future figure and (perhaps) a spiritual, rather than physical, temple.[28] For example, Mason argues with respect to the promise that the "Branch" will build the temple of Yahweh in Zech 6:13:

> Verse 13 might have been an original word to Zerubbabel, but it is now assigned to the role of a future messianic figure while, in the tradition also, Zerubbabel has been reduced, as he was in the Haggai framework, to the role of Temple builder alone (4:6–10). (Mason 1982a: 148)

In short, Zerubbabel did not turn out to be the Messiah, and so the tradition has been modified to transfer these messianic expectations to another figure.

The second position is that Zech 6:12–13 never referred to Zerubbabel, and instead was addressed at the outset to a future figure.[29] This position is argued in the 2000 monograph by Rose, *Zerubbabel and*

26. Most commentators recognize the overtones of the Davidic dynastic tradition in Zech 6, though contra Pomykala 1995: 53–60.

27. This phrase comes from Pola. For further on Pola's position, see n. 39.

28. For this view (with variations), see Wellhausen 1903: 5392; Mitchell 1912: 186–88; Lindblom 1962: 419; Laato 1992: 236–37; Mason 1982a: 148; 1998: 348–49; Bright 1980: 371; Carroll 1979; Beatty 1995: 11.

29. Cf. Tollington, who argues "Zechariah uses the צֶמַח motif to point away from current historical figures towards a future leader of the community" (1993: 172).

Zemah.[30] Rose (2000: 248–49) argues that "Zemah"[31] is not to be identified with Zerubbabel. Rather,

> Zemah [is] a future figure... The temple which Zemah will rebuild must then be interpreted as either a future temple, or an expansion of the present one. If Zemah is a future figure who will build the temple and rule, then the צמח oracles can be called messianic in the sense described in Chapter 1: expectations focusing on a future royal figure sent by God who will bring salvation to God's people and the world and establish a kingdom characterized by features like peace and justice.

Both of these positions share the assumption that Zerubbabel was (ultimately) not the "messianic" figure promised by Jer 23. It is this assumption which I seek to undercut. My position is that Zerubbabel is the "Branch" of Zech 6:12–13 precisely because he is a "messianic" figure who rebuilt the "house" of Yahweh[32] and through whom the "house" of David was re-established (to pick up the language of 2 Sam 7). My argument is that the double allusion in Zech 6:12–13 (to the Davidic "Branch" and to the temple-building-Son-of-David) is mutually interpreting. Taken together, they are announcing the restoration of the Davidic line in and through Zerubbabel, which would be demonstrated by his building of the temple.[33] That is to say, Zerubbabel is given the title "Branch" precisely because he is a Son-of-David-temple-builder (i.e. *a* messiah).

As noted above, it is important to distinguish between "a messiah" (which is what any ruling son of David was—i.e. Yahweh's anointed) and "The Messiah" (the final figure at the end of time who would bring salvation).[34] I suggest that interpreters have too quickly assumed that

30. See also Park's assessment of the Branch in Zechariah (2003: 160–67).

31. Rose does not translate צֶמַח as "Branch," instead transliterating it ("Zemah") as a personal name. Rose argues against the traditional translation "Branch" on the ground that the semantic range of צֶמַח only extends to vegetation which shoots from the ground. For a summary of this argument, see now Rose 2003: 176–78.

32. On this point, see similarly Floyd 2006b: 280–82.

33. This is similar to Lemaire, who argues that Zech 6:9–14 views the rebuilding of the temple as the pledge of the renewal of the Davidic dynasty—"le gage du renouvellement de la dynastie davidique" (Lemaire 1996: 55). This is also close to Siebeneck, who argues that "Zorobabel is given a messianic title in so far as the messianic promises pertaining to the Davidic dynasty are renewed in him" (1957: 321). According to Zech 6:12–15, the proof that Yahweh has restored the Davidic line in Judah is in the rebuilding of the temple by a son of David (i.e. Zerubbabel)—see Zech 6:15 and comments below.

34. My distinction between "a messiah" and "the Messiah" parallels the approach of Gillingham (1998). Gillingham makes a "distinction between the function of a

Zech 6 reflects a fully developed "Messianism," of the kind reflected in the definition of "messianic" given in the quote from Rose above. Those in the Christian interpretive tradition (where I myself stand) are—by definition—committed to the New Testament's proclamation that Jesus is the Messiah, but perhaps we have been guilty of anachronism by reading Zech 6:9–15 through the lens of our own (christologically shaped) messianic expectations.[35] Instead, to understand Zech 1–8 in its original context, one must ask the following question: What was the content of the "messianic expectation" in the early second temple period?[36]

Clearly, that expectation had been shaped by the promises of Jer 22, 23 and 33. As noted above, the promise of the "Branch" in Jer 23 is the answer to the problem of evil shepherds such as Jehoiachin. Jeremiah 22 announces the "end of the line" for Jehoiachin, but this is balanced by an announcement of the new beginning in Jer 23. Thus, the Jeremianic Branch is not necessarily describing "The Messiah" (in the sense of the ultimate end-of-history saviour figure). As John Barton notes,

> It is at least arguable that the prophecies of a new David in Jeremiah are meant to refer, not to a figure of the end-time, but to a new king who will be not the end of David's line but the beginning of a new dynasty. (Barton 1998: 374)

I wish to pursue a variation on the position suggested by Barton, and argue that the promises in Jer 23/33, of restoration (beyond judgment) of the Davidic line, find a *partial* fulfilment in Zech 6:12–13, while at the same time acknowledging that Zerubbabel falls short of a complete "fulfilment" of Jer 23 and 33. My argument is that the promises in Jer 23 and 33 are "messianic" in precisely the same way that 2 Sam 7 is messianic. There is an immediate (or partial) fulfilment to 2 Sam 7 in the person of Solomon, but Solomon did not exhaust the ultimate fulfilment of Yahweh's promises. Likewise, there is a fulfilment of the promises in Jer 23 and 33 in the person of Zerubbabel, although only partially so.[37]

messiah (lower case m), and the title Messiah (capital M). The former denotes the figure of the king and his dynastic rule; the latter, by contrast, presumes a once-for-all figure coming either at the end of time, or heralding it" (1998: 211).

35. For the argument that "Messianism" (in the sense of an eschatological salvific figure) does not develop until the late second or early first century B.C.E., see further Charlesworth 1992; Collins 1995; Fitzmyer 2007.

36. For opposite readings of the significance of the Davidic dynastic tradition and its relationship to "messianic" expectations, one may contrast Pomykala 1995 and Laato 1997, or Dumbrell 1978 and Petterson 2006.

37. It may be that Zech 6:12–13 hints at the nature of this "partial" fulfilment in the way in which the references to "*David's* throne" have been muted. As argued

This partial fulfilment with respect to Zerubbabel parallels the partial fulfilment of other promises of Yahweh, referred to above in relation to Zech 1–2.[38]

Thus, my answer to the "Zerubbabel problem" is to say that there is no problem! Zerubbabel is the "Branch" because he is the temple-building Davidic scion.[39] I offer four lines of evidence in support of this interpretation of Zech 6:12–13.

First, my reading allows these verses to make sense without emendation or re-interpretation. The most natural way to understand the promised

above, Zech 6:12–13 picks up (and reverses) the language of the decline of Jehoiachin, none of whose offspring would sit "upon the throne of David" (עַל־כִּסֵּא דָוִד). In Jeremiah, it is repeatedly stressed that the coming Branch would sit/rule on *David's* throne (see Jer 33:17, 21, 26). However, any reference to "David" is conspicuous by its absence in Zech 6:13: the Branch in Zech 6 does not sit upon *David's* throne (עַל־כִּסֵּא דָוִד), he sits upon *his* throne (עַל־כִּסְאוֹ). Perhaps this removal of the name of David is an acknowledgement that, even though Zerubbabel was the chief civic ruler in the land, a Persian-appointed governor is still something less that the fullness of the promises of Jer 23 and 33.

38. See my comments at the conclusion of the previous chapter.

39. There are a number of points of similarity between my argument and the argument of Pola, though there are also some important differences. We both wish to say that there is no "Zerubbabel problem." We alike argue that the chief significance of Zerubbabel's role is as the rebuilder of the temple, and that there is every reason to think that Zerubbabel did complete this task. Pola speaks of Zerubbabel's role in terms of a "functional messianism" ("funktionale Messianität," 2003a: 278), in the sense that Zerubbabel is, like David and Solomon, a temple builder. But, in Pola's view, Zerubbabel was nothing more than that. His Davidic credentials are necessary to legitimate the reconstruction of the temple, but there is no significance to his role beyond his initial patronage of the temple project.

Pola and I come to (partially) different conclusions because of the different weights which we give to the various traditions regarding kingship and priesthood. Pola argues that Zech 1–8 reflects *in particular* the Priestly Code in Ezekiel, in which (he argues) there has been a clear shift towards the role of the priests at the expense of the role of the Davidic monarchy. His views about the nature of the messianism in Zech 1–8 (see further n. 131 below) are an outworking of this assumption (see Pola 2003a: 275–81).

This is the point at which my path diverges from Pola. In my opinion, Pola's theory about the evolution of the tradition is too monochromatic, and does not do justice to the "blending" of the disparate traditions which we see generally (see, e.g., the conclusions to the previous chapter). In particular, instead of viewing the messianism of Zech 1–8 as an outworking of Ezek 40–48, I detect strong overtones from Jeremiah (esp. 23/33) which continue to have a strong Davidic expectation. As a result, I see a greater significance than Pola to the fact that Zerubbabel is the "restarting" of the Davidic line.

"temple building" in 6:12–13 is with reference to the second Jerusalem temple (built 520–515 B.C.E.), of which Zerubbabel is the promised temple builder (as explicitly identified in Zech 4:9). Those arguing for "position one" above (i.e. that Zech 6:12–13 was *originally* about Zerubbabel building the second Jerusalem temple, but this has now been redacted out[40]) need to posit an incompetent redactor, because whoever subsequently "fixed" Zechariah's mistaken messianism has not only left an incoherent text in Zech 6, but also failed to notice that a similar change should have been required in Zech 4:9. Those arguing for "position two" (i.e. future figure and future temple) must interpret these verses in tension with the wider context. Elsewhere in Zech 1–8, Yahweh's return to dwell in Jerusalem is linked to the rebuilding of the temple there (see §4.2 on Zech 1:16 and 8:3) and the emphasis throughout Zech 1–8 is on that physical temple. Thus, the suggestion that Zech 6:12–13 suddenly switches in focus to a "future" or "spiritual temple"[41] is incongruous.

Secondly, my interpretation of the significance of Zerubbabel is consistent with the manner in which Haggai (as a contemporary of Zechariah) understood the promises of Jeremiah. Both Hag 2 and Zech 6 allude to Jer 22 in a manner which stresses its imminent reversal. Haggai 2 alludes to Jehoiachin in the well known prophecy about the "signet ring." In Jer 22:24, Yahweh declares "Even if Coniah [= Jehoiachin]… were the signet ring (חוֹתָם) on my right hand, even from there I would tear you off." In Hag 2:23, Yahweh alludes to the language of this prophecy in order to reverse it—"I will take you, O Zerubbabel my servant…and make you like a signet ring (חוֹתָם); for I have chosen you."[42] That is, the books of Haggai and Zech 1–8, written at overlapping times, both contain an oracle of Yahweh which directly reverses the "Jehoiachin" prophecy of Jer 22.[43] My argument is that we should understand the passages in Hag 2:20–22 and Zech 6:9–15 congruently with each other, and see in both a prediction of the restoration of the

40. See n. 28 for proponents of this view.

41. For example, a new temple in the eschatological future (Baldwin 1972: 136–37), or a spiritual temple of which the physical temple was a symbol (Keil 1996: 554–55), or temple-building as a metaphor for building up God's faithful people (e.g. Mason 1977a: 63).

42. Contra Rose (2000: Chapter 7 passim) who argues that Hag 2 is not promising any royal role to Zerubbabel.

43. In addition to this parallel, it is also pertinent to note that Hag 2:23 uses the phrase "My servant Zerubbabel" (זְרֻבָּבֶל…עַבְדִּי), to which Zech 3:8's "My servant Branch" (אֶת־עַבְדִּי צֶמַח) is a near parallel.

Davidic line.[44] In Jer 22:30, Yahweh declares that Jehoiachin's "seed" would not succeed him as ruler over Judah. Zerubbabel was (according to 1 Chr 3:19)[45] Jehoiachin's grandson, which must surely have raised the question—Does Jer 22:30 apply against all successive generations of Jehoiachin's offspring (or, to borrow an argument from the Apostle Paul, "seeds"), or only against his direct progeny ("seed")?[46] Both Hag 2 and Zech 6 reflect the latter understanding, in that they hold out the hope for the imminent reversal of Jer 22 for the Davidic scion Zerubbabel.

Thirdly, my interpretation recognizes the significance of the role of temple builder, and of the royal connotation of this role. As can be seen in Mason's quote above ("Zerubbabel has been reduced…to the role of Temple builder alone"), some interpretations tend to underplay the significance of Zerubbabel being the temple builder, whereas our brief canvas of this biblical motif above suggests that kingship and temple building were integrally linked.[47] Furthermore, recent research into ancient Near Eastern building texts has highlighted the fact that the king played a pivotal role in the temple rebuilding rituals, and a number of scholars have helpfully applied insights from these texts to the interpretation of Zech 1–8.[48]

44. Contra, for example, Sauer (1967), who argues that Haggai and Zechariah had completely opposite expectations as regards to Zerubbabel. He argues that Haggai views Zerubbabel as a new beginning of the Davidic line, in contrast to Zechariah, who had a cultic interest in the establishment of the temple.

45. Unravelling the ancestry of Zerubbabel is complex. Zerubbabel is described as the "son of Shealtiel" in Hag 1:1, 12–14; Ezra 3:2, 8; 5:2; Neh 12:1. However, in 1 Chr 3:17–19 "Shealtiel, the son of Jehoiachin" is listed with no offspring, and instead, Zerubbabel is listed as the first son of Pedaiah, the brother of Shealtiel. The most reasonable explanations for this involve either levirate marriage or adoption. The uncertainties are compounded because the command of Jer 22:30 to "record this man (Jehoiachin) as if childless" may have had particular implications for a genealogy traced through him. See further Japhet 1982: 71–72 and Edelman 2005: 20–22.

46. There is an ambiguity to Jer 22:30 at this point, arising from a play on the word יִצְלַח to mean both "succeed" and "successor." Jehoiachin will not "succeed in his days" (לֹא־יִצְלַח בְּיָמָיו) and "there will not be a successor from his seed" (לֹא יִצְלַח מִזַּרְעוֹ). If the time reference of the first clause ("in his days") indicates the focus of the prophecy as a whole, then this suggests a prophecy against Jehoiachin's direct progeny (i.e. "seed").

47. See further Rooke 1998 on the "priestly" role of kings more generally.

48. See, e.g., Petitjean 1969; Petersen 1974; Halpern 1978; Laato 1992: 222–57; 1994; Hurowitz 1992; 2003; Boda 2006. From the ancient Near Eastern association between king and temple, the implication has sometimes been drawn that the messianic expectations came to be attached to Zerubbabel *because* he built the temple (see, e.g., Laato 1994: 67). In essence, the argument runs: since ancient Near

Fourthly, my interpretation (that Zerubbabel reverses Jer 22 and partially fulfils Jer 23 as the recommencement of the Davidic line) is borne out by history. According to the later biblical witness, the Davidic lineage does in fact run through Zerubbabel, after its abnormal hiatus in the days of Jehoiachin.[49]

To this point, I have argued for an interpretation of Zech 6:9–15 arising from its *intertextual* context. I now wish to demonstrate that this interpretation is also the one most consistent with what we know of the *historical* context.

I acknowledge the wider ongoing debates concerning the historical reconstruction of this period, including the issues of the political status of "Yehud" in the Persian empire,[50] the wider social, political and economic impetus for rebuilding the temple,[51] the nature and extent of possible conflict between returnees and "the people of the land,"[52] as well as some historical questions relating to the temple itself—including the relationship between Sheshbazzar and Zerubbabel and the two "refoundings," and the source of the impetus for the temple rebuilding. However, these debates need not detain us here, as they have been more than adequately canvassed by other scholars,[53] and the outcome of our present enquiry is not materially affected by the various alternatives. For the present purposes, we may safely proceed (with the majority of scholars, though contra Edelman[54]) on the basis that Zerubbabel was governor of the Persian province of Yehud ca. 520 B.C.E., and that the rebuilding of the

Eastern kings build temples, and Zerubbabel is building the temple, it is this which created the (mistaken) expectation that Zerubbabel was going to become the king. However, while I accept the importance of the connection between kingship and temple-building, Zech 1–8 suggests that the line of causality runs in the opposite direction—not that temple building made Zerubbabel the "Branch," but that Yahweh identifies Zerubbabel as the Branch because he was the son of David who would build Yahweh's house.

49. Note 1 Chr 3:19; cf. Matt 1:12; Luke 3:27. Contra Miller and Hayes 1986: 456. Regarding Zerubbabel's ancestry, see n. 45 above.

50. See further Carter 1999.

51. See further Blenkinsopp 1991. Cf. Niehr 1999: 234–35. See Weinberg 1992 for an analysis of this era which draws on the sociological model of the "citizen-temple community."

52. For an estimate of the number who remained in the land, and an analysis of this, see Barstad 1996.

53. See particularly Ackroyd 1968; Japhet 1982; 1983; 1991a; 1991b; Ahlström 1993; Berquist 1995; Bedford 1995; 2001; VanderKam 2004: 6–18; Grabbe 2000; 2004: 277–89.

54. Edelman 2005 argues for a redating of the temple-building project to the reign of Artaxerxes I.

temple began (or recommenced) under the leadership of Zerubbabel and Joshua at this time.

With respect to the historical specifics of this period, we must proceed with caution, acknowledging that our sources are very limited. In the past, this paucity of data has led to unwarranted speculation, sometimes based on dubious assumptions that various texts yield historical data about Zerubbabel. We may safely dismiss the suggestions of Smith that Zech 12 recounts Zerubbabel's assassination.[55] Equally unlikely is Haupt's claim that Ps 21 describes Zerubbabel's coronation as king.[56] Though an intriguing suggestion, I regard it as historically unlikely that Zerubbabel was ever appointed "king" over Judah/Yehud.[57] Others have drawn the inference that the messianic expectations raised by Haggai and Zechariah resulted in Zerubbabel's removal from power "probably the result of Persian intervention" (e.g. Albertz 1994: 2:454), or perhaps was subject to "a murderous plot by a power-hungry priesthood, followed by a cover-up" (Lewis 2005: 313). However, even the claim that Zerubbabel "mysteriously disappears" (Lewis 2005) is an exaggeration of the available evidence.[58]

55. Smith (1987: 87–88) suggests that Zech 12:10 ("the one whom they have pierced") refers to Zerubbabel, who "had been assassinated as the result of a conspiracy led by other members of the Davidic family...[to] get rid of a relative whose messianic pretensions would involve them in his ruin if he failed." See similarly Levin 1996. Cf. Waterman who argued that Zerubbabel "became the victim of the political propaganda of Haggai and Zechariah, and it brought his immediate liquidation" (1954: 73). Ackroyd (1958) rightly questions the conclusions which Waterman has drawn from the contemporary history of the Persian empire. See Lurie (1990–91) for the suggestion that Zerubbabel was accused of treason.

56. Haupt (1918) has argued that Zerubbabel was crowned as king in 519 B.C.E., on the assumption that Ps 21 is a celebration of Zerubbabel's coronation. However, this argument depends on highly speculative reconstructions of Zech 3, 4 and 6 and Pss 21, 24 and 110, which I find unconvincing.

57. This is advanced by Bianchi (1994) and Lemaire (1996). It is based on the argument that, at this stage in history, Judah (Yehud) was both a province *and* a vassal kingdom of Persia. With respect to Persian administration, Zerubbabel is a "governor" of a province, but indigenously, he is a vassal "king." On the use of the title "governor" (פֶּחָה) in connection with this claim, see further Meinhold 2001. Neihr notes that this historical reconstruction is not verifiable from sources, but regards it as "very likely" (1999: 231). However, as Albertz comments wryly, this argument "confuses the wishes for a monarchic restoration with its reality" (2003b: 8 n. 28).

58. We might just as justifiably say that Ezra, Nehemiah, Sheshbazzar and even Joshua the high priest "mysteriously disappear," because there is no record of the after-events of their lives...though most people do not thereby conclude that they have been assassinated or spirited away by their Persian overlords! It is more

On the available evidence, clearly Zerubbabel *was* present in Jerusalem for the refounding of the temple (Zech 4:9, see below) in 520 B.C.E., but not present when the sign-act in Zech 6:9–15 was given, since Joshua is crowned symbolically in his place (as argued above).[59] However, we should not leap to the conclusion that this "mysterious disappearance" indicates his premature demise, since the evidence of Ezra 5–6 indicates that Zerubbabel was again present in Jerusalem in time for the dedication of the temple in March 515 B.C.E.

The completion of the temple is recorded in Ezra 6:13–16. It is sometimes suggested that the fact that Ezra 6:14 (which says that the "elders of the Jews...finished building the temple") does not explicitly mention Zerubbabel by name at the temple completion is evidence of his absence in 515 B.C.E.[60] However, this argument cannot stand when this verse is read in its wider context. Ezra 6:14 is part of a continuous narrative which runs from Ezra 5:1 (see Williamson 1985: 72–73). Both Zerubbabel and Joshua are explicitly named in Ezra 5:2, and are then included in the collective set of the שָׂבֵי יְהוּדָיֵא ("elders of the Jews") in Ezra 5:5.[61] The most natural inference from the passage is that these same "elders of the Jews"—including both Zerubbabel and Joshua—complete the temple in Ezra 6:14.[62]

accurate to say that "Biblical history mysteriously disappears" from 515 to the mid 400's. We must recognize that the biblical record of the early Achaemenid period is very patchy, and that absence of evidence is not evidence of absence.

59. Furthermore, as we shall see in our examination of Zech 3:8, Yahweh's words "Behold, I am bringing my servant the Branch" implies that the Branch (Zerubbabel) is not present in Jerusalem at that time. This implication of the absence of the "Branch" is correctly noted by Tiemeyer (2006b: 31), though I do not agree with the conclusion which she draws from this (see further below §5.3.5 and n. 127).

60. See, e.g., Laato 1994: 64. Against this position, it should be noted that Japhet convincingly shows that there is a tendency in Ezra–Nehemiah to downplay the significance of the Davidic line by "democratizing" the role of leadership in favour of "the elders of the Jews" (Japhet 1982: 80–89). Thus, the absence of Zerubbabel's name in Ezra 6 is not so much evidence of his physical absence as of the theological tendencies of the author/editor of Ezra 6.

61. Furthermore, the decree of Darius (as recorded in Ezra 6:7) says "Let the governor of the Jews and the Jewish elders rebuild this house of God on its site," and in the next verse the phrase "elders of the Jews" is used in such a way that it clearly includes the "governor of the Jews" mentioned in the prior verse. See further Williamson 1985: 81–82.

62. I concur with the reasoning of Williamson (1985: 76), who writes, "In view of the narrator's method in this section, no weight should be put on the fact that they are not mentioned by name again (though cf. 6:7)... The silence about what happened to Zerubbabel should thus not be interpreted as implying that he was

Thus, Zerubbabel was present in Jerusalem in 520 B.C.E. for the refounding of the temple, was absent a few years later when the sign-act of Zech 6:9–15 occurred, and then was present again by 515 B.C.E. for the temple's completion.

As to why Zerubbabel was absent for a period, we have no solid data. However, my *speculation*, which is a variation on Ackroyd's (1968: 197), is that Zerubbabel was absent from Jerusalem during this time because he was part of a delegation to Darius concerning the temple building. According to Ezra 5:3–6, Tattenai attempted to intervene in the rebuilding progress by sending a delegation to Darius with a report.[63] My suggestion is that Zerubbabel was part of this delegation (or else separately goes to Babylon to argue the case before Darius), which seems likely given his involvement in the temple rebuilding and his role as governor.[64] While we should be very wary of building an historical

removed from office because of involvement in seditious activity or the like, as has sometimes been supposed. This is in any case most unlikely, since (a) Jeshua is not mentioned again either, though no one doubts that he continued in office, and (b) Darius explicitly confirmed Zerubbabel in office and allowed his work to continue after Tattenai's inquiry (6:6–7). This permission would not have been given had there been any suggestion of involvement in sedition."

The following scholars proceed on the assumption that Zerubbabel was present at the completion of the temple in 515bc: Galling 1964b: 148; Beyse 1972: 45–48; Williamson 1985: 76; Rose 2000: 33–36; Schmid and Steck 2001: 73; Pola 2003a: 275.

63. I anticipate that there might be some raised eyebrows at my use of the book of Ezra to construct the history of the period—see, e.g., the comments of Becking (2006). Most scholars would accept that Ezra 1–6 has been composed with reference to some sources. Williamson (1985: 73) argues that Ezra 5–6 has been composed by an author who had copies of two primary documents, and has constructed the narrative framework of the chapter by inference. In contrast, Grabbe (1998: 134) argues that only the letter of Tattenai is likely to be authentic. However, on either approach the point remains that there is documentary evidence of (at least) Tattenai's objection. Contra Bedford, who argues that the opposition is not historical, but instead a "late anti-Samaritan polemic" (2001: 279). For further on the opposition to the rebuilding, see Margalith 1991.

64. Darius's reply expresses his support for an unnamed "governor of the Jews" (Ezra 6:7). Although Ezra goes not explicitly use the title "governor" for Zerubbabel, clearly it is he who occupies this role at this stage in history (Hag 1:1 identifies Zerubbabel as "governor," in a prophecy which is dated prior to this delegation). Moreover, Sheshbazzar (who was governor from 537) is clearly no longer on the scene in 520, since the communication to Darius in Ezra 5:14 had to explain to the king who Sheshbazzar was. Clearly, Zerubbabel must have been appointed governor some time during or before 520 B.C.E.

reconstruction based on 1 Esdras and Josephus,[65] it should be noted that this reconstruction finds support from both of these sources.[66]

Whether or not this particular historical reconstruction to explain Zerubbabel's absence is persuasive, the fact remains that Zerubbabel was *temporarily* absent from Jerusalem during the temple rebuilding project. I suggest that this absence—and the corresponding uncertainty about the fate of the temple rebuilding project—is the historical background against which Zech 1–8 speaks its words of encouragement regarding the future.

The text of Zech 6:9–15 bears out the suggestion that Zerubbabel was away in Babylon at this time. Zechariah 6:15 promises that "the far-off-ones will come and build[67] the temple of Yahweh." I take it that the choice of the particular expression "the far-off-ones" has been shaped by Isa 60:9.[68] However, I submit that these "far off ones"—who will come from Babylon to build the temple—must include Zerubbabel, since

65. See Japhet (1983) for an account of the tendencies in 1 Esdras and Josephus which shape their presentation of the historical material with respect to Zerubbabel and Sheshbazzar.

66. Josephus refers to Zerubbabel's participation in the delegation sent: "So the Jews determined to send an embassage to king Darius, in favour of the people of Jerusalem… The ambassadors were Zorobabel…" (*Ant.* 11.9).

In 1 Esd 2–3 there is an entertaining story (which is repeated in Josephus, *Ant.* 11.3) about the wisdom of Zerubbabel in gaining the favour of Darius to rebuild the temple. The historical value of this episode is dubious (see Japhet 1983: 220), but it does speak of the high regard with which Zerubbabel was held in the era in which the story was composed, which is unlikely should he have been deposed or assassinated, and it may also preserve a memory that Zerubbabel has successfully intervened with Darius to bring about the temple reconstruction.

67. The Hebrew construction is literally "build in" (בנה ב). This construction occurs 20 times, typically with a place name following, with the ב taking a locative sense (e.g. "built in Jerusalem"). However, this locative sense (i.e. "build in the temple") does not fit the context here, where the temple is clearly not yet complete. The construction בנה ב occurs in 2 Kgs 16:18 with "the house" (i.e. probably the temple, or perhaps palace) as the indirect object, where it denotes a covered walkway built "at" the temple. The construction בנה ב occurs twice in Neh 4 (vv. 4, 11) where it apparently means nothing more than "building" (the wall). I take it that the phrase בנה ב in Zech 6:13 is a similar instance of this (later?) usage.

68. In the phrase "the far-off ones will come" (וּרְחוֹקִים יָבֹאוּ), there are probable echoes of Isa 43:6; 49:12, and/or Isa 60:4, 9—"they shall come" (בוא) "from afar" (מֵרָחוֹק). But this combination alone is not sufficient evidence of an allusion, since variations on this phrase are also used in a number of other texts to describe those who come from Babylon (e.g. 2 Kgs 20:14; Deut 29:21; Hab 1:8; Isa 39:3; cf. 1 Kgs 8:41). However, in the wider context, there are tantalizing echoes of Isa 60:9–10 which increase the likelihood of an allusion to this passage in Zech 6:9–15.

otherwise Zech 6:15 creates an obvious tension with both Zech 6:13 and Zech 4:9, which promise that "the Branch"/Zerubbabel will build the temple. If instead we take the reference in Zech 6:15 to include Zerubbabel, who has come from "far off," then the two parallel prophetic authentication formulae in Zech 4:9 and 6:15 work in exactly the same manner.[69]

In light of the intertexts of Zech 6:12–13, and the likely historical context, we are now in a position to consider the overall significance of the events described in Zech 6:9–15.

I suggest that the crowning in Zech 6:9–15 is a sign-act, with reference to both Joshua the high priest and also (in his absence) Zerubbabel, the temple-building "Branch." The prophet Zechariah is told to use the contribution[70] from some (named) returned exiles, and make crown(s) of silver and gold.

The decision as to whether to translate עֲטָרוֹת as "crown" or "crowns" is complex.[71] The word occurs twice in this passage, in variant forms. In Zech 6:11 the form is עֲטָרוֹת, and in 6:14 the form is עֲטָרֹת. In the latter case, the noun is followed by a verb in the singular ("and the crown shall be…"). Short of major textual emendation, there are three possibilities:

69. Although admittedly only oblique, there is another hint in the text of Zech 1–6 that Zerubbabel was absent during this time. The name "Zerubbabel" means "seed of Babylon." (See further Mitchell 1912: 186–87; Mowinckel 1956: 19–20, 120.) Zech 6:12 is best understood as involving an agricultural word-play on this name. Verse 12 says "he will sprout from his place (מִתַּחְתָּיו) and build the temple" (see Exod 10:23 for מִתַּחְתָּיו = "from his place"). Applying this to Zerubbabel, the "seed of Babylon" is currently in "his place" (i.e. Babylon, meeting with Darius), but the "seed" will "sprout" from his place and return to Jerusalem, to finish rebuilding the temple there. At this point, contra Siebeneck (1957: 326), who takes יִצְמָח מִתַּחְתָּיו as a word-play which refers to the descendants who will "sprout" from Zerubbabel.

70. In addition to the echo in this verse of Isa 60:9 (noted in n. 68), it is also interesting to note that Zech 6:11, "take silver and gold" (וְלָקַחְתָּ כֶסֶף־וְזָהָב), echoes Exod 25:3, "take from them gold and silver" (תִּקְחוּ מֵאִתָּם זָהָב וָכֶסֶף), given that Exod 25 describes the offerings for the original tabernacle (and given our conclusions elsewhere about the significance of the Exod 25 lampstand for the meaning of Zech 4). Cf. Meyers and Meyers 1987: 346–47. Viberg suggests a connection to the silver and gold of the plundering of the Egyptians in Exod 12:35–36 (2000: 162). I have already noted the theme of "plundering of the Egyptians" as an intertext of Zech 2:12; see §4.6.2 above.

71. Scholars have typically sought to resolve the issue of crown/crowns on redactional lines, suggesting that the text originally had referred to the crowning of Zerubbabel, but that the failure of messianic expectations surrounding Zerubbabel led to a revision of the passage to focus on Joshua instead. See, e.g., Mitchell 1912: 185–86, Amsler 1981: 108–9 and Redditt 1995: 256.

1. in both instances the reference is to a singular "crown";[72]
2. in both instances the reference is to plural "crowns";[73]
3. the first is plural, "crowns," the second is singular, "the crown."[74]

However, whichever approach we take, for the present purposes the outcome is very similar, because of the implication of Zech 6:14. According to Zech 6:14, after the crowning of Joshua, the crowns/crown/other crown are/is given to the returned exiles, to be a memorial in the temple of Yahweh. That is, there is a crowning for Joshua,[75] and a crown held as

72. See, e.g., Rose 2000: 47, Lipiński 1970: 34–35; Viberg 2000: 164–65. Rose argues that the וֹת ending on עֲטָרוֹת is not the marker of the feminine plural, but rather a rare, archaic feminine singular ending (Rose 2000: 83). Job 31:36 apparently has the word עֲטָרוֹת denoting a singular "crown." A variation on this approach is to take the plural form as denoting a singular object (like "scissors" in English). See, for example, Mason (1977a: 62), who suggests that the plural form may be because the crown was composed of two circlets.

73. On this view, Joshua is crowned with multiple crowns, whereby Joshua is commissioned in his own right as priest, as well as symbolically crowned in place of the absent Zerubbabel. See, for example, Ackroyd (1968: 196–200) who views Joshua as crowned proleptically on behalf of an absent Zerubbabel. Cf. Beyse 1972: 40; Conrad 1999: 126–27; Wallis 1972. Tollington (1993: 168) regards it as a representative crowning for the absent Branch. Problematic for this view is the non-agreement with the singular verb תִּהְיֶה in Zech 6:14. Wallis (1972: 236) argues that the singular in 6:14 is the result of an editorial smoothing of the text.

74. This is argued by Meyers and Meyers (1987: 349–53, 62–63). Their argument arises from the difference in form between עֲטָרוֹת and עֲטָרֹת. They suggest that עֲטָרֹת has been incorrectly vocalized, and the consonantal text instead should be repointed as the singular עֲטֶרֶת. As E. Meyers (1996: 129) notes, translating this second instance as a singular is supported both by the LXX and the Peshitta. In the view of Meyers and Meyers, the prophet Zechariah was to make two crowns, one silver and one gold. The first crown (which they take to be the silver one) is the one put on Joshua's head in Zech 6:11, and the other crown (the gold one) it to be put in the temple as a memorial, as described in Zech 6:14. See, similarly, VanderKam (2004: 41–42), and see Viberg (2000: 162) for a critique of the approach of Meyers and Meyers.

75. Contra van Hoonacker (1908: 631–32) who seeks to avoid the implications of a "crowning" for Joshua by emending בְּרֹאשׁ to לִפְנֵי, so that the crown is placed "before" Joshua, rather than on his head.

Though my interpretation here follows the consensus position of a "crowning" for Joshua, I note that there is another, very different, way of reading Zech 6:11b, one which arises from an intertext. I recognize that the typical translation of Zech 6:11 is problematic, for two reasons. First, the verse has no indirect object, though the context requires it—literally, "you shall set on the head [of Joshua]" (וְשַׂמְתָּ בְּרֹאשׁ). Most translations simply supply an indirect object—"you shall set *it* (i.e. the crown) on the head." Secondly, the rendering of בְּרֹאשׁ as "*on* the head" is also unusual. By

a sign of the promise of the coming Branch (who, as I have argued, is Zerubbabel).

The interpretation I suggest for this symbolic act (which will be substantiated by my examination below of Zech 3 and Zech 4) is as follows:

1. Joshua's "crowning" is part of his commissioning for his role as high priest, completing an action begun in Zech 3, when a "turban" was put on his head.[76]
2. The crown which is "for a memorial in the temple" symbolizes the future "crowning" of the (absent) Zerubbabel.[77]

The dual crowning thus anticipates the time when the "Branch" will have built the temple,[78] and the high priest will be administering it. This is the

comparison with Zech 3:5 (יָשִׂימוּ...עַל־רֹאשׁוֹ, "you shall place [a clean turban] on his head"), we might have expected עַל־רֹאשׁ, rather than בְּרֹאשׁ.

These difficulties give us warrant to see if any intertexts might be able to shed light on this phrase. It happens that the only other instance of the construction שִׂים + בְּ + רֹאשׁ occurs in Deut 1:13, where Moses says (of the leaders chosen from the tribes) "I will appoint them as your heads" (וַאֲשִׂמֵם בְּרָאשֵׁיכֶם). If we can take this verse as reflecting an idiomatic way of rendering this particular construction, then it suggests a very different interpretation for Zech 6:11—בְּרֹאשׁ becomes "as head" (or "in headship"), and the clause becomes "You shall set Joshua the high priest *in headship*."

On this reading, Zech 6:11b does not describe the "crowning" *per se*. However, in the immediate context, a reasonable inference is that the way that Zechariah appoints Joshua "in headship" is by putting (one of) the crowns on his head, and so this interpretation comes to the same end via a different route.

76. Both Zech 3:5 and 6:11 describe something "placed" (שִׂים) on the "head" (רֹאשׁ) of Joshua. On the semantic equivalence of שִׂים...עַל־רֹאשׁ and שִׂים... בְּרֹאשׁ, see Viberg (2000: 162–63). As I will demonstrate below in my analysis of Zech 3, according to Lev 8:9 the high priest is adorned with both "turban" and "crown," and so this "crowning" is the completion of the act begun earlier. Thus, the "crown" here is not a symbol of kingly authority, but rather (in light of Zech 3:7) as symbolic of Joshua's responsibility to govern (דִּין) Yahweh's house, and administer his courts (חָצֵר) (see below).

77. So also Petitjean 1969: 282–86. Cf. Floyd (2000: 406) who argues that the symbolic crowning of Zerubbabel is an expression of his "quasi-royal status...by virtue of his function as a temple builder."

78. Some scholars suggest that there is a contradiction between v. 12 (which posits a temple yet to be built) and v. 14, which requires a temple in which to place the memorial. However, this contradiction is more apparent than real. The tense of v. 14 is future—"the crown *will be*...as a memorial in the temple"—which does not imply that the temple was presently standing at the time the oracle was given. As Viberg (2000: 169) notes, there are other instances where there is a command to put something into a temple, where its construction is clearly still future (e.g. Ezra 5:15; Zech 5:11).

significance of the two figures in Zech 6:12–15, each on their own "throne" (i.e. ruling in their respective spheres), with a harmony between the two.[79] I will argue below that this same hope is reflected in the two olive trees which flank the lampstand in Zech 4, and in the promises made to Joshua in Zech 3.

Having used the intertexts and historical context of Zech 6:9–15 to derive my suggested understanding of this passage, I will now analyze Zech 3 and Zech 4, both in the light of these findings, and in the light of the further intertexts in each passage.

5.3. *Zechariah 3:1–10 in Light of Its Intertexts*

In Zech 3 Joshua the "high priest"[80] appears before the angel of Yahweh, with "the Satan" standing as Joshua's accuser in the heavenly court. Unexpectedly, the Satan is rebuked (3:2), while Joshua is reclothed and given promises by Yahweh (3:3–7). In addition, promises are made about "the Branch," a stone and the day of the removal of sin (3:8–10).

5.3.1. *Zechariah 3:1–2a—The Divine Council Scene*

As discussed above (see §3.2.2), and as noted by many commentators, the divine council scene in Zech 3 is strongly reminiscent of Isa 6.[81] Over and above the formal parallels already noted, there are also strong conceptual parallels which are not repeated elsewhere—both scenes involve a human being present in the heavenly court in an impure state, who is subsequently cleansed by an act of Yahweh.[82]

However, Isa 6 is not the only heavenly council scene which has influenced Zech 3. In a helpful article, Tidwell (1975) assesses the *Gattung* of the heavenly council scene, examining 1 Kgs 22, Isa 6, Isa 40 and Job 1–2, in addition to Zechariah.[83] Tidwell argues that

79. Cf. Petersen (1991: 137): "As I have already suggested, one key issue for the polity of reformed Judah was the relative power of the civil and religious leaders. Zechariah's visions held for relative equality between the two: Davidic pretender and high priest. Not so the oracles, which highlight the role of the Davidide, in a way similar to Haggai (Hag 2.20–23)."

80. There is a debate (not germane to the present enquiry) as to whether the title "high priest" (הַכֹּהֵן הַגָּדוֹל) was a revival of a pre-monarchic title, or a new coinage of the post-exilic era. See further Bailey 1951: Tollington 1993: 126–31; Rooke 1998: 194–96, 201–2; 2000: 150–51.

81. Cf. Tidwell 1975; Jeremias 1977: 203–6; Delkurt 2000: 189; Floyd 2000: 374.

82. On the divine council scene in Canaanite and early Hebrew literature, see Mullen 1980. On the council of Yahweh in Second Isaiah, see Cross 1953.

83. See also the analysis of Kee (2007), who adds Ps 82 and Dan 7:9–14 to this list of divine council scenes.

> The fourth vision [of Zechariah] stands in a particularly close conceptual relationship to the prologue of Job, and the two together present a very full and detailed picture of the council operating as a law court. (1975: 347)

In both Zech 3 and Job 1–2, we see the first appearances of "the Satan" (הַשָּׂטָן) functioning as a prosecuting counsel in the heavenly court. As argued above at §3.3.6, Job 1–2 is the prior work.[84] As such, the divine council scene in Zech 3 is an amalgam of imagery from both Isa 6 and Job 1–2.

The Satan is "rebuked" (גער) because Yahweh has chosen Jerusalem (הַבֹּחֵר בִּירוּשָׁלָםִ). The repetition of this reference to Yahweh's choice of Jerusalem (cf. see on Zech 1:17 and 2:16 above) integrates this vision with prior visions, signalling that the reclothing of, and promises to, Joshua are linked to Yahweh's return to dwell in Jerusalem.

5.3.2. *Zechariah 3:2b–5—Joshua and His Reclothing*

The imagery of these verses raises questions about the nature of Joshua's guilt and the implications of his reclothing, and about whether these matters apply to Joshua as an individual, as the representative head of the priesthood, or as the representative of all the people. These matters turn on the significance attached to the various intertexts of these verses.

Joshua the high priest is described as "a brand plucked from the fire" (אוּד מֻצָּל מֵאֵשׁ). Most commentators recognize this to be an echo of Amos 4:11 (אוּד מֻצָּל מִשְּׂרֵפָה),[85] though this point is disputed by Nurmela.[86] I take it that Zech 3 is a deliberate reversal of the imagery of Amos 4.[87]

84. It is possible that Ps 109:6, which says "Let an accuser stand at his right hand" (וְשָׂטָן יַעֲמֹד עַל־יְמִינוֹ), might also be an intermediate step in the development of this imagery. Cf. also Isa 6:2—seraphs "standing above."

85. See Baldwin 1972: 113; Meyers and Meyers 1987: 187; Stuhlmueller 1988: 78; Redditt 1995: 63; Delkurt 2000: 189; Boda 2004: 252; cf. Jeremias 1977: 207.

86. Nurmela dismisses the parallels between the two verses with a single comment "The contexts are, however, quite different, and both these passages may simply use an expression which was in current use in ancient Israel" (1996: 27–28). However, we should note that, for an expression supposedly in "current use," it has left very little trace. There is no other instance of the combination of the verb נצל "rescued" and the noun "firebrand" (אוּד—a rare word, only occurring otherwise in Isa 7:4), nor of any instance where this verb describes a rescue from fire (any synonyms). In light of the absence of any proof that this expression was in common use, I suggest that the more reasonable conclusion is that Zech 3:2 echoes Amos 4:11. Nurmela's reluctance to recognize a parallel because "the contexts are…quite different" is curious. Elsewhere, he frequently recognizes allusions which "reverse" other texts, and I take it the same kind of reversal is taking place in Zech 3.

87. So also Delkurt 2000: 189; cf. Jeremias 1977: 207.

But what is the significance of this allusion? The typical interpretation (which I support) is that it refers to Joshua's rescue from the "fire" of the judgment of exile.[88] However, Tiemeyer has recently sought to challenge this position, arguing that the exile in and of itself did not make people unclean, and that Joshua's guilt (and the guilt of the priesthood as a whole) is the result of their unorthodox worship. Her argument is based (in part) on the wider context of the Amos 4:11 allusion. She argues (following Barstad) that Amos 4:4–5 accuses the people of illegitimate sacrifices and idol worship, that the punishment of Amos 4:11 was in response to these specific "cultic" sins, and that the allusion to Amos 4 in Zech 3 "sought to convey that Joshua and the rest of the Judahite priesthood were guilty of similar sins" (2003: 7). However, in my view, this relies too much on a very particular reading of the context of Amos 4.[89] Instead, I take it that the point of the allusion to Amos 4 is not to make a statement about Joshua (hinting at the cause of his guilt in cultic malpractice), but to make a statement about Yahweh (who rescues—undeservedly—from the midst of judgment). For Zechariah's generation, that judgment had been the exile, and Joshua is part of the remnant which has survived and been "snatched from the fire." This rescue was not limited to Joshua, nor to the priesthood alone, but for the whole community. I agree with Tollington, that

> the identification of Joshua as the brand implies that he stands accused as representative of the entire community, not as an individual, and not as the figurehead of the priesthood. That the problem does not rest in Joshua himself is also apparent from the next stage of the vision. (1993: 155)[90]

There is another set of intertexts in these verses which concerns the reclothing of Joshua. In Zech 3:3–5, Joshua's filthy clothes are replaced with special garments, and, at Zechariah's direction,[91] a clean turban is

88. See, e.g., Jepsen 1948: 107; Chary 1969: 75; Baldwin 1972: 113–14; Jeremias 1977: 208; Amsler 1981: 81; VanderKam 1991: 555–56; Redditt 1995: 63; Rooke 2000: 140; Pola 2003a: 194.

89. Even if we grant the "cultic" nature of the sin in Amos 4:4–5 (which is by no means certain), it is clear that the weight of the condemnation of the chapter is in relation to the moral failings of Amos 4:1—"oppress the poor, crush the needy," and so on. For this reason, I do not accept the argument that the allusion to Amos 4 should be thought to have exclusive cultic connotations.

90. See also Beuken (1967: 284, 99) who argues that Joshua represents the people in this vision. He points to Gen 35:2 and Lev 16:3–4 as other passages in which a change of dress functions as an atoning rite. So also Siebeneck 1957: 319.

91. A number of commentators have been troubled by וָאֹמַר ("And I said") in v. 5, in that it involves the prophet Zechariah in issuing a directive to the heavenly attendants. As such, they have sought to modify or excise v. 5 to avoid this con-

put on his head. From the context of these verses, the word "filthy" (צֹאִי) clearly has moral (rather than hygienic) overtones, since the removal of the filthy clothes parallels the removal of sin/guilt (עָוֹן, v. 4).[92] But, over and above this "cleansing" from impurity, there is also a reclothing, which takes on a special significance in the light of the fact that it is a high priest who is being reclothed.

As Tiemeyer notes, "the Torah legislates that the high priest should change his garments on two occasions: at his inauguration and at the Day of Atonement" (2006b: 249). Although Zech 3 omits some of the specific terminology for the priestly regalia, the thematic parallels are still striking. When one searches for the theme "to place a turban on a head" (שׂים[93] + צָנִיף/מִצְנֶפֶת/צָנוּף + ראשׁ) and "clothing a [priest] with a garment" (לבשׁ[94] + בֶּגֶד + כֹּהֵן/אַהֲרֹן) then the best semantic links are with Exod 28–29, Lev 8 and 16, and Ezek 44:17–19. In this, I agree with the conclusion of Boda (2001: §2.1.2) that "the consistent use of vocabulary from priestly rituals strongly suggests that the scene reflects the investiture and atonement rituals of the high priest."[95]

clusion—see, e.g., Pola 2003b: 166. The versions take various approaches—the LXX omits the word entirely, while the Vulgate and Peshitta modify it to third person. However, the Naḥal Ḥever minor prophets scroll has a (partial) witness to this verse (see Tov 1990: 72–73) which Tov reconstructs as supporting the MT. I conclude that the MT's reading is the original, from which the other versions have been derived. When correctly understood, there is no "difficulty" with the MT. Tidwell has helpfully shown that one of the formal features of the "divine council" scene is the intervention of a participant: "The proceedings are always brought to a climax by the intervention of one particular participant—frequently a prophet—who settles the issue under discussion by his intervention, or who, by a sudden outburst or daring challenge, moves Yahweh, or his representative, to speak some decisive word or to inaugurate some decisive or fateful action" (Tidwell 1975: 354). In particular, the וָאֹמַר of Zech 3:5 echoes the וָאֹמַר of Isa 6:8. Thus, the prophet's interjection in Zech 3:5 is a standard feature of the form, and requires no textual emendation.

92. Jeremias (1977: 207–8) similarly argues that "filthy" is a reference to moral impurity. Tiemeyer (2003: 7) argues that צֹאִי means "ritual impurity," though the examples cited only prove that the word *can* have this connotation, and that it can also mean "moral impurity." *Targum Jonathan* offers the interpretation that "filthy" refers to an illicit marriage by Joshua and/or his sons; see further Gordon 1994: 108–16.

93. Exact matches in Exod 29:6 and Lev 8:4. Conceptual parallels in Exod 28:37; Lev 16:4; Ezek 44:18

94. Exact matches in Exod 29:5; Lev 16:4, 32; Ezek 44:17. See also Exod 40:13; Isa 52:1 (metaphoric).

95. Similarly, see also Jeremias 1977: 208 and Tiemeyer 2006b: 249.

These intertexts suggest that the reclothing of Joshua in Zech 3 is related to both the removal of guilt[96] and to the (re)institution of the priesthood. Rather than treating "atonement" and "investiture/commissioning" as alternative ways to interpret these verses, the intertexts help us to realize that they are complementary.[97] This conclusion is also supported by the intertextual connections with Isa 6 (as already noted), in that Isa 6 is likewise both a cleansing from sin and a commissioning. Thus in Zech 3 we see both the (re)commissioning of the high priest to his office and a ritual associated with the removal of sin. I shall return to this theme in my discussion of Zech 3:9, in relation to the Day of Atonement.

Before we leave the topic of Joshua's reclothing, it is necessary to address the significance of the fact that Joshua has a "turban" (צָנִיף) put on his head. It is sometimes suggested, on the basis of the parallelism of Isa 62:3,[98] that the word צָנִיף has "royal" overtones.[99] This, together with the fact that Zech 6:11 describes a "crowning" of the high priest, has led to the suggestion that Joshua's various headgear signify a transfer of royal authority to the priesthood. However, in Biblical Hebrew the "turban" (מִצְנֶפֶת/צָנִיף) does not have an intrinsic royal connotation[100]—it should be noted that the abovementioned "royal" overtones in Isa 62:3 only arise through the addition of the adjective מְלוּכָה. Likewise, a "crown" (עֲטָרָה) may or may not have royal connotations, depending on the context.[101] Furthermore, if we consider other synonyms for "crown" (in particular, נֵזֶר), it is clear that both kings and priests wore crowns.[102]

96. The language of "guilt removal" in Zech 3 is unusual. The combination "take away" (עבר, Hiphil) and "iniquity" (עָוֹן) only occurs in two other contexts: 2 Sam 24:10 (= 1 Chr 21:8) when David prays "cause the guilt of your servant to pass over" (אֶת־עֲוֹן הַעֲבֶר־נָא), and Job's cry in 7:21, "Why do you not pardon my transgression and *take away my iniquity*" (וְתַעֲבִיר אֶת־עֲוֹנִי).

97. See Beuken (1967: 284) for an example of an "investiture" approach. See Tollington (1993: 157) for an example of an "atonement" approach.

98. "You shall be a crown of beauty (עֲטֶרֶת תִּפְאֶרֶת)...and a royal turban (וּצְנִיף מְלוּכָה)."

99. See, e.g., Chary 1969: 77; Jeremias 1977: 210; Meyers and Meyers 1987: 192. See also Rooke (1998: 204–5) on the "question of the royal elements in the high priest's ceremonial garments."

100. See VanderKam 1991: 557 for his analysis on צָנִיף and מִצְנֶפֶת.

101. Tollington (1993: 167 n. 4) identifies the following passages as examples where the "crown" (עֲטָרָה) is used in a figurative sense to symbolize honour or status: Job 19:9; 31:36; Prov 4:9; 12:4; 14:24; 17:6; Isa 28:1, 3; 62:3; Lam 5:16; Ezek 16:12; 23:42.

102. See, e.g., 2 Sam 1:10; 2 Kgs 11:12; Ps 132:18 for נֵזֶר used with reference to the crown of a king. See, e.g., Exod 29:6; 39:30; Lev 8:9 for reference to the priest's "holy crown." Cf. Tollington 1993: 167 n. 5.

One text, which refers to both a turban and a crown, is particularly significant for our present enquiry. Leviticus 8:9 reads:

וישם את־המצנפת על־ראשו
וישם...ציץ הזהב נזר הקדש

> And you shall place the turban upon his head
> And you shall place [at its front] the golden rosette, the holy crown

I shall discuss this further below in connection with Zech 3:9, but for the present purposes we should note that the investiture of the high priest involved both a turban and a gold crown. Zechariah 3:5 has described the first phase of this process (יָשִׂימוּ צָנִיף טָהוֹר עַל־רֹאשׁוֹ), expressed in phraseology with a high degree of semantic equivalence to Lev 8:9 (cf. above). I will argue below that the engraved stone of Zech 3:9, together with the "crowning" of Joshua in Zech 6:11, are the second phase of this investiture process.

5.3.3. *Zechariah 3:6–7—Promises Made to Joshua*

In Zech 3:6–7 the angel of Yahweh gives Joshua a solemn charge.[103] The grammatical structure of that charge in v. 7 is a matter of some debate, with disagreement about which clauses belong to the protasis and which to the apodosis.[104] Clearly, the first two (marked by אם) are conditions for Joshua to meet, but are the next two (marked by וְגַם) further conditions,

103. Hiphil of עוד followed by בְּ, literally to "bring witness against." The verb occurs 40 times (39 Hiphil, 1 Hophal) and usually has negative overtones, being typically translated "warned, testified against." Tiemeyer translates this word "admonish." This translation in itself is unobjectionable, since the word "admonish" is derived from the Latin *admonēre* with the root meaning "to remind, warn," and so an admonition in English *can* mean a warning or reminder of duty (which is the sense that I understand עוד to have here). However, "admonish" (in English) can also have the negative connotation of "reproof" or "rebuke," and this is this sense in which Tiemeyer goes on to use the word, in that she argues (2003: 11) that the word עוד indicates Joshua's failure to adhering to the principles in Zech 3:6–7 (which supports her wider thesis about a "guilty priesthood"). However, the consensus is that עוד denotes not a "rebuke" for actual wrongdoing (so Tiemeyer) but a "solemn charge" (VanderKam 1991: 558; Meyers and Meyers 1987: 194; Redditt 1995: 64) or a "strong warning" (Boda 2004: 254).

104. Scholars who support a two statement protasis include Mitchell 1912: 154; Ackroyd 1968: 186–87; Chary 1969: 78; Baldwin 1972: 115; Amsler 1981: 78; Smith 1984: 198; Meyers and Meyers 1987: 194; VanderKam 1991: 558–59; Ollenburger 1996: 764; Floyd 2000: 372; Tiemeyer 2003: 12.

Scholars who support a four-statement protasis include Beuken 1967: 291–93; Petersen 1984a: 206–8; Tollington 1993: 158–60; Redditt 1995: 64–65; Rose 2000: 68–69; Boda 2004: 254.

or the consequences? That is, is Joshua commanded to do four things (walk in my ways...keep my requirements...rule my house... watch over my courts) and promised one ("access") or is he commanded to do two things and is promised the latter three? Though grammatical arguments can be mounted for both conclusions, I prefer the latter construction, both on grammatical[105] and contextual grounds,[106] though for the present purposes it does not materially affect my analysis one way or the other. More relevant for my present purpose is to consider the background to these phrases, as the suggestion is often made that (whether as conditions or consequences) they represent a transfer of royal prerogatives to the priesthood.[107] On closer examination, this claim cannot be sustained.

The first clause, "you shall walk in my ways" (בִּדְרָכַי תֵּלֵךְ), is deuteronom(ist)ic,[108] and broadly applied to Israelite society, not just to the king. The second clause, "you shall keep my requirements" (מִשְׁמַרְתִּי תִשְׁמֹר), has both a technical application to the priesthood (typically in connection with sanctuary/tabernacle/temple, especially in Ezek 40–48),[109] and an application to the people of God generally.[110] Thus, while it is true that the combination of all four terms דֶּרֶךְ + הלך + מִשְׁמֶרֶת + שׁמר only occurs in 1 Kgs 2:3, it is spurious to draw the conclusion from this that they were originally royal expectations, which Zech 3 has reapplied to the priesthood,[111] since the two constituent elements of this compound phrase already had antecedent application to the priesthood.[112]

The third clause is "you shall execute justice (תָּדִין) [in] my house." A number of scholars point to the expectation that the Davidic house would

105. The fact that the independent personal pronoun אַתָּה ("you") introduces both clause 3 and clause 4, serves to differentiate these clauses from clauses 1 and 2, which are not governed by an independent pronoun. This is noted by Rudolph 1976: 93 n. 7. See similarly Tiemeyer 2006b: 252.

106. Contextually, the third and fourth clauses—"govern in my house" and "keep my courts"—make more sense as a promise for the future (given that the temple reconstruction has not been completed), rather than a precondition for Joshua to keep in the present.

107. E.g. Meyers and Meyers 1987: 196. Similarly, Delkurt (2000: 189) argues "Hier werden Erwartungen, die in den König gesetzt werden, auf den Hohenpriester übertragen." For a refutation of this line of argument, see Rose 2000: 79–83.

108. E.g. Deut 5:33; 8:6; 10:12; 11:22; 13:6; 19:9; 26:17; 28:9; 30:16; Josh 22:5; 1 Kgs 2:3; 3:14; 8:58; 11:33, 38.

109. Lev 22:9; Num 1:53; 3:7–8, 28–38; 8:26; 9:19, 23; 18:3–5; 31:30, 47; Ezek 40:45–46; 44:8–16 (×5); 48:11; 1 Chr 23:32; 2 Chr 13:11.

110. Lev 18:30; Deut 11:1; 2 Chr 23:6; cf. Gen 26:5. It is applied to the king—only once—in 1 Kgs 2:3. See further Jeremias 1977: 213.

111. So, e.g., Delkurt 2000: 189.

112. See similarly Tiemeyer 2006b: 252–53.

"execute justice" (דין) (e.g. Jer 21:13; Pss 72:2; 110:6) and conclude that this function is now being transferred to the priesthood. However, this again goes beyond the evidence. The object of דין is "my house"—which in the context of Zech 1–8 clearly refers to the temple[113]—and nowhere do we see that the role of the monarchy is to execute judgment over/in the temple.[114] However, what we *do* see elsewhere, as VanderKam (1991: 559) notes, is that "some biblical passages do speak of the levitical priests as dispensing justice (Deut 17:9–11; 21:5; Ezek 44:24 [at the sanctuary]; 2 Chr 19:8, 11)."[115] I conclude that it is this priestly function which is being promised to Joshua.

The fourth clause is "you shall keep my courts" (תִּשְׁמֹר אֶת־חֲצֵרָי). In context, it is clear that "the courts" (plural) is referring to the temple as a whole. When one considers the 191 instances of חָצֵר, most conceive of the temple as having a single court.[116] However, in the book of Ezekiel the word is used 48 times (predominantly in Ezek 40–46) to describe the various courts (plural) which make up the temple complex.[117] In Ezek 40–46, it is the priests (and not the royal figure, "the prince," נָשִׂיא) who are to have charge (שׁמר) of the various courts (חָצֵר) of the temple.[118]

Thus, on the basis of the first four clauses, it cannot be said that Joshua is being commanded/promised anything more than the proper prerogatives of the priesthood.[119]

113. As noted recently by Tiemeyer, "the word ביתי is likely to mean 'My temple' due to the parallelism between ביתי and חצרי in the following verse" (2006b: 253 n. 22). So likewise Rudolph 1976: 93; Jeremias 1977: 214 n. 48, Petersen 1984a: 205; Tollington 1993: 158 n. 6; Hanhart 1998: 190; Rose 2000: 71 n. 82. Contra Rignell (1950: 120) and Marinkovic (1994: 99) who argue that "house" means "community."

114. I take it that דין here has it usual meaning of "execute justice," rather than a more general notion of "govern." So also Mason 1982a: 147; Meyers and Meyers 1987: 195; Tollington 1993: 159. Contra Jeremias (1977: 214–15) who argues that דין here refers to an administrative rather than juridical function. Contra also Tiemeyer (2006b: 253–54) who argues that Zech 3:7 gives Joshua's judicial function of "judging the temple" in the sense of judging the people of the temple (i.e. the priests).

115. See likewise Tollington 1993: 158–60.

116. See Exod 27; 28; 35; 40 where the "court" is always singular. See also Lev 6:9, 19; Num 3–4; Jer 19:14; 26:2.

117. Outside of Ezekiel, the concept of temple "courts" (plural) occurs only in Isa 1:12; 62:9; Neh 8:16; 13:7.

118. See, e.g., Ezek 40:44–45; 44:16–19; cf. 44:11, 14–15, 23–24; 45:4. Cf. also the role of "prince" and priest in Ezek 44–46. See Tiemeyer 2006b: 254.

119. It does not represent a transfer of royal prerogatives to the priesthood in order to strengthen it (so Mason 1977a: 147), nor is it an "an accommodation…to the political realities of the late sixth century" (Meyers and Meyers 1987: 196). See

This brings us to the final clause—"Then I will give you access (מַהְלְכִים)[120] among these standing ones."[121] Jeremias argues, on the basis of Jer 30:21, that this kind of access is a prerogative of the king, which is now being transferred to the priesthood (1977: 218). In contrast, Boda argues that "the only individuals who have access to the heavenly council are the prophets," and so this promise is "securing an enduring role for the prophet in the future operation of the temple cult" (2001: §2.3.1.4). However, against the contentions that Joshua is promised access *like a king* (per Jeremias) or *like a prophet* (per Boda), I argue for the (hardly radical) conclusion that Joshua is being promised access *like a priest*.[122] As has been demonstrated in the analysis of the intertexts of Zech 3:6–7 above, Ezek 40–48 has provided the dominant imagery for the four prior clauses. Ezekiel 40–48 also provides the intertextual key for Zech 3:7. In Ezek 40:46, the Zadokite priests are those who "draw near to Yahweh to serve him" (הַקְּרֵבִים...אֶל־יְהוָה לְשָׁרְתוֹ). The language in Zech 3:7—of "standing before Yahweh"—is idiomatic for "serving Yahweh."[123] This thematic parallel indicates that Joshua is being promised access *like a priest*, to draw near to serve the Lord. Zechariah 3:7 promises Joshua the proper prerogatives of the priesthood, as outlined in Ezek 40:46.

5.3.4. *Zechariah 3:8–10 in Its Historical Context(s)?*

Before we consider the details of Zech 3:8–10, it is necessary to consider the originality of Zech 3:8–10, since a number of scholars have detected

Rose (2000: 70–73) for the view that Zech 3:7 gives to Joshua nothing more than the power of administration of the temple. So similarly Beyse 1972: 101.

120. Contra Rendsburg 2002, who argues that מַהְלְכִים is an otherwise unattested Hebrew word for "sacrifices." This seems an unnecessary step when the form can be explained in other ways (see below).

121. Several scholars have challenged the traditional understanding of מַהְלְכִים as a "right of access" (from a plural of מַהֲלָךְ, "an accessway"—cf. Ezek 42:4; Jon 3:3, 4; Neh 2:6), arguing that the ancient versions suggest that we should read a Piel of the verb הלך, and should be instead translated "those who walk about." See Rose 2000: 73–83, followed by Boda 2001: §2.3.1.4. See also VanderKam 1991: 560. A slightly different approach is taken by Beuken 1967: 293–96, which is dismissed by Jeremias (1977: 217) as too complicated to be convincing. However, for the present purposes, the difference is only marginal, for Joshua is either promised direct access himself, or else those who "walk about" in the presence of Yahweh will be "given" to Joshua (which effectively amounts to an indirect access).

122. So likewise Sweeney 2000: 599–600; Petterson 2006: 61.

123. See comments below on Zech 4:14. This interpretation is borne out by the other visions in Zechariah, where those "standing" before the Lord are the members of his divine council, who carry out his commands.

various layers of redaction in these verses.[124] I submit that we should be wary about confident assertions about what is "original" and what is "redactional." As VanderKam notes, "[t]he fact that Petitjean and Meyers and Meyers on the one hand and Beuken on the other can come to the opposite conclusion about what is primary and what secondary, suggests that this sort of division is not based on very strong evidence" (1991: 562). For the most part, the different conclusions are entailed by assumptions about the text's historical context(s). For example, it is the assumption that the priesthood assumed great power in the "Chronistic" era which drives Beuken's conclusion that Zech 3:6–7 was added at that time. It is the (opposite!) assumption, that 3:8, 10 were added to transfer power *away from* the priests, which drives Petersen's conclusions (1984a: 214). It is the assumption that 3:8, 10 are too "messianic" and "eschatological" for (say) 518 B.C.E. which entails Redittt's conclusion that these verses are later additions.[125]

Instead, I propose that we let the wider context of Zech 1–8 shape the assumptions about context which we bring to the text. In particular, the promise of Zech 6:13, of harmony between ruler and priest, counts heavily against an historical reconstruction which seeks to pit rulers against priesthood in demarcation disputes over power. As I will demonstrate, there is a perfectly reasonable way of reading Zech 3:1–10 as a coherent unit in the context of (say) 519 B.C.E.[126] without the need to designate verses as secondary additions, or to posit incoherence in the text based on competing agendas.

124. For example, Petitjean (1969: 190–206), Meyers and Meyers (1987: 222) and Reventlow (1993: 54) argue that Zech 3:8–10 is a supplementary oracle. Petersen (1984a: 202) argues that 3:1–5 was the original vision, which was later extended by 3:6–7, 9, and then 3:8, 10. Redditt (1995: 62–63) and Tiemeyer (2006b: 30–31) argue for what amounts to Petersen's view reduced to two stages: Stage 1: 3:1–7, 9 and Stage 2: 3:8, 10 (which shifts the focus to the "messianic" Branch).

In contrast to these positions, which all treat Zech 3:8–10 (or 3:8, 10) as the last redactional layer, Beuken argues that the original oracle is 3:8–10, and 3:6–7 are the later addition (1967: 294–300). Different again is the position of Delkurt, who argues that Zech 3:9 is the later addition, which has come from the hand of a redactor who sought to connect Zech 3 (the purification of an individual) with Zech 5:5–11 (the national removal of sin) and Zech 4 (the 7 lamps). According to Delkurt, the redactor has taken Exod 28 as the crucial referent text for vv. 1–7, but has overladen the high priestly diadem with imagery from Zech 4, and thereby created a text which is "confused" (2000: 193–94).

125. Though this would seem to be refuted by the evidence of Hag 2:21–23, with the eschatological overtones of "shaking the heavens and earth" and the messianic overtones in the "signet ring" prophecy.

126. So similarly VanderKam 1991 and Pola 2003a: 186–221.

5.3.5. *Zechariah 3:8—A Sign of the Coming Branch*

As argued above, Zech 3:8 picks up the language of Jer 33:15 in speaking of a promised "Branch," and applies this at a time in history when Zerubbabel (the Branch) was temporarily absent (as in Zech 6:9–15).[127] Verse 8 is addressed to Joshua and the priesthood ("you and your associates who sit before you").[128] They are "men of portent" (אַנְשֵׁי מוֹפֵת).

127. Contra Tiemeyer, who argues that Zech 3:8b (the promise of the coming "Branch") must be a secondary addition to the chapter. Her argument is that the depiction elsewhere of Zerubbabel as the temple builder (4:6b–10a) together with the promise in Zech 6:12–13 that the Branch will build the temple fits the identification of Zerubbabel as the Branch, but that this is inconsistent with Zech 3:8b, since Zech 3:8b indicates that the Branch is *not* present in Jerusalem, whereas both Zerubbabel and Joshua *were* present in Jerusalem from 520 B.C.E. From this, Tiemeyer concludes that "Zech 3:8b was added at a later time when Zerubbabel was no longer an important presence in Judah. At that time, the expression 'branch' had ceased to refer to him as a person, and instead had come to carry messianic connotations" (2006b: 32).

I agree with the various premises in Tiemeyer's reasoning, but suggest that there is a better conclusion which can be drawn. Tiemeyer's argument hangs on the question of the presence/absence of Zerubbabel. She does not canvas the possibility (which I have argued for above) of a *temporary* absence of Zerubbabel—i.e. that Zerubbabel was present in 520 B.C.E. for the refounding of the temple, absent in 519 B.C.E. in order to argue the case for the temple before Darius, and present again for the completion in 515 B.C.E. This historical reconstruction obviates the need to posit any secondary additions to the text of Zech 3.

128. Most scholars accept that Joshua's "associates"—literally neighbours (רֵעַ)—are the priesthood. See, e.g., Mitchell et al. 1912: 155; Davis 1920: 265; Wellhausen 1963: 181; Beuken 1967: 289; Rudolph 1976: 99; Meyers and Meyers 1987: 198–99; Rose 2000: 150; Pola 2003a: 203–4; Boda 2004: 255; Tiemeyer 2006b: 33. Contra Petersen, who argues that there is little warrant for taking רֵעַ to be a group of priests, and instead suggests that they could equally be "important members of the newly revivified society in and around Jerusalem, quite possibly those who had recently returned from Babylon" (1984a: 209). However, while I note that the usual post-exilic description of the priesthood is the priest and his "brothers" (אָח—e.g. Ezra 3:2; Neh 12:7, 24), I also note that there is a fluidity to "neighbour/brother" terminology in Zech 1–8 which should make us cautious of reading too much into the particular choice of words here. For example, there is an interchange of terms between Zech 7:9, "each to his brother" (אִישׁ אֶת־אָחִיו), and the parallel expression in Zech 8:16, "each to his neighbour" (אִישׁ אֶת־רֵעֵהוּ). I suspect that the choice of רֵעַ terminology in the present context may have been to complement the expression "each to his neighbour" (אִישׁ לְרֵעֵהוּ) in Zech 3:10. Moreover, Petersen's suggestion does not do justice to the next phrase—"those seated before you" (הַיֹּשְׁבִים לְפָנֶיךָ). As noted by a number of scholars (see, e.g., Meyers and Meyers 1987: 198–99; Boda 2004: 255; Tiemeyer 2006b: 33), this phraseology suggests a company of people in subordinate rank to a head figure (see, e.g., Gen 43:33; 2 Kgs 4:38; Ezek 8:1; 14:1; 20:1; 33:31). In the context of a chapter about the

Of all the rich tradition of "signs" (מוֹפֵת) in the Hebrew Bible, the closest conceptual parallel to this is in Isa 8:18,[129] where Isaiah and his "children" (his disciples?, v. 16) are "for signs in Israel" (וּלְמוֹפְתִים בְּיִשְׂרָאֵל). These men in Isa 8:16–18 are signs to Israel of what it means to trust Yahweh and to follow his torah.

In Zech 3:8, Joshua is told that his associates are a sign *that* (כִּי) Yahweh will bring "my servant the Branch" (עַבְדִּי צֶמַח). However, in what sense is the priesthood a sign of the Branch? The lack of an obvious logical connection between the "sign of priesthood" and the Branch has puzzled some, and led to a variety of suggested alternatives. For example, Tiemeyer removes 3:8b as a secondary insertion, so that the "sign" of the priesthood in 3:8a instead points to the removal of sin (on the Day of Atonement) in 3:9 (2003: 2; 2006b: 240). Alternatively, Petersen argues for a translation which removes any causal or logical connection between the sign and the Branch.[130] However, there is no need to avoid

cleansing of the high priest, surely the people who are likely to be "seated before" a high priest are the rest of the priesthood, rather than (as argued by Petersen) some sort of Jerusalem council.

129. So similarly Mason 1977a: 51, VanderKam 1991: 560.

130. See Petersen (1984a: 209). The issue turns on how to translate the two clauses introduced by כִּי. I argue that the most natural construction is to take the first to be causative and the second a subordinating conjunction ("*for* [כִּי] they are men of portent *that* [כִּי] I am indeed bringing my servant the Branch"). In contrast, Petersen translates "*for* they are indeed men of portent! I am indeed bringing my servant," arguing that the first כִּי clause is an emphatic parenthesis, and the second כִּי is also an emphatic particle. Petersen argues that when a clause begins "Listen!" (שְׁמַע imperative), the word "behold" (הִנֵּה) introduces the actual oracle, which would mean that in this case the oracle commences with the words "I am bringing my servant..." As such, the intervening clause about the "men of portent" is not part of the oracle *per se*, and the כִּי which starts the second clause cannot be a connective (since there is now nothing for it to connect to).

However, this argument from the grammatical regularity of שְׁמַע...הִנֵּה clauses loses much of its persuasive force when it is realized that Zech 3:9 also has *another* הִנֵּה כִּי construction which breaks the very pattern that Petersen is arguing for, and which Petersen himself admits is "anomalous" (1984a: 211).

The flaw in Petersen's argument is the assumption that Zech 3:8 must be a שְׁמַע...הִנֵּה construction. There are numerous examples of שְׁמַע clauses where the content of the message is *not* marked by a הִנֵּה—see, e.g., Isa 44:1–2; 48:12; Jer 28:15; Ezek 2:8. I take it that Zech 3:8 is another example of this. In this case, each of the two subsequent הִנֵּה is emphatic in their respective clauses.

Moreover, Petersen's argument does not do justice to the wider way in which the word כִּי is used in conjunction with "signs and wonders" vocabulary. In short, we should typically expect a description of a "sign" to be followed by a clause which explains the sign. The following generalization is possible, based an examination of the connection normally implied by כִּי, if we let the wider context of Zech 1–6 inform our understanding of the role of the "Branch" (צֶמַח). As argued above, the climactic oracle in Zech 6:9–15 explains that the role of the "Branch" is to build the temple. Yahweh's act of recommissioning the priesthood in Zech 3 is necessarily in anticipation of the completion of the temple, in that the priesthood requires a temple in which to operate. This is made explicit in Zech 3:7, which says that Joshua will "rule *my house*" and "take charge of *my courts*." Thus, the recommissioning of the priesthood is a sign that Yahweh's house is about to become operative again, which in turn implies that the temple builder (צֶמַח) must be about to come and complete the construction.[131] It is in this sense that the priesthood is a "sign" that the "Branch" is coming, because (like the men of Isa 8:18) its very existence is a testimony that Yahweh will fulfil the sign and restore the temple.[132]

"sign" and "wonder" language in the Hebrew Bible: sign followed by בְּ = "a sign against" (e.g. Deut 6:22; Neh 9:10; Ps 135:9); sign followed by לְ = "a sign for" (e.g. Deut 34:11; Ezek 12:6; Ps 71:7); sign followed by אֲשֶׁר = "a sign which" (e.g. Num 14:11; Deut 4:34; 11:3); sign followed by כִּי = "a sign that." where כִּי gives the sign's content/result.

The following examples of the last category are relevant to the present enquiry: "The sign *that* I have sent you" (Exod 3:12); "As a sign upon your hand...*that* by the strength of his hand" (Exod 13:16); "A sign...*that* in six days Yahweh made [the heavens]" (Exod 31:17); "The sign...*that* Yahweh will do what he said" (2 Kgs 20:9); "What is the sign *that* I shall go up to the house of Yahweh?" (Isa 38:22); "The sign...*that* I will punish you" (Jer 44:29)

These examples establish that, where a "sign" is followed by the word כִּי, the most natural reading will be to translate the כִּי as "that." That is, כִּי introduces a clause which gives the content/result/meaning of the sign. For some examples of scholars who have taken the כִּי in this sense, see Wellhausen 1903: 5392; Hanhart 1998: 167; Redditt 1995: 66; Rooke 2000: 141. See further Boda 2004: 256 n. 22.

131. Contra Pola, who argues that the priests are themselves a sign of the eschatologically expected "Branch." Until then, the Branch is in their midst in a hidden way through the deposited crown in the temple: "Er ist in ihrer Mitte bzw. durch die deponierte Krone im Tempel in verborgener Weise präsent" (2003a: 280). Pola takes (in my view) an over-realistic view of the sign. With tongue in cheek, one might describe it as a "consubstantiated" messiah, who is in the midst of the priesthood "in, with, and under" the form of the crown.

132. Arrived at independently, my argument is similar to Rooke's at this point. Rooke argues that "for the cult to begin to function again, and to enable Joshua to carry out the role for which he has been prepared—including having charge of the Temple courts (3:7)—there must be a Temple, so that the vision is also an implicit promise of the Temple's restoration... Joshua himself is not given the task of Temple-building, but as restored high priest he and his friends are 'men of portent' (3:8) that there will be one able to build the Temple, namely the Branch" (Rooke 2000: 141).

5.3.6. *Zechariah 3:9—An Engraved Stone and the Removal of Sin*

Continuing the promise of Zech 3:8,[133] 3:9 describes a "single stone with seven eyes" which Yahweh has set before Joshua, and upon which Yahweh will "engrave its inscription." The verse concludes with Yahweh's promise to remove the iniquity of this land in one day.

There are no shortages of possible interpretations of this "single stone with seven eyes," whether in isolation, or in conjunction with the various stones and "seven lamps/eyes" in Zech 4. However, as VanderKam (1991: 562) notes, in recent years two views on the "stone" in Zech 3 have come to dominate—either that the stone is part of Joshua's high-priestly vestments, or that the stone is for the construction of the temple. I suggest that the intertexts of Zech 3:9 point toward the first of these alternatives.

The combination of "engrave an engraving" (פִּתּוּחַ + פתח) in Zech 3:9 echoes Exod 28, referring to either the two onyx stones engraved with the names of the twelve tribes in Exod 28:11, and/or to the engraved "rosette" (צִיץ) in Exod 28:36.[134] In contrast, there are no biblical parallels to engraving (פתח) a stone for use in temple construction.

There are other intertextual parallels connecting these two passages. In Zech 3:9, Yahweh says "I will remove the guilt" (מַשְׁתִּי אֶת־עֲוֹן) in connection with an engraved stone. This is semantically parallel to Aaron who "bears the guilt" (נָשָׂא...אֶת־עֲוֹן) in connection with an engraved rosette in Exod 28:38. In the wider context, the "pure" (טָהוֹר) turban of Zech 3:5 echoes the "pure" (טָהוֹר) gold rosette in Exod 28:36. Furthermore, Exod 28:29 (and cf. 28:12) tells us that, by wearing the breastpiece containing the two engraved stones, Aaron "bears" (נשׂא) the names of the twelve tribes "for a memorial" (לְזִכָּרֹן) before Yahweh. Likewise, the crown in Zech 6:14 is "for a memorial" (לְזִכָּרוֹן) in the temple of Yahweh. This adds weight to the suggestion made above of a connection between the turban of Zech 3 and the crown of Zech 6.

As noted above (§5.3.2), Lev 8:9 (which is a reading-together of Exod 28:36–37; 29:6; 39:30)[135] describes a two-part crowning for Aaron—first

133. Zech 3:9 begins with a similar כִּי הִנֵּה structure to 3:8b, suggesting that the two are parallel clauses that describe two related acts of Yahweh:

For—behold—(כִּי־הִנְנִי) I am bringing my servant the Branch…

For—behold—(כִּי הִנֵּה) the stone which I have set before Joshua…

134. The combination of פתח + פִּתּוּחַ in Zech 3:9 is found in Exod 28:11, 36 and otherwise only in Exod 39:6 (which is the outworking of Exod 28) and 2 Chr 2:6, 13 (which post-date Zech 1–8).

135. Exod 28:36–37 gives instructions for the making of a "rosette of pure gold" (צִיץ זָהָב טָהוֹר), engraved with the words "Holy to Yahweh," which is to be "upon the turban" (עַל־הַמִּצְנָפֶת). Exod 29 goes on to describe how Aaron is to be clothed

with a turban, followed by “the golden rosette, the holy crown” (צִיץ הַזָּהָב נֵזֶר הַקֹּדֶשׁ) which is put on the front of the turban. To those familiar with these intertexts, the placement of a turban on Joshua’s head in Zech 3:5 is an incomplete act, in as much that it requires “the golden rosette, the holy crown” to complete the investiture. Based on the intertextual connections between Zech 3:9 and Exod 28 noted above, I submit that the engraved stone in Zech 3:9 (presumably engraved with the phrase “Holy to Yahweh”) has the same function as the engraved rosette of the holy crown. In Zech 3:9, Yahweh gives this stone to Joshua, probably to be later incorporated into his “holy crown.” The crowning of Joshua in Zech 6:11 is thus the completion of his reinvestiture as high priest. Thus Zech 3:8 and 3:9 are both anticipatory acts—the reinstitution of the priesthood in 3:8 anticipates the coming temple builder, and the engraved stone in 3:9 is given in anticipation of the ultimate “crowning” of the high priest (cf. 6:11–14).

Another related set of intertexts arises in connection with the final clause of v. 9—“and I will remove the guilt of this land in one day” (וּמַשְׁתִּי אֶת־עֲוֹן הָאָרֶץ־הַהִיא בְּיוֹם אֶחָד). At a thematic level, a one-day removal of sin connects this verse with the sacrificial system in general, and the Day of Atonement in particular.[136]

with the various vestments whose construction is described in Exod 28. In Exod 29:6, the turban is to be put on Aaron’s head, and then “the holy crown” (אֶת־נֵזֶר הַקֹּדֶשׁ) is to be put “upon the turban” (עַל־הַמִּצְנֶפֶת). Since there is no mention of the “holy crown” in Exod 28, and the only element in Exod 28 which is put “upon the turban” (עַל־הַמִּצְנֶפֶת) is the “gold rosette,” the reasonable conclusion is that the holy crown and the gold rosette are either the same item (or perhaps that the rosette is part of the holy crown). This conclusion is supported by both Exod 39:30 and Lev 8:9: אֵת צִיץ הַזָּהָב נֵזֶר הַקֹּדֶשׁ (“The golden rosette, the holy crown,” Lev 8:9); אֶת־צִיץ נֵזֶר־הַקֹּדֶשׁ זָהָב טָהוֹר (“The rosette, the holy crown of pure gold,” Exod 39:30).

136. Although there are no exact verbal parallels to the phrase “I will remove the guilt” (מַשְׁתִּי אֶת־עֲוֹן), there are clear thematic parallels with the sacrificial system. Moreover, given the focus elsewhere in the chapter on the high priest and his role, it is likely that Zech 3:9 reflects the understanding reflected in (say) Lev 10:17, of a sin offering… “to take away (נשׂא) the guilt (אֶת־עֲוֹן) of the congregation, to make atonement for them (לְכַפֵּר עֲלֵיהֶם).” Furthermore, the Day of Atonement (Lev 16) in particular was *the* occasion for the removal of national guilt on a single day, and, as noted above, the high priest had to be dressed in his regalia on that day. All these connections suggest that the sacrificial system in general, and the Day of Atonement in particular, is the intertextual background for this phrase in Zech 3:9. So also Pola 2003a: 222; Boda 2004: 258; Tiemeyer 2006b: 249.

Furthermore, the vocabulary of “iniquity” (עָוֹן) connects this verse to Zech 3:4, recalling the taking away of Joshua’s iniquity (עָוֹן) by the exchange of his filthy clothes for pure ones (טָהוֹר). Although the vocabulary of impurity (טמא) is not used

5.3.7. *Zechariah 3:10—"In that day"*

Zech 3:10 describes a day of paradisiacal peace. Zechariah utilizes an image of peace and security from Mic 4:4 // 1 Kgs 5:5 (= ET 4:25)—"under vine and under fig tree" (תַּחַת גַּפְנוֹ וְתַחַת תְּאֵנָתוֹ)—but with a twist: it is not just individual enjoyment, but a shared experience. This picture reverses the conditions which Israel had experienced under judgment, when "each is set against their neighbour" (see Isa 3:5; Exod 32:27; Zech 7:10; 8:17; 14:13).[137]

Finally, there may also be wider intertextual connections to Jer 33 in this section. We have already noted the obvious allusion to the "Branch" of Jer 33:15, but we should also note that coming צֶמַח is promised "in those days" (Jer 33:15; cf. Zech 3:10, "in that day"), at a time when Yahweh had cleansed his people from all their guilt (עָוֹן) (Jer 31:34; 33:8; cf. Zech 3:9). Furthermore, this cleansing from sin ushers in an age of paradisiacal blessing (Jer 33:9–13; cf. Zech 3:10).

5.3.8. *Conclusions on Zechariah 3:1–10*

In the opening verses of this section the allusion to the brand snatched from the fire (a reversal of Amos 4) depicts Joshua as a representative of the remnant of the people who have returned from judgment (i.e. exile). Joshua's "filthy" clothes depict the guilt of exile, and the sustained allusions to Isa 6 reminds the reader that it is Yahweh who takes the initiative to remove sin/guilt/impurity, which is what is being symbolized in the reclothing of Joshua.

The promises made to the priesthood in Ezek 40–48 provide the dominant imagery for the conditions and promises of Zech 3:6–7. By sustained allusion, Zech 3 invokes the promises of the restoration of the priestly function promised in Ezek 40–48.

in Zech 3:1–7, clearly this is implied by the adjective "filthy" (צֹאִי). Thus, if we read the cleansing of Joshua as in some way proleptic of the purification of the land, then perhaps it is not drawing too long a bow to understand the "iniquity of the land" in terms of its impurity caused by the sin of the people (for טמא and אֶרֶץ, see Lev 18:25, 27, 28; Num 35:34; Jer 2:7; Ezek 36:18). Cf. Tiemeyer, who distinguishes between the sin of the priesthood and the sin of the land. She argues that Zech 3 speaks of the purification of a guilty priesthood, with Joshua standing as a representative of the Judahite priesthood, who together have become unclean, "possibly due to idolatry and unorthodox worship… The only solution in this situation is a divine intervention where the high priest is purified (vv. 3–5), followed by the celebration of the Day of Atonement when the guilt of the land is erased" (2003: 14).

137. For a detailed examination of the motif of "brother against brother," see Good 1992, as well as the discussion below on Zech 7:10 and 8:17.

In the final section (Zech 3:8–10), Zechariah combines allusions to various texts from Exod 28 and Lev 8, 16 and Jer 33 to stress the reinstitution of the priesthood in a reconstructed temple, climaxing on a "Day" (probably the Day of Atonement) when God's people can again have their sins forgiven and experience God's blessings.

5.4. *Zechariah 4 in Light of Its Intertexts*

Zechariah 4 begins with words which reinforce the conclusion that Zech 3 was an original part of the night-vision sequence. That the interpreting angel "returned" (שׁוב) presupposes an absence from the previous vision (which is only the case if Zech 3 was the prior vision). Furthermore, the fact that the episode begins with the prophet being "roused" (עור)[138] from sleep acknowledges that the immediately preceding episode is of a different character to the other visions.

5.4.1. *On the Integrity of the Chapter as a Whole*

On most analyses, the chapter falls into three main sections:[139]

vv. 2–5	vision report (and dialogue) about a lampstand and two olive trees
vv. 6–10	oracle about Zerubbabel building the temple? / oracle about seven eyes?
vv. 11–14	an interpretation of the two olive trees

In the above schema question marks have been applied to the second section because many commentators since Wellhausen have routinely considered Zech 4:6b–10aβ to be an insertion into a text which originally read "And he answered and he said to me 'These seven are the eyes of Yahweh which range through the whole earth'."

Zechariah 4:6b–10aβ are clearly disjunctive with their context, because at first glance they do not seem to relate to the questions of vv. 2–5. However, it is important to realize that simply taking scissors to the text does not satisfactorily resolve the problem. Indeed, as van der Woude (1988: 238–39) has demonstrated, this approach actually raises more questions than it solves—it does not give a satisfying answer to where

138. Though expressed in different terminology, Jer 31:26 is a possible allusion, in that it gives the best conceptual match for a disjunctive "waking up" in the midst of prophetic activity—"At this I awoke and looked, and my sleep had been pleasant to me." Cf. Dan 7:1 (a dream, later written down).

139. Though for an alternate structure based on the placement of paragraph markers, see Van Amerongen 2005.

4:6b–10aβ originally stood, it leaves us with only half an interpretation (the seven spouts are explained, but not the lampstand itself), it removes the only promise of future weal (which is a feature of every other night-vision), and the supposed reconstruction of 4:6b and 10b produces textual transitions which are unprecedented.[140] Furthermore, the argument for redactional insertion raises the questions "when" and "why"?[141]

For these reasons, I propose to follow the lead of those commentators who seek to interpret vv. 6–10 in the context of Zech 4.[142] Given that the vision as a whole describes a lampstand and two olive trees, and that vv. 11–14 only give an interpretation of the two olive trees, I will proceed on the (not unwarranted) assumption that vv. 6–10 are in some way related to the interpretation of the lampstand with the seven spouts.

5.4.2. *Zechariah 4:2–5 (and 4:10b)—The Golden Lampstand*

There are two other places where the imagery of the golden lampstand (מְנוֹרַת זָהָב) is used, which might be possible intertexts to Zech 4—namely, the ten golden lampstands in Solomon's temple (1 Kgs 7:49), and the single lampstand in the tabernacle (Exod 25:31–39; 37:17–24; 39:37; Lev 24:4; Num 8:4). However, the further description in Zech 4:2 of "seven lamps" makes it clear that the single tabernacle lampstand is on view, since a reference to the seven lamps (וְשִׁבְעָה נֵרֹתֶיהָ) only occurs in Exod 25:37; 37:23 and Num 8:2. Thus, our starting point is that the vision in Zech 4 is making a primary allusion to the tabernacle lampstand.[143]

140. As van der Woude (1988: 238–39) argues, "the alleged original transition from v. 6aα to v. 10b is not as smooth as has been suggested… If v. 10b were the sequel of v. 6aα, we would expect ʾēlleh šebaʿ (or šibʿā) ʿēnē yhwh, 'These are the seven eyes of the Lord', instead of šibʿā ʾēlleh ʿēnē yhwh, 'These seven are the eyes of the Lord'."

141. See, e.g., Niditch (1983: 94) who notes that these verses "must refer to Zerubbabel, whose rise and fall appears to have taken place within a very short period of time… Therefore, verse 6aβ–10a must be nearly contemporary with the vision itself. Perhaps these vss. did once belong elsewhere in the Zechariah material. Yet surely, any redactor would have realized how out of place they seem here, dividing the question from the answer by a lengthy excursus."

142. Some scholars regard Zech 4 as an original unity (see, e.g., Buzy 1918; van der Woude 1988: 238–39), whereas others treat the chapter as a literary unity, though acknowledging that there may have been earlier forms of the chapter (so Meyers and Meyers 1987: 242, 265–72; Tigchelaar 1996: 24; Fournier-Bidoz 1997; Floyd 2000: 381, 384). For the present purposes, the net result is the same.

143. That it is not to exclude the possibility that there is also a secondary influence of the Solomonic lampstands. For example, Meyers and Meyers argue that Zechariah's lampstand is "a conflation of the two traditions, the premonarchic and

The other terminology used in Zech 4 to describe the lampstand is without intertextual parallel. The lamps have "seven spouts" (if indeed "spouts" is how מוּצָקוֹת should be translated),[144] but nowhere else is the word "spouts" used in conjunction with a lampstand. Similarly, the phrase "a bowl[145] at its top" (וְגֻלָּה עַל־רֹאשָׁהּ) is nowhere else used in relation to a lampstand.[146]

The other main components of the vision are the two olive trees (וּשְׁנַיִם זֵיתִים). Though the "olive tree" (זַיִת) has multiple metaphoric and symbolic uses,[147] the conclusion which we have already reached regarding the lampstand helps to constrain the possibilities of its use in the present context. There is one, and only one, set of allusions which explain both the lampstand and the olive trees—in Exod 27:20 (and cf. Lev 24:2), the Israelites are to bring "oil of olive, pure [and] clean (שֶׁמֶן זַיִת זָךְ כָּתִית) for

the preexilic" (1987: 233). In contrast, Petersen argues that the tabernacle lampstand (which Meyers and Meyers label "premonarchic") is in fact entirely the invention of a post-exilic priestly writer. "All references to a single m^enôrāh derive from literature that probably was written in the post-exilic period" (1984a: 218). Petersen's argument is that the Exod 25 lampstand is "markedly different from that described in Zech 4" and that "the differences outweigh the similarities" (1984a: 223). In my opinion, however, the differences which Petersen highlights, which are mainly omissions rather than contradictions, are not as significant as the similarities. Furthermore, the intertextual connections between Zech 3 and Exod 28 (see above) demonstrate that Zechariah has access to a tradition which encompassed the rules for tabernacle construction in Exod 25–30.

144. In Appendix 6 of my doctoral dissertation (Stead 2007), I argue that the "seven מוּצָקוֹת" may in fact be referring to the "lights" of the lamps rather than "pipes" or "spouts." However, for the present purposes the interpretation is not materially affected one way or another.

145. Or perhaps "branchwork." See Rignell (1950: 146–50), for whom the גֻּלָּה refers to the curved branchwork of the menorah, rather than to a bowl supplying oil.

146. It should be noted that a similar construction is found in 1 Kgs 7:41 to describe the tops of the temple pillars. As Niditch notes, this correspondence may be incidental, because a saucer-shaped feature was a common ancient Near Eastern design element, though I agree with her comment that גֻּלָּה "Is a rare term…and the possibility of an intentional link between temple and menorah cannot be ruled out" (1983: 105). However, this adds little to our understanding of the significance of the lampstand.

147. For example, oil for anointing, oil as a symbol of abundance, olive harvest as a metaphor for judgment/remnant, a place (Mount of Olives) and oil used in a parable about kingship (Judg 9). Ps 52:10 (ET v. 8) has imagery that initially looks relevant to our enquiry—"a verdant olive tree in the temple." However, on closer analysis, the metaphor is another instance of the olive used as a symbol of abundance, though I would be prepared to concede, if pressed, that Ps 52:10 may have influenced the particular tree chosen for the metaphor in Zech 4.

the light (לַמָּאוֹר)."[148] This complex allusion to Exod 25–27 in Zech 4 provides us with a first key to making sense of the vision, in that the function of two olive trees must be (in some way) to provide oil to the lamp of the lampstand. However, these allusions only take us so far, in that they reveal the connections between the symbols, but they do not tell us what the symbols symbolize. We, like Zechariah, are left asking "What are these things?" (Zech 4:4).

To answer this question, we must partially anticipate the conclusions yet to be drawn regarding Zech 4:6–10 and 4:11–14. However, for the sake of the clarity of the following discussion, I shall give an overview of the interpretation I intend to defend. The two dominant interpretations of the lampstand are either that it symbolizes Yahweh (because of the apparent connection with his "eyes" in 4:10)[149] or that it symbolizes the worshipping community.[150] However, I will argue for a third option, which is that the lampstand symbolizes the temple. This third option is not without scholarly support.[151]

My interpretation stems from recognizing the effect of an "insertion" (in a literary sense, whether or not in a redactional sense) of an oracle about temple-building, at the point at which the reader is expecting an answer to the question "What is the lampstand?" If Zech 4:6aβ–10a can make any sense in their context, it can only be by providing an implicit answer to this question—that is, that the lampstand symbolizes the restored and re-established temple. Thus, with reference to the various elements of the vision, 4:6aβ–10a explains the lampstand (the lampstand is the rebuilt temple), v. 10b explains the seven lamps (and/or the seven מוּצָקוֹת) as "the seven eyes of Yahweh," and vv. 11–14 explains the two

148. In context, the "light" (מָאוֹר) is clearly the light of the lampstand. See also Exod 35:14 and Num 4:9. The consistent imagery in these texts is of one lampstand (מְנֹרָה) with multiple lamps (נֵרֹת) which constitutes one light (אֶת־מְנֹרַת הַמָּאוֹר or simply הַמָּאוֹר). Zechariah replicates this imagery.

149. See, e.g., Rignell 1950: 175; Jeremias 1977: 181; Chary 1969: 85; Petersen 1984a: 234. See Niehr (1999: 238) for the argument that the lampstand fulfilled the function of a cult symbol of Yahweh's presence in the Second Temple.

150. See, e.g., Boehmer 1938: 360–64; Baldwin 1972: 124; Rudolph 1976: 109. The chief argument for this position stems from the fact that the sons of oil provide oil to the lampstand, making Yahweh dependent on Joshua and Zerubbabel. Rudolph rejects this as blasphemous (see below). See Rose (2000: 179) for a list of those who adopt both of these options. See Strand 1982 for the view that the lampstand symbolizes Zerubbabel.

151. The following scholars have argued that the lampstand symbolizes the temple (or some part thereof): Buzy 1918: 166–67; Rost 1951: 220; Bullough 1953: 693; Niditch 1983: 104; Bakon 1989: 155. Rose argues that "the lampstand is meant to be the temple or the worshipping community" (2000: 182).

olive trees. The correspondence between vision element and interpretation is shown in the following table:

Vision (Zech 4:2–3)	*Interpretation (Zech 4:6–14)*
A lampstand, all of gold, and a bowl upon the top of it	*Either unexplained, or explained by 4:6–10a* The hands of Zerubbabel have laid the foundation of this house; his hands shall also complete it (Zech 4:9)
seven lamps on it—seven, and seven מוצקות for the lamps which are on the top of it	These seven are the eyes of Yahweh, which range through the whole earth (Zech 4:10b)
And by it there are two olive trees, one on the right of the bowl and the other on its left	"What are these two branches of the olive trees, which pour out the oil through the two golden pipes?"... Then he said, "These are the two sons of oil who stand before the Lord of the whole earth" (see Zech 4:12–14)

5.4.3. *Zechariah 4:6–10a—The Word of Yahweh to Zerubbabel*

In the midst of the angel's explanation of the lampstand, lamps/lights and olive trees, we find a "word of Yahweh to Zerubbabel" (Zech 4:6aβ–10a). While there is no small debate about the precise meaning of the details in these verses (in particular relating to the various stones and the "mountain" and their relationship to ancient Near Eastern building practices), there is broad agreement about their overall significance. The "word of Yahweh" is an assurance that Zerubbabel will complete—by Yahweh's spirit—the rebuilding of the temple at Jerusalem.

This oracle to Zerubbabel begins with Yahweh's assurance that he will build "not by might, nor by power, but by my spirit," which may be an echo of Ps 33:16.[152]

Zechariah 4:7 then describes a "great mountain" (הַר־הַגָּדוֹל) which shall be "like a plain" (לְמִישֹׁר) before Zerubbabel. This same word occurs otherwise only (in full form לְמִישׁוֹר) in Isa 40:4 and 42:16. The most likely intertext for Zech 4:7 is Isa 40:4—"every mountain (הַר) and hill

152. Ps 33:16 is the only other instance of the combination "not by might/power" (לא+בְּ+חַיִל+כֹּחַ): "A king is not saved by the greatness of might (חַיִל) nor a warrior by greatness of power (כֹּחַ)." An examination of the wider context of Ps 33 reveals a number of other thematic connections with this pericope. Ps 33:6 describes God's creative power by the word of the Lord (דְּבַר יְהוָה) and by his Spirit (רוּחַ); cf. Zech 4:6. Furthermore, the psalm is a reminder that this power is at work to defend and uplift his people in their times of difficulties and oppression by their enemies (33:10–15). Ps 33 ends with an encouragement to trust the Lord amidst difficulties (33:20–22). The effect of this echo of Ps 33 in Zech 4 is to invoke the assurance of the Lord's unstoppable plans in the rebuilding the temple through Zerubbabel. Laato (1994: 66) also draws a connection between Zech 4:6 and Ps 33.

be made low; the uneven ground shall be like a plain (לְמִישׁוֹר)."[153] The vocabulary in Zech 4, describing Zerubbabel's actions in building the temple, recalls the restoration and return promised in Isa 40.

However, what should we make of the significance of the "great mountain" in Zech 4? Many commentators treat it either as the pile of debris from the old temple (we might say "a mountain of rubble"),[154] or as a metaphor for the difficulties which Zerubbabel faces in the rebuilding effort (perhaps, colloquially, "a mountain of trouble").[155] However, there are no biblical instances of the word הַר being used in either of these general senses. There is, however, biblical precedent for the word הַר being used as a metaphor for world powers arrayed against God's people. In Jer 51:25, Yahweh says about Babylon "Behold, I am against you, *O destroying mountain*" (הַר הַמַּשְׁחִית). Similarly, in Isa 41:11–15, the enemies of Israel who wage war against her are "mountains" (Isa 41:15) whom Israel will thresh and crush.[156] On this basis, and in light of the intertextual echo noted above from Isa 40:4, I conclude that the "great mountain" facing Zerubbabel is the world power which opposes the temple building.[157] On the historical reconstruction offered above, this is Persia (at least potentially), in that Zerubbabel has gone as part of a delegation to convince Darius not to oppose the rebuilding of the temple.[158]

After the "great mountain" has been reduced to a plain, Zerubbabel will bring out the "*top stone*." *Top stone* is literally אֶת־הָאֶבֶן הָרֹאשָׁה.

153. Nurmela (1996: 65–66) categorizes Zech 4:7 as a "probable allusion" to Isa 40:4 and Isa 42:16. This connection is also noted by Galling (1964b: 140) and Tollington (1993: 145–46).

154. See, e.g., Galling 1964b: 141–42; Petitjean 1969: 258–63; Halpern 1978: 170; Tollington 1993: 148–49; Tigchelaar 1996: 47; Sweeney 2000: 608; Pola 2003a: 117. Laato (1994: 64, 66) sees it possibly as a reference to rubble as well as a metaphor for opposition.

155. See von Rad (1982: 2:285), who reads "adverse factors which look like towering mountains." Cf. Baldwin 1972: 121; Floyd 2000: 381; Webb 2003: 91–92.

156. The following commentators have understood the "mountain" in Zech 4:7 to signify a world power, or world powers: Sellin 1942–43: 69–70; Rignell 1950; Rost 1951: 220. Elliger (1963: 126) identifies the opposing powers as the Samaritans.

157. Contra van der Woude, who reduces its meaning to "a general statement: no mountain, however great and impressive, can ultimately venture to compete with Zion!" (1988: 240).

158. This identification of the "mountain" as a metaphor for a world power (in this case, Persia) also makes best sense in light of the grammar of Zech 4:7. The verse begins מִי־אַתָּה הַר־הַגָּדוֹל—literally "*Who* are you, O great mountain?" Commentators wishing to find an impersonal object are forced to translate מִי as "what?" instead of the more natural "who?"

The noun רֹאשָׁה is a *hapax*, but the other nouns in the ראשׁ family suggest two possible lines of meaning. If רֹאשָׁה is more like ראשׁ ("head"), then the stone is the "top stone" (perhaps the capstone at the head of the building). But if רֹאשָׁה is analogous to רִאשׁוֹן ("first") and רֵאשִׁית ("beginning"), then the stone is the "first stone" (i.e. a foundation stone).

A number of scholars have built on the work of Ellis (1968) on foundation deposits in ancient Near Eastern temple construction to argue that the הָאֶבֶן הָרֹאשָׁה was the foundation stone of the temple, akin to the *libitu maḫrītu* in the Mesopotamian *kalû* ritual.[159] In this ritual, the *libitu maḫrītu* was a stone removed from the foundation of a former temple, which was incorporated as a deposit in the foundation of the new temple, in an elaborate refounding ceremony.

As indicated above, I think that there is merit in understanding Zech 4 against the general background of ancient Near Eastern temple-building texts.[160] However, the attempts to interpret Zech 4:6–9 against the specific details of the *kalû* ritual "runs against the grain" of the details in Zech 4. According to the dates in Hag 2:18 and Zech 1:7, the temple foundations were (re)laid two months prior to Zechariah's night-visions.[161] This accords with Zech 4:9, which says that "the hands of Zerubbabel have founded—(יִסְּדוּ) *past tense*—the temple." Furthermore, according to Zech 4:7, Zerubbabel will bring out the הָאֶבֶן הָרֹאשָׁה at a future point in time.[162] Thus, the הָאֶבֶן הָרֹאשָׁה cannot be a "foundation deposit" (which was the function of the *libitu maḫrītu* in the *kalû* ritual).[163]

159. For scholars who have pursued this approach, see Petitjean 1969: 251–63; Lipiński 1970; Halpern 1978; Petersen 1974; 1984a: 240–44; Meyers and Meyers 1987: 246–49; Laato 1994.

160. See Hurowitz 1992 for a helpful analysis of more than twenty extra-biblical building accounts, covering Sumerian, Old Babylonian, Assyrian, Neo-Babylonian, Mesopotamian mythology and Northwest Semitic sources. Hurowitz then focuses on 1 Kgs 5–9, and concludes that "this building account…is strikingly similar in its structure to the extra-biblical stories" and that "[t]he same can be said about other biblical building accounts [including]…the restoration of the temple" (1992: 311).

161. Hag 2:18 dates the refounding to the twenty-fourth day of the ninth month (of the second year of Darius—see Hag 2:10). Zech 1:7 is dated to the twenty-fourth day of the eleventh month—i.e. two months later.

162. In order to maintain the *kalû*-inspired interpretation, Laato (1994: 63) re-sequences the passage by breaking it into two separate oracles, with vv. 6–7 uttered prior to the founding ceremony, and vv. 8–10a at some time after. This temporal adjustment is only necessary to support this particular interpretation.

163. This likewise counts against the suggestion that the "great mountain" is the debris from the old temple, since one presumes that this must have cleared away before the laying of the foundation stone.

Moreover, the argument that הָאֶבֶן הָרֹאשָׁה is equivalent to the *libitu maḫrītu* is by no means conclusive. Petersen says that *libitu maḫrītu* ("the first/former brick") is "a semantic parallel to *hāʾeben hāroʾšāh*" (1984: 240). However, this is to prejudge the very issue at hand. Clearly, the words themselves are not linguistic cognates, and so the "semantic parallel" depends on whether one takes רֹאשָׁה as "head" or "first."

The closest intertextual parallel to הָאֶבֶן הָרֹאשָׁה in Zech 4:7 is Ps 118:22, that describes a rejected "stone" (אֶבֶן) becoming "head of the corner" (רֹאשׁ פִּנָּה). The stone in Ps 118:22 is not a "foundation stone" but a "capstone."[164] Taking the stone in Zech 4:7 to be a crucial stone in the last stages of construction also accords with the context, since Zech 4:9 anticipates Zerubbabel's completion of the temple. For this reason, I (tentatively) conclude that the stone in Zech 4:7 is the "top stone."[165]

Zerubbabel will bring out the top stone to sounds of "grace, grace to it" (חֵן חֵן לָהּ). This is an unusual usage of the word חֵן, which in this instance must be taken as an imprecation that Yahweh would bless this stone with special honour.[166]

Zechariah 4:9 promises that Zerubbabel will be the one to complete the temple. The word for "complete" (בצע) in Zech 4:9 is unusual[167]—literally "Zerubbabel's hands will 'finish-off' (תְּבַצַּעְנָה) the temple."[168]

164. The stone identified as the "head of the corner" in Ps 118 is different from the "foundation cornerstone" in Jer 51:26 and Isa 28:16. The latter stones are clearly foundation stones because of the parallelism in their respective contexts. For the argument that רֹאשׁ פִּנָּה in Ps 118 means "capstone," see further Jeremias 1929; 1937; Cahill 1999. See also Derrett (1968), who argues it is a "cornerstone" bridging the top of two walls. Contra McKelvey (1962), who argues that it is a foundation stone; cf. Siegert 2004.

165. So also Baldwin 1972: 121–22; Mason 1977a: 55; Achtemeier 1986: 126; Hurowitz 1992: 261 n. 2.

166. See Ps 84:12 (ET v. 11), for example, for the parallelism between grace (חֵן) and honour (כָּבוֹד). See also Ps 45:3 (ET v. 2) for a connection between grace and blessing. There is perhaps an intertextual echo of the thought of Jer 31:23—"Once more they shall use these words…when I restore their fortunes: 'Yahweh bless you, O abode of righteousness, O holy hill!'"

167. The verb בצע occurs 16 times, typically meaning "cut off" or "finish off." However, Isa 10:12 provides a parallel where the word clearly has the more neutral sense of "finish" (וְהָיָה בְּהַר צִיּוֹן כִּי־יְבַצַּע אֲדֹנָי אֶת־כָּל־מַעֲשֵׂהוּ)—though even in that context it is Yahweh "finishing" his judgment!

168. Elsewhere, this word typically has a negative connotation, but perhaps here it is intended as an ironic reversal of Lam 2:17—"Yahweh has done what he purposed; he has finished (בצע) his word." In the wider context of Zech 1–8, Yahweh has announced a new word—not a message of judgment, but of restoration, and this is what Zerubbabel will "finish" by the completion of the temple. The completion of

Zechariah 4:10 speaks of those who "scorn the day of small things."[169] On the basis of the descriptions in Hag 2:3 and Ezra 3:12, I assume (with most) that this is a reference to the day of the refounding of the temple, when the people were disappointed by the scale and grandeur of the new temple compared to its predecessor.[170] By means of this oracle, Yahweh gives an assurance that these people shall rejoice and that they shall see the "tin-stone" (אֶת־הָאֶבֶן הַבְּדִיל) in the hand of Zerubbabel. Some scholars argue by analogy from ancient Near Eastern building texts that this is another reference to a foundation deposit.[171] However, this view creates sequencing difficulties, since the founding of the temple occurred in the past, while Zech 4:9 anticipates the "tin stone" in Zerubbabel's hand at a future point in time. There are two other main options. Some commentators follow the Vulgate, Targum and LXX, and see the "tin stone" as a weight used in construction (e.g. a plummet).[172] Others follow the Syriac's ܠܟܐܦܐ ܕܦܘܪܫܢܐ ("stone of separation") and repoint הַבְּדִיל so as to derive it from the verb בדל ("separate"), either as a passive participle (הַבָּדִיל)[173] or, by a small emendation of the consonantal text, as the Hiphil infinitive absolute (הַבְדֵּל),[174] to render it as a "stone of separation," perhaps a stone set aside from the old temple to be the capstone for the new.[175] However, on either of these two options, this stone in the hands of Zerubbabel is a sign of the near completion of the temple.

5.4.4. *Zechariah 4:11–14—The Interpretation of the Two Olive Trees*

Zechariah 4:11–14 begins with the prophet Zechariah asking about the significance of the two olive trees in his vision.[176] In the vision, the two

the temple by Zerubbabel will authenticate that "word" now given through the prophet Zechariah.

169. After the verb בוז, the preposition ל denotes the object being "scorned." See. e.g., 2 Kgs 19:21(= Isa 37:22); Job 12:5; Prov 11:12; 13:13; 23:9; Song 8:1. The sense of the combined construction בוז ל is "contempt for."

170. See, e.g., van der Woude 1988: 242. Cf. Beckwith 2004: 72, who lists Ezra 3:12–13; Hag 2:3 and Tobit 14:5 as passages which indicate the disappointment at the beginnings of the Second Temple.

171. See Halpern 1978: 172–73; Petersen 1984a: 244; VanderKam 1991: 566.

172. See, e.g., Mitchell 1912: 191.

173. So Galling 1964b: 144; Bruehler 2001. Bruehler argues (2001: 439) that "*qātîl* forms are often 'adjective(s) used substantivally with a passive meaning to denote duration in a state'" (citing GKC §84.l).

174. So Rudolph 1976: 111 n. 1.

175. See, e.g., Edelman (2005: 125) for the argument that it is a "separated stone" set aside from the original temple.

176. Since Zechariah does not continue to ask about the lampstand, the implication is that what the angel has already said has made the meaning of the lampstand

olive trees stand on either side of the lampstand.[177] Zechariah 4:12 provides additional details, though this verse is notoriously difficult to translate. Literally,

> what are the two stalks of the olive trees (מַה־שְּׁתֵּי שִׁבֲּלֵי הַזֵּיתִים)
> which are in the hand of the two golden pipes (אֲשֶׁר בְּיַד שְׁנֵי צַנְתְּרוֹת הַזָּהָב)[178]
> the ones pouring out the gold from them? (הַמְרִיקִים מֵעֲלֵיהֶם הַזָּהָב)[179]

As with most commentators, I will proceed on the basis that the "gold" in the last clause refers to the colour of the oil from olive trees (in that it is otherwise difficult to make sense of "gold flowing from oil trees"), and that בְּיַד ("in the hand of") in the second clause has an instrumental sense. On this basis, Zech 4:12 describes two olive trees from which come two golden pipes, with golden oil pouring forth. That is, whatever we might make of the details of the verse (and about which I acknowledge some uncertainty) it is clear that the overall picture is of olive trees from which oil pours out. The wider context of the vision (esp. Zech 4:2–3) makes it clear that the oil pours into a bowl which supplies the lamps on the lampstand.

The interpreting angel explains the symbolism of this in Zech 4:14—"These are the two sons of oil" (אֵלֶּה שְׁנֵי בְנֵי־הַיִּצְהָר), "who are standing before the Lord of all the earth" (הָעֹמְדִים עַל־אֲדוֹן כָּל־הָאָרֶץ). There are two key issues which arise in the interpretation of this verse.

sufficiently clear. This further reinforces the conclusion above that the function of Zech 4:6–10b is to explain that the temple is the lampstand.

177. The locations of the trees are "upon the right" (עַל־יְמִין) and "upon its left" (וְעַל־שְׂמֹאולָהּ). However, the use of the preposition עַל does not mean that the olive trees are "above" the lampstand. The context does not warrant that עַל be given locative sense of "above." It is clear from the parallel description of the olive trees in Zech 4:3 (מִימִין הַגֻּלָּה וְאֶחָד עַל־שְׂמֹאלָהּ׃) that עַל־יְמִין and מִימִין are synonymous (and מִימִין has the normal sense of "at the right"). In the wider context, the same expression in Zech 3:1 cannot mean "above," in that this would imply that Joshua is standing *above* the Satan.

178. The word צַנְתְּרוֹת is a *hapax*, but typically presumed to be related to צִנּוֹר "pipe, spout, conduit" (which itself is only found in 2 Sam 5:8, referring to the water conduit into Jerusalem) and Ps 42:8 (Yahweh's water-spouts). Wolters argues that this derivation of "pipes" from צַנְתְּרוֹת is dubious, and instead suggests the meaning "oil pressers" (2000: 94). In his rendering, Zech 4:12 describes "streaming olive twigs which are in the hands of the olive pressers" (2000: 111–13). For the present purposes, either meaning leads to much the same result, in as much that on either approach, the function of the olive trees is to provide oil to the lampstand.

179. Though מֵעַל can mean "above" or "up from" (e.g. Gen 1:4; 17:22), it can also mean simply "from" (see, e.g., Gen 13:11), which is a better rendering in the present context (especially given the conclusions in n. 177 about the meaning of עַל in Zech 4:11).

First, what does the phrase "the two sons of oil" signify? Most translations give this phrase a "messianic" significance by rendering it "the two anointed ones."[180] However, there are good reasons for not translating this phrase as "anointed."

Rose (2000: 188–94) has argued that the word for "oil" (יִצְהָר) is the wrong word to use for "anointing oil," which is always שֶׁמֶן.[181] This argument from vocabulary is perhaps not as strong as Rose suggests,[182] but I grant that it is one indication against the translation "anointed." However, a stronger argument against the "anointed" interpretation is that the direction of flow of oil is the wrong way around—those who are "anointed" receive oil, whereas in Zech 4, it is clear that the function of the olive trees is to give oil.[183] It is perhaps this very implication which has encouraged some commentators to adopt the "anointed" interpretation, so as to avoid the implication that Yahweh is reliant on human beings for "oil supply." For example, Rudolph argues (1976: 109) that it is blasphemous to suggest that the two sons of oil feed and fortify Yahweh.[184] We shall return to this issue below when I offer an explanation of what it is that the two sons of oil do. For the present purposes, however, we should note that the clear implication of Zech 4:12 is that the olive trees pour out oil, rather than receive it. This must shape our reading of Zech 4:14.[185]

For these reasons, I conclude that the phrase should be translated "the two sons of oil,"[186] and that their function (in the manner explained below) is to provide oil to the lampstand.

180. So RSV, NASB, JPS, ESV, and cf. NIV "two who are anointed."

181. See similarly van der Woude 1974: 264; Tollington 1993: 177; Boda 2001: §3.3.1.1.

182. As noted above in the comments on the olive trees in Zech 4:3, a key intertext of the oil/lampstand imagery is the phrase "pure oil of beaten olive for the lamp" (שֶׁמֶן זַיִת זָךְ כָּתִית לַמָּאוֹר) in Exod 27:20 (// Lev 24:2). That is, the word for lamp oil is שֶׁמֶן, and by implication, the sons of "oil" (יִצְהָר) in Zech 4:14 are providing שֶׁמֶן to the lamp. If this is the case, then this is the same type of oil used for anointing (also שֶׁמֶן), which means that there is no qualitative difference between "anointing oil" and "lamp oil."

183. See Boda 2001: §3.3.1.1. See also Seybold (1974a: 66–67) who argues that the significance of the olive trees is that they provide oil to the lamp. Niditch (1983: 87) argues that the oil connects to both the temple cult and anointing.

184. See similarly van der Woude 1974: 266.

185. It is interesting to note that Rudolph excises Zech 4:12 as a secondary addition, which has the effect of removing the apparent "blasphemy" of human beings supplying "oil" to Yahweh.

186. So also van der Woude 1974: 265.

The second key issue is: Who are the "two sons of oil" who "stand before the Lord"? Most commentators identify these two figures as Joshua and Zerubbabel.[187] However, Boda has questioned this identification, arguing from 1 Kgs 22:19 that the phrase "standing before (עמד…על) Yahweh" denotes a prophetic role (Boda 2001: §3.3.1.2). On this basis, Boda identifies Haggai and Zechariah as the "two sons of oil."[188]

Boda's argument relies on the particular significance to the use of the preposition עַל, without allowing for the fact that עַל is elsewhere used in Zech 1–8 in peculiar ways.[189] As noted by Ehrensvärd (2003: 180), Zech 6:5 uses the expression הִתְיַצֵּב עַל ("to present themselves *before*") where we might have expected to find the more usual combination הִתְיַצֵּב לִפְנֵי.[190] Clearly, there is no semantic distinction between the two phrases. Similarly, in Zech 3:1, the Satan is "standing at (the) right" (עֹמֵד עַל־יְמִינוֹ) of Joshua, where there is no special significance to the preposition עַל. In context, the phrase הָעֹמְדִים עַל־אֲדוֹן in Zech 4:14 clearly

187. See, e.g., Mitchell 1912: 165; Rignell 1950: 171; Wellhausen 1963: 182; Elliger 1963: 111; Galling 1964b: 137; Wallis 1972; van der Woude 1974: 95; Mason 1977a: 48; Petersen 1984a: 231; Smith 1984: 205; Tollington 1993: 176–77; Hanhart 1998: 289–302; Floyd 2000: 387. Cf. Rose (2000: 177–207) who argues that it refers to a future high priest and forthcoming messianic "Sprout," and Delkurt (2000: 213–20) who argues that the "two" figures are Judah and Israel.

188. Boda's argument claims more than the evidence permits. If, as he argues, 1 Kgs 22:19 should be determinative of what the construction "standing" (עמד) "by" (עַל) must always mean, then it is only the angelic hosts who "stand by" Yahweh. On Boda's own evidence, there is no instance where this combination of words is used of a prophet. It is only by extension that Boda is able to bring in the prophetic role, arguing that "Micaiah had access to this scene." On the role of prophet and the divine council, see further Nissinen 2002. Boda's use of the example of Micaiah shifts the grounds of argument, in that the focus is no longer on the specific construction עמד + עַל, but rather the inference that עמד + עַל implies access to the heavenly council. Boda (2001: §3.3.1.2) makes the claims that "the prophet was the one human allowed into this privileged position." However, the exclusivity of this claim cannot be sustained. Clearly, there are other humans who are granted access to the heavenly council. In the context of the book of Zechariah, there is an obvious example in Zech 3. In Zech 3:1, Joshua "stands before" (עֹמֵד לִפְנֵי) the angel of Yahweh (who speaks as Yahweh himself in Zech 3:2). Moreover, in Zech 3:7, Joshua is promised access among "those who stand here" (הָעֹמְדִים הָאֵלֶּה). Thus, it is not only prophets who have access to the heavenly council (if indeed that is what עמד + עַל implies).

189. See, e.g., the discussion above in relation to the phrase עַל־יָמִין (n. 177) and מֵעֲלֵיהֶם (n. 179).

190. See, e.g., Exod 8:15; 9:13; Deut 9:2; Josh 24:1; 1 Sam 10:19. The form of the phrase found in Zech 6:5 (הִתְיַצֵּב עַל) is also found in Job 1:6; 2:1 (×2). See further my argument below in §6.4 that Zech 6:5 alludes to Job 1–2 at this point.

denotes those who are "standing before" Yahweh.[191] Accordingly, in order to determine what this means we might validly look at phrases which are *semantically* equivalent to this (whether or not they use the word עַל). The *concept* of "standing before Yahweh" has both a long history and definite meaning (though expressed in a variety of forms). For example,

Deut 18:7	he ministers in the name of Yahweh...like all his fellow Levites who stand there before Yahweh (העמדים שם לפני יהוה)
Ps 134:1	all the servants of Yahweh, who stand in the house of Yahweh (העמדים בבית־יהוה)
Neh 12:44	the Levites who minister (= "stand," העמדים)

From the parallelism of these verses, we may conclude that "standing before Yahweh" is idiomatic for "serving Yahweh."[192] Thus, what is being promised is *not* (per Boda) that the "two sons of oil" will have access to the divine council, but rather that they are servants of Yahweh.

In the context of the book of Zechariah, it is clear that these two individuals must be Joshua and Zerubbabel, since they are the only two individuals so described elsewhere in Zech 1–8.[193] Joshua is the subject of Zech 3, and Zerubbabel is explicitly named as the temple builder in the oracle of 4:6–10 (and, as I have argued above, is the "Branch" of 6:9–15). Elsewhere, both Joshua and Zerubbabel are promised roles in which they *serve* Yahweh (Joshua in serving as high priest—see Zech 3:7, and Zerubbabel as "my *servant* the Branch"—see Zech 3:8).

In what sense, then, do Zerubbabel and Joshua "serve Yahweh"? (Or, to put the question in the symbolic language of the vision: How do these two olive trees provide oil to the lampstand?) If we recall the earlier conclusion that the lampstand symbolizes the temple, then the answer is that the Zerubbabel and Joshua do this by their service to and in the

191. The parallel with Zech 6:5 is again instructive. Zech 6:5 reads הִתְיַצֵּב עַל־אֲדוֹן כָּל־הָאָרֶץ ("presenting themselves before the Lord of all the earth") where עַל stands in place of the expected לִפְנֵי. Similarly, Zech 4:14 has a very similar phrase, הָעֹמְדִים עַל־אֲדוֹן כָּל־הָאָרֶץ, which I argue should be translated "those standing before the Lord of all the earth."

192. In addition, we might also add another line of evidence. Those who "stand before" a human king are his servants (see Judg 3:19; 1 Kgs 12:8).

193. This point weighs heavily against Boda's interpretation. If Zechariah and Haggai were the two sons of oil, it is difficult to see how Zechariah's readers could have come to this conclusion, since Haggai is not mentioned by name, and only obliquely referred to once in Zech 8:9. For similar reasons, I also reject the suggestion of Barker (1977) that the two figures are Joshua and a rival priest.

temple. Zerubbabel "provides oil" to the temple through his role in building it, and Joshua "provides oil" through his role as high priest in the temple. This interpretation is not open to the "blasphemy" objection as raised by Rudolph (as noted above), in that it is Yahweh's house (rather than Yahweh himself) receiving the "oil" from the olive trees.

This conclusion—that Zerubbabel and Joshua are the sons of oil through their service to Yahweh's house—is not dissimilar to that argued by Rost more than half a century ago, who argued that the lampstand symbolized the temple, and that the oil was the cult in the temple:

> Aber, könnte man nun einwenden, sollten wirklich die Lampen als Augen Jahwes auf den Dienst der beiden Männer Zerubbabel und Josua angewiesen sein ? Sollte der Bau des Tempels und die Einrichtung und Durchführung des Kults wirklich nötig sein, um die Leuchtkraft der Augen Jahwes zu sichern? Es scheint mir unausweichlich zu sein, dies als Meinung des Sacharja herauszustellen. (1951: 220)

5.5. *Drawing the Threads Together*

The argument of this chapter is that Zech 3, Zech 4 and Zech 6:9–15 are mutually interpreting when read against a number of identifiable intertexts.

The key theme which connects these three passages and their intertexts is the theme of "restoration." The interwoven message is of a restored priesthood (Zech 3), a restored temple (Zech 4) and a restored Davidic line (Zech 6:9–15).

Many commentators wish to read these passages as describing "something new"—whether that be an emergent political "diarchy" between king and priest,[194] or the historical ascendancy of the priesthood over the monarchy,[195] or perhaps even a (later) redactional transference of power from monarchy to priesthood.[196] In contrast, the intertexts of these passages suggest that what is being promised is not something "new" but a restoration of a previous ideal, which had been lost as a consequence of the exile.

194. So Petersen 1984a: 234; Meyers and Meyers 1987: 276; Mason 1998: 348–49; Tollington 1993: 175.

195. See, for example, Hanson, who regards Zechariah as documenting the "expand[ing] authority of the Zadokite priests so as to encompass areas earlier controlled by prophets and kings. The history of the growth and transmission of the book of Zechariah thus gives us a glimpse of the development of the Jewish community from a diarchy under a Davidic prince and a Zadokite priest to a hierocracy under a Zadokite functioning as high priest" (Hanson 1987b: 498).

196. So Beuken, see §5.3.4 above.

The intertexts of Zech 3 demonstrate that the high priest Joshua is being promised a restoration of the proper prerogatives of the priesthood (governing Yahweh's courts, ministering before Yahweh etc.) and his re-clothing is not in "royal" robes and turban but rather in the regalia of a high priest. The key intertexts for Zech 3 are various "priestly" texts (esp. Exod 28–29; Lev 8; 16; Ezek 40:46; 44:17–19) combined with corruption and purification imagery from Amos 4 and Isa 6. The message of Zech 3 is of the restoration of a priesthood which has been stained by sin and exile, again giving a hope for a future day (probably the first Day of Atonement after the completion of the temple) when the sins of all the people of the land can again be dealt with. Furthermore, in Zech 3:8–10 the recommissioning of the priesthood is a proleptic sign that the "Branch" (the temple builder) is going to come and complete his task, in that a priesthood requires an operative temple. A restored priesthood is a promissory sign of a restored temple.

This theme of a restored temple is taken up in Zech 4, in a vision of a lampstand (temple) with seven lamps. The light from these lamps is identified with the seven eyes of Yahweh which rove throughout the world. The key intertexts for Zech 4 are various passages in Exodus, Leviticus and Numbers which explain the significance of the lampstand and its (olive) oil, and the passages which explain the significance of "standing before Yahweh." The message of Zech 4 develops the promise of the preceding night-visions (see esp. Zech 1:16; 2:14; cf. 8:3) of Yahweh's return to dwell in Jerusalem in the rebuilt temple. The vision, with its "operative" lampstand, depicts the time when there will be an "operative" temple in which Yahweh is present. Thus the message of the vision is a word of assurance that the temple will indeed be completed. The "inserted" oracle to Zerubbabel makes exactly the same point. Though initially jarring to the reader, this oracle is in fact congruent with the message of the chapter. At the point at which we as readers are expecting the answer to the question "What is the lampstand?," we are given an oracle of reassurance that Zerubbabel will complete the temple. By means of this juxtaposition, the implicit answer to the question is given—the lampstand is the completed temple. The remaining verses in Zech 4 explain the two olive trees. Zerubbabel and Joshua together are the "two sons of oil." This is not a messianic designation, but rather an acknowledgement of their role in serving Yahweh in and through the restoration of the temple and its cultus.

In Zech 6:9–15 the restoration of the Davidic line is promised. The key intertexts of this passage are 2 Sam 7, on the "messianic" significance of the builder of Yahweh's temple, and Jer 22, 23 and 33, which describe the termination of the Davidic line in the person of Jehoiachin (Jer 22) and the promise of a future restoration by the "Branch" (Jer 23), working in harmony with a (restored) Levitical priesthood (Jer 33). In Zech 6:9–15, the temple-builder—Zerubbabel—is given this messianic appellation because he is the beginning of fulfilment of the promise of Jer 23/33. The time of rejection of Jehoiachin and his (immediate) offspring has ended, and a new hope for the Davidic line has been restored. The message of Zech 6:9–15 parallels the declaration of Haggai that Zerubbabel will be Yahweh's signet ring (Hag 2:23, reversing the rejection of Jehoiachin in Jer 22:24).

From what we may legitimately infer from history, the three specific promises given about the "Branch" in Zech 6:9–15—that he would come "from his place," that he would build the temple, and that he would sit on his seat and rule—were all fulfilled in the person of Zerubbabel.[197] In these chapters, Zechariah announces Yahweh's intention to restore the priesthood (Zech 3), the temple (Zech 4) and the Davidic line (Zech 6:9–15).

197. As indicated above, I infer that Zerubbabel was the (unnamed) "governor of the Jews" in Ezra 6:7 who returned to Jerusalem under royal sanction from Darius to rebuild the temple, and that Zerubbabel continued to rule (as governor) over Jerusalem for some time after this. As noted by Floyd (2006b: 271–73), most modern interpreters have held that Zechariah had promised something more than this—that Zerubbabel would be king, and that there was widespread disappointment because this prophecy has "failed." Floyd questions whether this dominant view is a valid reading of the evidence of the text, or merely a projection of a "disappointment theory" which owes more to anti-Semitism/anti-Judaism than it does to biblical scholarship.

Chapter 6

Zechariah 5:1–6:8

6.1. *Introduction*

In the previous chapters we have seen the benefit of an intertextual approach to Zech 1–8. We have seen how the various identified "intertexts" have both clarified and added layers of meaning to our understanding of Zechariah's message. However, others have claimed that an "intertextual" approach to Zech 1–8 must necessarily produce multiple, competing meanings, which ultimately cannot be resolved, resulting in a text of indeterminate meaning.[1] I will examine this issue in the present chapter in relation to the visions in Zech 5–6. The final three night-visions contain imagery which is, on any analysis, bizarre. The strangeness of this imagery has generated a plethora of interpretations. If ever there were passages where the intertexts could lead us into interpretive confusion, it would be these. However, we shall see that, instead of creating a confusing plurality of meanings, the intertexts of these visions help to limit and clarify the interpretive options, even if they do not offer complete interpretive certainty.

My rationale for treating the last three night-visions together is that they share a common direction of movement—"going out" (יצא). Zechariah 5:1–4 describes a flying scroll containing "the curse which is *going out*" (הָאָלָה הַיּוֹצֵאת), 5:5–11 describes "the ephah which is *going out*" (הָאֵיפָה הַיּוֹצֵאת), and 6:1–8 describes "four chariots *going out*" (אַרְבַּע מַרְכָּבוֹת יֹצְאוֹת).[2] Neither the use of this verb, nor an "outwards" direction of movement, is paralleled in the preceding night visions.[3] The focus of

1. See Love 1999. Love argues that Zech 1–8 frequently appears to suggest intertextual sources for discerning its meaning, but then fails to provide this promised cessation of the signifying chain when the significance of the suggested "key" to decipherment is considered. Love maintains that Zech 1–8 leaves us with a "metaphor stew" (1999: 137). He argues that the intertexts in Zech 1–8 help to create an "evasive" text which defies attempts to wrest meaning from it.

2. This is also noted by Floyd 2000: 329.

3. It should be noted that the first vision does not describe horses going out into the world, but rather the return of the horses once they have completed their mission.

the earlier visions is oriented towards Jerusalem: visions 1–3 express Yahweh's intention to return to Jerusalem to dwell there, and to overthrow the "horns" so that his people can flee from "Babylon" (back to Zion). Similarly, visions 4–5 describe events which are centred on Jerusalem—Yahweh's renovation of the priesthood and promised reconstruction of the temple. In contrast to the first five night-visions, which are directed towards or in Jerusalem, the final three night-visions are directed outwards, suggesting that these three night-visions are together describing the outworking of the first five night-visions: Yahweh's return *to Jerusalem* will mean the rooting out of perjury and theft (5:1–4), the departure of the "wickedness" of the woman in the ephah (5:5–11), and the going out of Yahweh's chariots into all the world (6:1–8).

6.2. *Zechariah 5:1–4—The Flying Scroll*

The fact that the crimes of "false swearing" (שׁבע...לַשֶּׁקֶר) and "stealing" (גנב) are emphasized in both v. 3 and v. 4 suggests that this combination might be a good place to begin our search for possible intertextual connections.

There are several other passages where these words or their synonyms appear in combination. These parallels are shown in the following table:

Zech 5:4	הגנב ו...הנשבע בשמי לשקר	*The thief and...the one swearing falsely in my name.*
Jer 7:9	הגנב רצח ונאף והשבע לשקר	Will you *steal*, murder, commit adultery, *swear falsely*...
Lev 19:11–12	לא תגנבו ולא־תכחשו ולא־תשקרו איש בעמיתו ולא־תשבעו בשמי לשקר	You shall not *steal*; you shall not deal falsely, and you shall not lie to one another, and you shall not *swear falsely in my name*
Exod 20:15–16	לא תגנב לא־תענה ברעך עד שקר	You shall not *steal* You shall not *bear false witness* against your neighbour
Deut 5:18–19	ולא תגנב ולא־תענה ברעך עד שוא	And you shall not *steal* And you shall not *bear false witness* against your neighbour
Hos 4:2	אלה וכחש ורצח וגנב	Swearing and *lying* and murder, and *stealing*...
Hos 7:1	פעלו שקר וגנב יבוא	They deal *falsely* and the *thief* enters in...

Jeremiah 7:9 is the only other place where these words are used in the same verse. In Lev 19 the words are in contiguous verses, and Lev 19 also shares in common the word בִּשְׁמִי ("in my name"), which is not

present in Jer 7:9. Stealing and false witness also occur beside each other in the Decalogue, and in Hosea in lists of unethical behaviour, though using some different vocabulary to Zech 5:4.

A number of commentators have argued for a primary connection between Zech 5:3–4 and the Decalogue. For example, Petersen argues:

> These two forms of infractions, reformulated as they seem to have been by Zechariah, represent the major parts of the Decalogue; swearing falsely by Yahweh's name counts as a violation against the deity, whereas stealing represents a violation of the social order. These two cases are significant because they represent the two basic forms of infraction included in the Decalogue, crimes against Yahweh and crimes against humanity. (1984a: 252)[4]

Similarly, Meyers and Meyers argue that Zechariah is "citing the decalogue" (1987: 284). A significant number of commentators understand the contents of the scroll as in some way related to Israel's covenantal obligations imposed by the law.[5]

Delkurt is critical of those who regard Zech 5:3–4 as a summary of the Decalogue. He argues—contra Petersen—that the kind of activity implied by "false swearing" (שׁבע...לַשָּׁקֶר) is not related to the third commandment ("bearing Yahweh's name in vain"), but to the ninth commandment ("false witness"), and as such, Zechariah's scroll relates only to commands in the second table of the ten commandments, and so cannot be a "summary" of the whole (1999b: 197). Moreover, Delkurt also objects to the more general argument, as expressed for example in Meyers and Meyers, that Zechariah is "citing" any part of the Decalogue, on the grounds that the words used in Zech 5 deviate substantially from the words used in the Decalogue (in either form), which counts against the assumption of quotation (1999b: 198). Instead, he draws attention to the fact that both Jer 7:9 and Lev 19:11–12 have much closer vocabulaic connections to Zech 5:3–4, and so are more likely to be its source. Delkurt discounts Lev 19 from consideration, on the grounds that he regards it as a post-exilic text which postdates Zech 5,[6] and concludes therefore that Jer 7 is the source behind Zech 5.

4. Rignell (1950: 186), Hanhart (1998: 340–50) and Floyd (2000: 389) similarly relate the two crimes to the two "tables" of the Decalogue.

5. See, e.g., Floyd 1996: 57: "The torah scroll contains covenantal norms that serve as a basis for the newly emerging Jewish communal identity." See similarly Conrad 1999: 114: "The social infractions of stealing and swearing falsely echo stipulations of the decalogue." Also Mitchell 1912: 169: "…the two tables of the covenant…" Cf. Baldwin 1972: 127 and Smith 1984: 208.

6. Delkurt's argument (see 1999b: 200–203) is that Hos 4:2 and Jer 7:9 are the source for both the Decalogue and the holiness code. Since Wellhausen, there has

In common with Delkurt, I agree that Jer 7 is the primary intertext for the thief and false-swearer in Zech 5:1–4, both on the basis of the similarities in lexical form, and because of the connections with Jer 7 elsewhere in Zechariah.[7] However, in contrast to Delkurt's "exclusive dependency" approach, I also recognize connections with the Decalogue, as well as with Lev 19. That is, where Delkurt is arguing "either/or," I am arguing for a "both/and" approach.

I recognize that there are polarized positions on the relative priority of Decalogue and the Prophets. For example, Delkurt argues that Hos 4:2 and Jer 7:9 are the source for the Decalogue prohibitions, whereas Weiss (1990: 67–68) and Miller (1989: 235) argue precisely the opposite—that Hos 4 and Jer 7 reveal traces of the Decalogue—on exactly the same evidence. This diversity is a reflection of different positions on the dating of the Decalogue (and perhaps also some now-questionable assumptions about the inferiority of "law" to the prophets). While some scholars regard the entire Decalogue as a late creation,[8] and others regard the entirety as early, a majority would recognize an original core, while allowing for the possibility of (post-)exilic expansion.[9] Since the Decalogue's stipulations about stealing and false witness are clearly not commandments which have undergone "expansion," there is no necessary reason to date them to a late period. Thus it is not unreasonable to proceed on the basis that the author of Zech 5 is aware of the Decalogue prohibitions against theft and false swearing.

The position which I seek to defend is that Zech 5:1–4 contains a primary allusion to Jer 7, but this has been nuanced by secondary allusions, in particular to the Decalogue. My reason for making this secondary connection is based on the similarities between Zech 5:3 and the form of the third commandment. In Exod 20:7 (and likewise Deut 5:11), the prohibition against bearing Yahweh's name in vain concludes

been a long running assumption of the priority of the prophets over the law, and Delkurt continues this trend. However, his argument cannot be supported by the evidence that he cites. Even if one might accept Delkurt's opening assertion that the final form of the Holiness Code in Lev 19 is a late development (1999b: 201), this still leaves open the question of the dates of the individual elements of Lev 19. I shall develop this point below.

7. See my comments in the next chapter on the sustained allusion between Jer 7 and Zech 7.

8. Recent examples of scholars arguing for a late creation of the Decalogue include Himbaza (2004), who regards the Decalogue as a postexilic summary of older books of law, and Lang (2003), who argues for the creation of the Decalogue in three stages, commencing in the exilic period.

9. See, e.g., Greenberg 1990: 110.

"Yahweh will not acquit…" (לֹא יְנַקֶּה). The same verb (נקה) is used twice in Zech 5:3, and not otherwise in any of the other passages listed above as possible intertexts. Zechariah 5 and the Decalogue thus share common vocabulary, the combination of which is very rare: the verb נקה used in connection with false witness is only otherwise found in Prov 19:5–9. While there is some debate as to the precise meaning of נקה in Zech 5:3,[10] it would seem clear from context that the word must at least have a neutral sense (i.e. the thief will be *adjudged* according to the scroll) if not a negative sense (i.e. the thief will be *purged out* on the basis of the scroll), which is an inversion (perhaps here done with deliberate irony)[11] of the way the word is being used in its positive sense ("acquitted") in the Decalogue. The use of this shared vocabulary in this way adds weight to the argument that Zech 5:3 is framed in order to recall the Decalogue. In addition, I also suggest that Zech 5:4 alludes to Lev 19 as well, on the basis of the close echo of the phrase "swearing falsely in my name." We can best explain all the particularities of the crimes listed in Zech 5:3–4 by recognizing it as a composite allusion to Jer 7; Exod 20/Deut 5 and Lev 19. No single intertext can account for all the distinct phraseology in Zech 5:3–4, but taken together, they all do. In Zech 5:3–4 we do not have merely one allusion, but a complex re-use of various streams of tradition, woven together.

I suggest that Zech 5:3–4 has been framed in such a way as to recall what Yahweh has already said before—as expressed in both the Law and

10. In terms of grammatical form, נִקָּה might either be a Niphal or Piel. According to *HALOT*, the נקה in Piel means "to leave unpunished," or "to declare to be free from punishment" (i.e. to acquit), and clearly this is the sense in which it is used in the Decalogue. However, if this sense were applied to Zech 5:3, then the thief and perjurer are "acquitted" by the flying scroll, which is at odds with the destruction of their houses in the next verse. Though Meyers and Meyers attempt to offer an interpretation which seeks to sustain this meaning (see 1987: 286), ultimately their argument is less convincing than the typical interpretation that comes from reading נִקָּה as a Niphal.

According to BDB, נקה in the Niphal can mean "cleaned out" or "purged out." BDB cites Isa 3:26 and Zech 5:3 as instances of this usage. (*HALOT* recognizes this sense in Isa 3:26 and 1QIsa 65:3, but emends the text of Zech 5:3 to turn it into an interrogative—instead of מִזֶּה כָּמוֹהָ נִקָּה, "from this, according to it they will be purged out," the text would then become מִי זֶה כָּמוֹהָ נִקָּה. This produces an awkward sentence—literally, "[the thief] who is this according to it will be acquitted?"). I submit that the sense of the Niphal attested in Isa 3:26 (and 1QIsa 65:3) is to be preferred for Zech 5:3 as well, since it does not require this awkward emendation.

11. For an example of an ironic inversion, see Jer 34:17, which states that because of the failure of the people "to proclaim freedom" (לִקְרֹא דְרוֹר) for each other, Yahweh will proclaim "freedom" for them—freedom to (die by) the sword etc.

the Prophets—about theft and perjury. I take it that these particular crimes are listed in Zech 5 because they represent, as they do in Jer 7 and Hosea, typical examples of breaches of the ethical demands of Yahweh's covenant law. The flying scroll in Zech 5:1–4 demonstrates that these ethical standards—as expounded and applied at an earlier stage of Israel's history—will continue to apply, and be enforced by Yahweh, in the midst of the post-exilic community.

6.2.1. *The Curse-Bearing Scroll*

The nature of this vision can be further elucidated by other background texts which make sense of this curse-bearing scroll. The word for scroll in Zech 5:1–2 (מְגִלָּה) occurs only otherwise in Jer 36 (×14); Ezek 2–3 (×4) and Ps 40:8 (ET 40:7).[12] Whether or not we may legitimately draw a direct connection between Zechariah's flying scroll and the scroll of Yahweh's words consumed by the prophet in Ezek 2–3, and/or Jeremiah's scroll containing "all Yahweh's words" in Jer 36, these antecedent texts would suggest, as a minimum, that the מְגִלָּה in Zech 5 contains Yahweh's words in written form (the full expression is typically "a scroll of writing," מְגִלַּת־סֵפֶר).

In addition, Zech 5:2 says of the flying scroll "This is the curse…" (זֹאת הָאָלָה). When one searches for other biblical texts for a *written* "curse" (אָלָה), there are two types of passages which might be possible intertexts of Zech 5.

The first is Deut 29:19 (ET 29:20), which refers to "every curse written in this book" (כָּל־הָאָלָה הַכְּתוּבָה בַּסֵּפֶר). This verse comes within the wider context of Deut 28–30, which describes the curses for covenant malfeasance (and the blessings for covenant obedience). I take it that Jer 11:1–8; Dan 9:11 and 2 Chr 34:24 are all further instances of this kind of a written curse, stemming from Yahweh's covenant law, as expressed in Deut 29. I shall use the label "curses of the covenant" as a shorthand way of referring to this type of written curse.

The second type of written curse is instanced in Num 5, which relates to a woman accused of adultery. In Num 5, the priest directs the woman to pronounce curses upon herself should she have committed adultery (Num 5:19–21), and then puts these curses in writing, washes off the curses with the "water of bitterness," and then makes the woman drink the water which now contains the curse (Num 5:23–24). We might describe this as "curses for false oaths of acquittal." Rudman argues that this second kind of curse lies behind Zech 5:1–4:

12. On this, see further Freedman 1990: 42–43.

> In such cases where an oath of innocence is involved, a false declaration of innocence theoretically leads to the activation of the attendant curses (אלת/אלה) which the accused has called down on his/herself [*sic*]. This would appear to be the situation envisioned in Zech 5,3. (Rudman 2000: 198)

However, I regard it as unlikely that this second kind of a curse underlies Zech 5:1–4. While Num 5 shares the themes of "curse" and "oath," there is no reference to theft, which is the other specific crime identified in Zech 5. Rudman's analysis attempts to address this problem by combining the two sins into one—"the perjured thief" (2000: 199)—positing a situation in which a thief (rather than an adulterous woman) has sworn an oath before a priest falsely declaring his innocence (see 2000: 197). However, if this were the case, then it does not explain why Zech 5 should specifically describe a penalty for the thief, since (on this analysis) the curse is attached only to the perjury. Moreover, the curse in Num 5 is not directly borne by the scroll (as it is in Zech 5) but by the water which the woman consumes. For these reasons, Rudman's argument that Zech 5 is a curse of this second type is not compelling.

Instead, we may conclude that the flying scroll in Zech 5:1–4 is a vivid representation of the "curses of the covenant." This allusion must surely have taken on a special poignancy for that early post-exilic generation who understood the exile to have been the outworking of the Deuteronomic curses of the covenant, in that it graphically shows the post-exilic generation that the kind of curses listed in Deut 28–30 will continue to apply for covenant law breakers in their day.[13]

In Zech 5, the power of this covenant curse is given a dramatic edge by a secondary allusion to the events of the Passover. In Zech 5:3–4, the curse goes out (יצא) "over all the land"[14] (עַל־פְּנֵי כָל־הָאָרֶץ)[15] and enters

13. In the next chapter I shall demonstrate that there are a number of other allusions to the "covenantal" themes in Deut 28–30. These allusions strengthen the case for an allusion to Deut 29:1 in the present instance.

14. Petersen (1984a: 249) argues for the translation "all the earth" rather than "all the land," arguing that that this phrase is used elsewhere in Zech 1–8 in the wider sense. However, the evidence is more ambiguous than Petersen's argument allows. Granted, in Zech 1 and 6—when referring to the ambit of the heavenly horses—the phrase clearly means "earth" (as Petersen notes). However, in Zech 5:6, the same phrase is used to refer to "the iniquity *in all the land*." This land is contrasted with the "land of Shinar" (Zech 5:11), where the iniquity is to be deposited, which strongly suggests that the use of כָל־הָאָרֶץ in Zech 5:6 is referring to iniquity in the land of Judah. Similarly, in Zech 3:9, the removal of the guilt of "this land" (הָאָרֶץ־הַהִיא) clearly refers to Judah. That being so, there is no overriding pattern to the usage of the phrase כָל־הָאָרֶץ in Zech 1–8 which determines *a priori* whether it should be rendered "land" or "earth." This translation decision must be resolved by

into the house (וּבָאָה אֶל־בֵּית) of the thief and the perjurer, in order to destroy. The language and imagery used is strongly reminiscent of that used to describe the first Passover in Exod 11–12:

Passover (Exod 11–12)	*Zech 5:3–4*
Yahweh will "go out" (יצא) in the midst "of all the land of Egypt" (בְּכָל־אֶרֶץ מִצְרָיִם) (Exod 11:4–6)	the curse "goes out" (יצא) "over all the land" (עַל־פְּנֵי כָל־הָאָרֶץ)
The destroyer will not "*enter your house* to strike" (לָבֹא אֶל־בָּתֵּיכֶם) (Exod 12:23)	...*enters into the house* (וּבָאָה אֶל־בֵּית)...to consume it.

This allusion to the Passover calls to mind Yahweh's power to carry out that which he had promised to do.[16] The implication is that Yahweh himself will enact the curses of his covenant, with all the inescapability of the Passover event.

A number of the phrases in Zech 5:3–4 are suggestive of further allusion, but, because of overlapping possibilities, it is difficult to come to a definitive conclusion. The destruction of "both its timbers and stones" (וְאֶת־עֵצָיו וְאֶת־אֲבָנָיו) in Zech 5:4 might point to Ezek 26:12—"houses destroyed...*stones and timbers* (וַאֲבָנַיִךְ וְעֵצַיִךְ)...," in which case it is simply a metaphor for complete destruction.[17] However, as Rudman (2000: 199) has noted, this phrase is also similar to Num 14:45, which describes what a priest must do when he finds a house infected by a leprous disease—"He shall tear down the house, both its stones and its timbers" (וְנָתַץ אֶת־הַבַּיִת אֶת־אֲבָנָיו וְאֶת־עֵצָיו). While it is tempting to argue for an intertextual connection with Num 14 (with the implication

the immediate context. In the context of Zech 5:1–4, the application of the covenant law is presumably limited to the people of Yahweh, which suggests that "land" is the better translation (so also Baldwin 1972: 126–27), rather than, as Petersen has it, a covenant which goes across the whole "earth," but only operates on Judahites, whether they happen to be in Syria-Palestine or in the Diaspora. Furthermore, the intertextual parallels with Exod 11–12 (see below) are also suggestive of the narrower interpretation.

15. The phrase "upon the face of the land" (עַל־פְּנֵי כָל־הָאָרֶץ) is common in Genesis (see, e.g., Gen 1:29; 7:3; 8:9; 11:4, 8, 9; 41:56) to refer to events affecting the whole land/earth. The phrase is similarly used in Deut 11:26–28; 1 Sam 30:16; 2 Sam 18:8; Dan 8:5.

16. I have elsewhere detected an intertextual connection between Zech 2:13 (ET 2:9) and the Exodus tradition, with respect to the theme of the former slaves "plundering the Egyptians" (see §4.6.2 above). This intertextual connection to Exod 12 increases the likelihood of an allusion here.

17. And see also Hab 2:11–12: "The stones of the wall will cry out, and the beams of the woodwork will echo it. Woe to him who builds a city with bloodshed and establishes a town by crime!" This gains weight in light of the allusions to Hab 2 in Zech 1–2 (see §4.6.4).

that Zech 5 is nuanced by overtones of "uncleanness," whereby theft and perjury have defiled the land like a disease and must be "purged"), I concede that the evidence for a connection to Num 14 is not compelling, and must remain merely a tantalizing possibility.

Similarly, there are several passages which might be the source of the language of a curse which "consumes" (כלה) in Zech 5:4, the most likely being Deut 28:21 (a pestilence that "consumes"), and Jer 5:2–3 (Yahweh "consumes" those who swear falsely).[18] However, the most we can say is that these are all "possible" (or suggestive) intertexts.

In summary, the clear intertexts of Zech 5:1–4 give us a firm basis to conclude that the flying scroll is a representation of Yahweh's covenant law, as reflected in both the Law and the Prophets, of which theft and perjury have been selected as typical instances. Thus, even though the theme of "Yahweh's covenant law" is not explicitly spelled out in 5:1–4, the intertextual links have brought in this theme by association. We might say that the covenantal theme is implicit in the intertexts. I shall argue in the next chapter that Zech 7–8 makes this implicit theme explicit.

The vision which the prophet sees affirms that the curses of the covenant will continue to be in effect within the post-exilic community, against any who would break Yahweh's law, and that punishment will come upon law breakers with all the suddenness and devastation of the judgment which fell on Egypt in the Passover.[19] The return of Yahweh to dwell with his people at Jerusalem (Zech 1–4) means that the covenant law now goes out (from Zion?) against covenant breakers across all the land.

6.3. *Zechariah 5:5–11—The Woman in the Ephah*

Zechariah 5:5–11 describes a vision of a woman (identified as "wickedness") confined in an ephah. The ephah is borne by stork-winged women towards Shinar (i.e. Babylon) where a "house" is to be built for it. There is much that is puzzling about the imagery of this vision. However, the key to understanding this passage is to read Zech 5:5–11 in the twin contexts of its "intratexts" (i.e. Zech 1–8) and its intertexts (the wider

18. The following verses have the verb "consume" (כלה) with people as the object: Exod 32:12; Num 17:10; Deut 28:21; Isa 1:28; Jer 5:2–3; 9:15; 14:12; 16:5; 44:27; 49:17; Ezek 5:12–13; 7:8; 13:14–15; 20:13.

19. In contrast, Delkurt comes to a very different conclusion as to the function of Zech 5:1–4. Delkurt argues that Zech 5 alludes to Jer 7 in order to provide an explanation of the delay in the promised salvation, in that the same crimes that had led to the destruction of the temple in Jeremiah's day where still continuing in Zechariah's day—see Delkurt 1999b: 204–5.

biblical background to which it alludes). I will argue that the intratexts and intertexts of Zech 5:5–11 intersect in such a way as to reveal that Zech 5:5–11 depicts an "anti-ark" borne by "anti-cherubs," to be put in an "anti-temple" in an "anti-Jerusalem."

6.3.1. *Anti-Temple in an Anti-Jerusalem*

There are clear connections between Zech 5:11 (especially in the phrase "to build a house for it in the land of Shinar") and the theme of temple-building in Zech 1–8. In Zech 1:16, Yahweh announces his return to Jerusalem, and that "my house shall be built in it" (בֵּיתִי יִבָּנֶה בָּהּ). Yahweh's promise of the rebuilding of the house (i.e. "the temple," הַהֵיכָל) is reaffirmed in Zech 8:9. It is through rebuilding this temple that Yahweh will return to dwell in Jerusalem (Zech 8:3). As argued above, Zech 1–4 describes the implications of the rebuilding of Yahweh's house in Jerusalem. Read in this context, Zech 5:11 (especially given its poignant location in "Shinar") cannot be anything but a deliberate antithesis to this dominant theme. That is, Zech 5:11 describes an "anti-temple."[20]

6.3.2. *Anti-Cherubs*

What, then, should we make of the winged creatures in Zech 5? There is nothing obvious in the wider context of Zech 1–8 which helps to unravel their meaning,[21] so we must look to the intertexts of Zech 5:5–11 to make sense of this.

These creatures have "wind in their wings" (רוּחַ בְּכַנְפֵיהֶם). This phrase is evocative of the winged cherubs in Ezekiel's visions in Ezek 1–11, where there is a close connection between the movements of Yahweh's winged cherubs and the "wind" (or "spirit," רוּחַ). We are first introduced to these creatures in Ezek 1:4–6 and 1:20–24, and it is these same creatures which Ezekiel sees in Ezek 10 (see esp. 10:16–21), bearing the heavenly chariot on which Yahweh departs from the temple. Ezekiel's imagery would appear to be a development of the imagery of

20. This "cultic" flavour to the word "house" in Zech 5:11 is confirmed by the fact that the ephah is placed on "a pedestal" (מְכוֹנָה) at the end of v. 11. The word מְכוֹנָה occurs 25 times, and the other 24 instances all describe cultic "pedestals"—see 1 Kgs 7; 2 Kgs 16; 25; Ezek 3:3; Jer 27; 52; 2 Chr 4. See Seybold (1974a: 75 n. 54) for a similar argument that the phrase "on its pedestal" in Zech 5:11 has cultic overtones.

21. The only possible connection with these "winged women" elsewhere in Zech 1–8 is the "flying scroll" of Zech 5:1–4, on the basis of the repetition of the motif of flight. However, this connection is not strong, given that the vocabulary of "flying" (עוּף) is not repeated in Zech 5:5–11.

the Ark of the Covenant, which had two cherubs atop it,[22] upon which Yahweh sat as the one "enthroned between the cherubim."[23] In several passages elsewhere, Yahweh is said to have mounted a cherub and flown on the wings of the wind.[24] It would appear that the winged cherubim in Ezek 10 are a further development of this imagery. This "cherub" imagery from Ezekiel helps us to understand the winged creatures in Zech 5. The women with "wind in their wings" who bear the ephah away from Jerusalem towards Babylon are a parody of Yahweh's heavenly attendants in Ezek 10, who bore him away from Jerusalem (see Ezek 11:23). The winged creatures in Zech 5:5–11 are "anti-cherubim," who serve, not the living God, but rather serve iniquity personified.

The likelihood of a deliberate echoing of the imagery of Ezekiel's opening chapters in Zech 5:5–11 is further strengthened by a number of close correspondences in vocabulary:

- In Zech 5:11, the winged women lift (נשׂא) the ephah basket "between earth and heaven" (בֵּין הָאָרֶץ וּבֵין הַשָּׁמָיִם). Exactly the same thing is said in Ezek 8:3—the spirit lifts (נשׂא) Ezekiel "between earth and heaven" (בֵּין־הָאָרֶץ וּבֵין הַשָּׁמַיִם). This combination of words occurs nowhere else in the Hebrew Bible.[25]
- As Schnocks notes (1996: 62), there is also a particularly close formal parallel between the visions in Ezek 8 and Zech 5:5–11. Both passages say: "And he said to me "Lift up your eyes" (וַיֹּאמֶר אֵלַי שָׂא נָא עֵינֶיךָ),[26] and "And I lifted my eyes…and behold" (וָאֶשָּׂא עֵינַי…וְהִנֵּה).[27]
- In Zech 5:8, the woman in the ephah is identified as "wickedness" (רִשְׁעָה). I shall discuss this imagery in more detail below, but for the present purposes we need note only that the word רִשְׁעָה occurs just 15 times,[28] and among these, Ezek 5 and Zech 5

22. Exod 25:18–20; 1 Kgs 6:23–29.

23. See, e.g., 1 Sam 4:4; 2 Sam 6:2; Pss 80:1; 99:1; Isa 37:16.

24. 2 Sam 22:11 = Ps 18:10; cf. Ps 104:3 where clouds (not cherubs) are his chariot.

25. This point is also made by Schnocks (1996: 61). The only other verse which is remotely close in form is 2 Sam 18:9, which describes Absalom hanging between "heaven and earth." However, not only is the sequence of "earth and heaven" reversed, but this passage also does not have the verb נשׂא.

26. See Zech 5:5 and Ezek 8:5. Ezek 8:5 also includes the phrase בֶּן־אָדָם.

27. Note these further minor differences between Ezek 8:5 and Zech 5:9: וָאֶשָּׂא עֵינַי דֶּרֶךְ צָפוֹנָה וְהִנ ("And I lifted my eyes *to the way of the north* and behold," Ezek 8:5); וָאֶשָּׂא עֵינַי וָאֵרֶא וְהִנֵּה ("And I lifted my eyes *and looked* and behold," Zech 5:9)

28. Deut 9:4, 5; 25:2; Ezek 5:6; 18:20, 27; 33:12, 19; Isa 9:17; Mal 1:4; 3:15, 19; Prov 11:5; 13:6; Zech 5:8.

are the only two passages where wickedness is personified. Likewise, it is only in these two passages that wickedness is described by means of a symbolic act.

- In Zech 5:6, the ephah is described as "their iniquity" (עֲוֹנָם; text emended).[29] Ezekiel 4:4 describes Ezekiel's symbolic act on behalf of the house of Israel, by which he bears "their iniquity" (עֲוֹנָם).

These connections suggest that the opening chapters of Ezekiel are key intertexts of Zech 5:5–11. I agree with Schnocks (1996: 63) that Zech 5:5–11 is an inner-biblical response to Ezek 8, but (on the basis of the wider connections noted above with Ezek 4, 5 and 10) I wish to take this conclusion further and argue that Ezek 1–11 taken as a whole is the appropriate background against which to understand the imagery of Zech 5:5–11.[30]

More specifically, my argument is that Zech 5:5–11 is something of a reversal of Ezek 1–11. Ezekiel 1–11 describes the departure of Yahweh from Jerusalem because of the idolatry (Ezek 8), iniquity (Ezek 4) and wickedness (Ezek 5) of his people, and his departure is attended by winged creatures riding on the wind. But, now that Yahweh is returning to dwell in Jerusalem, idolatry/iniquity/wickedness is being forced to depart, in a parody of Yahweh's earlier departure. I agree with the conclusion of Floyd (1996: 66), that

> ...the woman flying off in the ephah mimics one theophanic flight of Yahweh in particular. In one of Ezekiel's visions, Yahweh left Jerusalem and came to Babylon in much the same way, borne on his chariot throne by winged cherubim (Ezekiel 10).

29. MT reads עֵינָם, from עַיִן ("eye"), whereas the LXX and Syriac reflect a Hebrew *Vorlage*—עֲוֹנָם. The form עֵינָם is the singular noun with third masculine plural suffix. This is unusual. It is only otherwise attested in Isa 13:18 (עֵינָם), and in a variant form in Ps 73:7 (עֵינֵמוֹ). The usual form is either a *dual* with a plural suffix (e.g. עֵינֵיהֶם "their eyes"—49 times) or the dual with a singular suffix (e.g. עֵינָיו, "his eyes"—128 times). In terms of the meaning of the word here in Zech 5:6, the singular is unexpected, since eyes are usually dual in form (both grammatically and physiologically!).With most commentators, I think it is likely that the text originally read עונם not עינם (i.e. that a scribal error has confused waw for yod), and that the original reading was "their iniquity." In contrast to MT's unusual עֵינָם, the form עֲוֹנָם is frequently attested (33 times). In the context of Zech 5, the meaning "their iniquity" makes much better sense than "their eye."

30. Regardless of the redaction history of Ezek 1–11, it is not unreasonable to suppose that these chapters had reached their present form by the time that Zech 5:5–11 was written. See further §3.3.2.

I agree with a number of other scholars that Zech 5:5–11 is something of a mock theophany, parodying the transport of Yahweh by his heavenly attendants.[31]

6.3.3. *Anti-Ark*

There is another layer of intertextual connections in Zech 5:5–11 which aids our understanding of these verses, by showing that the ephah is a parody of the Ark of the Covenant. While one might have inferred this from the association between the cherubim and ark (noted above), there are some additional lexical links that make this connection explicit, by association with 2 Sam 7. In Zech 5:9, the woman is "dwelling in the midst of the ephah" (יוֹשֶׁבֶת בְּתוֹךְ הָאֵיפָה). In 2 Sam 7:2, "the ark of God is dwelling in the midst of a tent" (וַאֲרוֹן הָאֱלֹהִים יֹשֵׁב בְּתוֹךְ הַיְרִיעָה). This combination of "dwelling in the midst" (used in this symbolic way) occurs nowhere else.[32]

Furthermore, David's plan to build a temple prompts the response of Yahweh, "Are you the one who will build a house for me to dwell in?" (הַאַתָּה תִּבְנֶה־לִּי בַיִת לְשִׁבְתִּי, 2 Sam 7:5).[33] As already noted above, Zech 5:11 picks up (antithetically) this imagery of "building a house," a central theme in Zech 1–8. As noted in the previous chapter, 2 Sam 7 is a foundational passage for the later biblical tradition regarding the significance of "building a house."

If it can be taken as established that the ephah in Zech 5:5–11 functions as some form of a parody of the Ark of the Covenant, then another intertext can be suggested, one which helps to explain the curious phrase in Zech 5:7—כִּכַּר עֹפֶרֶת—usually translated "lead disk" or "lead cover." The word כִּכַּר can mean "disk" (and especially a "disk" of bread, i.e., a loaf),[34] but the typical use of this word is in the phrases כִּכַּר זָהָב ("a talent of gold") and כִּכַּר כֶּסֶף ("a talent of silver"). The grammatical construction of כִּכַּר followed by a metal occurs more than 50 times (out of the 68 instances of the word). For this reason, the most natural

31. See likewise Jeremias 1977: 198–200; Floyd 1996; Boda 2004: 307–8.

32. The combination of ישב and תָּוֶךְ occurs in 23 verses, but only in Zech 5 and 2 Sam 7 in this sense. Schnocks (1996: 61–62) draws a connection between Ezek 8:3, which describes "the dwelling (מוֹשַׁב) of the image-of-jealousy there (שָׁם) in the temple," and Zech 5:7, which describes "the woman dwelling (יוֹשֶׁבֶת) in the ephah," together with Zech 5:11, which refers to the ephah being put "there (שָׁם) in Shinar." While this link is attractive (and not inconsistent with my wider argument), the lexical links to 2 Sam 7 are stronger.

33. I note the interchangeability of the notion of "the ark of God dwelling" (2 Sam 7:2) with "Yahweh himself dwelling" (2 Sam 7:5).

34. See, e.g., Exod 29:23; Jer 37:21; Judg 8:5; Prov 6:26

interpretation of the phrase כִּכַּר עֹפֶרֶת in Zech 5:7 is "a talent of lead." However, interpreters tend not to use this translation because the context of Zech 5 makes clear that the phrase must refer to the lid of the ephah, and a "talent" of lead would be much too big/heavy.[35] As a result, the consensus translation of this phrase is "disk of lead" or similar. And yet, on this interpretation, the reason for the use of the peculiar phrase כִּכַּר עֹפֶרֶת remains an enigma.

However, when we recognize the ephah as an anti-ark, the wider imagery associated with the Ark of the Covenant (as particularly seen in Exod 25) suggests a significance in the use of the phrase כִּכַּר עֹפֶרֶת. The cover of the ark was the כַּפֹּרֶת (usually translated "mercy seat" or "atonement cover"—see Exod 25:17). I suggest that כִּכַּר עֹפֶרֶת is a pun on כַּפֹּרֶת (or perhaps כְּכַפֹּרֶת "like-a-mercy-seat"—if one says the words aloud, the similarities are apparent). Just as the ark has its cover (a כַּפֹּרֶת made of the most valuable metal—gold), so too the anti-ark has a cover, but with a name which is a parody of its counterpart (it is only "like a mercy seat"), and, instead of gold, it is made of the least valuable metal—lead.[36]

Zechariah 5:5–11 makes an intertextual use of Exod 25 (esp. vv. 8–22) to picture the ephah basket as a grotesque parody. In sharp contrast to the ark (a container for the testimony), with its gold "atonement cover" and winged pair of cherubs, Zech 5:5–11 describes an ephah (a container for "wickedness"), with a leaden cover and a winged pair of stork-women.

In summary, then, the intratexts and the intertexts of Zech 5:5–11 combine to provide a sufficient conceptual framework for making sense of the passage as a whole. The key *intratexts* are those passages in Zech 1–8 which help us to understand the significance of the phrase "to build a house" in Zech 5:11, and the key *intertexts* are Ezek 1–11; 2 Sam 7 and

35. A cover which weighed a "talent" would be disproportionate to the weight of the contents of an ephah. An ephah had a capacity of 22 litres, and was a "dry" measure for products like grain. For the sake of a comparative calculation, if we assume the ephah to have had a roughly cylindrical shape, then a 22 litre ephah might have had a 30 cm diameter and a height just over 30 cm. A talent is estimated to have weighed between 50 and 58 kg. A 30 cm diameter ephah-cover made from "a talent of lead" would have been almost 6 cm thick. (The specific gravity of pure lead is 11.3437 g/cm^3.) The cover would have weighed almost four times as much as an ephah full of grain (assuming the grain to have a specific gravity around 0.7 g/cm^3).

36. In the various lists of metals which include lead, lead and tin always rank as the last two—e.g. Num 31:22; Ezek 22:18–20; 27:12—and in all but one instance, lead is last in the list. The "value ranking" of the various metals would seem to be in the order gold, silver, bronze, iron, tin, and lastly lead.

Exod 25, which help us to recognize the ephah basket as an anti-ark borne by anti-cherubs to an anti-temple in an anti-Jerusalem.

I am not suggesting that these intratexts and intertexts completely determine the meaning of this passage, only that they constrain it. As will become apparent below, there are a number of features of Zech 5:5–11 where we lack sufficient data to be certain about their precise significance.

6.3.4. *The Contents of the Ephah*

One of the features in which we might find a range of possible meanings is the contents of the ephah-basket. In Zech 5:7, the cover of the basket is lifted, and "there was one woman" (וְזֹאת אִשָּׁה אַחַת).[37] The interpreting angel then further explains in Zech 5:8 that "this is wickedness" (זֹאת הָרִשְׁעָה).

The typical interpretations of this metaphor can be broadly divided into two camps—those which understand the woman in terms of a feminine-personified metaphor for sin (e.g. Eve, Jerusalem, the prostitute, menstrual uncleanness etc.),[38] and those which understand the woman to represent idolatry in one form or another. Of the latter approach, the best case would seem to be for "Asherah," on the grounds that her name (אֲשֵׁרָה) is a near anagram for the word "wickedness" (רִשְׁעָה) in Zech 5:8,[39] and there is ample biblical precedent of mocking foreign deities by the use of parodies of their names.[40] Also supportive of the case for

37. In this phrase, זֹאת is functioning as a demonstrative—see GKC §136d.

38. *Eve*: Jones (1962: 82), *Jerusalem*: Barker (1978: 24), *Prostitute*: Mitchell (1912: 173), *Menstrual uncleanness*: Mason (1977a: 58).

39. The shift from "wickedness" (רִשְׁעָה) to "Asherah" (אֲשֵׁרָה) requires the substitution of א for ע. However, as Meyers and Meyers point out, the difference between these consonants would not be heard. Meyers and Meyers (1987: 302–3) and Uehlinger (1994: 101–2) are proponents of this view. Also, it should be noted that רִשְׁעָה in Zech 5:12 is preceded by the article, and so, even with out the consonantal rearrangement, הָרִשְׁעָה sounds very similar to אֲשֵׁרָה. Middlemas (2005: 93–95) is reluctant to identify this figure with Asherah in particular, but regards it as likely that it depicts a female deity.

40. For example, the condemnation in Amos 8:14 of those "swearing by the *guilt* (אַשְׁמַה) of Samaria" would appear to be a pun on the name of the deity Ashimah (אֲשִׁימָא)—see 2 Kgs 17:30. Another well-known example is the replacement of the name "Baal" ("Lord") with "Bosheth" ("shame"), as evidenced in name substitutions: Esh-Baal (1 Chr 9:39) is otherwise known as Ish-bosheth (2 Sam 2:8), Jerub-Baal is changed to Jerub-Besheth (compare Judg 9:28 and 2 Sam 11:21), and see likewise Merib-Baal (1 Chr 9:40)/Mephibosheth (2 Sam 9:6). See also the parallelism drawn between "Baal" (בַּעַל) and "shame" (בֹּשֶׁת) in the prophets—Jer 11:13; Hos 9:10. Another example is the mocking renaming of the bronze serpent as

"Asherah" are the intertextual connections between Ezek 8 and Zech 5 noted above. In Ezek 8:3–6, the cause of Yahweh's departure from Jerusalem was the "idol of jealousy which provokes jealousy" (סֵמֶל הַקִּנְאָה הַמַּקְנֶה) which stood within the temple at Jerusalem. Though Ezekiel does not identify this idol as Asherah, it is reasonable to assume this to be the case. Manasseh had established an idol of Asherah (פֶּסֶל הָאֲשֵׁרָה) in the temple,[41] and although this idol was removed by Hezekiah (see 2 Kgs 23:6), there is evidence that the worship of Asherah continued in Jerusalem well into the period recorded in Ezek 8,[42] which makes it likely that a re-introduced Asherah idol is the "idol which provokes to jealousy" seen by Ezekiel.

If the "woman in the ephah" represents Asherah—perhaps an Asherah figurine—then Zech 5:5–11 describes the deportation of idolatrous worship from Jerusalem, as the antithesis of Ezekiel's vision. Whereas Ezek 1–11 had described how idolatry had triggered Yahweh's departure from the city, now it is the return of Yahweh to Jerusalem which triggers the removal of idolatry.

While I find this second line of interpretation highly suggestive, in the end one must conclude that there is simply not sufficient evidence to choose definitively between these two lines of interpretation—quite simply, Zech 5:5–11 could be about the removal of sin (personified as a woman) or it could be about the removal of idolatry (personified as, or perhaps in the form of, an idol figurine). But this does not necessarily mean that we must abandon all hope of making sense of this passage. The important thing to realize is that these two lines of interpretation are not mutually exclusive alternatives but different points along a scale from general to particular, which yield differing nuances of interpretation, but

"Nehushtan" (נְחֻשְׁתָּן), meaning "thing of brass" (see 2 Kgs 18:4), which involves a play on the similarity of the words "serpent" (נָחָשׁ) and "bronze" (נְחֹשֶׁת). It may also be that Ashtaroth (עַשְׁתָּרוֹת, see 1 Sam 31:10) (= Astarte) became Ashtoreth (עַשְׁתֹּרֶת, 1 Kgs 11:5) through being repointed with the vowels of "bosheth" (בֹּשֶׁת). For another possible pun, see Merodach-Baladan (מְרֹדַךְ־בַּלְאֲדָן) in Isa 39:1 which becomes Berodach-Baladan (בְּרֹאדַךְ־בַּלְאֲדָן) in 2 Kgs 20:12. The former means "Marduk has given a son," but in the latter, the name of the Babylonian deity "Marduk" has been altered to Berodach (בְּרֹאדַךְ). This is typically regarded as merely a textual corruption (though this must then assume a double error—both the substitution of ב for מ as well as the insertion of א). However, it is possible that the alteration is a deliberate mocking of the name "Marduk"—for example, בְּרֹאדַךְ could be read as בָּרִיא ("fatness") and דַּךְ ("crushed"). On this point, see also Delcor 1975: 144.

41. See 2 Kgs 21:7; in 2 Chr 33:7 this in called a סֶמֶל, which is the same word as used in Ezek 8:3.

42. See esp. Jer 7:18; 44:17–25; the "Queen of Heaven" is a title for Asherah.

which come to the same ultimate conclusion, especially in light of the intertexts of Zech 5:5–11. Taking our lead from Ezek 1–11, the reason for the departure of Yahweh from Jerusalem was because of the idolatry (Ezek 8) *and* iniquity (Ezek 4:4) *and* wickedness (Ezek 5:6) of his people. Suppose we follow the first line of interpretation, and say that Zech 5:5–11 is about the removal of sin in general, then we must also say that this necessarily entails the removal of idolatry in particular as well. Alternatively, should we say that Zech 5:5–11 is specifically about the removal of idolatry, it is clear from the biblical witness that idolatry is a paradigmatic example of sin. Moreover, the immediate context (particularly Zech 5:1–4) makes clear that Yahweh's return to Jerusalem will result in the banishment of all sin, not just idolatry.

On this basis, we may safely conclude that Zech 5:5–11 is about the removal of idolatry—and perhaps sin in general—from Jerusalem, consequent upon Yahweh's return to the city.

6.3.5. *The Ephah*

Another enigmatic feature of Zech 5:5–11 is the ephah itself. Given the conclusion above that the ephah is an "anti-ark," we can dismiss those interpretations which are inconsistent with this broad framework.

For example, the suggestion that the ephah is a coffin,[43] a prison,[44] a lead-lined container for the disposal of evil[45] or a pun on the Sumerian

43. For example, as argued by the "prosecution" in Edelman (2003: 337), "the *ʿêpâ* was used as a coffin by members of the Neo-Babylonian elite in the sixth and fifth centuries BCE," citing Zorn (1993) in support of this position. However, Edelman's prosecutor has fudged the evidence somewhat. Zorn does *not* say that "the *ʿêpâ* was used as a coffin"—Zorn's articles (Zorn 1993; 1997) both concern what Zorn describes as a "Mesopotamian-style 'bathtub' coffin" (1997: 219). Zorn does not describe this as "ephah," nor is it a reasonable extension of his conclusions, given the size of the coffins described. For example, Zorn describes one of these bathtub coffins in Megiddo Tomb no. 37—"The coffin is 67 cm wide and 57 cm deep at the rim; the excavators were unable to discover its length" (1997: 217). If we make a very conservative guess at a length of 60 cm—many of the other examples cited in Zorn (1997) are closer to 100 cm—then the capacity would be at least 229 litres, which is more than 10 times the size of an ephah. The ephah is one tenth of the homer (see Ezek 45:11), and the homer is typically estimated around 220 litres—see Meyers and Meyers 1987: 295–96. An ephah was a small container for measuring (and transporting) dry produce—perhaps a wooden or pottery container, or even a woven basket. One would have thought that there was sufficient difference between a 22 litre ephah basket and a 220 litre clay bathtub not to confuse the two items. There is no evidence to suggest that the ephah was used for funeral rites.

44. Delcor (1975: 140–43) cites the Hittite myth of Telepinu, in particular noting examples of imprisonment in bronze cauldrons with tin lids. Delcor draws a connection between this and the ephah with its lead cover: "Il y a donc une certaine

E-pa[46] can be readily discounted, in that they are based on (sometimes highly tenuous) parallels with extra-biblical material which are not supported by any parallels in the biblical corpus. These interpretations offer little to help explain the significance of the ephah in Zech 5–11.

There would seem to be two possible lines of significance to the ephah—either its association with equitable trade, and/or its size. These two possibilities correlate with the twin possibilities noted above in our discussion of the contents of the ephah.

---

ressemblance entre le récipient décrit par Zacharie et les chaudrons des incantations hittites au couvercle de plomb ou d'étain" (Delcor 1975: 142). However, Delcor's argument can be turned against itself. As Delcor rightly notes, the ephah is itself not made out of lead. It was probably made of wood or pottery—the typical containers in Israelite households appear to have been either earthenware (כְּלִי־חֶרֶשׂ) or wooden (כְּלִי־עֵץ). Metal vessels are typically described in connection with temple use. For example, compare the regulations in Lev 15:21 (for the purification of household vessels, which only contemplates wood and pottery items) with Lev 6:21 (which gives instructions for the purification of cultic vessels, referring to both pottery and bronze vessels). Delcor argues for a similarity between Zech 5 and the Hittite myth based on the fact that, in each case, the lid is made of a different material to the container. However, the same evidence points more strongly in the opposite direction. It is a striking point of dissimilarity that the Hittite cauldron is metal and the ephah is not. Should Zech 5:5–11 be an allusion to the Hittite cauldrons, one would have expected a metal container. The other difficultly with Delcor's suggested interpretation is the size of the cauldron *vis-à-vis* the ephah. The bronze cauldron was clearly large enough to imprison a man; why then use "an ephah" (only about 22 litres in capacity) to allude to this?

45. Wright (1987: 263–64) notes Hittite parallels (particularly the Telepinu myth, as also cited by Delcor) in which evil is consigned to the nether world in a bronze kettle and sealed with a lid. Wright concludes that Zech 5:5–11 "appears to derive from Near Eastern (specifically Hittite or North Syrian?) methods of disposing of evils in sealed containers" (1987: 273). Delcor (1975: 142–43) argues that, "Le plomb pour les Hittites avait la propriété magique d'être impénétrable aux esprits. Cela est illustré par une série d'incantations hittites selon lesquelles les esprits sont emprisonnés dans des chaudrons en bronze du monde souterrain fermés avec des couvercles de plomb. On peut supposer que le couvercle de l'épha avait des propriétés analogues". Again, counting against Delcor's suggestion of the parallel with Zech 5 is the fact that only the lid, and not the ephah itself, is made of lead. If the impenetrable qualities of lead are so important, then one would expect that the whole container should be lead-lined.

46. Marenof argues that the "ephah" of Zech 5 has nothing to do with a measuring basket, but refers to a room or shrine at the top of a Babylonian temple. Marenof (1932: 265) notes that the name of a Babylonian Zikkurats was *E-pa* (meaning "the summit house"). He suggests that "the name *E-pa*, which is of Sumerian origin, became a loan word in the Assyrian language, and from the Assyrian into other Semitic Languages."

If the ephah contains "sins," then the significance of the choice of the word "ephah" is that it is reminiscent of the sins of the people in their unjust dealings with each other. More than one quarter of the instances of the word אֵיפָה are connected with condemnation of the "dishonest ephah" (i.e. an ephah of non-standard size; see Lev 19:36; Deut 25:14–15; Amos 8:5; Mic 6:10; Ezek 45:10–11; Prov 20:10). Moreover, it is the אֵיפָה in particular that has this connotation, much more so than any other instrument of measure. This may explain the choice of the word "ephah" in this context. The Targum on Zech 5:6 makes this kind of "economic" interpretation explicit.[47] On this interpretation of Zech 5, the sins of the people are sealed up and deported in an instrument of their sin. There is thus a poetic justice in the use of the imagery of the ephah.

However, if the ephah contains "idolatry," then the significance of the ephah would seem to be in the smallness of the measure. It is much too small to hold a woman, so it must be a representation of one (perhaps a statuette of Asherah)—the point being that this "woman" can be fully contained inside a 22 litre container. The Ark of the Covenant had a capacity around 400 litres, but in contrast this "anti-ark" is only a fraction of its size. Moreover, Yahweh was not contained within the ark, or even the temple—indeed, as Solomon declares of Yahweh in 1 Kgs 8:27, "even the highest heaven cannot contain you" (וּשְׁמֵי הַשָּׁמַיִם לֹא יְכַלְכְּלוּךָ). In this interpretation, then, the significance of the choice of the "ephah" is its paltry size—this god can fit within a mere ephah, and can be constrained within it.

However, perhaps it is not necessary to decide between these two alternatives, should we also recognize Amos 8 as further intertext to Zech 5. Amos 8, like Zech 5, describes a symbolic vision involving a container.[48] In Amos 8, it is a "basket of fruit" (כְּלוּב קָיִץ) which symbolizes the "end" that has come for Israel ("fruit," קַיִץ, is a pun on the word "end," קֵץ). The reasons given in Amos 8 for Israel's end are twofold—its economic exploitation (vv. 4–7) and its idolatry (v. 14). In each case, there is a suggestive connection with Zech 5:[49]

47. *Targum Jonathan* paraphrases Zech 5:6's "the ephah" as "those taking and giving in measures of falsehood" (see Cathcart and Gordon 1989: 196; Sperber 1992: 483).

48. There are other symbolic/metaphoric uses of containers—for example, Jeremiah's baskets of figs (Jer 24) and cup of wrath (Jer 25:15), and Ezekiel's cooking pot (Ezek 24) etc.—but Amos 8 and Zech 5 bear the closest conceptual parallels.

49. Another parallel between the two passages is the common vocabulary of "cast" (שׁלך Hiphil)—the woman is "cast" into the basket in Zech 5:8, and the dead are "cast" in every place in Amos 8:3

- The example of economic exploitation in Amos. 8:5 is the "dishonest ephah"—"making the ephah small and the shekel great" (לְהַקְטִין אֵיפָה וּלְהַגְדִּיל שֶׁקֶל).
- The example of their idolatry is "swearing by the guilt of Samaria" (Amos 8:14) where "guilt" (אַשְׁמָה) is apparently a play on Ashima (אֲשִׁימָא), much as "wickedness" (רִשְׁעָה) in Zech 5:8 is a pun on "Asherah" (אֲשֵׁרָה).[50]

My suggestion is that the word "ephah" in Zech 5:5–11 has been chosen because it connects with both of these themes in Amos 8, in which another basket was symbolic of the sins of both economic exploitation and idolatry. If this argument is found convincing, then it means that we can offer a "both–and" interpretation—the ephah in Zech 5:5–11 symbolizes both sin in general and idolatry in particular.

6.3.6. *Other Details in the Vision*

The intertexts of Zech 5:5–11 help to narrow the field of possible interpretations, but there are still some incidental features of the vision which remain perplexing. For example, why do the winged ephah-bearers have "wings like wings of a stork" (כְנָפַיִם כְּכַנְפֵי הַחֲסִידָה)? What is the significance of the stork? Is it (as Boda 2004: 307 suggests) because the stork is an unclean bird? Or is it, as Mitchell (1912: 174) suggests, because the stork is a strong and high-flying migratory bird, suitable for carrying this cargo to "Shinar"? Or it is both (so Petersen 1984a: 260)? Or is it (as suggested by Glazier-MacDonald 1998: 246) a word-play between "stork" (חֲסִידָה) and "faithful" (חָסִיד)? The short answer is—we do not know, because of the paucity of intertexts.[51]

However, a degree of indeterminacy at this level of detail does not render the vision unintelligible. Clearly, this vision parodies the temple-building theme in the wider context of Zech 1–8, and alludes to Ezek 1–11; 2 Sam 7 and Exod 25 in order to depict the ephah basket as anti-ark borne by anti-cherubs to an anti-temple in an anti-Jerusalem. Further allusions to Amos 8 and Ezek 8 help us to realize that the ephah symbolizes the iniquity and idolatry of the people, which is being deported from Jerusalem as a consequence of Yahweh's return.

50. See nn. 39 and 40 above.

51. There are only six references to the חֲסִידָה. In two verses, it is mentioned as an unclean bird (Lev 11:19; Deut 14:18), in two other verses it is noted as a migratory/high-flying bird (Jer 8:7; Ps 104:17) and in two more (Job 39:13; Zech 5:9) the significance of the bird is uncertain.

6.4. *Zechariah 6:1–8—The Four Chariots*

Zechariah 6:1–8 is the final of the eight night-visions, and completes the "outwards" movement which commenced in the sixth vision and was developed in the seventh.

Zechariah 6:1–8 also picks up and develops the allusions to Job 1–2 which began in the first night-vision. As we saw in Zech 1:10, the role of the horses was "to patrol in the earth" (לְהִתְהַלֵּךְ בָּאָרֶץ), which (as argued above at §4.3.1.1) is a clear allusion to Job 1:7 and 2:2, which describe one who comes from roving "in the earth" (בָּאָרֶץ) "and from patrolling in it" (וּמֵהִתְהַלֵּךְ בָּהּ).[52] This allusion to Job 1–2 is continued in Zech 6:7, where the horse chariots go out "to patrol in the earth" (לְהִתְהַלֵּךְ בָּאָרֶץ three times in Zech 6:7). In a further development of this allusion, the horses in Zech 6 perform a parallel function to the heavenly attendants in Job 1–2. The "sons of God" in Job 1–2 come "to present themselves before Yahweh" (לְהִתְיַצֵּב עַל־יְהוָה). Similarly, these horses go out "from presenting themselves before Yahweh" (מֵהִתְיַצֵּב עַל־אֲדוֹן).[53] Zechariah 6:1–8 consolidates and develops the imagery of the heavenly attendants in Job 1–2.[54]

The last night-vision also shares with the first the motif of coloured horses patrolling the earth, though it is important to note the differences as well as the similarities. The last night-vision strongly emphasizes the number four (אַרְבַּע)—"four chariots" (6:1), the description of each of the four chariots (6:2–3), and the "four winds/spirits of heaven" (6:5)—whereas the first night-vision does not mention the number four.[55] In contrast, it lists only three horse colours—red, sorrel and white (אֲדֻמִּים שְׂרֻקִּים וּלְבָנִים, Zech 1:8)—as against the four listed colours in the last

52. The Hithpael infinitive construct of the verb הלך occurs only in Job (1:7; 2:2), Zechariah (1:10; 6:7 [×3]) and only otherwise in Prov 6:22 and Ps 56:14. Only in Job and Zechariah does this construction occur in the context of a "divine council" scene.

53. The Hithpael infinitive construct of the verb יצב occurs only in Job (1:6; 2:1 [×2]); Zech 6:5 and only otherwise in 2 Sam 21:5 and 2 Chr 20:6. 2 Chr 20 is later, and in 2 Sam 21:5 the verb is not followed by the preposition עַל. Moreover, the more "typical" expression is הִתְיַצֵּב לִפְנֵי (see, e.g., Exod 8:15; 9:13; Deut 9:2; Josh 24:1; 1 Sam 10:19). The expression הִתְיַצֵּב עַל which occurs in Job 1–2 and Zech 6:5 only otherwise occurs in 2 Chr 11:13.

54. So also Tiemeyer 2006a: 190.

55. I agree with Reventlow 1992: 182–86 as to the significance of the number four in this vision, though I remain unconvinced by his argument that the four chariots are the four winds of heaven.

night-vision—red, black, white and "dappled grey" (אֲדֻמִּים...שְׁחֹרִים...לְבָנִים...בְּרֻדִּים אֲמֻצִּים, Zech 6:2–3). In its use of the number four to symbolize the whole world, the last night-vision is closer in thought to the second night-vision with its four horns and four craftsmen.

The other obvious difference between the first and last visions is that the coloured horses in Zech 6:1–8 are drawing chariots, whereas in Zech 1:7–12 they are not. "Chariots" (מַרְכָּבוֹת) add a bellicose overtone which is absent from the first vision. The biblical instances of chariots in Yahweh's service (only in Hab 3:8; Joel 2:4–5; Isa 66:15)[56] suggest the image of Yahweh as divine warrior, riding out to save his people by the defeat of their enemies. The militaristic overtones of "chariots" (מַרְכָּבוֹת) are strengthened by the way in which this word is used in Haggai, especially given our conclusions elsewhere, that the author of Zech 1–8 draws on Haggai.[57] In Hag 2:22–23, Yahweh announces that he is about to shake the earth and overthrow the strength of the nations and their "chariots." In Zech 6:1–8 we can perhaps see the outworking of this promise, as Yahweh subdues the nations by sending out his own chariots.

On the basis of these similarities and differences, we can conclude that, while both the first and the last visions describe the same heavenly emissaries in Yahweh's service, in each instance they are sent out with a different purpose. In the first vision, they had been sent out on a "reconnaissance mission," whereas in the last they are to go out as the "host" (i.e. army) of "Yahweh of Hosts."[58]

56. Niditch argues for a connection to the "chariot of fire" in 2 Kgs 2:11, and views the chariots not as vehicles of war, but as serving "a boundary-crossing function, linking this world to the next" (1983: 156). However, it should be noted that the vocabulary is different. 2 Kings uses the word רֶכֶב, whereas Zech 6 uses the word מֶרְכָּבָה, which is the word typically used elsewhere to describe a "war chariot." I take it that the chariots in Jer 4:11–12 are the chariots of Babylon, not the chariots of Yahweh (notwithstanding the fact that Babylon's chariots execute Yahweh's judgment). But perhaps we should not draw too strong a distinction at this point, because the "chariots of Yahweh" may well be a development from the imagery of Jer 4:11–12.

57. We have already seen in the previous chapter (see §5.2) that Haggai and Zechariah shared a common "messianic" expectation for Zerubbabel. We shall see in the next chapter (see §7.6.3) that Zech 8:10–13 describes the covenant blessings in terms of agricultural fecundity by allusion to Hag 1–2.

58. "Yahweh of Hosts" (יְהוָה צְבָאוֹת) is a title which emphasizes that Yahweh is the ruler over the hosts (i.e. armies) of heaven. This title is used with rhetorical effect in Zech 1:12—having learnt from the patrolling angel that the nations (who have oppressed God's people) are still at rest and dwelling securely, the angel cries out "Yahweh *of Hosts*, How long…?," thus entreating Yahweh to send out his hosts to act for his people's sake. See further my comments on the "re-enthronement of

The mission which the latter group performs is "to cause my spirit to rest in the land of the north" (הֵנִיחוּ אֶת־רוּחִי בְּאֶרֶץ צָפוֹן). Commentators are divided as to whether to give this phrase a positive or negative connotation. Some have understood it to mean that Yahweh's chariots go out to bring Yahweh's presence, in the sense of divine rule, over the powers of the north.[59] Others (myself included) understand the phrase in a negative sense, in that Yahweh's spirit is resting there in anger, and/or that his anger is given rest by the execution of judgment.[60] The argument for the negative connotation is based on the fact that the wind (רוּחַ) of Yahweh is sometimes an expression of his wrath, and that the context of this vision (with its bellicose overtones of "war chariot" imagery) makes this reading more likely. In particular, Ezekiel uses the wind of Yahweh in this way. For example, in Ezek 13:13, Yahweh declares "I will make a stormy wind (רוּחַ) break out in my anger" (וּבִקַּעְתִּי רוּחַ־סְעָרוֹת בַּחֲמָתִי). There are also notable parallels in phraseology between the two books, which are even more significant in the light of the conclusions above about the re-use of Ezek 1–11. The construction "cause my spirit to rest on…" (הֵנִיחוּ אֶת־רוּחִי בּ) is very similar to Ezekiel's phrase "I will cause my anger to rest on…" (הֲנִחֹתִי אֶת־חֲמָתִי בּ).[61] I argue that, if we understand Zech 6:8 in the context of its Ezekielian intertexts, then it is clear that the spirit of Yahweh resting on the land of the north has negative connotations—Yahweh's spirit rests there in judgment.[62]

Recognizing this broad framework helps us to make sense of some of the more obscure details in Zech 6:1–8. In Zech 6:1, the four chariots come "from between the two mountains (מִבֵּין שְׁנֵי הֶהָרִים), and the mountains [were] mountains of bronze (וְהֶהָרִים הָרֵי נְחֹשֶׁת)." There have been a number various interpretations suggested for this imagery.

A number of commentators connect these mountains with the dwelling place of God, on the basis of apparent parallels with ancient Near Eastern

Yahweh Sabaoth" in §4.4 above. The final night-vision is an intratextual response to the entreaty of the first.

59. See, e.g., Niditch 1983: 156: "In our opinion, the actual battle is now over, however, and the chariots and horses are not headed to holy war, but to certify Yahweh's victory by establishing his rule over the land of the north." See similarly Rothstein 1910: 194; Sellin 1922: 518; Galling 1964a: 121; Mason 1977a: 60–61; Meyers and Meyers 1987: 331.

60. So (with variations) Ackroyd 1968: 183; Rudolph 1976: 125; Petersen 1984a: 271; Boda 2004: 323–24.

61. See Ezek 24:13 and similar constructions in Ezek 16:42; 21:22; 22:20. Reventlow (1992: 188) makes a similar argument from these verses in Ezekiel, and also refers to Ezek 5:13; 24:13. This parallel also noted by Floyd 2000: 397.

62. A similar conclusion is reached by Jeremias 1977: 27.

mythology: in particular with the Mesopotamian sun-god Shamash emerging (sometimes on a chariot) from between two mountains.[63] However, "*bronze*" mountains per se are not a feature of the Shamash myth, leading to a variety of conjectures as to why these particular mountains are "bronze."[64]

A different line of interpretation attaches more significance to the word "bronze," making a connection with the two massive bronze pillars which stood at the entrance to the Solomonic temple (1 Kgs 7:15).[65] Seybold (1974a: 69) combines the mythological and the temple-pillar interpretations by arguing that the pillars of the temple in Jerusalem are symbolic of the divine mountains demarcating the abode of the deity. Supportive of what might, at first glance, seem to be an unlikely interpretation is the fact that the "bronze pillars" are typically listed together with the "bronze sea."[66] Clearly, the bronze sea in the temple is not a literal "sea," and some have argued that it is a representation of the primordial floodwaters—*ein Abbild der Ur flut* (Fohrer 1963). So too (the argument goes) the bronze pillars likewise have a cosmological significance, representing the primal mountains. However, this argument is ultimately not compelling, precisely because the "pillars" are designated as "pillars" (i.e. unlike the bronze "sea," they are never referred to as "mountains," and there is no hint anywhere that they have a special cosmological or representational significance).

Instead of ancient Near Eastern myths or temple furniture providing the key to Zech 6:1, I submit that the intertexts of Zech 6 might provide a better conceptual background to this imagery of the bronze mountains. While I readily concede that the interpretation I am about to offer requires a degree of conjecture, I hasten to stress that this is also true of the two interpretations already discussed.

63. For documents, see *ANET* 683–85. For examples of scholars following this approach, see Mitchell 1912: 177; May 1938: 75; Horst 1964: 100; Chary 1969: 105; Meyers and Meyers 1987: 319–20; Boda 2004: 318–19. For a detailed treatment of the theme of the "cosmic mountain," see Clifford 1972.

64. One popular view is that the mountains are "bronze" because of their shiny appearance, as reflecting the radiant glory of God. Cf. Niditch, who argues for a connection with the "bronzeness" of the divine beings in Ezek 1:7; 40:3 and Dan 10:6, commenting: "Like the bronzeness of the divine beings, the bronzeness of the cosmic mountains implies a quality of fiery, divine power, indeed the presence of the deity" (1983: 155).

65. See, e.g., Rothstein 1910: 167–8.

66. The temple furnishings are typically described as "the bronze pillars, the movable stands and the bronze Sea"—see 2 Kgs 25:13, 16; 1 Chr 18:8; Jer 27:19; 52:17, 20. Cf. 1 Kgs 7 for a variation of this sequence.

My conjecture is that the significance of Yahweh's chariots emerging "from between the two [bronze] mountains" in Zech 6:1 is that Yahweh has burst through the mountains. I suggest that this imagery arises from an intertextual conflation of Isa 45:2 and Hab 3. In Isa 45:2, Yahweh declares that "I will level the mountains[67] and break down the doors of bronze (נְחוּשָׁה)." Habakkuk 3 describes Yahweh the divine warrior riding forth to rescue his people, with shattering consequences for the geographic features in his path:[68]

Hab 3:6	[Yahweh] has split[69] the everlasting mountains (ויתפצצו הררי־עד)
Hab 3:9	You split the earth with rivers (נהרות תבקע־ארץ)
Hab 3:10	Mountains saw you and writhed (ראוך יחילו הרים)

According to Hab 3:8, it is particularly Yahweh's chariots (מַרְכְּבוֹת) and horses (סוּסִים) which are the agents of his destruction. The same vocabulary of chariots and horses is repeated in Zech 6:1–8, in a similar context. I acknowledge the high degree of speculation in this, but I suggest that the bronze doors and levelled mountains of Isa 45 have been conflated into the "bronze mountains" which Yahweh has split forth before him. Perhaps also the mountains in Zech 6:1 are described as "bronze" to denote their strength and permanence (cf. "the everlasting mountains" of Hab 3:6) and hence of Yahweh's strength in being able to split the mountains and come forth from between them.[70]

67. My translation of "mountains" follows 1QIsa 45:2 (והררים) and LXX (ὄρη); MT has "exalted ones/things" (וַהֲדוּרִים), which is Qal passive participle of הדר. The MT probably arose though a scribal confusion between resh (ר) and daleth (ד).

68. This imagery is not unique to Habakkuk. See, for example, Mic 1:2–4—"Yahweh is coming from his dwelling place… The mountains melt beneath him and the plains will split." See also Nah 1:5: "The mountains quake before him and the hills melt." The clearest example of "mountain splitting" is Zech 14:4: "and the mount of olives shall be split in half."

69. Reading this as the Hithpoel of the verb פצץ, "shattered, split" (rather than פוץ, "scattered"). The other two instances of the verb פצץ in Job 16:12 (Pilpel) and Jer 23:29 (Poel) suggest that the word means "divide in two" (note particularly the parallel in Job 16:12) or "to split" (Jer 23:29, describes the action of a hammer on a rock face).

70. In tracing the theme of Yahweh-the-mountain-splitter to Hab 3, I take a different route to Hurowitz. Hurowitz (1999) argues that the "mountain splitting" theme in Zech 14:4 is a projection into the end time and transfer to Jerusalem of an etiological tale of the formation of the Levantine Rift Valley, between the Lebanon and the Ante-Lebanon reflected in the *Epic of Gilgamesh*'s account of the ancient battle between Enkidu and Humbaba. *Epic of Gilgamesh* Tablet 5 reads (in part) "The ground split open with the heels of their feet, as they whirled around in circles

Another puzzling element of the vision in Zech 6:1–8 is the description in vv. 6–8 of the direction to which the chariots "go out." The uncertainty arises in relation to the direction of travel of the white horses—do they go "westward" (so NIV, RSV, NRSV) or "northwards" (so ASV, NASB, JPS, ESV)? The MT says that the white horses go out "to the rear of them" (אֶל־אַחֲרֵיהֶם). If this phrase means "after them," then the antecedent noun is the black horses, with the implication that the white horses follow them in the same direction (i.e. northwards). On the other hand, Rudolph (1976: 123) has argued that the phrase means something like "towards their behinds" (i.e. backwards), which he takes to imply a westwards direction. Althann has rightly questioned whether the phrase can have the meaning which Rudolph suggests (1988: 67–68), and offers his own suggestion that the phrase means "to their end" in the sense of "destination," which he assumes to be westwards (1988: 69). Other scholars suggest various emendations to the MT to arrive at a westwards direction.[71]

However, it needs to be noted that those who argue for the "westwards" direction (by whatever route) are proceeding on the basis of a questionable assumption. The assumption is that, since the black horses head north and the speckled horses head south, then the white horses should likewise be headed towards a (different) cardinal point, as it would be asymmetrical to have two teams headed northwards. However, I make two observations which undercut the strength of that assumption. First, the directions in v. 6 are not cardinal points, strictly speaking, but rather the "land of the north" and the "land of the south." This might only seem like a semantic quibble, but in fact the difference is very significant. The "land of the north" has already been singled out for special mention in Zech 2:10 (ET 2:6):

> "Come! Come! And flee from the land of the north" (מארץ צפון) declares Yahweh, "for I have scattered you like the four winds of heaven (ארבע רוחות השמים)."

Zechariah 2 and Zech 6 both refer to "the land of the north" and the "four winds of heaven," legitimating the reading of these two passages together. In the light of this, it becomes less surprising that two chariot teams should be dispatched towards the land of the north, since this is the direction of the captivity of Yahweh's people.

The second observation which I wish to make against the assumption of "symmetry" is that the vision as a whole is not symmetrical. There are

Mt. Hermon and Lebanon split." However, there is little else in the context to suggest a connection with Zech 14, and even less with Zech 6:8.

71. For example, Mitchell (1912: 180) emends the text to get the necessary direction.

four chariot teams mentioned in 6:1–3, but only three of the four are mentioned in v. 6. Furthermore, in v. 8, it is only those who went to the "land of the north" who cause Yahweh's spirit to rest there. There is no corresponding report about the "land of the south" (to say nothing of "east" and "west").[72] This suggests that the chariot teams are not sent out on a single, universal mission to the four points of the compass, but rather that the focus of the passage is on a particular mission to give Yahweh's Spirit rest against the land of the north.

For these reasons, I conclude that there is nothing to overturn the natural translation of אֶל־אַחֲרֵיהֶם as "after them," with the implication that the white horses follow the black horses to the north.[73]

We have seen that the intertexts of Zech 6:1–8 help to clarify the meaning and significance of the final night-vision. Zechariah 6:1–8 picks up and extends an allusion begun in the first night-vision in relation to the heavenly emissaries in Job 1–2. Zechariah 6:1–8 combines this allusion to Job with the theme of "Yahweh's chariots," which gives a bellicose edge to the role of Yahweh's emissaries. Habakkuk 3 in particular was identified as providing the background for both the "horses and chariots" of Yahweh, and (together with Isa 45:2) for the symbolism of Yahweh bursting out from between the mountains of bronze in Zech 6:1, as the hosts of the divine warrior ride out to overthrow his foes. This understanding of the task of the black and white horses is confirmed by the fact that they "give Yahweh's Spirit rest" (when that phrase is properly understood against the background of a passage like Ezek 24:13). This mission is particularly directed against the "land of the north" (for which Zech 2:10 provides the conceptual background).

6.5. *Conclusion*

The final three night-visions combine to describe the progressive outworking of the consequences of Yahweh's return to dwell in Jerusalem. The flying scroll symbolizes the outworking of the curses of Yahweh's covenant law in banishing sin from the post-exilic community. The woman in the ephah denotes the removal of idolatry and other sin, and its relocation towards Shinar (Babylon). The final night-vision completes

72. Moreover, it would seem that v. 7 and v. 8 are referring to different teams of horses. In 6:7, it is only the [speckled-]grey horses which go out to "patrol" the earth (like the horses of the first vision), whereas in 6:8 "those which went out to the north" (which I take to encompass both the white and black horses) go out bent on conquest.

73. So McComiskey 1992: 1109; Floyd 2000: 400; Hahlen 2000: 253.

this sequence,[74] with Yahweh's Spirit being made to rest upon the land of the north.

The final three night-visions describe what might be termed the "negative" consequences of Yahweh's return to Jerusalem. The idolatry and other sin which had been so vexatious to Yahweh in the past will now be rooted out, shipped out and finally wiped out.[75] It is important to note that, strictly speaking, there is no "positive" side to these visions, in the sense that there is neither the promise of good things for God's people nor an explicit command for the people to respond in any particular way—these visions are simply the unilateral declaration of what is necessarily going to happen as a consequence of Yahweh's return.

It remains for Zech 7–8 to establish the positive implication of Yahweh's return, particularly in terms of the ethical responses required in view of Yahweh's return to dwell in Jerusalem. This is the subject of the following chapter.

6.6. *Intertextuality and Strategies of Containment*

I conclude this chapter by reflecting on the claims of "radical indeterminacy" with which the chapter began. As I noted, in recent years there has been a growing argument that texts do not have a single determinate meaning, but rather offer a plurality of interpretations, as a necessary consequence of their "intertextuality." Any text is a "tissue of quotations drawn from the innumerable centres of culture" (Barthes 1977: 146), and the sheer breadth of possibilities means that the reader is confronted with a plethora of interpretive possibilities. For example, Beal argues:

> Every text—as an intersection of other textual surfaces—suggests an indeterminate surplus of meaningful possibilities. Interpretation is always a production of meaning from that surplus. (Beal 1992: 31)

74. It is important to read the final night-vision as the sequel to the previous one, otherwise Zech 5:5–11 is open to the criticism that it implies that "Yahweh is in effect the founder and patron of some idolatrous cult" (Floyd 1996: 62). However, reading Zech 5:5–11 and 6:1–8 in sequence makes it clear that Yahweh is not sanctioning idolatry in Babylon, but rather has removed it to there, so that he can destroy it there. In the past, when idolatry and other sins were present in Jerusalem, Yahweh's anger against these practices had resulted in the destruction of the city and the withdrawal of his presence. The message of these visions is that Yahweh's wrath against idolatry and other sin will still come with destructive force, but it will fall in another place, rather than in Jerusalem.

75. In the past, the consequence of Yahweh's vexation was that (in the words of Jer 32:31) "this city has so aroused my anger and wrath that I must remove it from my sight." Now it is the sin and idolatry that is being removed.

To explore this issue, I will focus on Zech 5:5–11. I choose this passage in particular because of the specific claims made about the radical indeterminacy of Zech 5:5–11 in a recent article by Diana Edelman.

In her article, Edelman incorporates a representative cross-section of scholarly views on Zech 5:5–11 into a hypothetical court case. In her article, Yahweh is on trial for murdering his wife, Asherah. In his putative defence, Yahweh relies on the vast plurality of interpretations of these verses. Yahweh argues that this passage is deliberately multivalent (with the implication that the prosecution cannot convict him, since their case requires a single, "right" interpretation).[76] The same approach to Zech 1–8 more widely is reflected in the works by Love and Conrad, who offer their own "readings" of Zech 1–8, which are acknowledged to be just that—*a* "reading," not *the* "meaning."[77]

Timothy Beal has argued that, as a matter of expediency, readers must limit the infinite possibilities of a text in order to arrive at an interpretation, and that they do so based on their own ideology:

> Movement from the indeterminate "general text" to particular practices of intertextual reading demands that one ask about the ideological limits, or "strategies of containment,"[78] that make interpretation possible. (1992: 29)

76. Edelman's approach is both original and clever. However, while its rhetoric may well be appropriate for a defence lawyer, in the field of biblical scholarship we must beware of arguments which elevate rhetoric above substance. The defence takes the form of a deliberate obfuscation, where the reader is left bewildered by catalogue after catalogue of alternate interpretations. In these lists, there is little evaluation of the relative strengths of the various interpretations of Zech 5:5–11, so that interpretations which are exegetically unlikely, anachronistic and even tendentious are given equal (and in some cases, more) weight than interpretations which have greater merit. Moreover, by putting words in the mouth of Yahweh, Edelman can "authorize" a particular interpretation—for all of Yahweh's denials and plural interpretations, the reader is led to think "doth Yahweh protest too much?" Edelman's rhetoric argues to a conclusion (i.e. that Zech 5:5–11 probably *is* about Yahweh's "murder" of his co-deity Asherah), which cannot be sustained exegetically.

77. See, e.g. Conrad 1999: 17 and Love 1999: 40–47. A related approach is taken by Pyper, who argues that Zechariah is a difficult text to read, because it is an enactment of the difficulty of reading prior texts—"In the post-exilic world, where the authoritative but enigmatic text has taken the place of fallible prophecy, the dilemmas of faith become the dilemmas of the incompetent reader, confronted with a tradition whose surface meanings seem at odds with the realities of the social and political world" (2005: 500).

78. Beal's phrase "strategies of containment" is an allusion to Fredric Jameson. Jameson argues that a strategy of containment is a narrative construct which "allows what can be thought to seem internally coherent in its own terms, while repressing the unthinkable which lies beyond its boundaries" (Jameson 1981: 53 cf. 10).

In short, intertextual readings lead to multiple interpretations, and readers choose their preferred interpretation on ideological grounds.

However, in the light of our analysis of the woman in the ephah in Zech 5:5–11, we have seen a very different "strategy of containment" (if one will pardon an atrocious pun). We have seen that Zech 5:5–11 is indeed formed through the "intersection of other textual surfaces" (to quote Beal), but far from creating an indeterminate surplus of meaning, the intersection of these other texts instead has the effect of narrowing down the interpretive possibilities. If Zech 5:5–11 were read in absolute isolation, then these six verses could be made to mean almost anything. However, we have seen that the textual echoes in this passage suggest the intertexts by which it is to be understood. When read against these intertexts, the passage has a more limited range of meanings.

Moreover, the most reasonable interpretations of Zech 5:5–11 will be those which lie within the region circumscribed by the points of intersections of its various intertexts.

To use a geometric analogy, if we represent the possible range of meanings of a single metaphor as a line, then a passage with (say) three different metaphors, each drawing on distinct intertexts, might look something like this. The interpretations which are consistent with all three metaphors will lie inside the triangle in the middle:

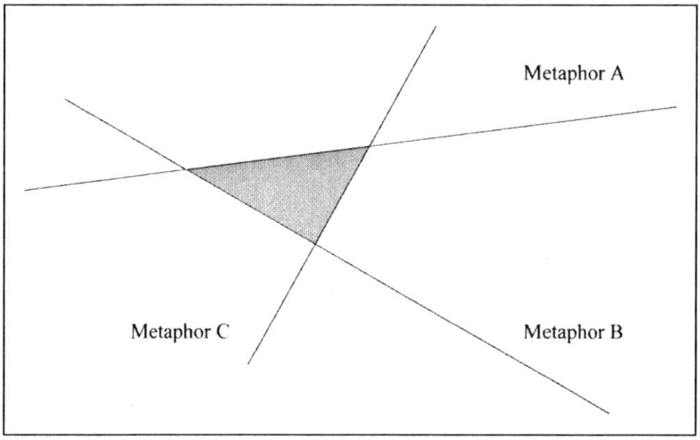

We have seen that the intratexts and the intertexts of Zech 5:5–11 provide a sufficient conceptual framework for understanding this passage. The key *intratexts* are those passages in Zech 1–8 which help us to understand the significance of the phrase "to build a house" in Zech 5:11, and the key *intertexts* are Ezek 1–11; 2 Sam 7 and Exod 25, which help us to recognize the ephah basket as an anti-ark borne by anti-cherubs to an anti-temple in an anti-Jerusalem. My argument is that this conceptual framework gives us a basis for determining which interpretations are more reasonable than others. Zechariah 5:5–11 is *not* adrift in an ocean of radical indeterminacy, in which a plurality of interpretations means that the reader must choose-their-own-adventure (contra Edelman and Love). Rather, the range of valid interpretations is limited to those which co-inhere with the framework. As noted above, I am not suggesting that the intratexts and intertexts completely determine the meaning of this passage, only that they "constrain" it (or "contain it," if you will again pardon the pun). There are other features of Zech 5:5–11 where we lack sufficient data to arrive at a single determinate meaning, but their features are only incidental (and, indeed, may have no intrinsic significance), and certainly do not make the field of interpretations as hopelessly ambiguous as some scholars have suggested. Intertexts are a help—not a hindrance—in narrowing the interpretive possibilities of a passage such as Zech 5:5–11.

Chapter 7

ZECHARIAH 7–8

7.1. *Introduction*

My aim in this chapter is to establish that Zech 7 and 8 are crucial for understanding the message of Zech 1–8 as a whole, in as much as they provide the link between the "cultic" focus on the temple rebuilding (*inter alia*) and the "ethical" parts of the message.

For much of the past century the study of exilic and post-exilic prophecy has languished in a backwater, a situation largely attributable to Wellhausen's dichotomy between "ethical monotheism" and "cultic religion." Ezekiel and Zech 1–8 in particular, with their obvious interest in the temple and other cultic matters, are (to Wellhausen) clear examples of a degeneration into cultic religion.[1] At the points where these prophets do apparently reflect an ethical concern, these words are not their own, but a mere imitation of the "true" prophets of old.[2] Wellhausen's effect on the study of Zech 1–8 has been long lasting.[3]

1. Wellhausen's most memorable rhetoric was directed against Ezekiel, "the priest in prophet's mantle" (1885: 59), though Zechariah and Haggai are clearly tarred with the same brush, in Wellhausen's view.

2. "We may call Jeremiah the last of the prophets: those who came after him were prophets only in name. Ezekiel had swallowed a book (iii.1–3), and gave it out again... Zechariah speaks of the old prophets as a series which is closed, in which he and those like him are not to be reckoned" (Wellhausen 1885: 403–4).

"[Ezekiel] is the connecting link between the prophets and the law. He claims to be a prophet, and starts from prophetic ideas: but they are not his own ideas, they are those of his predecessors which he turns into dogmas. He is by nature a priest, and his peculiar merit is that he enclosed the soul of prophecy in the body of a community which was not political, but founded on the temple and the cultus" (Wellhausen 1885: 421).

3. Writing in 1982, Mason noted the continuing negative effect of Wellhausen's view on the study of the "prophets of the restoration." Mason himself has a much greater appreciation for the way in which "ethical and cultic concerns were held together in the preaching of the second temple" (Mason 1982a: 149).

More recently, however, there has been a growing recognition of the importance of ethics in the argument of Zech 1–8.[4] For example, Boda (2003b: 51) argues that the effect of the addition of Zech 1:1–6 and 7:1–8:23 is that Zech 1–8

> ...in its final form transcends the agenda of temple rebuilding by accentuating the ethical agenda of two key exilic traditions: the literary tradition of the prophet Jeremiah and the oral tradition of penitential prayer.

Boda's recognition of the ethical agenda of Zech 1–8 is something which I heartily endorse. However, at the same time, I wish to extend the discussion somewhat, by exploring the relationship between "cult" and "ethics" in Zech 1–8. To demonstrate the ways in which Zech 7–8 links cult and ethics together, I will analyze a number of key allusions in these chapters, showing that these chapters are composed of "double-allusions." By "double allusion," I mean that these chapters allude—simultaneously—both to other texts in Zech 1–6, and also to texts outside Zechariah.[5] That is, Zech 7–8 has both "intratexts" and "intertexts," and it is reading these chapters in the context of both which provides the clue to linking cult and ethics in Zech 1–8.

In this chapter I will treat Zech 7–8 as a unity. Whether or not some parts of these chapters originally existed as independent literary units, clearly they have been brought together at some stage into their present form. The indications are that this redaction occurred before the completion of the temple in March 515 B.C.E.[6] In the absence of any evidence to the contrary, it is reasonable to assume that these chapters were composed in essence by Zechariah himself, some time between December 518 B.C.E. (the date implied by Zech 7:1) and March 515 B.C.E.

4. On this point, see also Floyd 2000: 412–14.

5. For some examples of Zech 8 echoing the words and themes of Zech 1–6, see Tollington 1993: 28.

6. Cf. the conclusion of Tollington 1993: 47 that (apart from 8:23) all of Zech 7–8 probably derives from the prophet Zechariah prior to the completion of the temple. Furthermore, while I recognize the differences in form between 8:1–13 and the material which surrounds it, I regard all of this material as coming from the hand of Zechariah, and having reached its present form prior to 515 B.C.E. Contra (Boda 2003a: 402), who argues that Zech 8:1–13 was added in a subsequent redaction. My rationale for this dating is that Zech 8:3 presupposes that Yahweh is not yet "dwelling in the midst of Jerusalem," and, as I will argue below, this indicates that the temple construction is not yet complete. Furthermore, this section ends in Zech 8:9–13 with an exhortation to "let your hands be strong," clearly relating to the (still future) rebuilding of the temple (see Boda 2006: 237 n. 106). There would seem to be no reason for these verses to have been added at any point after the temple had been completed—a point similarly made by Meyers and Meyers 1987: 381.

7.2. *A Question of Fasting—The Framework for Zechariah 7–8*

All the material in Zech 7–8 is set within a framework established by a question about fasting. The section opens in 7:2–6 with the question, which is finally answered in 8:19.

Zechariah 7:2–3 describes a delegation from Bethel[7] which comes to Jerusalem[8] to "entreat the favour of Yahweh" (לְחַלּוֹת אֶת־פְּנֵי יְהוָה)[9] and ask whether they should continue to "mourn" (בכה) and "abstain" (נזר) in the fifth month.[10] The prophet responds by rephrasing their enquiry in terms of "fasting" (צום) and "lamenting" (ספד) (Zech 7:5),[11] and

7. I take it that בֵּית־אֵל is the subject of verb in Zech 7:2—literally "Bethel sent Sharezer, and Regem-melech and his men." Contra Hyatt (1937), who argues that the phrase בֵּית־אֵל שַׂר־אֶצֶר in Zech 7:2 should be read as a personal name, based on neo-Babylonian attestation of the name Bīt-ili-shar-uṣur.

8. This location is implied by the fact that they come to speak to "the priests of the house of Yahweh" (Zech 7:3). This reference to "the house of Yahweh" does not necessarily mean that the temple has been rebuilt. This same phrase is used in Ezra 2:68 to describe the temple in its ruined state—"When they came to the house of Yahweh (לְבֵית יְהוָה)..." Similarly, see also Hag 1:2, 4, 8 and 14 and Jer 41:5, which all speak of "Yahweh's house" in referring to the building in its unreconstructed state. The reference to the "house of Yahweh" here in Zech 7:3 must fall into this same category of use, since Zech 8:9 makes it clear that the temple reconstruction is not yet complete.

9. The threefold repetition of the phrase "entreat the favour of Yahweh" in 7:2, 8:21 and 8:22 is noteworthy. Literally, it means "to make favourable the face of Yahweh" (לְחַלּוֹת אֶת־פְּנֵי יְהוָה). The author of Zech 7–8 is clearly aware of the more typical לְבַקֵּשׁ אֶת־יְהוָה ("to seek Yahweh") since this construction also appears (twice) in Zech 8:21–22. Given this deliberate use of the more unusual phrase to frame Zech 7–8, it is important to investigate whether any antecedent uses of the phrase "entreat the favour of Yahweh" might be significant for our understanding of Zech 7–8. In its various forms, this phrase only occurs twelve times, three of which are in Zech 7–8, and otherwise only in Exod 32:11; 1 Kgs 13:6 (×2); 1 Sam 13:12; 2 Kgs 13:4; 2 Chr 33:12; Dan 9:13; Jer 26:19; Mal 1:9. There are also four other instances in the more general form "seek the face" (i.e. without "Yahweh")—see Job 11:19; Prov 19:6; Pss 45:13; 119:58. The phrase typically occurs in negative contexts, suggesting that one seeks the "face" of Yahweh because Yahweh's face has been turned away in anger. The paradigmatic example is Exod 32:11—Yahweh had announced his intention to let his anger burn and destroy his people, but "Moses sought the favour of Yahweh." Of the possible prior instances of this phrase, the most likely intertext for Zech 7–8 is Jer 26:19, on the basis of other allusions to Jer 26 in Zech 7–8 (see Boda 2003b: 60).

10. On the social function of the fasts in Zech 7–8, see Hoffman 2003.

11. סָפוֹד is an infinitive absolute which continues the action of a preceding finite verb (see GKC §113z).

broadens the enquiry to include the fast of the seventh month. The answer to their question is finally given in Zech 8:19. Yahweh declares that the fasts (צוֹם, cognate noun to the verb in 7:5) in the fifth and seventh month (and the fasts in the fourth and tenth months as well) will become joyful and glad occasions. The progression is completed in Zech 8:20–23 by the promise that people from many cities will come to Jerusalem to "entreat the favour of Yahweh" (same phrase as in 7:2), and this same phrase is repeated again in Zech 8:22 to describe many peoples and strong nations in pilgrimage to Jerusalem. This follows a chiastic pattern.

A	7:2	People from Bethel coming to Jerusalem to entreat the favour of Yahweh
B	7:3–6	Ritual fasting (?)
B′	8:19	An answer concerning fasting—the fasts will turn to feasts
A′	8:20–22	Nations and cities coming to Jerusalem to entreat the favour of Yahweh

The prophet's initial reply in Zech 7:5–6 is enigmatic. While the first part of 7:5 is relatively straightforward, the last clause is far from clear. The words הֲצוֹם צַמְתֻּנִי are recognizable as the sequence interrogative + infinitive absolute[12] + perfect verb, which could be translated "Did you indeed fast…?"[13] However, the pronominal suffix on צַמְתֻּנִי is unexpected, since the root צום ("to fast") is intransitive. The literal translation "you fasted me" makes little sense. The sense adopted by almost all commentators is "You fasted *for* me"[14] (as though עָלַי צַמְתֶּם, by analogy with Ezra 4:16), though the routes to this conclusion are many and varied.[15] Also unusual is the first person pronoun אָנִי which completes the phrase,

12. In form, הֲצוֹם could also be the interrogative הֲ prefixing the noun צוֹם. However, in context, this is unlikely as it produces an awkward transition to the following verb, reading literally "Is a fast—you fasted me."

13. For similar constructions, see Gen 37:8, 10; 43:7; Num 22:37, 38; Judg 11:25; Isa 50:2; Jer 3:1; 14:19; 40:14; Ezek 18:23. See also GKC §113q.

14. See, e.g., Petersen 1984a: 285; Boda 2004: 358; Floyd 2000: 421.

15. GKC (§117x) argues that usage has allowed the verb צום to shift from intransitive to a transitive form, which has allowed the indirect object to be "directly subordinated in the form of an accusative suffix." Ewald §315b argues that Zech 7:5 must be an accusative suffix, citing analogies with Neo-Syriac, Persian, Armenian and Coptic. Meyers and Meyers argue that the pronominal suffix is a dative suffix, which is "quite common in poetry and also in the case of elevated prose" (1987: 389). Though I find none of these explanations entirely satisfactory (in as much as they seem to be a conclusion in search of a justification), I am at a loss to offer a better alternative.

though this is not without parallel elsewhere.[16] The translation of Zech 7:6 is less problematic, though it is not clear what significance we should attach to the switch from perfect to imperfect tense.[17] We might translate 7:5–6 (with most commentators) as follows:

When you fasted and mourned...	כי־צמתם וספוד...
was it indeed *for me* that you fasted?	הצום צמתני אני
And when you [*shall?*] eat and drink,	וכי תאכלו וכי תשתו
are not you the ones who are eating and drinking?	הלוא אתם האכלים ואתם השתים

However, even having established this translation, this still leaves the most vexing question: What is the rhetorical effect of these two questions? These questions are not directly answered in Zechariah, but are instead followed by a third question: "Were not these the words which Yahweh proclaimed by the former prophets...?"

One factor which can aid us in understanding Zech 7:5–7 is the wider parallels between Zech 7 and Zech 1. As many commentators have recognized, there are clear verbal and thematic parallels between Zech 7:7–14 and 1:1–6, and there is also the same sequence of ideas in each of the two passages.[18] (This is summarized in the table appearing overleaf.)

The "intratextual" parallels help us to understand the rhetorical force of Zech 7:5–7. First, it is clear that, when Zech 7:7 refers to the words proclaimed by "the former prophets," the reference is cataphoric (i.e. pointing forward to 7:9–10), rather than attributing the two preceding questions of 7:5–6 to the former prophets, since this is how the reference to the former prophets functions in Zech 1:4.[19]

Furthermore, the intratextual parallels with Zech 1 suggest that the rhetorical questions in Zech 7:5–6 should be given a negative edge. The appeal to the "former prophets" in both passages serves to stress that Yahweh requires a certain ethical response on the part of his people (which the generation of "the fathers" had failed to achieve, because of their refusal to listen and repent).

16. GKC §135e lists this as an example of a personal pronoun added to give emphasis to a verbal suffix. The other examples cited by GKC are בָּרֲכֵנִי גַם־אָנִי ("Bless me, even me also!") in Gen 27:34, and אֲנִי הִנְנִי ("I—I myself") in Ezek 6:3; 34:11; 34:20.

17. Floyd (2000: 422) regards the imperfect as denoting a "whole pattern of consumption at any and all times." In contrast, Mitchell 1912: 200 treats it as denoting a future time of eating and drinking.

18. See, e.g., Meyers and Meyers 1987: lii–liii; Tollington 1993: 208–9; Boda 2003a: 403.

19. So similarly Mitchell 1912: 200 and Floyd 2000: 423, 25.

Feature	*Zech 1:1–6*	*Zech 7:7–14*
Recalling the proclamation (קרא) of the former prophets (הנביאים הראשׁנים)	1:4a Do not be like your fathers, to whom the *former prophets proclaimed…*	7:7 Were not these the words that Yahweh *proclaimed* by the *former prophets…*
Near quotation of a designated "former prophet" (= Jeremiah)	1:4b Turn from your evil ways and from your evil deeds *(alluding to Jer 25:4–5; see the analysis at §2.8 and §4.2 above)*	7:9–10 Render true judgments, show kindness and mercy to one another; do not oppress the widow, the orphan, the alien, or the poor; and do not devise evil in your hearts against one another *(alluding to Jer 7:5–6; see below)*
The people's response—they would not hear (שׁמע) or listen (קשׁב)	1:4c But they did not *hear* (שׁמע) or *listen* (קשׁב) to me	7:11–12 But they refused to *listen* (קשׁב), and turned a stubborn shoulder, and stopped their ears from *hearing* (שׁמע). They made their hearts hard in order not to hear the law and the words that Yahweh of Hosts had sent by his spirit through the former prophets.
Exceeding wrath (קצף)	1:2 Yahweh wrathed *wrath* (קצף) upon your fathers	7:12 Therefore great *wrath* (קצף) came from Yahweh of Hosts.
Consequences	1:5–6 Your fathers, where are they? And the prophets, do they live forever? But my words and my statutes, which I commanded my servants the prophets, did they not overtake your fathers?	7:13–14 Just as, when I called, they would not hear, so, when they called, I would not hear and I scattered them with a whirlwind among all the nations that they had not known. Thus the land they left was desolate, so that no one went to and fro, and a pleasant land was made desolate.

From this, we may legitimately infer that the answer to the question in Zech 7:3 about the continuation of "ritual fasting" is that what really matters to Yahweh is justice, kindness and mercy (see Zech 7:9–10). For this reason, I conclude that the implicit function of the first two rhetorical questions must somehow be a critique of the fasting practices of the past "seventy years"; it is as if they are saying "The fasts have not been for Yahweh's sake—they are for your own sakes, just like eating and drinking."

In addition to these *intra*textual links which shape our understanding of Zech 7, there are two probable *inter*textual parallels which further nuance our understanding of the passage as a whole.

Zechariah 7:3–5 echoes the vocabulary of fasting and lament in Joel 2:12. The original enquiry in Zech 7:2 was framed in terms of "weeping" (בכה) and "abstaining" (נזר), which is paraphrased (in reverse order) in Zech 7:5 in terms of "fasting" (צום) and "mourning" (ספד). While no other passage has all four terms, Joel 2:12–13 has three of the four:[20]

> Return to me with all your heart with *fasting*, *weeping*, and *mourning* (ובבכי ובמספד ובצום). Rend your hearts and not your garments.

We have already noted a large number of connections between Joel 2 and Zech 1–2 (see §5.4). Of particular relevance to the present enquiry is the similarity between the first half of this clause—"Return to me"—and Zech 1:3. Another point of commonality between the two passages is the similar stress on "inward" versus "outward," reflected in Joel's call to "Rend your hearts and not your garments," and Zechariah's call to the kind of moral reformation Yahweh requires in response to a question about ritual fasting.

A second possible intertext is Isa 58.[21] The commonalities between Zech 7 and Isa 58 are not so much at the level of vocabulary (though it is only in these two passages that a *hê* interrogative is used to form a question about fasting), but rather at the thematic level. Both passages take a negative view of the fasting of the people—the implication of Zech 7:5 is that that they have not been "fasting for Yahweh," and likewise in Isa 58:5 their fast is not "a day acceptable to Yahweh." In each passage, their observance of "ritual" fasting[22] is held in contrast to their

20. The only other two passages with a combination of three terms are: 2 Sam 1:12, "mourned and wept and fasted" (וַיִּסְפְּדוּ וַיִּבְכּוּ וַיָּצֻמוּ); and Esth 4:3, "fasting and weeping and mourning" (וְצוֹם וּבְכִי וּמִסְפֵּד). The mourning for Saul's death in 2 Sam 1 is contextually unlike the mourning in Zech 7, and the passage from Esther post-dates Zech 1–8.

21. Tiemeyer (2006b: 94–96) argues that Zech 7:4–7 should be understood in the context of Isa 58, and reads Zech 7 as a critique of fasting done without a corresponding commitment to social justice. The parallels with Isa 58 are also argued by Webb (2003: 119–21), and cf. Baldwin (1972: 144), who asks "[c]ould it be to [Isa 58] that Zechariah refers in verse 7? The theme scarcely occurs in the prophets generally acknowledged to be pre-exilic (but *cf.* Ps 34:18; Joel 1:14; 2:12)."

22. "Ritual" in that it occurs on prescribed days (see Zech 7:5; cf. Isa 58:5).

failure to observe the ethical behaviour which Yahweh requires (see Zech 7:9–10; cf. Isa 58:6–10). Furthermore, in light of Zechariah's focus on the restoration of Jerusalem, it is interesting that Isa 58 also stresses the restoration of the "ancient ruins" (58:12).[23]

The effect of both of these intertexts is to reinforce the point being made by the intratextual parallel with Zech 1. What matters to Yahweh is not the (past) observance of seventy years of ritual fasts, but the (present) ethical transformation of his people. As we shall see below, the ethical standards which "the fathers" failed to achieve (Zech 7:9–10) are the same ethical standards which the present generation are now being called upon to demonstrate (cf. 8:16–17).

7.3. *The Intratexts of Zechariah 8*

In the preceding section, we have seen that Zech 7 contains a number of intratextual parallels to 1:1–6, and have argued that we should read Zech 7 in the light of 1:1–6. In this section, I will argue that a similar intratextual relationship is also true for Zech 8 and the visions and oracles in Zech 1–6.

Zechariah 8 contains a number of very clear allusions to the visions and oracles of Zech 1–6. In 8:2, Yahweh says "I am jealous for Zion with great jealousy" (קִנֵּאתִי לְצִיּוֹן קִנְאָה גְדוֹלָה). This is a clear echo of 1:14, "I am jealous for Jerusalem and Zion with great jealousy" (קִנֵּאתִי לִירוּשָׁלַ͏ִם וּלְצִיּוֹן קִנְאָה גְדוֹלָה), in that there are no other verses in the biblical corpus with the phrase "great jealousy" (קִנְאָה גְדוֹלָה). Yahweh's words in Zech 8 begin with a deliberate echo of the first night-vision.

In Zech 8:3, Yahweh says "I am returning to Zion, and will dwell in the midst of Jerusalem" (שַׁבְתִּי אֶל־צִיּוֹן וְשָׁכַנְתִּי בְּתוֹךְ יְרוּשָׁלָ͏ִם).[24] This is an echo of 1:16, "I am returning to Jerusalem" (שַׁבְתִּי לִירוּשָׁלַ͏ִם), combined with 2:14 (ET 2:10), "I will dwell in your midst" (וְשָׁכַנְתִּי בְתוֹכֵךְ) (where "your" refers to Zion). This combination of words (i.e. Yahweh's return to dwell in Zion/Jerusalem) is not paralleled outside of Zech 1–8.[25]

23. There are clear parallels between Isa 44:26; 58:12a and 61:4: "And of the cities of Judah, 'They shall be *rebuilt*, and I will *raise up* their *ruins*'" (Isa 44:26); "And your ancient *ruins* shall be *rebuilt*; you shall *raise* up the foundations of *many generations*" (Isa 58:12a); "They shall *build up* the ancient *ruins*, they shall *raise up* the former devastations; they shall repair the ruined cities, the devastations of *many generations*" (Isa 61:4).

24. On my "present continuous" translation of שַׁבְתִּי as "I am returning," see the discussion at §4.2 above.

25. Though, as argued in §5.2, this is a thematic reflection of Ezek 40–43.

These intratextual connections between Zech 1–6 and Zech 7–8 are crucial for informing the reader as to how the overall message is to be understood, in that Zech 7–8 both re-iterates and extends Zech 1–6.

As has been seen above in the analysis of Zechariah's night-visions, Yahweh's "return to dwell" at Jerusalem/Zion is intimately connected with the rebuilding of the temple.[26] I have already quoted the first part of Zech 1:16, where Yahweh says "I am returning to Jerusalem." In the same verse, Yahweh continues "My house will be built in it" (בֵּיתִי יִבָּנֶה בָּהּ). What is announced programmatically in the first vision is reinforced in the two central visions in the night-vision sequence. As discussed above, Zech 4 describes the completed temple using the symbolism of a lampstand, flanked by two olive trees (representing Joshua and Zerubbabel). These two are singled out, because Zerubbabel is the promised "Branch" who will rebuild the temple of Yahweh, and Joshua is the high priest who will lead the re-established priesthood in the restored temple (Zech 3). These two figures also feature in the climactic oracle in Zech 6:9–15, which completes the night-vision sequence. In short, the night-visions describe the restoration of Zion, centred on a restored temple.[27]

Zechariah 8:3 makes an unmistakable allusion to this central theme in Zech 1–6, stressing that the means by which Yahweh returns to "dwell" in Zion will be through the rebuilding of the temple at Jerusalem. The future tense of "I will dwell" and "will be built" suggests that, at the time of writing, the goal of Yahweh's return has not yet been reached.

The remainder of Zech 8 contains numerous parallels to the night-visions and oracles, though more at a thematic, rather than verbal, level.

Zechariah 8:4–8 describe a repopulated Jerusalem, with streets full of playing children, which comes about because Yahweh will save his people from East and West and bring them back to Jerusalem. The two visions and their associated oracle in Zech 2 describe the same scene (albeit in a visionary mode): Yahweh overthrowing the "horns" (i.e. nations) (Zech 2:1–4 ET 1:18–21) so that his people can return back to Jerusalem (2:10–11 ET 2:6–7), with the result that Jerusalem will be so populous that it cannot be measured or contained by a wall (2:8–9 ET 2:4–5; cf. 1:17).[28]

26. Contra Marinkovic (1994: 90), who argues that "not one of the nightvisions as such is connected with the temple as such or with its reconstruction." Marinkovic (rightly) perceives the thematic importance of the return of Yahweh to Jerusalem, but argues that this is unrelated to the reconstruction of Yahweh's house.

27. On the centrality of the temple to night-vision sequence as a whole, see also Hanson 1987a.

28. The absence of verbal links between Zech 8:4–8 and Zech 2 might be because there is another layer of allusion operating in Zech 8. As I have argued elsewhere

In the light of this promised restoration, Zech 8:9 says, "Let your hands be strong" to the generation who were present "in the day of the (re)founding[29] of the house of Yahweh" (בְּיוֹם יֻסַּד בֵּית־יְהוָה, 8:9b). In context, the implication of the exhortation is clear—they are to "let their hands be strong" to complete the rebuilding of the temple. This stress on the founding and completion of the temple echoes the thought of 4:6–10,[30] particularly the oracle about Zerubbabel in 4:9—"The hands of Zerubbabel founded this house and his hands will finish it" (יְדֵי זְרֻבָּבֶל יִסְּדוּ הַבַּיִת הַזֶּה וְיָדָיו תְּבַצַּעְנָה).

The language of Zech 8:14—particularly of Yahweh "purposing" (זמם) destruction because of "wrath" (קצף) at "their fathers" (אֲבֹתֵיכֶם)—echoes Zech 1:2, 6. However, as Zech 8:15 makes clear, Zechariah's hearers are not to be subject to the same fate as their fathers. Zechariah 8:15 picks up the theme of the "reversal of wrath" developed in Zech 1:12–17. There are verbal links which reinforce this thematic connection: Zech 1:12–15 announces that Yahweh will no longer withhold mercy from *Jerusalem* (יְרוּשָׁלַםִ) and the cities of *Judah* (יְהוּדָה); instead, he declares, "My cities shall again overflow from the *good* (טוֹב)" (1:17). There is a verbal echo of this in Zech 8:15, in the promise of Yahweh "to do *good* to *Jerusalem* and to the house of *Judah*" (לְהֵיטִיב אֶת־יְרוּשָׁלַםִ וְאֶת־בֵּית יְהוּדָה).[31]

To this point in Zech 8 the intratextual links have been confined to Zech 1–4. At Zech 8:16–17, however, we strike something new, with a connection to Zech 5. Zechariah 8:16–17 is an ethical directive to Zechariah's generation: to speak the truth, render justice, devise no evil and love no false oath. While there are a number of similarities between Zech 8:16–17 and 7:9–10 (which I shall discuss below), there is also a connection with the flying scroll of 5:4. In the same way that the scroll

(Stead 2009), Zech 8:4–8 is part of a sustained allusion to Lam 2. In Lam 2:10–11, the elders of Daughter Zion (זִקְנֵי בַת־צִיּוֹן) sit (ישב) in lament, the young girls with heads bowed to the ground (הוֹרִידוּ לָאָרֶץ רֹאשָׁן), and children faint "in streets of the town [i.e. Jerusalem]" (בִּרְחֹבוֹת קִרְיָה). In reversal of this image, in Zech 8:4–5, the "elders" (זְקֵנִים וּזְקֵנוֹת) "shall again sit" (עֹד יֵשְׁבוּ) in the streets of Jerusalem (בִּרְחֹבוֹת יְרוּשָׁלָםִ), and the children shall play in "the streets of the city" (וּרְחֹבוֹת הָעִיר). Zechariah inverts the imagery of Lam 2 in order to declare the end of the exile.

29. I agree with Andersen (1958) that יסד in this context does not mean "founding" *de novo*, but rather the resumption of work on a previously founded temple. Cf. Gelston 1966; Rudolph 1976: 46; Tollington 1993: 152.

30. For further points of commonality between Zech 4:6–10 and Zech 8:9–13 in connection with ancient Near Eastern temple-founding ceremonies, see Boda 2006.

31. The verbal links alone are not compelling evidence, since the combination of Jerusalem, Judah and "do good" are not without parallel elsewhere.

acts against the one who swears falsely (לַשָּׁקֶר...הַנִּשְׁבָּע), Zech 8 condemns the false oath (שְׁקֶר שְׁבֻעַת).[32] This rare combination of words links the chapters, and this link is further reinforced by the observation that both Zech 8 and Zech 1–5 follow the same progression of thought—each begins with the time of wrath ended and Yahweh's return to dwell (Zech 1–4 and 8:1–15) and then moves to what might be termed the "ethical implications" of this return of Yahweh (Zech 5 and 8:16–17).

Zechariah 8:18–19 returns to the question of fasting with which Zech 7 began, and then the chapter concludes in Zech 8:20–23 with a passage that describes the nations taking the initiative to come in pilgrimage to Jerusalem. This final section echoes a theme introduced in Zech 2:15 (ET v. 11), as shown in the following table:[33]

2:15 Many nations shall join themselves to Yahweh on that day, and shall be my people; and I will dwell in your midst.	8:22 Many peoples and strong nations shall come to seek Yahweh of Hosts in Jerusalem, and to entreat the favour of Yahweh. 8:23 … "Let us go with you, for we have heard that God is with you."

At the same time, this conclusion to Zech 8 also "ends at the same point" as the final night-vision, in as much that both sections end with a focus on the nations, although the direction of movement and implications are inverted—in Zech 6:1–8, Yahweh's Spirit goes out to "rest" (in judgment)[34] on the nations, whereas in 8:20–23 the nations come in to seek the favour of Yahweh.[35]

32. The only passages predating Zech 1–8 which speak of false oaths (using these words or cognates) are Lev 5:22–24; 19:12; Jer 5:2; 7:9. These will be discussed in more detail below, where I conclude that Jer 7 is the likely source for both Zech 8:16–17 and Zech 7:9–10, as it was for Zech 5:4.

33. The phraseology of Zech 8 differs from Zech 2, probably under the influence of the intertextual connections between Zech 8 and Isa 2 (and/or Mic 4).

34. See §6.4 for my view on Zech 6:8 in the context of its Ezekielian intertexts.

35. I analyzed the intertextual connection between Zech 8:20–22 and Isa 2:4 at §2.8 (example 4). For the sake of completeness, I should also note the possible intertexts of Zech 8:23, as I will not be focusing on this verse in my analysis below. Zech 8:23 would appear to be a combination of various intertexts: (1) the imagery of "ten men grasping" a Jew (יַחֲזִיקוּ עֲשָׂרָה אֲנָשִׁים) is thematically similar to Isa 4:1, in which "seven women will grasp a man" (הֶחֱזִיקוּ שֶׁבַע נָשִׁים בְּאִישׁ); (2) the specific vocabulary of "grasping the hem" (הֶחֱזִיקוּ בִּכְנַף) echoes 1 Sam 15:27, which describes Saul "grasped the hem of the robe" of Samuel (וַיַּחֲזֵק בִּכְנַף־מְעִילוֹ); (3) the phrase "all the tongues of the nations" (מִכֹּל לְשֹׁנוֹת הַגּוֹיִם) is an echo of (or is echoed by) Isa 66:18, when Yahweh gathers "all the nations and tongues" (כָּל־הַגּוֹיִם וְהַלְּשֹׁנוֹת), which similarly occurs in the context of the pilgrimage of the nations to Jerusalem

7.4. *Zechariah 7–8: A Recapitulation of Zechariah 1–6*

So far in this chapter I have highlighted the "intratextual" connections between Zech 1–6 and Zech 7–8, and demonstrated a number of repeated themes. The combined effect of the intratexts in Zech 7–8 is to create a parallel structure between Zech 1–6 and Zech 7–8, with Zech 7–8 recapitulating the message of Zech 1–6, albeit in a different mode. Or to put this another way, the same message which Zech 1–6 makes via a sequence of eight visions is made in a more prosaic form in Zech 7–8:[36]

Yahweh's wrath against the fathers and its consequences	*Yahweh's return to dwell in Jerusalem, consequent upon the rebuilding of the temple*	*Implications for his people*	*Implications for the nations*
1:1–6	1:7–4:14; 6:9–15	ch. 5	6:1–8
7:1–14	8:1–15	8:16–19	8:20–23

The effect of the "intratextual" connections is to bind the two sections of Zech 1–8 together. The repetition of phrases and ideas from Zech 1–6 in Zech 7–8 signals that these chapters are dealing with the same concerns as the earlier chapters. The "panelling"[37] of these two parallel accounts suggests that they are to be read together to get the complete picture.[38]

When we read both "panels" together, it is apparent that Zech 7–8 adds important nuances to the way we should understand the meaning of Zech 1–6. Most significantly for present purposes, it suggests that the central concern of Zech 1–8 is not "temple building" *per se*, but rather Yahweh's return to dwell in the midst of Jerusalem,[39] and that the

(cf. Isa 66:18–20); (4) the report "God is with you" (עִמָּכֶם אֱלֹהִים) may be an echo of the "Immanuel" (עִמָּנוּ־אֵל) promise of Isa 7:14; 8:10 (cf. Petitjean 1969: 437).

36. A similar conclusion is reached by Petersen—"The oracles in Zech 7–8 rehearse in a less symbolic way issues broached in the visions and their oracular responses" (1984a: 123)—and Conrad (1999: 137)—"Zechariah's answer [in Zech 7–8] mirrors that of the first two sections (1:1–6:15), concerning what Zechariah had seen two years earlier." Cf. also Ollenburger 1996:789–90.

37. "Panelling" (in literary studies) is a metaphoric adaptation of the triptych of the art world. A triptych consists of three joined panels that tell a single story. In literary studies, the metaphor is used to describe the way in which parallel accounts interrelate to form a composite whole. My exposure to the term comes from Webb (1987: 178). See O'Connell (1992) on the panelling in Deuteronomy.

38. This parallel schema differs in some respects from the one proposed by Boda (2003a: 403), who parallels Zech 1:1–6 with 7:1–14 + 8:14–23.

39. That Zech 1–8 is principally concerned with Yahweh's return to dwell with his people is apparent from a comparison of Zech 8:1–15 with Zech 1–4—many of the same themes are there, but the emphasis in 8:1–15 is on the return to dwell, rather than the temple-building project.

"return" of Yahweh carries with it important ethical implications for the people of God.

To this point in my argument I have stressed the intratextual connection between Zech 1–6 and Zech 7–8. However, notwithstanding these close connections, there are also significant points of difference between the two sections. Zechariah 7–8 is not just saying the same thing over again, but is actually stressing a different point in the process of recapitulation. To hear this difference, we have to be sensitive not merely to *intra*texts but also to the *inter*texts of Zech 7–8.

7.5. *The Intertextual Connection Between Zechariah 7:7–14 and Jeremiah 7*

In Zech 7:7 there is what amounts to an intertextual "search warrant." The question "were these not the words which Yahweh proclaimed by the hand of the former prophets?" invites a search for the possible sources of the prophetic words which follow in Zech 7:9–10.[40] The second half of 7:7 gives us a time marker as to when these words were proclaimed—"when Jerusalem was inhabited and at ease, along with the towns around it, and when the Negeb and the Shephelah were inhabited." This phraseology is strongly reminiscent of the book of Jeremiah, which, alone among the prophets, has the only other instances of the combination "Jerusalem / surrounding cities / Negeb / Shephelah" (see Jer 17:26; 32:44; 33:13). And indeed, when we search for a parallel for the putative message of "former prophets" in Zech 7:9–10, by far the closest connection is with Jer 7:5–6, which is demonstrated below:[41]

40. As argued above at §7.2, Zech 7:7 is cataphoric, not anaphoric. A possible argument against this is that Zech 7:7 ends with a petucah (פ) and Zech 7:8 thus begins a new section, marked with the formula "the word of the Yahweh came to Zechariah, saying..." Wellhausen argued for the deletion of Zech 7:8 because what follows in v. 9 is the word of Yahweh to the former prophets introduced in Zech 7:7 (see 1963: 187). However, this is to miss the significance of the formula in Zech 7:8. The effect of Zech 7:8 is to affirm that the prophet Zechariah has received the words in 7:9–10 as a revelation from Yahweh, rather than merely from citing Scripture. Zech 7:9–10 is not so much Zechariah's summary of Jeremiah, but Yahweh's own summary of what he had said previously through Jeremiah.

41. A number of commentators have made this connection. Nurmela (1996: 69–72) lists this as a "sure" allusion. See similarly Boda 2004: 360. Petersen (1984a: 290) notes the strong connections, but hesitates over assigning literary dependence on the grounds that Jer 7 may be a late composition. Mitchell regards this verse as Zechariah's summary of the teaching of the former prophets—"the gist of their instruction"—and includes Jer 7 as a possible source for Zechariah's call to social

Zech 7:9–10	*Jer 7:5–6a*
משפט אמת שפטו וחסד ורחמים עשו איש את־אחיו ואלמנה ויתום גר ועני אל־תעשקו	תעשו משפט בין איש ובין רעהו אם־עשו גר יתום ואלמנה לא תעשקו
Render true justice and kindness and mercy *to one another; do not oppress the widow, the orphan, the alien, or the poor…*	if you truly *do justice with one another, if you do not oppress the alien, the orphan, and the widow…*

Though far from being a word-for-word quotation, the nature and extent of the parallels is typical of Zechariah's pattern of allusion.[42] In these verses there would also appear to be "overtones" from other passages.[43] Furthermore, not only does Zech 7:9–10 allude to Jer 7:5–6, but there are also wider parallels between the two chapters, parallels which make a compelling case for seeing a sustained allusion between Zech 7:7–13 and Jer 7.[44] Almost every major concept in Zech 7:9–13 has it conceptual parallel (and often its verbal parallel) in Jer 7, as the table opposite demonstrates.

Jeremiah 7 is commonly recognized to be made up of multiple oracles (typically divided 7:1–15, 16–20, 21–29, 30–34). On this analysis, Zech 7 is alluding to a form of the book of Jeremiah which already contained at least the first three of these oracles.[45]

virtues (1912: 201). In contrast, Sweeney (2000: 644), who argues that vv. 9b–10 "relate especially to Isa 1:16–17." However, the limited extent of the parallels with Isa 1 makes for a less compelling case for allusion than that for Jer 7.

42. Zechariah's pattern of allusion was analysed above at §2.8.

43. For example, the last phrase—"to devise (חשב) evil (רַע) in your hearts (לְבַב)"—would appear to be an echo of Jer 18:12: "We will follow our own devising (מַחֲשָׁבָה), and each…his evil (רַע) heart (לֵב)." The command to show "mercy" (חֶסֶד) could reflect Mic 6:8 and/or Amos 5:14, 24—see Watts 1972: 333, who also identifies echoes of Isa 1:16–17. See similarly Smith 1984: 225–26.

44. For an analysis of the use of Jeremiah's deuteronomistic prose in Zech 7–8, see Boda 2003b: 55–61. I go beyond Boda in arguing for a connection to Jer 7 in particular, as against Jeremiah's deuteronomistic prose more generally.

45. A factor that increases the likelihood of an explicit allusion to Jer 7 in this chapter is the fact that there are other allusions to Jer 7 in the wider context of Zech 1–8. The clearest allusion is the flying scroll of Zech 5:1–4, which contains prohibitions against the one who steals (גנב) and the one swearing falsely (הַנִּשְׁבָּע…לַשָּׁקֶר). Jer 7:9 is the only other instance of these terms being used in the same verse, and I concur with a number of other commentators who register an allusion at this point between Zech 5 and Jer 7; see further §6.2 above, and see, e.g., Nurmela 1996: 67; Delkurt 1999b; Tigchelaar 1996: 82; Boda 2004: 360. Cf. Meyers and Meyers 1987: 284–85.

Zech 7	*Jer 7*
7:9–10 Render true justice and kindness and mercy to one another; do not oppress the widow, the orphan, the alien, or the poor and do not devise evil in your hearts against one another.	7:5–6 *(see analysis above)* if you truly do justice with one another, if you do not oppress the alien, the orphan, and the widow, or shed innocent blood in this place
7:11–12 But they refused to listen, and turned a stubborn shoulder, and stopped their ears from hearing. They made their hearts hard…in order not to hear the law and the words which Yahweh of Hosts had sent by his spirit through the former prophets	7:24 And they did not listen nor open the ear, and walked in stubbornness of heart" 7:25 Not paying attention to Yahweh, who sent "my servants the prophets"
7:12 Therefore great wrath came from Yahweh of Hosts.	7:20 wrath and anger will be poured out 7:29 this generation is under his wrath
7:13 Just as, when I called, they would not hear, so, when they called, I would not hear…	7:13 I spoke, and you did not listen, and when I called you, you did not answer 7:16 Yahweh says "For I will not listen" to Jeremiah's prayers for people.

The extent of these connections strongly suggests that Zech 7:7–14 alludes to Jer 7.[46] Though the section as a whole contains much distinctive Jeremian phraseology in general,[47] I suggest that when Zechariah's

46. While Jer 22:3 also shares some features with Zech 7, Jer 7 has a greater number of correlations.

47. In particular, I note the following:

Zech 7:7: Prosperity (שָׁלֵו)	Jer 22:21 (שַׁלְוָה)
Zech 7:7: Negeb and Shephelah	Recalls Jeremiah's promises of restoration—Jer 17:26; 32:44; 33:13
Zech 7:10: poor (עָנִי)	Jer 22:16 (עָנִי), cf. Jer 5:28 (synonym: אֶבְיוֹן)
Zech 7:11: They made their hearts adamant (שָׁמִיר)	Jer 17:1, perhaps refracted through the lens of Ezek 3:7–9
Zech 7:14: for a desolation (לְשַׁמָּה)	Jeremiah has 20 of the 33 instances of this phrase—Jer 2:15; 4:7; 18:16; 19:8; *25:9, 11, 18, 38*; 29:18; 42:18; 44:12, 22; 46:19; 48:9; 49:13, 17; 50:23, 3; 51:29, 41. Of these, Jer 25 is the best candidate as the source, given that the phrase is repeated four times (highlighted above), given also that this passage is also alluded to elsewhere: Zech 1:4 = 25:4, and the "seventy years" (Zech 1:12; 7:5 = Jer 25:11–12)

audience heard him speaking these words, as being "the words spoken through the former prophets," they would have connected his words with Jer 7 in particular. If we can take it as sufficiently established that Zech 7 alludes to Jer 7, then it is possible to go on to ask the more important question: What might be the significance of a particular allusion to Jer 7?

Jeremiah 7:1–15 is the famous "temple sermon," and of particular significance for the present enquiry is the direct connection made there between "cult" and "ethics." Jeremiah had preached to a generation that was treating the temple as a talisman (Jer 7:4, 10–11), believing that Yahweh would never allow the destruction of the house where he had caused his name to dwell (7:10–14). As such, the people walked with impunity in their evil ways and deeds (7:5), in theft, murder, falsehood, idolatry and so on (7:9), thinking that they could still come to the temple to worship Yahweh (7:2, 10). Jeremiah 7:1–15 is a polemic against a "mechanistic" view of the temple which regarded the building itself as a guarantee of the presence of Yahweh, independent of the ethical behaviour of the people of God.

What, then, is the rhetorical effect of an allusion to Jeremiah's temple sermon in the present context of Zech 7? As noted above, Zech 7 begins with an enquiry about whether to end the ritual fasts of "these seventy years" (7:5). As noted above in the discussion on Zech 1:12, the "seventy years" denotes the period of temple destruction, which (in the historical context of 518 B.C.E.) had almost run their course. The assumption behind the enquiry is that fasting will no longer be required once the seventy years are up and the temple is rebuilt. However, that assumption betrays the same kind of "mechanistic" view of the temple which is so roundly criticized in Jer 7, in that it presupposes a direct correlation between the physical temple and the presence of Yahweh. Their enquiry presumes:

> No Temple = Yahweh not dwelling with his people → Fasting and mourning
> Temple = Yahweh dwelling with his people → No fasting/mourning needed

The rhetorical effect of the allusion to Jer 7 is to warn Zechariah's generation against adopting the "temple = God-in-a-box" mentality of their forebears. The mere completion of the temple will not guarantee the return of Yahweh to dwell with his people. It must be accompanied by

Zech 7:14: pleasant land (אֶרֶץ חֶמְדָּה)	Same phrase in Jer 3:19 (only otherwise in Ps 106:24)
Zech 7:14: I stormed them (וְאֵסָעֲרֵם) to the nations	Jer 30:23//23:19—behold the storm of Yahweh (הִנֵּה סַעֲרַת יְהוָה)

the ethical transformation of the people of God. The allusion to Jer 7 stresses that Yahweh's ongoing presence with his people demands an ethical response.[48] Zechariah 7 says, in effect, "The fathers (i.e. Jeremiah's generation) failed to make this response, and look what happened to them!" That which the fathers had failed to achieve (7:9–10) is the same standard which Zechariah's generation is now called to live up to.

Zechariah 8:16–17 is an intratextual echo of Zech 7:9–10, where the ethical standard formerly proclaimed to the "fathers" (7:9–10) comes to be applied to Zechariah's generation (8:16–17), as shown in this table:

Zech 7:9–10 The words (הַדְּבָרִים) proclaimed by the former prophets	*Zech 8:16–17* These are the words (הַדְּבָרִים) *you* shall do
	Speak truth, *each to his neighbour* (אִישׁ אֶת־רֵעֵהוּ)
Render true judgments (מִשְׁפַּט אֱמֶת שְׁפֹטוּ) show kindness and mercy, *each to his brother* (אִישׁ אֶת־אָחִיו) Do not oppress the widow, the orphan,	*Render* (שִׁפְטוּ) in your gates *judgments of truth* (וּמִשְׁפַּט שָׁלוֹם)
the alien, or the poor; *and do not devise evil in your hearts each against his brother*	*do not devise evil in your hearts, each against his neighbour*

Without Zech 7–8, it might be possible to read the night-visions of Zech 1–6 (see esp. 1:16; 2:14–17 = ET 2:10–14) in a mechanistic fashion, as though a rebuilt temple must automatically mean that Yahweh will again be dwelling in the midst of his people. However, Zech 7–8 adds an important nuance to the way that we read the book as a whole. While Zech 1–6 is clearly very interested in the temple reconstruction, this is not to be taken as an end in itself. The sustained allusion to Jer 7 in Zech 7 makes clear that the ethical transformation of Yahweh's people is essential. As a whole, the message of Zech 1–8 is that Yahweh is returning to dwell with his people in Jerusalem (Zech 8:3), and expects them to return to him with morally transformed lives. At the end of the day, what will turn the "fasts" into "feasts" is not the mere completion of the temple after "these seventy years," but the ethical transformation—especially expressed in terms of "truth" and "peace"[49]—brought about by Yahweh's return to dwell in their midst.

48. Cf. Tigchelaar (1996: 82) who also notes points of connection between Zech 1–8 and Jer 7:1–15, and concludes "The explicit textual details of Jer 7:1–15 would fit most appropriately in the text and context of Zechariah's sermon."

49. See Zech 8:19, especially in relation to the keywords אֱמֶת and שָׁלוֹם in the context of 8:16–17.

Another important effect of the allusion to Jer 7 is that it brings in "covenantal" overtones, which are not otherwise explicit in Zech 7. As Jer 7 makes clear, Yahweh's wrath at the fathers is because their evil ways are a forsaking of the stipulations of the covenant, which were given on the day he had "brought them out of the land of Egypt" and had said to them "I will be your God and you shall be my people" (Jer 7:22–23). I shall develop my argument as to the significance of these "covenantal" overtones after my analysis of the intertexts of Zech 8.

7.6. *The Intertexts of Zechariah 8*

For all of the commonality between Zech 8 and Zech 1–6 (as discussed in §7.3), it is also vitally important to note the points at which there are *no* explicit parallels in Zech 1–6, and determine the significance of this fact. In this section, I will demonstrate that a chief point of difference between Zech 1–6 and Zech 8 is that Zech 8 contains intertextual connections to numerous "covenant" themes which are (apparently) absent in Zech 1–6.

7.6.1. *"They will be my people and I will be their God"*

The "covenant formula" (וְהָיוּ־לִי לְעָם וַאֲנִי אֶהְיֶה לָהֶם לֵאלֹהִים) occurs in Zech 8:8b, where it is connected to Yahweh's gathering of his people back to Jerusalem. The formula occurs nowhere else in Zech 1–8.[50] Outside of Zechariah, this covenant formula (or part thereof) occurs in Deuteronomy (six times), Jeremiah (eight times) and Ezekiel (five times),[51] and then only otherwise in four places.[52] The connection between "I will be their God" and Yahweh bringing his people back to Jerusalem which we see in Zech 8:8 is a typical feature of both Jeremiah and Ezekiel, where this connection is expressed in explicitly covenantal (i.e. בְּרִית) terms.[53] Whether or not the author of Zech 8:8 had a particular

50. The only phrase that is close is Zech 2:15 (ET 2:11), which says that many nations "will be my people" (וְהָיוּ לִי לְעָם). However, this is the exception that proves the rule, as this is a promise for the nations, not for Israel.

51. Most of the instances in Deuteronomy only have the first clause of the covenant formula—see Deut 4:20; 7:6; 14:2; 26:18; cf. 27:9. Deut 29:12 does have both clauses, but not in the typical form. In contrast, Jeremiah and Ezekiel usually have both clauses in the typical form—see Jer 7:23; 11:4; 13:11 (לִי לְעָם לִהְיוֹת only); 24:7; 30:22; 31:1, 33; 32:38; Ezek 11:20; 14:11; 36:28; 37:23, 27.

52. Exod 6:7; Lev 26:12; 2 Sam 7:24 (paralleled in 1 Chr 17:22).

53. See Jer 24:6–7; 30:18–22; 31:1–5, 33; 32:37–40, and Ezek 11:17–20; 36:24–30; 37:21–28, and note especially the references to Yahweh's covenant (בְּרִית) in Jer 31:31–33; 32:30; Ezek 37:26.

text from Jeremiah and/or Ezekiel in mind, the use of this formula in Zech 8:8b is clearly evocative of the covenantal “thought world” as it finds expression in Deuteronomy/Jeremiah/Ezekiel. This is not a feature of Zech 1–6.

7.6.2. *Deuteronomy 28–30—Blessings and Curses of the Covenant*

Not only is the covenant formula conspicuous by its absence in Zech 1–6, but Zech 1–6 also lacks any explicit parallels to the covenant “blessings and curses” which are found in Zech 8.[54]

The clearest explicit example of the phenomenon is in Zech 8:13—“Just as you have been a curse among the nations (קְלָלָה בַּגּוֹיִם)...so I will save you and you will be a blessing (בְּרָכָה).” The interplay we see here between “blessing” (בְּרָכָה) and “cursing” (קְלָלָה) recalls the “words of the covenant” (דִּבְרֵי הַבְּרִית, Deut 28:69 = ET 29:1) given through Moses, as particularly expressed in Deuteronomy (see esp. Deut 28; 30:1–7; cf. 11:26–32). I regard the language of Zech 8:13—“a curse among the nations” and “blessing”—as a primary allusion[55] to Deut 30:1, on the basis that Zech 8:14 and Deut 30:1 are the only two verses where “blessing” (בְּרָכָה), “curse” (קְלָלָה) and “in (all) the nations” (בְּ +גּוֹי) occur together.[56]

A further example of this theme occurs in Zech 8:10, which alludes to the blessings and curses listed in Deut 28. Deut 28:6 promises blessings “when you come in (בוא) and go out (יצא),” followed directly by the promise that “enemies will smitten before you” (Deut 28:7).[57] This combination of themes is picked up (in reverse) in Zech 8:10: “There was no peace from the *enemies* for the *one going out* (יצא) and the *one*

54. Though on the “covenant” implications of the flying scroll in Zech 5, see footnote 59 below.

55. In addition, there may also be a secondary allusion to the covenant with Abraham. It is tempting to trace the unusual phrase “and you will be a blessing” (בְּרָכָה וִהְיִיתֶם) in Zech 8:13 back to the covenant with Abraham as recorded in Gen 12:2—“you will be a blessing” (בְּרָכָה וֶהְיֵה). However, while Gen 12:2 is the closest match, there are other partial parallels, including:

Deut 7:14:	“and you will be blessed among all peoples” (בָּרוּךְ תִּהְיֶה מִכָּל־הָעַמִּים)
Ezek 34:26:	“I will give them…a blessing” (וְנָתַתִּי...בְּרָכָה)
Isa 19:24:	“Israel will be…a blessing in the midst of the earth” (יִהְיֶה יִשְׂרָאֵל...בְּרָכָה בְּקֶרֶב הָאָרֶץ)

56. Jer 26:6 and 44:8 are only partial parallels, linking “cursing” and “nations.”

57. For the parallel curses to these blessings in Deut 28, see Deut 28:19 (“when you come in [בוא] and go out [יצא]”) and Deut 28:25 (“Yahweh will cause you to be smitten before your enemies”).

coming in (בוא).” Similarly, Zech 8:10 concludes with the reminder that Yahweh had set each against his neighbour. Though not paralleled in phraseology, this is thematically reflected in the description of the out-working of the curse in Deut 28:53–57, where a man is turned against brother and mother against her own children, events described using horribly graphic terms.

One might also detect more general allusions to Deut 28 in Zech 8:12, with the promise of “fruit of the vine” and the “produce of the ground” (Zech 8:12a; cf. Deut 28:4, 11, 18, 33, “fruit of your ground,” וּפְרִי אַדְמָתְךָ), and the promise of heavens that give their dew (Zech 8:12b; cf. Deut 28:12, “heavens giving rain,” הַשָּׁמַיִם לָתֵת מְטַר), and the promises that the people will possess all these blessings (Zech 8:13c; cf. the curse in Deut 28:30–33 that the people will not enjoy the fruits of their fields because they will be given to their enemies). However, while I would recognize that Deut 28 is the ultimate precedent for the expression of the covenantal blessing in these terms, I will argue in the next section that there are even closer connections between Zech 8:12 and the book of Haggai. The book of Haggai has picked up these covenantal blessings from Deut 28 (and elsewhere) and expressed them in its own particular idiom, which is then alluded to by Zechariah. Or, to put this in another way, Zech 8:12 alludes to the Deuteronomic blessings and curses, as mediated via Haggai.

In short, the intertexts used in Zech 8 depict the exile as the out-working of the curses of the covenant and announce Yahweh’s intention to reverse this and usher in a time of blessing, also expressed in covenantal terms.[58] In contrast, the concept of the blessings and curses of the covenant is not explicitly reflected in Zech 1–6.[59] Zechariah 1–6 does not directly connect the seventy years of exile with the covenant curses, and the promised restoration is not pictured in terms of the covenant blessings. Again, this is a significant point of contrast with Zech 7–8.

7.6.3. *Blessings in Terms of Material Prosperity (Haggai)*

Zechariah 8:10–13 describes the “blessings” which Yahweh is about to give in terms of material prosperity and agricultural fecundity. These

58. See similarly Petersen 1984a: 307–9.

59. The vocabulary of “blessing” (ברך and cognates) occurs frequently (almost 400 times) across the biblical corpus, but never in Zech 1–6. Furthermore, there are no references to “curse” (קְלָלָה) in Zech 1–6, and the only synonym occurs in Zech 5:3, where the flying scroll has a curse (אָלָה) on it. I have argued above (§6.2.1) that this written curse has covenantal overtones (through association with Deut 29:1). However, we should note that this covenantal theme is only implicit via the intertext, rather than explicit in the text itself.

blessings are the blessings of the covenant (which is again a feature not paralleled in Zech 1–6).

While we might trace the general theme of "material blessings" to a number of covenant texts (e.g. Deut 28, as noted above), there is one particular place where the text of Zech 8 directs us to look. Zechariah 8:9 refers to the words of the "prophets who were present at the founding of the temple," which clearly refers to the prophet Haggai (and perhaps also to Zechariah's own prophesying).[60] This reference to the prophet Haggai is followed in the next three verses with what I take to be unmistakable echoes of the book of Haggai:

Zech 8:10:	there was no reward for man or beast
Hag 1:11:	a drought on "man and beast and all the toil of their hands"
Zech 8:12:	the earth (אֶרֶץ) shall give its yield (יְבוּל) and the heavens (שָׁמַיִם) shall give their dew (טַל)
Hag 1:10:	Therefore the heavens (שָׁמַיִם) above you have withheld the dew (טַל), and the earth (אֶרֶץ) has withheld its yield (יְבוּל)
Zech 8:10:	Before these days (לִפְנֵי הַיָּמִים הָהֵם)
Hag 2:15:	From this day forward (מִן־הַיּוֹם הַזֶּה וָמָעְלָה)
Zech 8:9:	the day of the founding of the house of Yahweh of Hosts, the temple (בְּיוֹם יֻסַּד בֵּית־יְהוָה צְבָאוֹת הַהֵיכָל)
Hag 2:18:	the day when the foundation of the temple of Yahweh was laid… (הַיּוֹם אֲשֶׁר־יֻסַּד הֵיכַל־יְהוָה שִׂימוּ)

Other scholars have noted these and other connections with Haggai.[61]

60. So Petersen 1984a: 305. Contra Conrad 1999: 145–47, who argues—on the basis that the phrase "by the hand of the prophets" (מִפִּי הַנְּבִיאִים) refers to written prophecy—that it must refer to the words of the former prophets, read out at temple rededication. However, see Tollington (1993: 63–64) for a comprehensive analysis of the significance of the phrase "by the hand of," and see Meyers and Meyers (1987: 419–20) for a better analysis of this phrase in the context of Zech 8.

61. For other scholars who have noted these connections, see Wellhausen 1963: 187; Ackroyd 1968: 214; Petersen 1984a: 307; Meyers and Meyers 1987: 417–23; Tollington 1993: 30; Nurmela 1996: 178–80. Contra (Beuken 1967: 165–66), who suggests that the commonalities between Hag 1:10 and Zech 8:12 are evidence that both passages were added by the hand of a Chronistic redactor notwithstanding the fact that, as Beuken acknowledges, there is nothing in these verses themselves to link them with a Chronistic milieu. Contra also Nogalski (1993: 264–66), who argues that the theme of agricultural blessing has been added to both Haggai and Zech 8 as part of the editorial activity in creating the Book of the Twelve. In his view, Zech 8:12 is "a deliberate attempt to conform a prophetic writing to the hermeneutical paradigm in Joel [2:18–3:5]" (1993: 266). The arguments of both Beuken and Nogalski are not compelling because they do not account for other allusions to Haggai in Zech 8, including those noted above.

Furthermore, there are other links with Haggai in Zech 8:13:[62]

Zech 8:13:	Let your hands be strong (חזק)
Hag 2:4:	Be strong (חזק)
Zech 8:13:	Do not be afraid (אל־תיראו)
Hag 2:5:	Do not be afraid (אל־תיראו)
Zech 8:13:	You will be a blessing (ברכה)
Hag 2:19:	I will bless you (ברך)

In addition to these allusions to Haggai, there is also a probable echo of Haggai's "remnant" language. The word "remnant" (שְׁאֵרִית) does not appear at all in Zech 1–7, but now appears three times in the space of seven verses (Zech 8:6–12) in the context of these other allusions to Haggai. Furthermore, the phraseology in each case—"the remnant of this people" (שְׁאֵרִית הָעָם הַזֶּה)—echoes Haggai's phrase "the remnant of the people" (שְׁאֵרִית הָעָם, Hag 1:12, 14; 2:2).[63]

The significance of these allusions to the book of Haggai stems from the fact that Haggai is an explicitly "covenant-centric" book. Though not using the word "covenant" (בְּרִית), Haggai alludes unmistakeably to the Sinai covenant when describing "the word which Yahweh *cut* (כרת)[64] in the coming out from Egypt" (בְּצֵאתְכֶם מִמִּצְרַיִם, Hag 2:5). Haggai 2:5 grounds the assurance of Yahweh's present good purposes by stressing the continuance of the Sinai covenant with that present generation. Furthermore, Hag 2 makes unmistakeable allusions to the language of the blessing and curses of the covenant in Deuteronomy.[65]

The effect of the implicit reference to Haggai in Zech 8:9, followed by this string of allusions in 8:10–13, is to connect together the messages of

62. See Conrad 1999: 146–47, who also notes similar connections to Haggai.

63. I regard this as a "probable" allusion because it is also possible that it alludes to the same phrase in Jer 31:7. Jer 31:7 and the instances of this phrase in Haggai are the only places where the phrase "remnant of the people" is connected to God's restoration of his people expressed in terms of material blessings. Apart from the later occurrence in Neh 7:71, the only instances of the phrase "remnant of the people" (הָעָם שְׁאֵרִית) are in Jer 41:10, 16 and Zeph 2:9, none of which use the phrase consonant with the context of Zech 8.

64. The word כרת has clear associations with covenant establishment, across the range of biblical literature—see Gen 15:18; 21:32; 26:28; Exod 34:10; Deut 5:2; 28:69; 31:36; Isa 28:15; 55:3; Jer 34:13; Ezek 34:25; 1 Kgs 5:26; 2 Sam 3:12; Ezra 3:10; Ps 89:4 etc.

65. Hag 1:11: blight on grain (דָּגָן), wine (תִּירוֹשׁ), oil (יִצְהָר) = Deut 28:51; Hag 2:17: strike (נכה) with blight and mildew (בַּשִּׁדָּפוֹן וּבַיֵּרָקוֹן) = Deut 28:22; Hag 2:19: vine (גֶּפֶן), fig (תְּאֵנָה), pomegranate (רִמּוֹן), oil (זַיִת) = Deut 8:8; Hag 2:19: I will bless you (אֲבָרֵךְ) (cf. the keyword of Deut 28:1–14).

both prophets. By allusion to the book of Haggai, Zech 8 recalls and affirms the covenant-centric message of a prophetic contemporary,[66] which further strengthens the covenantal overtones in Zech 8. In contrast, Zech 1–6 does not use this concept of "covenant blessings" expressed in terms evocative of Haggai. In Zech 1–6, the effect of Yahweh's return to dwell is principally described in terms of a repopulated city. In the one place at which Zech 1–6 does describe the people *per se* (rather than their city), the phrase used does not have covenantal associations, but instead is a generic image of safety—"sitting under vine and fig tree" (Zech 3:9; cf. 1 Kgs 5:5; Mic 4:4; Isa 36:16 = 2 Kgs 18:31).

7.6.4. *Covenant Blessings in Terms of the "Restoration" in Jeremiah 30–31*

While the "blessings" in Zech 8:10–13 have strong echoes of Deut 28–30 and Haggai, the other verses in Zech 8 have much stronger connections to the promises of Jeremiah, particularly in Jer 30–31:[67]

Zechariah		*Jeremiah*	
8:3	… Jerusalem shall be *called the faithful city*, and the mountain of Yahweh of Hosts shall be *called* the *holy mountain*	31:23	Once more they shall use these words … "Yahweh bless you, *O abode of righteousness*, O *holy mountain*"
8:4–5	Thus says Yahweh of Hosts: Old men and old women shall again sit in the streets of Jerusalem, each with staff in hand because of their great age. And the streets of the city shall be full of boys and girls rejoicing in its streets	30:19	From them will come songs of thanksgiving and the sound of rejoicing. I will make them many, and they shall not be few. (30:20) Their children will be as in days of old. (31:13) Then shall the young women rejoice in the dance, and the young men and the old shall be merry

66. The fact that these parallels with Haggai are largely confined to Zech 8 counts against the suggestion that these apparent connections are nothing more than a common style of the prophets of the restoration. If these themes were merely the common preaching stock-in-trade of this era, we might expect to see them across all of Zech 1–8, rather than confined to a section which explicitly refers to the preaching ministry of Haggai.

67. I am not the first to recognize the connections between Zech 8 and Jer 30–31. Petersen argues that the motifs in Zech 8:4–5, "those of a city rebuilt, of many people, and of children playing, are shared by Jer 30:18–21" (1984a: 300). Similarly Mason (1977a: 69) regards these verses as "fulfilling" Jer 30:18–21. Cf. Beuken 1967: 176–77 and Petitjean 1969: 373–74.

Zech		Jer	
8:6	Thus says Yahweh of Hosts: Even though it seems impossible to the remnant of this people in these days, should it also seem impossible to me		(Cf. Jer 32:17: Nothing is impossible for God)
8:7	Thus says Yahweh of Hosts: I will *save my people from* the east country and from the west country	31:7	Save, *O Yahweh, your people*, the remnant of Israel
		31:8	See, I am going to *bring them from* the land of the north
8:8	*I will bring them* to live in Jerusalem *They shall be my people and I will be their God*, in faithfulness and in righteousness	31:1	*I will be the God* of all the families of Israel, and they shall be my people

The allusions in Zech 8:10–13 to Deuteronomy and Haggai have already been discussed above in §7.6.2 and §7.6.3, but in the present context I note also these distinctively Jeremian concepts and phraseology in the same verses.

Zech		Jer	
8:10	there were no wages for *man or beast…*	31:16	there are wages for your work
8:11–12	But now I will not deal with the *remnant of this people* as in *the former days*, For *the seed of peace*, the vine shall yield its fruit	31:7	*your people, the remnant* of Israel
		31:27	*The days are surely coming*, says Yahweh, when I will sow the *house of Israel and the house of Judah* with *the seed of man and the seed of beast*
8:13	Just as you have been a cursing among the nations, *O house of Judah and house of Israel*, so I will save you and you shall be a *blessing. Do not be afraid…*	30:10	*Do not be afraid*
8:14	For thus says Yahweh of Hosts: Just as I *purposed* to bring disaster and *did not relent…* 8:15 so again I have purposed in these days to do good to Jerusalem and to the house of Judah; do not be afraid	30:24	The fierce anger of Yahweh will *not turn back* until he has executed and accomplished the *purposes* of his mind.
		31:28	And just as I have watched over them to pluck up and break down, to overthrow, destroy, and bring evil, so I will watch over them to build and to plant, says Yahweh

The promised restoration in Zechariah is very similar to Jer 30–31, with the obvious difference that what Jer 30–31 says across two chapters is compressed into a handful of verses in Zech 8. Given the extent of the parallels between these two passages, there can be little doubt that Zech 8 is a deliberate "appropriation" of Jeremiah's programme of restoration.

Recognizing this parallel between Jer 30–31 and Zech 8 is tremendously significant for the present enquiry, for two reasons. First, at the heart of the promised restoration in Jer 30–31 is the promise of a new "covenant" (Jer 31:31–34). The allusion to these chapters to Zech 8 further reinforces the theme of "covenant."[68]

Secondly, in Jer 30–31, every mention of the rebuilding of Jerusalem (and by implication, its temple) is set within the context of covenant promises (see Jer 30:18–22; 31:1–4, 31–39). That is, the rebuilding of Zion is an outworking of God's covenant relationship with his people. It is via the background established by Jer 30–31 that the reader of Zechariah is able to establish the link between temple-building and the covenant.

In short, my argument is that Zech 8 alludes to "covenant" themes from Deuteronomy, Haggai and Jeremiah. Furthermore, the above analysis has shown that these "covenantal overtones" are something additional, not otherwise *explicitly* paralleled in Zech 1–6. I stress the word "explicitly," because I intend to argue in a moment that covenantal themes are present in Zech 1–6, albeit implicitly.

7.7. *Conclusion*

In the above examination of the intertexts of Zech 7 and 8 we have seen that Jer 7 is the key intertext behind the warning from "the former prophets" alluded to in Zech 7:7–14, and that Zech 8 makes a number of allusions to covenant texts (in particular Deut 28–30; Jer 30–31; Hag 1–2). The effect of these allusions in Zech 7–8 is to make explicit certain themes which are only implicit in Zech 1–6.

In Zech 1–6, the promised restoration is pictured in terms of a "restored city" (i.e. Jerusalem), whereas in Zech 7–8 this same truth is described in terms of a "restored covenant" (and all the blessings that this entails). My point is not that there are two competing concepts of "restoration" in the book, but rather that Zech 7–8 makes explicit that Yahweh's actions are the outworkings of the covenant, which is a

68. Petitjean (1969: 380) argues that the references to "covenant" in Zech 8 pick up Jeremiah's promise of a "new" covenant. In contrast, Petersen (1984a: 303) argues that "no new covenant is promised," and instead that Zech 8 is promising the continuation of the covenant of old. Supportive of Petersen's position is the fact that some of the most distinctive elements of the new covenant in Jer 31:31–34 (e.g. "law written on their hearts," "they all shall know me" etc.) are not picked up in Zech 8. I agree with Petersen that Zech 1–8 is declaring the restoration (or perhaps the continuing relevance) of the "old ordinances."

message that is only implicit in Zech 1–6. However, once Zech 7–8 has "attuned" us to this theme, it is possible to understand Zech 1–6 in a new light, and to draw to the surface what had been implicit all along. We can demonstrate this process with reference to Deut 28. As noted above, Deut 28 is a key intertext of Zech 8. Having identified this, we now can hear several "resonances" of this text in the traces of Deut 28 in Zech 1–6.

For example, if we ask the question "Why did the exile occur?," on our first reading of Zech 1–6 we might have answered, "Because of Yahweh's wrath at the evil ways and evil deeds of the fathers" (Zech 1:4). Zechariah 7–8 does not dispute this, but adds the extra nuance to the answer "...which was the outworking of the curses of the covenant." I stress that Zech 7–8 is not saying something different to Zech 1–6, but rather drawing out a message that was there all along in Zech 1–6, though only implicitly so, by virtue of its intertexts. In particular, we have already noted that Zech 1:6 alludes to Deut 28 (see esp. vv. 15, 45), in that these are the only two places where we find "statutes" (חֻקָּה / חֹק) which "overtake" (נשׂג). As noted by Meyers and Meyers, this allusion to Deut 28 serves to remind Zechariah's hearers that the cause of the exile was the curses embedded within the Deuteronomic covenant (1987: 101).[69] Zechariah 7–8 makes this "curses of the covenant" theme explicit—even though it was there, embedded in Zech 1:6, for those with "ears to hear" its intertexts.

Similarly, if we ask the question, "What is Yahweh about to do?," Zech 1–6 gives us the answer "Choose Jerusalem and return to dwell in the rebuilt temple on Zion." Zechariah 7–8 adds a covenantal overtone to this answer: "they will be my people and I will be their God." But again, this is only making explicit what is already there implicitly in the intertexts of Zech 1–6. Zechariah 6:15 promises the rebuilding of the temple of Yahweh, and concludes with a near-quotation of Deut 28:1: "this will happen if you diligently obey the voice of your God."[70] This intertext, which (in its wider context) links to all the blessings of the covenant, reminds us that the return of Yahweh to dwell is because of his covenant promise to bless his people.

Lastly, if we ask the question "What will be the outworking of Yahweh's action?," Zech 1–6 gives us an answer in terms of a restored

69. See similarly Petitjean (1969: 46): "Se heurtant à la négligence ou à la rébellion, les «paroles» divines se sont transformées en malédictions frappant la communauté. La pensée de Zacharie rejoint un thème majeur du Deutéronome et de la théologie deutéronomique de l'histoire."

70. Deut 28:1 has been recast in the plural form in Zechariah.

city (rebuilt, overflowing with people etc.) whereas Zech 7–8 answers in terms of a restored covenant (and particularly in terms of the blessings of the covenant *à la* Deut 28, Haggai and Jer 30–31). But again, that which is explicit in Zech 7–8 was already there implicitly in Zech 1–6. For example, the promise in Zech 2:8 (ET 2:4) of an "abundance of man and beast" is a thematic echo of Deut 28:11, that Yahweh will "make the fruit of womb and beast abound."

7.8. *Recapitulation and Final Conclusions*

To recapitulate my argument thus far: Zech 7–8 is composed of both "intratexts" (allusions to Zech 1–6) and "intertexts" (allusions to other biblical texts).

The effect of the *intratexts* is to weld the two parts of the book into a single unit. By picking up the key themes of Zech 1–6—in sequence—Zech 7–8 demonstrates that it is addressing the same subject matter. This encourages us to read the two "panels" of the book against each other, and let each nuance our understanding of the whole. For example, without Zech 7–8, it might be possible to construe Zech 1–6 as a book merely about temple-reconstruction, and to miss the significance of the traces of other texts in Zech 1–6 which allude to the covenant. The effect of the addition of Zech 7–8 (read in the context of the book as a whole) is to make clear that the emphasis is actually on Yahweh returning to dwell with his people. Zechariah 1–6 and Zech 7–8 are not offering different views of the "restoration" so much as answering different questions about the restoration. Zechariah 1–6 is answering the questions "What?," "When?" and "For Whom?" Zechariah 7–8 is much more concerned with the "Why?" question. In Zech 7–8, the theme of covenant is in the foreground to explain why Yahweh is about to do what he is about to do, and how his people should now be responding.

The effect of the *intertexts* in Zech 7–8 is to introduce a new layer of meaning to the argument of the book as a whole:

- Zechariah 1–6 stresses the restoration of Zion, centred on a rebuilt temple. However, this temple-centric focus in Zech 1–6 is nuanced by the warning in Zech 7 based on what had happened to an earlier generation who had trusted in that "house" and an empty cultic religion (made via allusion to Jer 7). The dwelling of God with his people is not guaranteed by the mere presence of a temple, because an ethical response is also required from God's people. An earlier generation had ignored this, to their peril. Without having to use the explicit words, Zech 7 clearly warns "Do not be like them!"

- Zechariah 1–6 announces Yahweh's "unconditional" return to dwell in his house in Jerusalem. This is nuanced by Zech 8, which explains this "dwelling Zechariah" in covenantal terms—that is, the promise "I will dwell with my people" is the out-working of "I will be their God and they shall be my people." Zechariah 8 makes clear that Yahweh's return to dwell in the temple is because of the continuation of the covenant, and that this carries with it the requirement that the people make an ethical response to the stipulations of the covenant.

We are now in a position to answer the question with which this chapter began: What is the relationship between "cult" and "ethics"? In both Zech 7 and Zech 8, it is the intertexts which provide the key to understanding the connection between cult and ethics. The connection between cult and ethics is that they both flow from the covenant. Yahweh's return to dwell in the rebuilt temple ("cult") is because of the continuation of the covenant ("I will be your God" = "I will dwell"). At the same time, the covenant also demands a response from the people of God ("ethics"). Diagrammatically, the situation can be presented as follows:

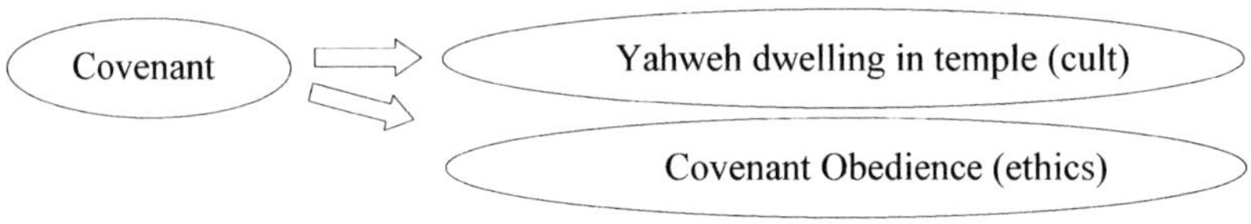

Yahweh's covenant relationship with his people is foundational for both cult and ethics in the book of Zechariah. This conclusion, which is otherwise only implicit in Zech 1–6, is made explicit in Zech 7–8. Zechariah 7–8 (and particularly its intertexts) are critical for shaping our understanding of Zech 1–8 as a whole.

In short, the message of Zechariah is not "Ethics" → "Cult" (e.g. "live ethically *so that* Yahweh will dwell in the temple again"),[71] nor "Cult" → "Ethics" (e.g. Yahweh's presence in the temple results in a

71. Boda comes close to suggesting this when he argues that a later hand has added Zech 8:1–13 "to remind the people of the picture of the restoration that had been promised but had not yet arrived; that is, they remind the reader that the reason these promises remain unfulfilled in that the people are replicating the patterns of the earlier generation" (2003a: 400–401). See also Smith (1984: 228) "Fasting and temple-building are not enough. The heart and actions of God's people must be right or God will withdraw."

holy people),[72] but that both cult *and* ethics stem from a covenantal relationship between God and his people. Zechariah 1–8 maintains a dual focus on cult and ethics because both are an outworking of a restored covenant relationship.

Rather than regarding cult and ethics as somewhat in tension (*à la* Wellhausen), the intertexts used in Zech 7–8 demonstrate a parallel relationship between the two—the message of Zech 1–8 is the restoration of Yahweh's covenant relationship with this people, which has the twin consequences that Yahweh will return to dwell with his people (in the rebuilt temple) *and also* that God's people must live in accordance with the covenant, which is demonstrated by an ethical response. Both calls for human action in the book ("Build the temple" and "Live ethically") are predicated on God's prior action in returning in covenant faithfulness to his people.

72. For example, Petersen 1984a: 299: "Divine initiative—rather than particular human efforts—seems critical to this author's view of postexilic restoration." Similarly, Ollenburger 1996: 739: "Moral transformation is the result (not the precondition) of God's return." Also Sweeney 2000: 643: "Zechariah calls for such [ethical] action on the part of the Judean community as a means to qualify them for entry into the soon-to-be-rebuilt Temple and participation in its cultic service."

Chapter 8

CONCLUSIONS

The focus of this investigation has been on the intertextual re-use of "the former prophets" in Zech 1–8.

In Chapter 4, we examined the allusions in Zech 1–2. It was demonstrated that two features of these chapters are *sustained allusions* (i.e. the repeated references to another "background" passage, which stretch across multiple passages in Zechariah) and *composite metaphors* (the simultaneous allusion to imagery from multiple source passages).

Zechariah 1–2 uses a sustained allusion to Lam 2 to provide the metaphors which are to be systematically reversed as Yahweh acts to restore his people (the "measuring line" is used to rebuild rather than to judge, the "horns of the nations" are now the ones being cast down, Yahweh himself will be their "wall of fire" rather than the one who destroys their wall with fire, and so on).

Zechariah 1–2 also makes sustained allusions to both Jer 48–51 and Ezek 38–39 to provide the background imagery which allows the reader to comprehend Yahweh's impending judgment on the nations, who are about to face a time of reversal.

Zechariah 1–2 combines elements of the programme of restoration in Ezek 40–48, Jer 30–33 and Isa 40–55 (especially Isa 54), to reveal that Yahweh is about to "return" to his people, by returning to dwell in the temple in Jerusalem, which will reverse the devastation of the exile and usher in a time of paradisiacal blessing. Joel 2 offered the same kind of hopes to a post-exilic generation, but, in picking up elements of Joel 2, Zech 1–2 has recast these with a more optimistic tone.

The cumulative effect of the sustained and combined allusions in Zech 1–2 is to remind Zechariah's first hearers that the long-awaited return of Yahweh to dwell with his people was imminent. Zechariah 1–2 anticipates the fulfilment (or reversal, as appropriate) of particular words of "the former prophets" in the near future.

In Chapter 5 we examined the allusions in Zech 3–4 and 6:9–15. It was demonstrated that Zech 3, Zech 4 and Zech 6:9–15 are mutually interpreting when read against a number of identifiable intertexts and when read in the particular historical context ca. 519 B.C.E. The interwoven message is of a restored priesthood (Zech 3), a restored temple (Zech 4) and a restored Davidic line (Zech 6:9–15).

The intertexts of Zech 3 demonstrate that the high priest Joshua is being promised a restoration of the proper prerogatives of the priesthood, which had been lost as a consequence of sin and exile. The key intertexts for Zech 3 are various "priestly" texts, especially Exod 28–29, Lev 8 and 16, and Ezek 40:46 and 44:17–19, together with corruption and purification imagery taken from Amos 4 and Isa 6. The engraved stone given to Joshua is to be part of the "holy crown" of the high priest, anticipating Joshua's later crowning in Zech 6:11. The recommissioning of the priesthood is a proleptic sign that the "Branch" (the temple builder) is going to come and complete his task, in that the priesthood requires an operative temple. A restored priesthood is a promissory sign of a restored temple.

The intertexts of Zech 4 help us to see that the lampstand symbolizes the temple, and that the seven lights symbolize Yahweh's presence in the temple. The key intertexts for Zech 4 are Exod 25–27, which explain the significance of the temple/tabernacle, lampstand and its (olive) oil, and Deut 18:7, which explains the significance of "standing before Yahweh." Zechariah 4 is addressed to a point in history between the commencement of the rebuilding of the temple and its completion, and spoken at time when the absence of Zerubbabel had led to uncertainty about the fate of the temple rebuilding project. Zechariah 4 develops the promise of the preceding night-visions (see esp. Zech 1:16; 2:14; cf. 8:3) of Yahweh's returning to dwell in Jerusalem once the temple has been rebuilt. Zerubbabel and Joshua together are the "two sons of oil," a designation which acknowledges their role in serving Yahweh in and through the restoration of the temple and its cultus.

In Zech 6:9–15, the restoration of the Davidic line is promised. The key intertexts for this passage are 2 Sam 7 and Isa 44–45 (on the messianic significance of the builder of Yahweh's temple) and Jer 22, 23 and 33, which describe the termination of the Davidic line in the person of Jehoiachin (Jer 22) and the promise of a future restoration of the Davidic line by the "Branch" (Jer 23), working in harmony with a (restored) Levitical priesthood (Jer 33). In Zech 6:9–15, the temple-builder—Zerubbabel—is given this messianic appellation because he is the beginning of fulfilment of the "Branch" promise of Jer 23 and 33. The time of rejection for Jehoiachin and his (immediate) offspring has ended, and a new hope for the Davidic line has been restored.

In Chapter 6 we examined the allusions in Zech 5:1–6:8. The key intertexts for the vision of the flying scroll (5:1–4) are Jer 7 and Deut 29, combined with elements of the Exodus tradition (Exod 11–12). The intertextual connections to these passages bring "covenantal" overtones to Zech 5:1–4, which are not otherwise explicit in the text. Based on this, we concluded that the flying scroll is a representation of Yahweh's covenant law, as reflected in both the Law and the Prophets, of which theft and perjury are selected as typical instances. The vision affirms that the curses of the covenant will continue to be in effect within the post-exilic community, against any who would break this law, and their punishment will come with all the suddenness and devastation of the judgment which fell on Egypt in the Passover.

The key intertexts of the vision of the woman in the ephah (Zech 5:5–11) are Ezek 1–11, 2 Sam 7 and Exod 25. Reading Zech 5:5–11 in the context of these intertexts helps us to recognize the ephah basket as an "anti-ark" borne by "anti-cherubs" to an "anti-temple" in an "anti-Jerusalem." The vision stands in juxtaposition to a key theme in Zech 1–4—Yahweh's return to dwell in his house in Jerusalem. Further allusions to Amos 8 and Ezek 8 indicate that the "ephah" contains a representation of the idolatry and/or other iniquity of the people, which is being banished as a consequence of Yahweh's return to Jerusalem.

The vision of the chariots in Zech 6:1–8 both continues and develops the allusions to Job 1–2 begun in the first night-vision. However, the last vision differs from the first because the intertextual roots of the "war chariots" suggest that this image has bellicose overtones, and hence that "Yahweh's spirit resting on the north" has negative consequences for that land. In the preceding night-vision, idolatry and other sins had been relegated to Shinar, and it remains for the last night-vision to depict the final state of that land. We noted that the imagery in Zech 6:1–8 of Yahweh's chariots emerging from between bronze mountain remains obscure, and has spawned interpretations which are, in my opinion, highly speculative. I then proceeded to offer my own—also highly speculative!—view that the imagery in 6:1–8 is an intertextual conflation of Isa 45:2 and Hab 3, depicting the hosts of Yahweh bursting out from between the mountain of bronze, riding out to overthrow his foes. The night-visions have thus come "full-circle," from Zech 1:11 in which the whole earth (except Jerusalem) is at rest, to Zech 6:8, in which Yahweh's spirit rests in judgment on the land of the north.

In Chapter 7 we examined the intertexts in Zech 7–8. It was argued that these chapters are composed both of intratexts (i.e. self-referential allusions to Zech 1–6) and intertexts. The effect of the *intratexts* is to weld the two parts of the book into a single unit, because Zech 7–8 addresses—in sequence—the same issues raised by Zech 1–6. However, in addressing these same matters, Zech 7–8 gives answers with a different nuance. Without Zech 7–8, it might be possible to construe chs. 1–6 as a book merely about temple reconstruction, and to overlook the significance of echoes of other texts in Zech 1–6 which allude to the covenant. However, the effect of Zech 7–8 is to make explicit that the emphasis of Zech 1–8 as a whole is on Yahweh returning to dwell with his people. Zechariah 1–6 and 7–8 are not offering different views of the "restoration" so much as answering different questions about the restoration. Zechariah 1–6 answers the questions "What is Yahweh about to do?," "When?" and "For whom?" Although Zech 7–8 does address these issues, it is much more concerned with the "Why?" question. The different nuances in Zech 7–8 are brought out by its intertexts.

The key intertext in Zech 7 is a sustained allusion to Jer 7. I have argued that Jer 7 in particular is behind the warning from the "former prophets" alluded to in Zech 7:7–14. The effect of this allusion to Jeremiah's temple sermon (with its critique of trust in the physical presence of the temple) is to stress to Zechariah's generation that the mere completion of the temple will not guarantee the return of Yahweh to dwell with his people. Instead, it must be accompanied by the ethical transformation of the people of God. What will turn the "fasts" into "feasts" is not the reconstruction of the temple after "these seventy years," but an ethical reformation—especially in terms of "truth" and "peace"—brought about by Yahweh's return to dwell in their midst.

The key intertexts in Zech 8 are passages from Deuteronomy, Haggai and Jeremiah, the allusions to which stress the outworking of God's covenant with his people. The language of the blessings and curses of the covenant alludes to Deut 28–30. Zechariah 8 understands the exile to have been the outworking of the curses of the covenant, and announces Yahweh's intention to reverse this and to usher in the promised blessings instead. The particularization of these blessings in terms of material prosperity and agricultural fecundity alludes to Hag 1–2. The wider implications of this restored covenant are expressed in terms of echoes of Jer 30–31. Zechariah 8 is a deliberate "appropriation" of some key elements of Jeremiah's programme of restoration. The combined effect of the intratexts and intertexts of Zech 7–8 is to nuance the message of Zech 1–8 as a whole, stressing that it is not about temple building per se, but the restoration of Yahweh's covenant with his people, and the ethical response required from them. In Zech 1–8, "cult" and "ethics" are *not* in tension. Rather, these chapters announce the restoration of Yahweh's covenant relationship with his people, with the implication that Yahweh will return to dwell in the rebuilt temple ("cult") *and also* that his people must return to him in an ethical response of obedience ("ethics"). Both calls for human action in the book ("Build the temple" and "Live ethically") are predicated on God's prior action in returning in covenant faithfulness to his people.

Zechariah 8 ends with an allusion to Isa 2:3, describing the pilgrimage of the nations to Jerusalem.[1] Because the theme of "the nations" has been touched on in a number of chapters, I have held back from drawing final conclusions about this theme until this point. But now, with the evidence of the intertexts of Zech 1–8 before us, we may conclude that there are two facets to Zechariah's view of the nations. On the one hand, the allusion in Zech 8:21–22 to Isa 2:3 offers a future to the nations which is unmistakably positive, as is the promise of Zech 2:15 (ET 2:11),[2] which points to the day when those from many nations will be "joined" to Yahweh. Indeed, Zech 2:15 goes beyond anything else in the Hebrew Bible in explicitly applying the "covenant formula" (וְהָיוּ לִי לְעָם) to the nations. However, on the other hand, we have also detected a negative view towards the nations, although in many cases the critique of the nations is "hidden" behind an intertext. For example, we have argued that the imagery of Yahweh's spirit "resting" on the north (Zech 6:8) would have been understood by biblically literate hearers as a bad thing, though it is otherwise ambiguous. Similarly, we saw that the ultimate fate of the "horns" in 2:1–4 (ET 1:18–21) is only revealed through a recognition of its intertexts, and that the "mountains" opposing Zerubbabel in Zech 4:7 refers to world powers, for those with "ears to hear" the echo of Jer 51:25/Isa 41:11–15. Likewise, I have suggested that references to "Babylon" and "Shinar" have taken on a metaphoric—rather than literal—referent. If we combine all this evidence, I conclude that Zech 1–8 both warmly embraces all from the nations who would come to Jerusalem to join themselves to Yahweh, but affirms that all nations who continue in their opposition to Yahweh will be overthrown. I have noted that the intertexts have been used to "encode" a layer of meaning for those familiar with the wider prophetic tradition, which would not be apparent to the uninitiated. I can only speculate as to why Zechariah would have done this—although the possibility comes to mind that his message in its present form would be less likely to offend any Persian overlords, while at the same time being perfectly clear to his intended audience.

1. See further §2.8 (example 4).

2. As I concluded at §4.6.3, Zech 2:15 is a composite allusion to Isa 56/Isa 14 and Isa 2:3.

In the light of this evidence of the allusions in Zech 1–8, it is now possible to synthesize from this some conclusions regarding the nature of the intertextuality of Zech 1–8 and the hermeneutical implications which this raises.

As discussed in Chapter 2, textual re-use spans "citation," "quotation," "allusion," "echo" and perhaps even "trace." Our investigations have shown that Zech 1–8 rarely, if ever, uses citation or direct quotation, instead preferring more *oblique references to other texts*. However, once the analysis moves into the realm of "allusion" and "echo," we have moved into the realm of "probability" rather than "certainty" when it comes to connections between texts. I do not expect that I will convince every reader about every textual connection I have detected—indeed, I have indicated that there are some "intertexts" about which I have not even convinced myself![3] However, I have built my argument on those "allusions" and "echoes" which I have assessed to be "likely."[4]

The analysis above has demonstrated that one of the features of the intertextuality of Zech 1–8 is *sustained allusion*. In addition to the examples already highlighted in relation to Zech 1–2 (see §4.7), we have also seen that there are repeated allusions across the breadth of Zech 1–8 to Exod 25–27; Deut 28–30; 2 Sam 7; Isa 54; Jer 30–33 and Ezek 40–48. The effect of these sustained allusions is to establish the dominant textual backgrounds by which the particulars of Zech 1–8 are to be understood. To illustrate the concept of a sustained allusion, one might consider Milton's *Paradise Lost*.[5] It would be to miss the point entirely to recognize that Milton's work contains a few scattered allusions to Gen 1–3. The reality is that Gen 1–3 (and a plethora of other biblical passages) provides the conceptual framework for the work as whole. I suggest that Zech 1–8 is another such work which depends upon sustained allusion in order to be understood.

While many scholars recognize that Zechariah contains a number of allusions, not enough work has been done on the way in which complexes of allusions work together to create a textual background which

3. For example, that the chariots emerging from bronze mountains in Zech 6:1–8 is an intertextual conflation of Isa 45:2 and Hab 3.

4. My assessment of "likelihood" was both cumulative and iterative—as I pursued my research, repeated discoveries of multiple "possible" echoes (e.g. Lam 2) amounted to a cumulative case for a "probable" allusion. Furthermore, as my research progressed, I developed an increasing sensitivity for the "typical" ways in which Zech 1–8 re-uses texts, which "fed into" my understanding of what constituted a "likely" allusion or echo.

5. For a penetrating analysis of "echoes" (biblical and otherwise) in Milton, see Hollander 1981.

makes the book intelligible.[6] We have seen that Zech 1–8 contains what we might call "meta-intertextuality"—that is, sustained background allusions which stretch across multiple chapters of the book. There are repeated allusions to a limited range of chapters which must be more than accidental. While many of these allusions have been individually recognized by other scholars, no one has examined their composite effect, and instead have tended to treat Zechariah as a repository of texts plucked more-or-less at random from the biblical corpus. However, the sustained allusions give warrant for reading Zechariah against the wider context of the specific passages being alluded to. My assumption is that Zechariah's audience did this more-or-less subconsciously, in the same way in which a modern reader of *Paradise Lost* automatically brings what they recall of the narrative of Gen 1–3 to their reading of Milton. In Zech 1–8, the explicit references to other texts function as triggers which alert the reader to the wider context of those verses. However, many modern readers do not have the same familiarity with the Hebrew Bible, and consequently the echoes do not trigger any recall, but leave the reader confused.[7] Recognizing the importance of sustained allusions in Zech 1–8 has important implications for how contemporary readers should approach the book. In order to understand Zech 1–8, one must read the various background passages and absorb their worldview and, only then, seek to read Zech 1–8 with this background in mind. The sustained allusions demonstrate that Zech 1–8 is a text "written with other texts-in-the-mind,"[8] and so we need to read it with the same texts in mind.

Another feature of the intertextuality of Zech 1–8 is the combination of allusion from multiple source passages into a *composite metaphor*. Zechariah 1–8 picks up *elements of* the programme of restoration from Isa 40–55; Jer 30–33 and Ezek 40–48. I stress the phrase "elements of" in order to focus on the fact that Zech 1–8 picks up some parts, but not others, of the promises of "the former prophets." For example, it picks up the Ezekielian promise of Yahweh's return to dwell in the temple, but without endorsing the full "construction blueprint" of Ezek 40–48.

6. Though Delkurt (2000) makes an important contribution in noting the multitude of allusions in Zechariah to one particular book (Isaiah).

7. One might consider the average modern reader coming across the phrase "My servant the Branch." I take it that Zechariah's first audience—as a community on the edge of their seats waiting for the fulfilment of Jer 23—would automatically have recognized the significance of this allusion, whereas I suspect that the average modern reader would have little idea about the allusion or its contextual significance

8. This phrase is an intertextual nod to Fishbane (1985: 435)—see below for the full quotation.

Similarly, Zech 1–8 picks up Jeremiah's hope of a restored Davidic line, but not the promise of a rebuilt city wall (Jer 31:38–39; cf. Zech 2:8 = ET 2:4) or the promise of a "new" covenant (Jer 31:31–34).[9] Or again, it picks up Isaiah's promise of a restored and enlarged Zion, but stresses this in terms of the multitude of its people (Isa 54:3) rather than in terms of a city wall rebuilt in sapphire and ruby (Isa 54:11–12). This is not to suggest that Zech 1–8 contradicts these former prophets at any point, but rather that only some elements of these earlier prophecies are understood to apply to the particular historical context of Zech 1–8. That is, Zech 1–8 is a particular appropriation of the words of the "former prophets," as they apply in the immediate post-exilic context. To put it in the negative, Zech 1–8 is *not* claiming that everything which Isaiah, Jeremiah and Ezekiel had ever promised was about to be fulfilled the moment the temple was completed. Zechariah 1–8 is a selective application of the promises of the former prophets.[10]

In a musical composition, "counterpoint" is the musical texture resulting from the combination of individual melodic lines. This provides a useful analogy to describe Zech 1–8. Zechariah 1–8 is a counterpoint of certain strains from the melody-lines of the former prophets, played together to create a new symphony, with these multiple melodies now brought together in a new harmony. Or to say the same thing in the language of Bakhtin, Zech 1–8 is a dialogical discourse created through the interaction of multiple voices. As Zech 1–8 "speaks again" the voices spoken in the past, it does not seek to overthrow or drown out those voices with its own, but is a selective re-vocalization of these earlier words, and the process of selection has the effect of transforming (or perhaps better, "recontextualizing") those words for a different era.

As indicated in my introductory literature review, the re-use of the prophetic tradition in Zech 1–8 has previously been examined in terms of "prophecy" and "fulfilment" (or non-fulfilment). While I do not wish to sidestep this issue—and indeed I will return to this precise question at the end of this conclusion—it is necessary to acknowledge that its intertextuality goes far beyond a "flat" model of "promise and fulfilment."

9. Conspicuous by its absence in Zech 1–8 is any mention of the law being "written on the hearts" and "put into the minds," which are key distinctives of the new covenant. See further §7.6.4 above. I agree with Petersen (1984a: 303) that Zech 1–8 describes the restoration of the Deuteronomic covenant, with the "old ordinances" remaining in force (cf. Zech 7:9; 8:16), rather than the inauguration of the new covenant.

10. See further the analysis of "the prophets of the restoration" by Mason. He notes that the "three prophets of the restoration...show considerable creativity in their selection and use of earlier material and traditions" (1982a: 142).

For example, the reapplication and reversal of Ezek 38–39 (whereby Yahweh will do to "Gog" what Gog has done to Israel) is not a "fulfilment" of the original text, but rather a typological inversion. Likewise, the application to Joshua of the imagery from Amos 4:11 of a burning stick snatched from the fire is not an "exegesis" of Amos 4 in its original context. If one can use the language of fulfilment at all, it is at best a "typological fulfilment." If we approach Zech 1–8 with a (modernist?) desire for a literal, contextual and sequential interpretation of other texts, we may well overlook many instances of Zechariah's textual "play." Zechariah 1–8 often offers what might be described as a "prophetic" interpretation—that is making a new prophetic statement by applying old texts to a new context in new ways. Though it lies well beyond the scope of this work to even begin to explore this, it would appear that Zech 1–8 lies along a trajectory which entails both the midrashic practices of later Judaism and the interpretive practices of the New Testament.[11]

Zechariah 1–8 is *written with texts-in-the-mind.* This description derives from Fishbane:

> [C]reators of aggadic exegesis appear to live with 'texts-in-the-mind'—that is, with texts (or traditions) which provide the imaginative matrix for evaluating the present, for conceiving of the future, for organizing reality (the inchoate, the negative, the possible), and even for providing the shared symbols and language of communication." (1985: 435)

However, it should be noted that Fishbane is describing "aggadic exegesis." While Fishbane's comment aptly describes the role of texts/traditions in Zech 1–8, Zech 1–8 is different from "aggadic exegesis." There is an increasing tendency to argue that there was a "transformation from prophecy to exegesis during the second temple period" (Sommer 1996a: 47).[12] However, my investigations have shown that Zechariah is still very much himself a "prophet" and not merely an exegete of the former prophets. That is, Zechariah speaks a genuine revelatory "new" word from Yahweh, one which (paradoxically) comes via a reiteration of the written words of the "former prophets." Zechariah writes with the texts of the former prophets in mind, to an audience with these same

11. For example, the book of Revelation does to Zech 1–8 what Zechariah did to "the former prophets." To pick just one example, the two olive trees and *two* lampstands of Rev 11:4 are an obvious "play" on the two olive trees and *one* lampstand of Zech 4, but Rev 11:4 is not thereby giving us an exegesis of the "single determinative meaning" of Zech 4. The imagery of Zech 4 has been *adapted* and *reapplied* in Revelation.

12. This is typically associated with the "end of prophecy," which most would date to after the time of Zech 1–8. For a different perspective, see Floyd 2006a.

texts in mind. Zechariah uses these texts to invoke what Assman calls a "cultural memory," in order to "introduce into the present something distant and alien" (2006: 16).[13]

Another feature of the intertextuality of Zech 1–8 is that it is *historically conditioned*. The re-activation of certain words of the former prophets in Zech 1–8 has occurred at a particular point in history. It has been argued that the most appropriate historical context against which to understand the allusions of Zech 1–8 is the one suggested by the three dating formulae in the book (i.e. ca. 520–518 B.C.E.). To read the allusions of Zech 1–8 against a different historical context (e.g. reading the promises to Joshua in Zech 3 in the context of a "chronistic milieu") runs the risk of distorting how the allusion should be understood. Furthermore, the message of the intertexts in Zech 1–8 suggests a very particular historical context. As we have seen in Chapters 4 and 5, the intertexts combine to stress a strong "restoration" focus, with a positive tone. This counts against a number of the suggested historical reconstructions of the period. As Bedford (2001: 10–23) notes, much of the recent research on the social history of Achaemenid Judah has interpreted the biblical texts of this period—including Zech 1–8—through the prism of "conflict," whether that be a conflict between repatriates and "people of the land,"[14] or between "theocrats" and "visionaries,"[15] or between monotheists and syncretists,[16] to pick three dominant examples. However, as we have seen, the evidence of the intertexts of Zech 1–8 offers no support for these historical reconstructions. For example, against Hanson's view, Zech 1–8 is pro-temple, pro-messiah, *and* pro-the imminent return of Yahweh to dwell in the midst of his people, and has a positive tone which does not suggest a community torn apart by conflict.[17] The intertexts of Zech 1–8 suggest that the community has every reason to be confident about the immediate future.

We have found that the intertextuality of Zech 1–8 is dominated by the thought-world of *"the former prophets" and of the book of Deuteronomy*. That is not to say that Zechariah is not aware of other traditions.

13. For more on the concept of "cultural memory," see Assmann 1995: 130.

14. See, e.g., Blenkinsopp 1990; 1991; Berquist 1995: 26–29, 74–79; and cf. Margalith 1991.

15. Hanson (1979) argues that the post-exilic community was rent by struggles between hierocratic and visionary circles for control of the Jerusalem temple.

16. Smith 1987: 11–42.

17. I echo the view of E. Meyers (1987: 510), who argues (contra Hanson) that Yehud enjoyed a period of internal stability at this time. He comments about Hanson that "[h]is reconstruction of postexilic history has more to do, in my opinion, with the fifth century than with the sixth" (1987: 518 n. 6).

Indeed, it has been argued above that Zech 1–8 alludes to, *inter alia*, the exodus tradition, the Decalogue, and especially the material in the book of Exodus and Leviticus regarding the tabernacle furnishings and high-priestly regalia. However, the dominant influence on Zech 1–8 is "the former prophets" and their theological viewpoint, which Zech 1–8 presumes its audience will be sufficiently familiar with—so much so that they can recognize echoes without explicit citation. It also presumes (without narrating or explaining) key events in Israel's history, including the destruction of the temple, the exile and the return from exile. Zechariah 1–8 is not as interested in the past "events" of Israel's salvation history so much as the future "promises" of Yahweh through his prophets. The distinction which I am seeking to make can be seen most clearly by way of comparison with Neh 9. If we may assume for the sake of argument that Neh 9 was written sometime in the "early Persian period,"[18] then these two works are written at (broadly) similar stages in history. Both are deeply intertextual in nature, but there are important differences in the texts being alluded to. The prayer in Neh 9 provides a rehearsal of Israel's history, spanning creation (9:5–6), Abraham (9:7–8), Egypt/Sinai/wilderness (9:9–21), conquest and settlement (9:22–28), right through to exile (9:29–31). As Boda notes, "the prayer presupposes the Pentateuch in a very similar form to that possessed today" (1999: 186). The prayer in Neh 9 establishes the sinfulness of the "fathers" by a comprehensive allusion to the events of Israel's history. Zechariah 1–8 has no such rehearsal of events, even though it has a very similar understanding with respect of the sins of the fathers—for example, compare Neh 9:29b and Zech 7:11.[19] In contrast, what is present in Zech 1–8 is what is absent in Neh 9—allusions to the specific promises of Yahweh given through the former prophets to restore his people. In short, Zech 1–8 is more like an "intertextual prophecy," whereas Neh 9 is (in part) more like an "intertextual history."

18. Boda's monograph on Neh 9 makes a strong case for an early Persian period dating. In a traditio-historical analysis, Boda argues that Neh 9 is part of the tradition of "Penitential Prayers," and that its original *Sitz* pre-dated the careers of Ezra and Nehemiah. Boda argues for a setting in the early restoration era, around the time of Haggai and Zechariah (1999: 189–95). Though I favour the generation or so after Zechariah as the more likely *Sitz* for the tradition in Neh 9 (based on the greater incidence of Late Biblical Hebrew features in Neh 9 *vis-à-vis* Zech 1–8), it still remains that the two works were composed in a similar era.

19. Compare: "They turned a *stubborn shoulder* (וַיִּתְּנוּ כָתֵף סוֹרֶרֶת) and stiffened their neck and *would not hear* (וְלֹא שָׁמֵעוּ)" (Neh 9:29b); "But they refused to listen, and *turned a stubborn shoulder* (וַיִּתְּנוּ כָתֵף סֹרֶרֶת), and stopped their ears *from hearing* (מִשְּׁמוֹעַ)" (Zech 7:11). On these similarities, see further Boda (1999: 177–78).

A further feature of the intertextuality of Zech 1–8 is that these chapters are an interweaving of self-referential allusions ("*intratexts*") and *intertexts*, and that both work together to establish the framework of meaning for the text. The implication of this is that the contemporary reader must understand the book in that double context. In the above analysis of Zech 1–8, we have seen that the intratextual connections between Zech 1–6 and Zech 7–8 have the effect of binding the two parts together, in such a way that the intertexts of Zech 7–8 can then shape the way in which the work as a whole is read.

Recognizing intertexts also aids our understanding of Zech 1–8 in other ways. Zechariah is a "gapped text," and its intertexts help fill in the gaps. Furthermore, *intertexts can import additional layers of meaning*, by drawing implications from background passages which are not explicitly present in the passage in Zech 1–8. For example, the conclusion that the scroll in Zech 5:1–4 depicts Yahweh's "covenantal law" is an implication of the intertexts, rather than something which is explicit from the "bare" text of Zech 5:1–4. Similarly, Zech 2:1–4 is ambiguous as to the ultimate fate of the "horns" (i.e. nations), but the intertexts to this passage make clear that all oppressive nations will be destroyed. The intertexts of Zech 1–8 add another layer of meaning to the text.

Another hermeneutical implication of the intertexts in Zech 1–8 is that they help create a framework for *limiting the range of possible meanings*. For example, the vision of the man with the measuring rod only "makes sense" when read against Ezek 40, and likewise, the significance of the reclothing of Joshua only "makes sense" when understood against various priestly texts. Without the framework established by the intertexts, many parts of Zech 1–8 would remain enigmatic. Furthermore, the greater the number of intertexts which have been combined, the more the field of possible meanings is delineated. In this, I come to the opposite conclusion to Mark Love. Love argues that the plethora of allusions in Zech 1–8 creates a "metaphor stew," resulting in a text which evades a determination of meaning. In contrast, we have seen that the effect of "compound" intertexts is in fact to narrow the field of possible meanings. While I would be the first to admit that there are still some parts of the vision of the woman in the ephah in Zech 5:5–11 which I find enigmatic, all is not lost! The fact that there are *multiple* intertexts is an aid, rather than a hindrance, because these other texts help to limit the possible interpretations, and to give shape to the interpretation of the vision as a whole. For example, the phrase "to build a house for it in Shinar" (5:11) might denote any kind of house, but the confluence of this with intertexts suggestive of the ark, of cherubs, and of other "tabernacle" imagery makes it clear that this "house" must be some kind of (anti-)temple. We have found that an intertextual hermeneutic—far from producing a limitless surplus of possible meanings—provides a means for recognizing the textual limits of meaning.

In my "intertextual" hermeneutic, I acknowledge the role of author, text and reader in the production of meaning. The *author* has "encoded" (to pick up the language of Eco) a message in a *text*, and part of the way in which this encoding works is via allusions to other texts. As a result, the *reader* has an irreducible role to play, in that meaning is not "produced" until the reader puts text and intertext together, which is a process which occurs in the mind of the reader. However, this also means that the role of the reader is *constrained* by text and intertext—the text itself imposes the "limits of interpretation." A reader is not free to take any random texts and rub them together and watch the sparks fly. All "readings" of a text are not equal—there will be better or worse "readings," depending on the capacity of a reader to recognize the *relevant* intertexts. What is *relevant* depends on one's goal. *If* our goal as readers is to reach the meaning of a text as encoded by its author for its original context—and I acknowledge that this need not necessarily be one's goal, but it is my goal—*then* the intertexts against which we read (say) Zech 1–8 must be shaped by an understanding of the historical situation and an estimation of the texts knowable to the prophet Zechariah at this time—a contextual intertextuality! The fact that this kind of an intertextual approach produces results which aid in our understanding helps to commend it over other kinds of intertextual hermeneutics.[20]

In the light of these conclusions on the extent, nature and effect of Zechariah's intertextuality, we may return to the question with which we began: What does Zechariah do with the promises of the classical prophets? Are they applied to his generation, are they taken as referring to a yet still future era, or are the promises transposed into "apocalyptic"?

Our investigations have led to the conclusion that Zechariah alludes to the classical prophets to affirm that *some of* their promises are about to be fulfilled. We find no evidence in Zech 1–8 of a transferral of these prophetic hopes into a (proto-)apocalyptic eschatology (with Collins; contra Cook and Gese), nor that the "messianic" hope is projected into a future era, or attached to a future figure (contra Rose, Pola and Petterson). Zechariah 1–8 applies the classical prophets with an "imminent" eschatology, rather than a futurist or apocalyptic one.

20. For example, the intertextual hermeneutic of Mark Love in the end leaves us with an "unreadable" text and a "frustrated reader." One must ask the question: Does the lack of meaningful "results" arise because of a flawed text (which is what Love concludes, arguing that we need a new hermeneutic for reading the unreadable as such) *or* does it reflect a flaw in the approach pursued?

However, that raises another question: What should we make of the apparent gap between promise and fulfilment? We have seen that Zech 1–8 invokes the words and themes of the classical prophets to depict the transformation of Zion consequent upon Yahweh's return to dwell in his house (Zech 1–2), the restoration of the priesthood and the messianic work of temple-building (Zech 3–4), the banishment of sin and idolatry (Zech 5–6) and the restoration of the covenant and its consequent blessings (Zech 7–8). While I have argued above that key promises relating to temple and priesthood and Davidic line were indeed fulfilled, the historical reality of life after the completion of the temple fell far short of the life of blessings and security which Zech 1–8 seems to promise. In 515 B.C.E., where was the plundering of "Babylon" by her slaves? Where was each man inviting his neighbour to share vine and fig tree? Where were the streets repopulated with children? Where were the ten men from every language and nation taking hold of a Jew by his robe to go in pilgrimage to Jerusalem?[21]

This question of "fulfilment" (or otherwise) has been raised in a number of the exegetical chapters, but it has been left hanging until now. I have done this deliberately, because it seems to me that this is what Zech 1–8 does. Zechariah 1–8 does not answer our questions about fulfilment, except to the extent that the fourfold prophetic validation formula ("Then you will know that Yahweh of Hosts has sent me")[22]—which ties prophetic authenticity to the outworking of historical events—implies that whoever has preserved these words clearly believed the prophet to have in fact been validated by subsequent history. But how is this so? Zechariah 1–8, in and of itself, leaves us hanging in suspense.

I wish to suggest that this observation might give us the best explanation of the relationship (both literary and historical) between Zech 9–14 and Zech 1–8. Zechariah 9–14 provides the resolution to the questions left hanging by Zech 1–8.

21. Floyd (2006b) has strongly critiqued the "disappointment theory" of prophecy, which argues that the prophetic hope arises as a result of unfulfilled prophecies. To disprove this theory, he examines as a test case whether there are "failed prophecies" of a future king in Zech 1–8. As I have already indicated above in Chapter 5, I heartily agree with Floyd's conclusion on this particular point—that it is a mistake to speak of "disappointed messianic expectations" *vis-à-vis* Zerubbabel.

However, from this test case, Floyd goes on to draw conclusions which assume "the fulfillment of all the prophecies in chapters 1–8" (2006b: 289). This takes the evidence of a single test case too far. As I have argued above, there *are* elements of the prophecies of Zech 1–8 which remain unfulfilled. Below I shall offer my own account for explaining the canonical response to the "unfulfilled" prophecies.

22. Zech 2:13, 15 (ET 2:9, 11); 4:9; 6:15.

Zechariah 9–14 is addressed to a later era than 518 B.C.E. (the date in 7:1), in that it presupposes that the temple has been rebuilt (9:8) and a time when the leadership of Joshua and Zerubbabel (which is affirmed and endorsed in Zech 1–8) has been replaced by corrupt leadership and worthless shepherds (10:3; 11:4–17).[23] Zechariah 9–14 is addressed to a generation struggling in this situation (being "fleeced" by their shepherds, we might say—cf. Zech 11:16), who must surely have compared the promises of Zech 1–8 with their present situation, and wondered "Is this all that we can expect?!" While Zech 9–14 demonstrates a continuity of many of the themes from Zech 1–8, there is also a marked eschatological shift in the time for the fulfilment of these promises. Whereas Zech 1–8 stresses the imminent (if partial) fulfilment of the classical prophets, Zech 9–14 stresses that the ultimate fulfilment of these prophets lies still yet in its future. Zechariah 9–14 does not contradict what has been said in Zech 1–8, but goes on to affirm that what has been said before is not the end of the story, and that there are important things which need to be heard by a subsequent generation.

In making this argument I am charting a parallel course to that which was argued by Mason in 1976. Mason examined the relationship between Zech 9–14 and Zech 1–8, and argued that there is a continuing line of tradition between the two, especially in the prominence of the Zion tradition (9:9; cf. 2:14 = ET 2:10), the cleansing of the community (3:5; cf. 13:1), universal salvation (9:6–7; 14:16–21; cf. 8:20–22), the appeal to the former prophets (1:2–6; 7:11–14; cf. the allusion to Jer 14 in Zech 10:1–2), and the provision of leadership as a sign of the new age. He suggests that in Zech 9–14 the "same essential spirit and outlook of proto-Zechariah" finds expression, though with respect to their expectations of leadership, they had become disillusioned with human leadership and looked instead for an eschatological intervention of God himself (see Mason 1976: 238).[24] Though I agree with the general thrust of Mason's

23. How much later is a matter of debate (and not strictly relevant to my enquiry). With most, I am not persuaded by those who argue for third- and second-century dates on the basis of the reference to Javan (i.e. Greece) in Zech 9:13. There is nothing in the text of Zech 9–14 that would preclude a dating of, say, 480 B.C.E. ± 30 years. Similarly, the question of authorship is not relevant to the present enquiry, and (from the point of view of intertextuality) it is not possible to distinguish between a school of Zechariah's disciples applying his message in a changed context vs. the prophet Zechariah (as an older man) reapplying his own prophecy to a new generation.

24. Robinson 1895: 84–88; Childs 1979: 482–85; and Meyers and Meyers 1993: 27 are among those who stress the continuity of thought between Zech 1–8 and 9–14.

conclusion, I arrive there via a slightly different route, arising out of observations regarding intratexts and intertexts.[25]

8.1. *Intratexts and Intertexts Again*

In Chapter 7 I argued that Zech 7–8 establishes its relationship with Zech 1–6 by means of a series of *intra*texts (i.e. allusions to Zech 1–6). The function of these intratexts is to entwine tightly the message of these blocks of material. At the same time, Zech 7–8 also relies on *inter*texts to introduce themes (particularly "covenantal" themes) which are not otherwise explicit in Zech 1–6. The intratextual allusions confirm the connection and continuity between the texts, so that the intertexts of Zech 7–8 can nuance the meaning of Zech 1–8 as a whole.

I wish to suggest that there is the same kind of intratext/intertext dynamic at work in Zech 9–14. A paradigmatic example of this can be seen in the relationship between Zech 2:14 and 9:9a.[26] Zechariah 9:9a is a clear *intra*textual allusion (in the context of the book of Zechariah as a whole) to Zech 2:14 (ET 2:10):[27]

Zech 2:14 (=ET 2:10)	Sing and rejoice, O daughter of Zion, for behold, I am coming and I will dwell in your midst, declares Yahweh.
Zech 9:9a	Rejoice greatly, O daughter of Zion! Shout aloud, O daughter of Jerusalem! Behold, your *king* will come to you...

Given this intratextual allusion, it is important to note the significant transformations which have occurred in the process of re-use. First, the (future tense) promise that Yahweh "will dwell" in Zech 2:14 is not repeated in 9:9. This is significant observation, given the central importance the theme of "Yahweh dwelling in Jerusalem" in Zech 1–8. Not only is this promise absent from Zech 9:9, but the promise that Yahweh

25. For a different, though complementary, argument to my own, see Floyd (2003: 242), who argues that Zech 9–11 offers a reinterpretation of Zech 1–8. See also De Vries (2003: 265–70) on differences between the "futurism" in Zech 1–8 and Zech 9–14, and Meyers 1995 on the differences between Zech 1–8 and 9–14.

26. This parallel is also discussed by Floyd 2006b: 287–89. For further analysis on the points of contact between the two passages, as well as the shift in rhetorical function, see Schultz 2003: 36–37.

27. In the light of the discussion above on the intertexts to Zech 2:14 (see §4.6.3), it is significant to note that the phrase "behold {X} is coming" (הִנֵּה + בוא) occurs in both Zech 2:14 and Zech 9:9, since this is not a feature in Isa 12:6; Zeph 3:14–15 or Joel 2:23. This suggests that Zech 9:9 is not just a co-incidental or independent re-use of the same tradition, but rather that Zech 9:9 is a deliberate reflection on Zech 2:14.

will "dwell" (שׁכן) is entirely absent from Zech 9–14. The conclusion that we can draw from this is that, subsequent to the temple's completion, Yahweh is indeed now dwelling with his people.[28] At one level, then, Zech 9:9 is an implicit affirmation that what Zech 1–8 has promised (cf. Zech 1:16) has in fact occurred.

However, there is another transformation in this verse, which shifts the ultimate fulfilment to the future. Whereas Zech 2:10 anticipated the coming of Yahweh, Zech 9:9a now anticipates the future coming of a king.[29] We have observed above (on Zech 3–4) that Zech 1–8 avoids all mention of the word "king," even though at the same time affirming Zerubbabel as the continuation of the Davidic dynasty. Zechariah 9:9 knows no such reticence in proclaiming a message with clear messianic overtones, but shifts this to an undetermined point in the future.[30]

Zechariah 9 alludes to Zech 2, and in the process transforms it, in two dimensions. In a sense, Zech 9 looks back at Zech 2 and says "yes, ...but"—"Yes, what Zech 2 has promised has happened, but the final day for rejoicing is still yet future, and that day will only come when Yahweh's king comes to Jerusalem."

In contrast to the positive tone of Zech 1–8, Zech 9–14 has more pessimistic overtones (cf. Redditt 1989). Zechariah 9–14 is addressed to a generation in distress, caused by bad leadership, and anticipates a time of struggle and opposition ahead, though still confident in the ultimate triumph of Yahweh and his people on the final day, affirming that what was promised in Zech 1–8 will find its ultimate fulfilment "on that day."

The imminent eschatology of Zech 1–8 has been affirmed by Zech 9–14, but at the same time tempered and recast in terms of an ultimate fulfilment at a future point in time. Zechariah 9–14 provides the resolution to the questions about the fulfilment of prophecy left hanging by Zech 1–8.

28. Supportive of this conclusion is that Yahweh "goes out" (יצא) from Jerusalem to fight as its divine warrior (Zech 14:3).

29. That this is a human figure is beyond doubt, given the fact that 9:9b describes him as riding on a donkey.

30. The "indeterminate" messianism of Zech 9–14 does not carry the same political risk, in terms of the response of the Persian overlords, as compared to a message about a governor becoming "king." For an interesting example of the perceived political risk in a slightly later generation, refer to Neh 6:5–8.

BIBLIOGRAPHY

Achtemeier, E. R. 1986. *Nahum–Malachi*. Atlanta: John Knox.

Ackroyd, P. R. 1952. The Book of Haggai and Zechariah 1–8. *JJS* 3:151–56.

———. 1958. Two Old Testament Historical Problems of the Early Persian Period. *JNES* 17:13–27.

———. 1967. History and Theology in the Chronicler. *Concordia Theological Monthly* 38:501–15.

———. 1968. *Exile and Restoration: A Study of Hebrew Thought of the Sixth Century BC*. London: SCM Press.

Aejmelaeus, A. 2002. Jeremiah at the Turning-Point of History: The Function of Jer. xxv 1–14 in the Book of Jeremiah. *VT* 52:459–82.

Ahlström, G. W. 1993. *The History of Ancient Palestine from the Palaeolithic Period to Alexander's Conquest*. Sheffield: JSOT Press.

Ahroni, R. 1977. The Gog Prophecy and the Book of Ezekiel. *HAR* 1:1–27.

Aichele, G., and G. A. Phillips. 1995. *Intertextuality and the Bible*. Atlanta: Scholars Press.

Albertz, R. 1994. *A History of Israelite Religion in the Old Testament Period*. London: SCM Press.

———. 2003a. Darius in Place of Cyrus: The First Edition of Deutero-Isaiah (Isaiah 40.1–52.12) in 521 BCE. *JSOT* 27: 371–88.

———. 2003b. The Thwarted Restoration. Pages 1–17 in Albertz and Becking 2003.

Albertz, R., and B. Becking, eds. 2003. *Yahwism After the Exile: Perspectives on Israelite Religion in the Persian Era*. Assen: Van Gorcum.

Albright, W. F. 1969. *Archaeology and the Religion of Israel*. 5th ed. Garden City, N.Y.: Anchor Books.

Allan, N. 1982. The Identity of the Jerusalem Priesthood During the Exile. *HeyJ* 23:259–69.

Allen, G. 2000. *Intertextuality: The New Critical Idiom*. London: Routledge.

Allen, L. C. 1976. *The Books of Joel, Obadiah, Jonah and Micah*. London: Hodder & Stoughton.

Althann, R. 1988. The Destination of the White Horses in Zechariah 6:6. *OTE* 1:65–71.

Amerongen, M. van. 2005. The Structure of Zechariah 4: A Comparison Between the Divisions in the Masoretic Text, Ancient Translations, and Modern Commentaries. Pages 191–209 in *Layout Markers in Biblical Manuscripts and Ugaritic Tablets*. Edited by M. C. A. Korpel and J. M. Oesch. Assen: Van Gorcum.

Amsler, S. 1972. Zacharie et l'origine de l'apocalyptique. Pages 227–31 in *Congress Volume: Uppsala, 1971*. Leiden: Brill.

Amsler, S. (with A. Lacocque and R. Vuilleumier). 1981. *Aggee; Zacharie 1–8; Malachie*. Neuchâtel: Delachaux & Niestlé.

Andersen, F. I. 1958. Who Built the Second Temple? *ABR* 6: 3–35.

Andersen, F. I., and A. D. Forbes. 1992. On Marking Clause Boundaries. Pages 181–202 in *Actes du troisième Colloque international Bible et informatique: Interprétation, herméneutique, competence informatique = Proceedings of the Third International Colloquium Bible and Computer: Interpretation, Hermeneutics, Expertise: Tübingen, 26–30 August 1991*. Association internationale Bible et informatique. Paris: Champion.

Applegate, J. 1997. Jeremiah and the Seventy Years in the Hebrew Bible: Inner-Biblical Reflections on the Prophet and His Prophecy. Pages 91–110 in *The Book of Jeremiah and Its Reception—Le Livre de Jérémie et sa Réception*. Edited by A. Curtis and T. Römer. Leuven: Leuven University Press.

Assmann, J. 1995. Collective Memory and Cultural Identity. *New German Critique* 65:125–33.

———. 2006. *Religion and Cultural Memory*. Stanford, Calif.: Stanford University Press.

Astour, M. C. 1976. Ezekiel's Prophecy of Gog and the Cuthean Legend of Naram-Sin. *JBL* 95:567–79.

Avalos, H. 1998. Daniel 9:24–25 and Mesopotamian Temple Rededications. *JBL* 117:507–11.

Avigad, N. 1976. *Bullae and Seals from a Post-Exilic Judaean Archive*. Jerusalem: Hebrew University Press.

Bailey, J. W. 1951. The Usage in the Post Restoration Period of Terms Descriptive of the Priest and High Priest. *JBL* 70:217–25.

Bakhtin, M. M. 1973. *Problems of Dostoevsky's Poetics*. Trans. R. W. Rotsel. Ann Arbor, Mich.: Ardis.

———. 1981. *The Dialogic Imagination: Four Essays*. Austin: University of Texas Press.

Bakon, S. 1989. Zerubbabel. *Dor le Dor* 18:148–56.

Baldwin, J. G. 1964. Tsemach as a Technical Term in the Prophets. *VT* 14:93–97.

———. 1972. *Haggai, Zechariah, Malachi*. London: Tyndale.

Barker, M. 1977. The Two Figures in Zechariah. *HeyJ* 18: 38–46.

———. 1978. The Evil in Zechariah. *HeyJ* 19:12–27.

Barr, J. 1995. The Synchronic, the Diachronic and the Historical: A Triangular Relationship? Pages 1–14 in de Moor 1995.

———. 2000. *History and Ideology in the Old Testament: Biblical Studies at the End of the Millennium*. Oxford: Oxford University Press.

Barstad, H. M. 1996. *The Myth of the Empty Land: A Study in the History and Archaeology of Judah During the Exilic Period*. Oslo: Scandinavian University Press.

Barthélemy, D. 1963. Les Tiqqune Sopherim et la Critique Textuelle de l'Ancien Testament. Pages 285–304 in *Congress Volume: Bonn, 1962*. VTSup 9. Leiden: Brill.

Barthes, R. 1977. *Image, Music, Text*. London: Fontana.

———. 1981. Theory of the Text. Pages 31–47 in *Untying the Text: A Post-Structuralist Reader*. Edited by R. Young. Boston, Mass.: Routledge & Kegan Paul.

Barton, J. 1986. *Oracles of God: Perceptions of Ancient Prophecy in Israel After the Exile*. London: Darton, Longman & Todd.

———. 1998. The Messiah in Old Testament Theology. Pages 365–79 in Day 1998.

———. 2001. *Joel and Obadiah: A Commentary*. Louisville, Ky.: Westminster John Knox.

Beal, T. K. 1992. Ideology and Intertextuality: Surplus of Meaning and Controlling the Means of Production. Pages 27–39 in Fewell 1992.

Beardsley, M., and W. Wimsatt. 1976. The Intentional Fallacy. Pages 1–13 in *On Literary Intention: Critical Essays*. Edited by D. Newton-De Molina. Edinburgh: Edinburgh University Press.

Beatty, B. 1995. Who Wears the Crown(S)? *Downside Review* 113:1–19.

Becking, B. 2006. Zerubbabel, Zechariah 3–4, and Post-Exilic History. Pages 268–79 in *Israel's Prophets and Israel's Past: Essays on the Relationship of Prophetic Texts and Israelite History in Honor of John H. Hayes*. Edited by B. E. Kelle and M. B. Moore. LHBOTS 446. New York: T&T Clark International.

Beckwith, R. T. 2004. The Temple Restored. Pages 71–79 in *Heaven on Earth*. Edited by T. D. Alexander and S. J. Gathercole. Carlisle: Paternoster.

Bedford, P. R. 1995. Discerning the Time: Haggai, Zechariah and the "Delay" in the Rebuilding of the Jerusalem Temple. Pages 71–94 in *The Pitcher is Broken: Memorial Essays for Gösta W. Ahlström*. Edited by S. W. Holloway and L. K. Handy. JSOTSup 190. Sheffield: Sheffield Academic Press.

———. 2001. *Temple Restoration in Early Achaemenid Judah*. Leiden: Brill.

Behrens, A. 2002. *Prophetische Visionsschilderungen im Alten Testament: Sprachliche Eigenarten, Funktion und Geschichte einer Gattung*. Munster: Ugarit-Verlag.

Ben Zvi, E. 1997. The Chronicler as Historian: Building Texts. Pages 132–49 in Graham, Hoglund and McKenzie 1997.

Ben Zvi, E., and M. Floyd, eds. 2006. *Utopia and Dystopia in Prophetic Texts*. Winona Lake, Ind.: Eisenbrauns. Helsinki: University of Helsinki.

Ben-Porat, Z. 1976. The Poetics of Literary Allusion. *PTL: A Journal for Descriptive Poetics and Theory of Literature* 1:105–28.

———. 1990. Forms of Intertextuality and the Reading of Poetry: Uri Zvi Greenberg's Bashaʾar. *Prooftexts* 10:257–81.

Bergey, R. 2003. The Song of Moses (Deuteronomy 32.1–43) and Isaianic Prophecies: A Case of Early Intertextuality? *JSOT* 28: 33–54.

Berquist, J. L. 1995. *Judaism in Persia's Shadow: A Social and Historical Approach*. Minneapolis: Fortress.

Beuken, W. A. M. 1967. *Haggai–Sacharja 1–8: Studien zur Überlieferungsgeschichte der frühnachexilischen Prophetie*. Assen: Van Gorcum.

———. 1989. Does Trito-Isaiah Reject the Temple? An Intertextual Inquiry into Isa 66.1–6. Pages 53–66 in Draisma 1989.

Beyse, K.-M. 1972. *Serubbabel und die Königserwartungen der Propheten Haggai und Sacharja: Eine historische und traditionsgeschichtliche Untersuchung*. Stuttgart: Calwer Verlag.

Bianchi, F. 1994. Le Rôle de Zorobabel et de la Dynastie Davidique en Judée du Vie Siècle au Iie Siècle Av. J.-C. *Transeuphratène* 7:153–65.

Bič, M. 1964. *Die Nachtgesichte des Sacharja: Eine Auslegung von Sacharja 1–6*. Neukirchen–Vluyn: Neukirchener-Verlag.

Blenkinsopp, J. 1990. A Jewish Sect of the Persian Period. *CBQ* 52:5–20.

———. 1991. Temple and Society in Achaemenid Judah. Pages 22–53 in Davies 1991.

———. 1995. *Wisdom and Law in the Old Testament: The Ordering of Life in Israel and Early Judaism*. Rev. ed. New York, Oxford University Press.

———. 2000. *Isaiah 1–39: A New Translation with Introduction and Commentary*. New York: Doubleday.

Block, D. I. 1992. Gog in Prophetic Tradition: A New Look at Ezekiel xxxviii 17. *VT* 42:54–72.

Bloom, H. 1973. *The Anxiety of Influence: A Theory of Poetry*. New York: Oxford University Press.

Boda, M. J. 1999. *Praying the Tradition: The Origin and Use of Tradition in Nehemiah 9*. Berlin: de Gruyter.

———. 2001. Oil, Crowns and Thrones: Prophet, Priest and King in Zechariah 1:7–6:15. *Journal of Hebrew Scriptures* 3: Article 10.

———. 2003a. From Fasts to Feasts: The Literary Function of Zechariah 7–8. *CBQ* 65: 390–407.

———. 2003b. Zechariah: Master Mason or Penitential Prophet. Pages 49–69 in Albertz and Becking 2003.

———. 2004. *Haggai, Zechariah*. Grand Rapids: Zondervan.

———. 2005. Terrifying the Horns: Persia and Babylon in Zechariah 1:7–6:15. *CBQ* 67:22–41.

———. 2006. From Dystopia to Myopia: Utopian (Re)Visions in Haggai and Zechariah 1–8. Pages 210–48 in Ben Zvi and Floyd 2006.

———. 2009. Hoy, Hoy: The Prophetic Origins of the Babylonian Tradition in Zechariah 2:10–17. Pages 171–90 in Boda and Floyd 2009.

Boda, M. J., and M. Floyd, eds. 2003. *Bringing Out the Treasure: Inner Biblical Allusion in Zechariah 9–14*. JSOTSup 370. London: Sheffield Academic Press.

———. 2009. *Tradition in Transition*. LHBOTS 475. London: T&T Clark International.

Boehmer, J. 1897. Wer is Gog von Magog? Ein Beitrag zur Auslegung des Buches Ezechiel. *Zeitschrift für wissenschaftliche Theologie* 40: 321–55.

———. 1938. Was Bedeutet die Goldene Leuchter Sach 4, 2? *BZ* 24: 360–64.

Bosshard-Nepustil, E. 1997. *Rezeptionen von Jesaja 1–39 im Zwölfprophetenbuch: Untersuchungen zur literarischen Verbindung von Prophetenbüchern in babylonischer und persischer Zeit*. Freiburg, Schweiz: Universitätsverlag.

Boyarin, D. 1990. *Intertextuality and the Reading of Midrash*. Bloomington: Indiana University Press.

Bright, J. 1980. *The History of Israel*. 3d ed. London: SCM Press.

Bruehler, B. B. 2001. Seeing Through the עינים of Zechariah: Understanding Zechariah 4. *CBQ* 63:430–43.

Buchanan, G. W. 1994. *Introduction to Intertextuality*. Lewiston, N.Y.: Mellen Biblical Press.

Bullough, S. 1953. Zechariah. Pages 545–54 in *A Catholic Commentary on Holy Scripture*. Edited by B. Orchard. London: Nelson.

Butterworth, M. 1992. *Structure and the Book of Zechariah*. JSOTSup 130. Sheffield: JSOT Press.

Buzy, D. 1918. Les Symboles de Zecharie. *RB* 15:136–91.

Cahill, M. 1999. Not a Cornerstone! Translating Ps 118,22 in the Jewish and Christian Scriptures. *RB* 106: 345–57.

Cameron, G. G. 1941. Darius and Xerxes in Babylonia. *The American Journal of Semitic Languages and Literatures* 58: 314–25.

Carroll, R. P. 1979. *When Prophecy Failed: Cognitive Dissonance in the Prophetic Traditions of the Old Testament*. London: SCM Press.

———. 1986. *Jeremiah: A Commentary*. London: SCM Press.

———. 1996. Jeremiah, Intertextuality and Ideologiekritik. *JNSL* 22:15–34.

Carter, C. E. 1999. *The Emergence of Yehud in the Persian Period: A Social and Demographic Study*. Sheffield: Sheffield Academic Press.

Cathcart, K. J., and R. P. Gordon. 1989. *The Targum of the Minor Prophets*. Edinburgh: T. & T. Clark.
Charlesworth, J. H. 1992. From Messianology to Christology: Problems and Prospects. Pages 3–35 in *The Messiah: Developments in Earliest Judaism and Christianity*. Edited by J. H. Charlesworth. Minneapolis: Fortress.
Chary, T. 1969. *Aggée, Zacharie, Malachie*. Paris: J. Gabalda.
Childs, B. S. 1979. *Introduction to the Old Testament as Scripture*. London: SCM Press.
———. 2001. *Isaiah*. Louisville, Ky.: Westminster John Knox.
Claassens, L. J. M. 2003. Biblical Theology as Dialogue: Continuing the Conversation on Mikhail Bakhtin and Biblical Theology. *JBL* 122:127–44.
Clark, D. J. 1982. The Case of the Vanishing Angel. *Bible Translator* 33:213–18.
———. 1994. Vision and Oracle in Zechariah 1–6. Pages 529–60 in *Biblical Hebrew and Discourse Linguistics*. Edited by R. D. Bergen. Winona Lake, Ind.: Eisenbrauns.
Clayton, J., and E. Rothstein, eds. 1991. *Influence and Intertextuality in Literary History*. Madison: University of Wisconsin Press.
Clements, R. E. 1965. *God and Temple*. Oxford: Blackwell.
———. 1996a. *Ezekiel*. Louisville, Ky.: Westminster John Knox.
———. 1996b. *Old Testament Prophecy: From Oracles to Canon*. Louisville, Ky.: Westminster John Knox.
Clifford, R. J. 1972. *The Cosmic Mountain in Canaan and the Old Testament*. Cambridge, Mass.: Harvard University Press.
Coggins, R. J. 1993. Prophecy—True and False. Pages 80–94 in McKay and Clines 1993.
———. 1996. Interbiblical Quotations in Joel. Pages 75–84 in *After the Exile: Essays in Honour of Rex Mason*. Edited by J. Barton and D. J. Reimer. Macon, Ga.: Mercer University Press.
———. 2000. Intertextuality in Joel. Pages 21–24 in *Joel and Amos*. Edited by R. J. Coggins. Sheffield: Sheffield Academic Press.
Coggins, R. J., A. Phillips and M. A. Knibb, eds. 1982. *Israel's Prophetic Tradition: Essays in Honour of Peter R. Ackroyd*. Cambridge: Cambridge University Press.
Collins, J. J. 1977. *The Apocalyptic Vision of the Book of Daniel*. Missoula, Mont.: Scholars Press.
———. 1979. The Jewish Apocalypses. *Semeia* 14:21–59.
———. 1995. *The Scepter and the Star: The Messiahs of the Dead Sea Scrolls and Other Ancient Literature*. New York: Doubleday.
———. 1998. *The Apocalyptic Imagination: An Introduction to Jewish Apocalyptic Literature*. 2d ed. Grand Rapids: Eerdmans.
———. 2003. The Eschatology of Zechariah. Pages 74–84 in Grabbe and Haak 2003.
Conrad, E. W. 1999. *Zechariah*. Readings: A New Biblical Commentary. Sheffield: Sheffield Academic Press.
———. 2003. *Reading the Latter Prophets: Toward a New Canonical Criticism*. JSOTSup 376. London: T&T Clark International.
Cook, S. L. 1995. *Prophecy and Apocalypticism: The Postexilic Social Setting*. Minneapolis: Fortress.
Cooke, G. A. 1936. *A Critical and Exegetical Commentary on the Book of Ezekiel*. Edinburgh: T. & T. Clark.
Crenshaw, J. L. 1995. *Joel: A New Translation with Introduction and Commentary*. New York: Doubleday.
Cross, F. M. 1953. The Council of Yahweh in Second Isaiah. *JNES* 12:274–77.

Culler, J. D. 2001. *The Pursuit of Signs: Semiotics, Literature, Deconstruction*. Repr., with a new preface by the author. London: Routledge.

Curtis, B. G. 1991. Eschatological Expectations and the Date Formulae in Haggai and Zechariah 1–8. Paper presented at the 43rd National Conference of the Evangelical Theological Society, November 21–23, 1991, Kansas City. Available at http://www.tren.com/e-docs/search.cfm?pETS-4334

Dahood, M. 1969. Hebrew–Ugaritic Lexicography VII. *Bib* 50:337–45.

Davies, P. R., ed. 1991. *Second Temple Studies 1: Persian Period*. JSOTSup 117. Sheffield: JSOT Press.

———. 1992. *In Search of "Ancient Israel"*. JSOTSup 148. Sheffield: Sheffield Academic Press.

———. 2003. Biblical Hebrew and the History of Ancient Judah: Typology, Chronology and Common Sense. Pages 150–63 in Young 2003.

Davis, J. D. 1920. The Reclothing and Coronation of Joshua: Zechariah iii and vi. *PTR* 18:256–68.

Day, J. 1995. Inner-Biblical Interpretation in the Prophets. Pages 230–46 in *The Place Is Too Small for Us: The Israelite Prophets in Recent Scholarship*. Edited by R. P. Gordon. Winona Lake, Ind.: Eisenbrauns.

———, ed. 1998. *King and Messiah in Israel and the Ancient Near East: Proceedings of the Oxford Old Testament Seminar*. JSOTSup 270. Sheffield: Sheffield Academic Press.

———. 2004. *In Search of Pre-Exilic Israel: Proceedings of the Oxford Old Testament Seminar*. T&T Clark International.

Day, P. L. 1988. *An Adversary in Heaven: Satan in the Hebrew Bible*. Atlanta: Scholars Press.

De Vries, S. J. 2003. Futurism in the Preexilic Minor Prophets Compared with that of the Postexilic Minor Prophets. Pages 252–72 in Redditt and Schart 2003.

Delcor, M. 1952. Les Sources du Deutero-Zacharie et ses procedes d'emprunt. *RB* 59:385–411.

———. 1975. La Vision de la Femme dans l'Epha de Zach, 5:5–11 à la Lumière de la Litterature Hittite. *Revue de l'Histoire des Religions* 187:137–45.

Delkurt, H. 1999a. Die Engelwesen in Sach 1,8–15. *BN* 99:20–41.

———. 1999b. Eine Zusammenfassung des Dekalogs in Sach 5,3f. Pages 193–205 in *Recht und Ethos im Alten Testament—Gestalt und Wirkung*. Edited by S. Beyerle, G. Mayer and H. Strauss. Neukirchen–Vluyn: Neukirchener Verlag.

———. 2000. *Sacharjas Nachtgesichte: Zur Aufnahme und Abwandlung prophetischer Traditionen*. Berlin: de Gruyter.

Depuydt, L. 1995. Evidence for Accession Dating under the Achaemenids. *Journal of the American Oriental Society* 115:193–204.

Derrett, J. D. M. 1968. The Stone that the Builders Rejected. Pages 180–86 in *Studia Evangelica*. IV. *Papers Presented to the Third International Congress on New Testament Studies held at Christ Church, Oxford, 1965*. 3d ed. Edited by F. L. Cross. Berlin: Akademie-Verlag.

Draisma, S., ed. 1989. *Intertextuality in Biblical Writings: Essays in Honour of Bas Van Iersel*. Kampen: Uitgeversmaatschappij J. H. Kok.

Driver, S. R. 1913. *An Introduction to the Literature of the Old Testament*. 9th ed. Edinburgh: T. & T. Clark.

Duhm, B. 1911. Anmerkungen zu den zwolf Propheten VII. Buch Sacharja I (Kapitel 1–8). *ZAW* 31:161–204.

Dumbrell, W. J. 1978. Kingship and Temple in the Post-Exilic Period. *Reformed Theological Review* 37:33–42.

Eagleton, T. 1983. *Literary Theory: An Introduction*. Oxford: Blackwell.

Eco, U. 1979. *The Role of the Reader: Explorations in the Semiotics of Texts*. Bloomington: Indiana University Press.

———. 1984. *Semiotics and the Philosophy of Language*. Basingstoke: Macmillan.

———. 1989. *The Open Work*. Cambridge, Mass.: Harvard University Press.

———. 1990. *The Limits of Interpretation*. Bloomington: Indiana University Press.

———. 1992. Between Author and Text. Pages 67–88 in Eco and Collini 1992.

Eco, U., and S. Collini, eds. 1992. *Interpretation and Overinterpretation*. Cambridge: Cambridge University Press.

Edelman, D. V. 2003. Proving Yahweh Killed His Wife (Zechariah 5:5–11). *BibInt* 11:335–44.

———. 2005. *The Origins of the "Second" Temple: Persian Imperial Policy and the Rebuilding of Jerusalem*. London: Equinox.

Ehrensvärd, M. 2003. Linguistic Dating of Biblical Texts. Pages 164–88 in Young 2003.

Eichrodt, W. 1970. *Ezekiel: A Commentary*. London: SCM Press.

Elliger, K., and A. Weiser. 1963. *Das Buch der zwölf kleinen Propheten*. 4th ed. Göttingen: Vandenhoeck & Ruprecht.

Ellis, R. S. 1968. *Foundation Deposits in Ancient Mesopotamia*. New Haven: Yale University Press.

Eslinger, L. M. 1992. Inner-Biblical Exegesis and Inner-Biblical Allusion: The Question of Category. *VT* 42:47–58.

Ewald, H. 1875. *Commentary on the Prophets of the Old Testament*. London: Williams & Norgate.

Fewell, D. N., ed. 1992. *Reading Between Texts: Intertextuality and the Hebrew Bible*. Louisville, Ky.: Westminster John Knox.

Finley, T. J. 1988. "The Apple of His Eye" (*babat ͑eno*) in Zechariah 2:12. *VT* 38:337–38.

Fischer, G. 1991. Jer 25 und die Fremdvölkersprüche: Unterschiede zwischen hebräischem und griechischem Text. *Bib* 72:474–99.

Fishbane, M. A. 1979. *Text and Texture: Close Readings of Selected Biblical Texts*. New York: Schocken.

———. 1985. *Biblical Interpretation in Ancient Israel*. Oxford: Clarendon.

———. 1986. Inner Biblical Exegesis: Types and Strategies of Interpretation in Ancient Israel. Pages 19–37 in *Midrash and Literature*. Edited by G. H. Hartman and S. Budick. New Haven: Yale University Press.

———. 1989. *The Garments of Torah: Essays in Biblical Hermeneutics*. Bloomington: Indiana University Press.

———. 1996. Inner-Biblical Exegesis. Pages 33–48 in *Hebrew Bible/Old Testament*. Edited by M. Sæbø. Göttingen: Vandenhoeck & Ruprecht.

———. 2000. Types of Biblical Intertextuality. Pages 39–44 in Lemaire and Sæbø 2000.

Fitzmyer, J. A. 2007. *The One Who Is to Come*. Grand Rapids: Eerdmans.

Floyd, M. H. 1996. The Evil in the Ephah: Reading Zechariah 5:5–11 in Its Literary Context. *CBQ* 58:51–68.

———. 2000. *Minor Prophets*. Grand Rapids: Eerdmans.

———. 2003. Deutero-Zechariah and Types of Intertextuality. Pages 225–44 in Boda and Floyd 2003.

———. 2006a. The Production of Prophetic Books in the Early Second Temple Period. Pages 1–25 in *Prophets, Prophecy, and Prophetic Texts in Second Temple Judaism*. LHBOTS 427. Edited by M. Floyd and R. D. Haak. New York: T&T Clark International.

———. 2006b. Was Prophetic Hope Born of Disappointment? The Case of Zechariah. Pages 268–96 in Ben Zvi and Floyd 2006.

Fohrer, G. 1962. Ehernes Meer. Page 372 in *Biblisch-Historisches Handworterbuch*, Vol. 1. Edited by B. I. Reicke and L. Rost. Göttingen: Vandenhoeck & Ruprecht.

Fournier-Bidoz, A. 1997. Des mains de Zorobabel aux yeux du Seigneur: Pour une lecture unitaire de Zacharie IV 1–14. *VT* 47:537–42.

Fowler, H. T. 1897. The Chronological Position of Joel Among the Prophets. *JBL* 16:146–54.

Freedman, D. N. 1990. The Flying Scroll in Zechariah 5:1–4. Pages 42–48 in *Studies in Near Eastern Culture and History*. Edited by J. A. Bellamy. Ann Arbor: University of Michigan Center for Near Eastern and North African Studies.

Friebel, K. G. 2001. A Hermeneutical Paradigm for Interpreting Prophetic Sign-Actions. *Didaskalia* 12:25–45.

Frolov, S. 2005. Is the Narrator Also Among the Prophets? Reading Zechariah Without Presuppositions. *BibInt* 13:13–40.

Fuller, R. 1990. Early Emendations of the Scribes: The Tiqqun Sopherim in Zechariah 2:12. Pages 21–28 in *Of Scribes and Scrolls*. Edited by H. W. Attridge et al. Lanham, Md.: University Press of America.

Galling, K. 1964a. Die Exilswende in der Sicht des Propheten Sacharja. Pages 109–26 in Galling 1964.

———. 1964b. Serubbabel und der Hohepriester beim Wiederaufbau des Tempels in Jerusalem. Pages 127–48 in Galling 1964.

———, ed. 1964c. *Studien zur Geschichte Israels im persischen Zeitalter*. Tübingen: Mohr.

Gelston, A. 1966. Foundations of the Second Temple. *VT* 16:232–35.

Gese, H. 1957. *Der Verfassungsentwurf des Ezechiel (Kap. 40–48): Traditionsgeschichtlich Untersucht*. Tübingen: J. C. B. Mohr (Paul Siebeck).

———. 1973. Anfang und Ende der Apokalyptik, Dargestellt am Sacharjabuch. *Zeitschrift für Theologie und Kirche* 70:20–49.

Gillingham, S. E. 1998. The Messiah in the Psalms. Pages 209–37 in Day 1998.

Glazier-MacDonald, B. 1998. Zechariah. Pages 247–49 in *Women's Bible Commentary*. Edited by C. A. Newsom and S. H. Ringe. Expanded ed. Louisville, Ky.: Westminster John Knox.

Goldman, Y. 1992. *Prophétie et royauté au retour de l'exil. Les origines littéraires de la forme massorétique du livre de Jérémie*. Freiburg, Schweiz: Universitätsverlag. Göttingen: Vandenhoeck & Ruprecht.

Good, R. M. 1982. Zechariah's Second Night Vision (Zech 2:1–4). *Bib* 63:56–59.

———. 1992. Zechariah 14:13 and Related Texts: Brother Against Brother in War. *Maarav* 8:39–47.

Gordon, R. P. 1975. An Inner-Targum Corruption (Zech. I 8). *VT* 25:216–21.

———. 1994. *Studies in the Targum to the Twelve Prophets: From Nahum to Malachi*. Leiden: Brill.

Grabbe, L. L. 1998. *Ezra–Nehemiah*. London: Routledge.

———. 2000. *Judaic Religion in the Second Temple Period: Belief and Practice from the Exile to Yavneh*. London: Routledge.

———. 2003. Prophetic and Apocalyptic: Time for New Definitions—and New Thinking. Pages 107–33 in Grabbe and Haak 2003.

———. 2004. *A History of the Jews and Judaism in the Second Temple Period*. LSTS 47. London: T&T Clark International.

Grabbe, L. L., and R. D. Haak, eds. 2003. *Knowing the End from the Beginning: The Prophetic, the Apocalyptic and Their Relationships*. JSPSup 46. London: T&T Clark International.

Graham, M. P., K. G. Hoglund and S. L. McKenzie, eds. 1997. *The Chronicler as Historian*. JSOTSup 238. Sheffield: Sheffield Academic Press.

Greenberg, M. 1983. *Ezekiel: A New Translation with Introduction and Commentary*. AB 22. Garden City, N.Y.: Doubleday.

———. 1984. The Design and Themes of Ezekiel's Program of Restoration. *Int* 38:181–208.

———. 1990. The Decalogue Tradition Critically Examined. Pages 83–119 in Segal and Levi 1990.

Gurney, R. J. M. 1981. The Seventy Weeks of Daniel 9:24–27. *EvQ* 53:29–36.

Hahlen, M. A. 2000. The Background and Use of Equine Imagery in Zechariah. *Stone-Campbell Journal* 3:243–60.

Halpern, B. 1978. The Ritual Background of Zechariah's Temple Song. *CBQ* 40:167–90.

Hanhart, R. 1998. *Sacharja*. Neukirchen–Vluyn: Neukirchener Verlag.

Hanson, P. D. 1979. *The Dawn of Apocalyptic: The Historical and Sociological Roots of Jewish Apocalyptic Eschatology*. Rev. ed. Philadelphia: Fortress.

———. 1987a. In Defiance of Death: Zechariah's Symbolic Universe. Pages 173–79 in *Love and Death in the Ancient Near East: Essays in Honor of Marvin H. Pope*. Edited by J. H. Marks and R. M. Good. Guilford, Conn.: Four Quarters.

———. 1987b. Israelite Religion in the Early Postexilic Period. Pages 485–508 in Miller, McBride and Hanson 1987.

———. 1987c. *Old Testament Apocalyptic*. Nashville: Abingdon.

Harris, S. L. 1995. *Proverbs 1–9: A Study of Inner-Biblical Interpretation*. Atlanta: Scholars Press.

Hatina, T. R. 1999. Intertextuality and Historical Criticism in New Testament Studies: Is There a Relationship? *BibInt* 7:28–43.

Haupt, P. 1918. The Coronation of Zerubbabel. *JBL* 37:209–18.

Hays, R. B. 1989. *Echoes of Scripture in the Letters of Paul*. New Haven: Yale University Press.

Hill, A. E. 1982. Dating Second Zechariah: A Linguistic Reexamination. *HAR* 6:105–34.

Himbaza, I. 2004. *Le Decalogue et l'histoire du texte: Etudes des formes textuelles du Decalogue et leurs implications dans l'histoire du texte de l'Ancien Testament*. Fribourg: Academic Press.

Hoffman, Y. 2003. The Fasts in the Book of Zechariah and the Fashioning of National Remembrance. Pages 169–218 in *Judah and the Judeans in the Neo-Babylonian Period*. Edited by O. Lipschitz and J. Blenkinsopp. Winona Lake, Ind.: Eisenbrauns.

Holladay, W. L. 1986. *Jeremiah 1: A Commentary on the Book of the Prophet Jeremiah, Chapters 1–25*. Hermeneia. Philadelphia: Fortress.

———. 1989. *Jeremiah 2: A Commentary on the Book of the Prophet Jeremiah, Chapters 26–52*. Hermeneia. Minneapolis: Fortress.

Hollander, J. 1981. *The Figure of Echo: A Mode of Allusion in Milton and After*. Berkeley: University of California Press.

Hölscher, G. 1924. *Hesekiel: Der Dichter und das Buch. Eine literarkritische Untersuchung*. Giessen: Töpelmann.

Holt, E. K. 1986. Jeremiah's Temple Sermon and the Deuteronomists: An Investigation of the Redactional Relationship Between Jeremiah 7 and 26. *JSOT* 36:73–87.

Hoonacker, A. van. 1908. *Les douze Petits Prophètes: Traduits et commentés*. Paris: J. Gabalda.

Horst, F. 1964. *Die zwolf Kleinen Propheten: Nahum bis Malachi*. 3d ed. Tübingen: J. C. B. Mohr (Paul Siebeck).

Hubbard, D. A. 1989. *Joel and Amos: An Introduction and Commentary*. Leicester: Inter-Varsity.

Hurowitz, V. 1992. *I Have Built You an Exalted House: Temple Building in the Bible in Light of Mesopotamian and Northwest Semitic Writings*. JSOT/ASOR Monograph Series 5. Sheffield: JSOT Press.

———. 1999. Splitting the Sacred Mountain: Zechariah 14:4 and Gilgamesh V, ii 4–5. *Ugarit-Forschungen* 31:241–45.

———. 2003. Restoring the Temple—Why and When? *JQR* 93:581–91.

Hurvitz, A. 1974. Date of the Prose-Tale of Job Linguistically Reconsidered. *HTR* 67: 17–34.

———. 1982. *A Linguistic Study of the Relationship Between the Priestly Source and the Book of Ezekiel: A New Approach to an Old Problem*. Paris: J. Gabalda.

———. 1988. Dating the Priestly Source in Light of the Historical Study of Biblical Hebrew a Century After Wellhausen. *ZAW* 100:88–100.

———. 1995. Terms and Epithets Relating to the Jerusalem Temple Compound in the Book of Chronicles: The Linguistic Aspect. Pages 165–83 in Wright, Freedman and Hurvitz 1995.

———. 1997. The Historical Quest for "Ancient Israel" and the Linguistic Evidence of the Hebrew Bible: Some Methodological Observations. *VT* 47:301–15.

———. 2000. Can Biblical Texts Be Dated Linguistically? Chronological Perspectives in the Historical Study of Biblical Hebrew. Pages 143–60 in Lemaire and Sæbø 2000.

Hyatt, J. P. 1937. A Neo-Babylonian Parallel to Bethel-Sar-Eser, Zech 7:2. *JBL* 56: 387–94.

Iser, W. 1971. Indeterminacy and The Reader's Response. Pages 2–45 in *Aspects of Narrative: Selected Papers from the English Institute*. Edited by J. H. Miller. New York: Columbia University Press.

Jameson, F. 1981. *The Political Unconscious: Narrative as a Socially Symbolic Act*. Ithaca, N.Y.: Cornell University Press.

Janzen, J. G. 1973. *Studies in the Text of Jeremiah*. Cambridge, Mass.: Harvard University Press.

Japhet, S. 1982. Sheshbazzar and Zerubbabel—Against the Background of the Historical and Religious Tendencies of Ezra–Nehemiah. *ZAW* 94:66–98.

———. 1983. Sheshbazzar and Zerubbabel—Against the Background of the Historical and Religious Tendencies of Ezra–Nehemiah: Part II. *ZAW* 95:218–29.

———. 1991a. "History" and "Literature" in the Persian Period: The Restoration of the Temple. Pages 174–88 in *Ah, Assyria: Studies in Assyrian History and Ancient Near*

Eastern Historiography Presented to Hayim Tadmor. Edited by M. Cogan, I. Ephal and H. Tadmor. Jerusalem: Magnes/Hebrew University.

———. 1991b. The Temple in the Restoration Period: Reality and Ideology Tr. S. Weitzman. *USQR* 44:195–251.

Jepsen, A. 1948. Kleine Beitrage zum Zwolfprophetenbuch III. *ZAW* 61:95–114.

Jeremias, C. 1977. *Die Nachtgesichte des Sacharja: Untersuchungen zu ihrer Stellung im Zusammenhang der Visionsberichte im Alten Testament und zu ihrem Bildmaterial*. Göttingen: Vandenhoeck & Ruprecht.

Jeremias, J. 1929. Kephale Gonias. *Zeitschrift fur die Neutestamentliche Wissenschaft* 30:264–80.

———. 1937. Eckstein-Schlussstein. *Zeitschrift fur die Neutestamentliche Wissenschaft* 36:154–57.

Jones, D. R. 1962. *Haggai, Zechariah, and Malachi: Introduction and Commentary*. London: SCM Press.

Joyce, P. M. 1995. Synchronic and Diachronic Perspectives on Ezekiel. Pages 115–28 in de Moor 1995.

Kaiser, O. 1983. *Isaiah 1–12: A Commentary*. 2d ed. London: SCM Press.

Kang, S.-M. 1996. The Authentic Sermon of Jeremiah in Jeremiah 7:1–20. Pages 147–62 in *Texts, Temples, and Traditions: A Tribute to Menahem Haran*. Edited by M. V. Fox. Winona Lake, Ind.: Eisenbrauns.

Kee, M. S. 2007. The Heavenly Council and Its Type-Scene. *JSOT* 31:259–73.

Keil, C. F. 1996. Zechariah. Pages 499–630 in vol. 10 of *Commentary on the Old Testament*. Reprint. Edited by C. F. Keil and F. Delitzsch. Peabody, Mass.: Hendrickson. (Originally published T. & T. Clark, 1866–91.)

Kessler, J. 2002a. *The Book of Haggai: Prophecy and Society in Early Persian Yehud*. Leiden: Brill.

———. 2002b. Building the Second Temple: Questions of Time, Text, and History in Haggai 1.1–15. *JSOT* 27:243–56.

Kline, M. G. 1991. The Structure of the Book of Zechariah. *JETS* 34:179–93.

Kloos, C. J. L. 1975. Zech 2:12: Really a Crux Interpretum? *VT* 25:729–36.

Klouda, S. L. 2002. An Analysis of the Significance of Isaiah's Use of Psalms 96–99. Ph.D. diss., Southwestern Baptist Theological Seminary.

Knibb, M. A. 1982. Prophecy and the Emergence of the Jewish Apocalypses. Pages 155–81 in Coggins, Phillips and Knibb 1982.

Koch, K. 1982. *The Prophets*. London: SCM Press.

Koenig, J. 1982. *L'hermeneutique analogique du Judaisme antique d'apres les temoins textuels d'isaie*. VTSup 33. Leiden: Brill.

Kohn, R. L. 2002. *A New Heart and a New Soul: Ezekiel, the Exile and the Torah*. Sheffield: Sheffield Academic Press.

Kristeva, J. 1969. *Semeiotike: Recherches pour une sémanalyse*. Paris: Seuil.

———. 1980. *Desire in Language: A Semiotic Approach to Literature and Art*. Oxford: Blackwell.

Kristeva, J., and T. Moi. 1986. *The Kristeva Reader*. Oxford: Blackwell.

Kutsko, J. F. 1997. The Presence and Absence of God in the Book of Ezekiel. Ph.D. diss., Harvard University.

Laato, A. 1992. *Josiah and David Redivivus: The Historical Josiah and the Messianic Expectations of Exilic and Postexilic Times*. Stockholm: Almqvist & Wiksell International.

———. 1994. Zachariah 4,6b–10a and the Akkadian Royal Building Inscriptions. *ZAW* 106:53–69.

———. 1996. *History and Ideology in the Old Testament Prophetic Literature: A Semiotic Approach to the Reconstruction of the Proclamation of the Historical Prophets*. Stockholm: Almqvist & Wiksell.

———. 1997. *A Star Is Rising: The Historical Development of the Old Testament Royal Ideology and the Rise of the Jewish Messianic Expectations*. Atlanta: Scholars Press.

Lang, B. 2003. Twelve Commandments—Three Stages: A New Theory on the Formulation of the Decalogue. Pages 290–300 in *Reading from Right to Left: Essays on the Hebrew Bible in Honour of David J. A. Clines*. Edited by J. C. Exum, D. J. A. Clines and H. G. M. Williamson. JSOTSup 373. London: Sheffield Academic Press.

Larkin, K. J. A. 1994. *The Eschatology of Second Zechariah: A Study of the Formation of a Mantological Wisdom Anthology*. Kampen: Kok.

Le Bas, E. E. 1950. Zechariah's Enigmatical Contribution to the Corner-Stone. *PEQ* 82:102–22.

———. 1951. Zechariah's Climax to the Career of the Corner-Stone. *PEQ* 83:139–55.

Lemaire, A. 1996. Zorobabel et la Judée à la Lumière de l'épigraphie (Fin du VI[E] S. Av. J.-C.). *RB* 103:48–57.

Lemaire, A., and M. Sæbø, eds. 2000. *Congress Volume: Oslo, 1998*. VTSup 80. Leiden: Brill.

Lemche, N. P. 1991. The Development of the Israelite Religion in Light of Recent Studies on the Early History of Israel. Pages 97–115 in *Congress Volume: Leuven, 1989*. Leiden: Brill.

———. 1998. *The Israelites in History and Tradition*. London: SPCK.

Leuchter, M. 2006. Tyre's "70 Years" in Isaiah 23,15–18. *Bib* 86:412–17.

Levenson, J. D. 1976. *Theology of the Program of Restoration of Ezekiel 40–48*. Cambridge, Mass.: Scholars Press for the Harvard Semitic Museum.

Lévêque, J. 1981. La Datation du Livre de Job. Pages 206–19 in *Congress Volume: Vienna, 1980*. Edited by J. A. Emerton. VTSup 32. Leiden: Brill.

Levin, S. 1996. Zerubbabel: A Riddle. *JBQ* 24:14–17.

Lewis, T. J. 2005. The Mysterious Disappearance of Zerubbabel. Pages 301–14 in *Seeking Out the Wisdom of the Ancients: Essays Offered to Honor Michael V. Fox on the Occasion of His Sixty-Fifth Birthday*. Edited by R. L. Troxel et al. Winona Lake, Ind.: Eisenbrauns.

Lindblom, J. 1962. *Prophecy in Ancient Israel*. Oxford: Blackwell.

Lipiński, E. 1970. Recherches sur le Livre de Zacharie. *VT* 20:25–55.

Lipton, D. 1999. *Revisions of the Night: Politics and Promises in the Patriarchal Dreams of Genesis*. JSOTSup 288. Sheffield: Sheffield Academic Press.

Love, M. C. 1999. *The Evasive Text: Zechariah 1–8 and the Frustrated Reader*. JSOTSup 296. Sheffield: Sheffield Academic Press.

Lowery, J. M. 1999. The Form and Function of Symbolic Vision Reports in the Hebrew Bible. Ph.D. diss., The Southern Baptist Theological Seminary.

Luckenbill, D. D. 1925. The Black Stone of Esarhaddon. *American Journal of Semitic Languages and Literatures* 41:165–73.

Lundbom, J. R. 1999. *Jeremiah 1–20: A New Translation with Introduction and Commentary*. AB 21A. New York: Doubleday.

———. 2004a. *Jeremiah 21–36: A New Translation with Introduction and Commentary*. AB 21B. New York: Doubleday.

———. 2004b. *Jeremiah 37–52: A New Translation with Introduction and Commentary*. AB 21C. New York: Doubleday.

Lurie, B. Z. 1988/89. The Vision in Zechariah 2:1–9. *Beit Mikra* 34:191–92.

———. 1990/91. What Happened to Zerubbabel? *Beit Mikra* 36:185–89.

MacKay, C. 1968. Zechariah in Relation to Ezekiel 40–48. *EvQ* 40:197–210.

Marenof, S. 1932. Note Concerning the Meaning of the Word "Ephah", Zechariah 5:5–11. *The American Journal of Semitic Languages and Literatures* 48:246–67.

Margalith, O. 1991. The Political Background of Zerubbabel's Mission and the Samaritan Schism. *VT* 41:312–23.

Marinkovic, P. 1994. What Does Zechariah 1–8 Tell Us About the Second Temple? Pages 88–103 in *Second Temple Studies 2*. Edited by T. C. Eskenazi and K. H. Richards. JSOTSup 175. Sheffield: JSOT Press.

Mason, R. A. 1973. The Use of Earlier Biblical Material in Zechariah 9–14: A Study in Inner Biblical Exegesis. Ph.D. diss., University of London. Pages 1–208 in Boda and Floyd 2003.

———. 1976. The Relation of Zech. 9–14 to Proto-Zechariah. *ZAW* 88:227–39.

———. 1977a. *The Books of Haggai, Zechariah and Malachi*. London: Cambridge University Press.

———. 1977b. The Purpose of the "Editorial Framework" of the Book of Haggai. *VT* 27:413–21.

———. 1982a. The Prophets of the Restoration. Pages 137–54 in Coggins, Phillips and Knibb 1982.

———. 1982b. Some Examples of Inner Biblical Exegesis in Zechariah 9–14. Pages 343–54 in *Studia Evangelica*. VII. *Papers Presented to the Fifth International Congress on Biblical Studies Held at Oxford, 1973*. Edited by E. A. Livingstone. Berlin: Akademie Verlag.

———. 1984. Some Echoes of the Preaching in the Second Temple: Tradition Elements in Zechariah 1–8. *ZAW* 96:221–35.

———. 1990. *Preaching the Tradition: Homily and Hermeneutics After the Exile; Based on the Addresses in Chronicles, the Speeches in the Books of Ezra and Nehemiah and the Post-Exilic Prophetic Books*. Cambridge: Cambridge University Press.

———. 1994. *Zephaniah, Habakkuk, Joel*. Old Testament Guides. Sheffield: JSOT Press.

———. 1998. The Messiah in the Postexilic Old Testament Literature. Pages 338–64 in Day 1998.

Mastin, B. A. 1976. Note on Zechariah 6:13. *VT* 26:113–16.

May, H. G. 1938. A Key to the Interpretation of Zechariah's Vision. *JBL* 57:173–84.

McCarthy, C. 1981. *The Tiqqune Sopherim and Other Theological Corrections in the Masoretic Text of the Old Testament*. Freiburg, Schweiz: Universitätsverlag. Göttingen: Vandenhoeck & Ruprecht.

McComiskey, T. E. 1992. *The Minor Prophets: An Exegetical and Expository Commentary*. Grand Rapids: Baker Book House.

McConville, J. G. 1993. *Judgment and Promise: An Interpretation of the Book of Jeremiah*. Leicester: Apollos. Winona Lake, Ind.: Eisenbrauns.

McHardy, W. D. 1968. Horses in Zechariah. Pages 174–79 in *In Memoriam Paul Kahle*. Edited by M. Black and G. Fohrer. Berlin: Töpelmann.

McKane, W. 1986. *A Critical and Exegetical Commentary on Jeremiah*. Edinburgh: T. & T. Clark.

McKay, H. A. 2005. The Horse in Warfare in Ancient Israel. Paper presented at the Annual Meeting of the SBL in Philadelphia, November 2005.

McKay, H. A., and D. J. A. Clines, eds. 1993. *Of Prophets' Visions and the Wisdom of Sages: Essays in Honour of R. Norman Whybray on His Seventieth Birthday*. JSOTSup 162. Sheffield: JSOT Press.

McKeating, H. 1993. *Ezekiel*. Old Testament Guides. Sheffield: JSOT Press.

McKelvey, R. J. 1962. Christ the Cornerstone. *NTS* 8:352–59.

Mein, A. 2001. *Ezekiel and the Ethics of Exile*. Oxford: Oxford University Press.

Meinhold, A. 2001. Serubbabel, der Tempel und die Provinz Jehud. Pages 193–217 in *Steine-Bilder-Texte: Historische Evidenz außerbiblischer und biblischer Quellen*. Edited by C. Hardmeier. Leipzig: Evangelische Verlagsanstalt.

Merrill, E. H. 1994. *Haggai, Zechariah, Malachi: An Exegetical Commentary*. Chicago: Moody.

Mettinger, T. N. D. 1982a. *The Dethronement of Sabaoth: Studies in the Shem and Kabod Theologies*. Lund: Gleerup.

———. 1982b. Yhwh Sabaoth—The Heavenly King on the Cherubim Throne. Pages 108–38 in *Studies in the Period of David and Solomon and Other Essays*. Edited by T. Ishida. Winona Lake, Ind.: Eisenbrauns.

———. 1993. Intertextuality: Allusion and Vertical Context Systems in Some Job Passages. Pages 257–80 in McKay and Clines 1993.

Meyers, C. L. 2003. *The Tabernacle Menorah: A Synthetic Study of a Symbol from the Biblical Cult*. 2d ed. Piscataway, N.J.: Gorgias.

Meyers, C. L., and E. M. Meyers. 1987. *Haggai, Zechariah 1–8: A New Translation with Introduction and Commentary*. AB 25B. Garden City, N.Y.: Doubleday.

———. 1992. Jerusalem and Zion After the Exile: The Evidence of First Zechariah. Pages 121–35 in *Shaarei Talmon*. Edited by M. Fisbane and E. Tov. Winona Lake, Ind.: Eisenbrauns.

———. 1993. *Zechariah 9–14: A New Translation with Introduction and Commentary*. AB 25C. New York: Doubleday.

Meyers, E. M. 1985. The Shelomith Seal and Aspects of the Judean Restoration: Some Additional Reconsiderations. *Eretz-Israel* 17:33–38.

———. 1987. The Persian Period and the Judean Restoration. Pages 509–21 in Miller, McBride and Hanson 1987.

———. 1995. The Crisis of the Mid-Fifth Century BCE: Second Zechariah and the "End" of Prophecy. Pages 713–23 in Wright, Freedman and Hurvitz 1995.

———. 1996. Messianism in First and Second Zechariah and the "End" of Biblical Prophecy. Pages 127–43 in *Go to the Land I Will Show You: Studies in Honor of Dwight W. Young*. Edited by D. W. Young, J. E. Coleson and V. H. Matthews. Winona Lake, Ind.: Eisenbrauns.

Middlemas, J. A. 2005. *The Troubles of Templeless Judah*. Oxford: Oxford University Press.

Millard, A. R. 1995. The Knowledge of Writing in Iron Age Palestine. *TynBul* 46: 207–17.

Miller, J. M., and J. H. Hayes. 1986. *A History of Ancient Israel and Judah*. Philadelphia: Westminster.

Miller, P. D. 1989. The Place of the Decalogue in the Old Testament and Its Law. *Int* 43:229–42.

Miller, P. D., S. D. McBride and P. D. Hanson, eds. 1987. *Ancient Israelite Religion: Essays in Honor of Frank Moore Cross*. Philadelphia: Fortress.

Mitchell, H. G. (with J. M. P. Smith and J. A. Bewer). 1912. *Haggai, Zechariah, Malachi and Jonah: Critical and Exegetical Commentary*. ICC. Edinburgh: T. & T. Clark.

Möhlenbrink, K. 1929. Der Leuchter im funften Nachtgesicht des Propheten Sacharja: Eine archaologische Untersuchung. *Zeitschrift des deutschen Palästina-Vereins* 52:257–86.

Moor, J. C. de, ed. 1995. *Synchronic or Diachronic? A Debate on Method in Old Testament Exegesis: Papers Read at the Ninth Joint Meeting of the Oudtestamentisch Werkgezelschap in Nederland en Belgie and the Society for Old Testament Study, Held at Kampen, 1994*. Leiden: Brill.

———. 1998. *Intertextuality in Ugarit and Israel*. Leiden: Brill.

Mowinckel, S. 1914. *Zur Komposition des Buches Jeremia*. Kristiania: Jacob Dybwad.

———. 1956. *He That Cometh*. Nashville: Abingdon.

Moyise, S. 2000. Intertextuality and the Study of the Old Testament in the New Testament. Pages 14–41 in *Old Testament in the New Testament: Essays in Honour of J. L. North*. Edited by S. Moyise. JSNTSup 189. Sheffield: Sheffield Academic Press.

Mullen, E. T. 1980. *The Divine Council in Canaanite and Early Hebrew Literature*. Chico, Calif.: Scholars Press.

Myers, J. M. 1962. Some Considerations Bearing on the Date of Joel. *ZAW* 74:177–95.

Naudé, J. A. 2003. The Transitions of Biblical Hebrew in the Perspective of Language Change and Diffusion. Pages 189–214 in Young 2003.

Newport, K. G. C. 1990. A Note on the "Seat of Moses" (Matthew 23:2). *AUSS* 28:53–58.

Newsom, C. A. 1996. Bakhtin, the Bible, and Dialogic Truth. *Journal of Religion* 76:290–306.

———. 2002. The Book of Job as Polyphonic Text. *JSOT* 97:87–108.

———. 2003. *The Book of Job: A Contest of Moral Imaginations*. Oxford: Oxford University Press.

Nicholson, E. W. 1970. *Preaching to the Exiles: A Study of the Prose Tradition in the Book of Jeremiah*. Oxford: Blackwell.

Niditch, S. 1983. *The Symbolic Vision in Biblical Tradition*. Chico, Calif.: Scholars Press.

Niehr, H. 1999. Religio-Historical Aspects of the "Early Post Exilic" Period. Pages 228–44 in *The Crisis of Israelite Religion: Transformation of Religious Tradition in Exilic and Post-Exilic Times*. Edited by B. Becking and M. C. A. Korpel. Leiden: Brill.

Nissinen, M. 2002. Prophets and the Divine Council. Pages 4–19 in *Kein Land für sich allein: Studien zum Kulturkontakt in Kanaan, Israel/Palästina und Ebirnari für Manfred Weippert zum 65. Geburtstag*. Edited by U. Hübner, M. Weippert and E. A. Knauf. Freiburg, Schweiz: Universitätsverlag. Göttingen: Vandenhoeck & Ruprecht.

Nogalski, J. D. 1993. *Literary Precursors to the Book of the Twelve*. Berlin: de Gruyter.

———. 1996. Intertextuality and the Twelve. Pages 102–24 in *Forming Prophetic Literature*. Edited by J. W. Watts and P. R. House. Sheffield: Sheffield Academic Press.

North, R. 1970. Zechariah's Seven-Spout Lampstand. *Bib* 51:183–206.

———. 1972. Prophecy to Apocalyptic via Zechariah. Pages 47–71 in *Congress Volume: Uppsala, 1971*. Leiden: Brill.

Nurmela, R. 1996. *Prophets in Dialogue: Inner-Biblical Allusions in Zechariah 1–8 and 9–14*. Åbo: Åbo Akademi University Press.

———. 2003. The Growth of the Book of Isaiah Illustrated by Allusions in Zechariah. Pages 245–59 in Boda and Floyd 2003.

O'Connell, R. H. 1992. Deuteronomy IX 7–X 7, 10–11: Panelled Structure, Double Rehearsal and the Rhetoric of Covenant Rebuke. *VT* 42:492–509.

O'Day, G. R. 1999. Intertextuality. Pages 546–48 in vol. 1 of *Dictionary of Biblical Interpretation*. Edited by J. H. Hayes. Nashville: Abingdon.

Odell, M. S. 2005. *Ezekiel*. Macon, Ga.: Smyth & Helwys.

Ollenburger, B. C. 1987. *Zion the City of the Great King: A Theological Symbol of the Jerusalem Cult*. Sheffield: JSOT Press.

———. 1996. Zechariah. Pages 735–840 in vol. 7 of *NIB*.

Oppenheim, A. L. 1968. The Eyes of the Lord. *JAOS* 88:173–80.

Orr, A. 1956. Seventy Years of Babylon. *VT* 6:304–6.

Park, S. H. 2003. An Examination of the Branch as a Messianic Motif with Attention Given to Branch Symbols on Coinage of the Mediterranean World. Ph.D. diss., Mid-America Baptist Theological Seminary.

Peachey, B. F. 1999. A Horse of a Different Colour: The Horses in Zechariah and Revelation. *ExpTim* 110:214–16.

Person, R. F. 1993. *Second Zechariah and the Deuteronomic School*. JSOTSup 167. Sheffield: JSOT Press.

Petersen, D. L. 1974. Zerubbabel and Jerusalem Temple Reconstruction. *CBQ* 36:366–72.

———. 1984a. *Haggai and Zechariah 1–8: A Commentary*. London: Westminster.

———. 1984b. Zechariah's Visions: A Theological Perspective. *VT* 34:195–206.

———. 1991. The Temple in Persian Period Prophetic Texts. Pages 125–45 in Davies 1991.

———. 2003. Zechariah 9–14: Methodological Reflections. Pages 210–24 in Boda and Floyd 2003.

Petitjean, A. 1969. *Les oracles du Proto-Zacharie: Un programme de restauration pour la communauté juive après l'exil*. Louvain: Impr. orientaliste.

Petterson, A. 2006. Behold Your King: The Hope for the House of David in the Book of Zechariah. Ph.D. diss., Queens University, Belfast.

Plöger, O. 1968. *Theocracy and Eschatology*. Oxford: Blackwell.

Pola, T. 2003a. *Das Priestertum bei Sacharja: Historische und traditionsgeschichtliche Untersuchung zur frühnachexilischen Herrschererwartung*. Tübingen: Mohr Siebeck.

———. 2003b. Form and Meaning in Zechariah 3. Pages 156–67 in Albertz and Becking 2003.

Polzin, R. M. 1976. *Late Biblical Hebrew: Toward an Historical Typology of Biblical Hebrew Prose*. Missoula, Mont.: Scholars Press for Harvard Semitic Museum.

———. 1989. *Samuel and Deuteronomist: A Literary Study of the Deuteronomic History: Part Two—I Samuel*. San Francisco: Harper & Row.

Pomykala, K. 1995. *The Davidic Dynasty Tradition in Early Judaism: Its History and Significance for Messianism*. Atlanta: Scholars Press.

Porten, B. 1968. *Archives from the Elephantine: The Life of an Ancient Jewish Military Colony*. Berkeley: University of California Press.

Powell, M. A. 1995. Do and Keep What Moses Says (Matthew 23:2–7). *JBL* 114:419–35.

Pyeon, Y. 2003. *You Have Not Spoken What Is Right About Me: Intertextuality and the Book of Job*. New York: Peter Lang.

Pyper, H. S. 2005. Reading in the Dark: Zechariah, Daniel and the Difficulty of Scripture. *JSOT* 29:485–504.

Rad, G. von. 1982. *Old Testament Theology*. London: SCM Press.

Redditt, P. L. 1986. The Book of Joel and Peripheral Prophecy. *CBQ* 48:225–40.

———. 1989. Israel's Shepherds: Hope and Pessimism in Zechariah 9–14. *CBQ* 51:631–42.

———. 1992. Zerubbabel, Joshua, and the Night Visions of Zechariah. *CBQ* 54:249–59.

———. 1995. *Haggai, Zechariah and Malachi*. London: Marshall Pickering. Grand Rapids: Eerdmans.

Redditt, P. L., and A. Schart, eds. 2003. *Thematic Threads in the Book of the Twelve*. BZAW 325. Berlin: de Gruyter.

Rendsburg, G. A. 2002. Hebrew Philological Notes (III). *HS* 43:21–30.

Renz, T. 2002. *The Rhetorical Function of the Book of Ezekiel*. Boston: Brill.

Reventlow, H. G. 1992. Tradition und Aktualisierung in Sacharjas siebentem Nachtgesicht: Sach 6,1–8. Pages 180–90 in *Alttestamentlicher Glaube und biblische Theologie*. Edited by J. Hausmann and H.-J. Zobel. Stuttgart: Kohlhammer.

———. 1993. *Die Propheten Haggai, Sacharja und Maleachi*. Rev. ed. Göttingen: Vandenhoeck & Ruprecht.

Richter, H. F. 1986. Die Pferde in den Nachtgesichten des Sacharja. *ZAW* 98:96–100.

Riffaterre, M. 1978. *Semiotics of Poetry*. Bloomington: Indiana University Press.

Rignell, L. G. 1950. *Die Nachtgesichte des Sacharja: Eine exegetische Studie*. Lund: C. W. K. Gleerup.

Robinson, G. L. 1895. The Prophecies of Zechariah with Special Reference to the Origin and Date of Chapters 9–14. *The American Journal of Semitic Languages and Literatures* 12:1–92.

Rooke, D. W. 1998. Kingship as Priesthood: The Relationship Between the High Priesthood and the Monarchy. Pages 187–208 in Day 1998.

———. 2000. *Zadok's Heirs: The Role and Development of the High Priesthood in Ancient Israel*. Oxford: Oxford University Press.

Rooker, M. F. 2003. *Studies in Hebrew Language, Intertextuality, and Theology*. Lewiston, N.Y.: Edwin Mellen.

Albertz and Becking 2003.

Rose, W. H. 2000. *Zemah and Zerubbabel: Messianic Expectations in the Early Postexilic Period*. JSOTSup 304. Sheffield: Sheffield Academic Press.

———. 2003. Messianic Expectations in the Early Postexilic Period. Pages 168–85 in Rost, L. 1951. Bemerkungen zu Sacharja 4. *ZAW* 63:216–21.

Roth, C. 1949. The "Chair of Moses" and Its Survivals. *PEQ* 81:100–11.

Rothstein, J. W. 1910. *Die Nachtgesichte des Sacharja: Studien zur Sacharjaprophetie und zur jüdischen Geschichte im ersten nachexilischen Jahrhundert*. Leipzig: J. C. Hinrichs.

Rudman, D. 2000. Zechariah 5 and the Priestly Law. *SJOT* 14:194–206.

———. 2001. Zechariah 8:20–22 and Isaiah 2:2–4//Micah 4:2–3: A Study in Intertextuality. *BN* 107–8:50–54.

———. 2003. A Note on Zechariah 1:5. *JNSL* 29:33–39.

Rudolph, W. 1976. *Haggai, Sacharja 1–8, Sacharja 9–14, Maleachi*. Gütersloh: Gütersloher Verlagshaus Mohn.

Sanders, J. A. 1999. Intertextuality and Canon. Pages 316–33 in *On the Way to Nineveh: Studies in Honor of George M. Landes*. Edited by S. L. Cook and S. C. Winter. Atlanta: Scholars Press.

———. 2000. Canon as Dialogue. Pages 7–26 in *The Bible at Qumran: Text, Shape, and Interpretation*. Edited by P. W. Flint and T. H. Kim. Grand Rapids: Eerdmans.

Sauer, G. 1967. Serubbabel in der Sicht Haggais und Sacharjas. Pages 199–207 in *Ferne und Nahe Wort: Festschrift Leonard Rost*. Edited by F. Maass. Berlin: Töpelmann.

Schaefer, K. R. 1993. Zechariah 14 and the Composition of the Book of Zechariah. *RB* 100:368–98.

Schmid, K. 2000. Innerbiblische Schriftauslegung. Aspekte der Forschungsgeschichte. Pages 1–22 in *Schriftauslegung in der Schrift. Festschrift für Odil Hannes Steck zu seinem 65. Geburtstag*. Edited by R. G. Kratz, T. Krüger and K. Schmid. BZAW 300. Berlin: de Gruyter.

Schmid, K., and O. H. Steck. 2001. Restoration Expectations in the Prophetic Tradition of the Old Testament. Pages 41–81 in *Restoration: Old Testament, Jewish and Christian Perspectives*. Edited by J. M. Scott. Leiden: Brill.

Schniedewind, W. M. 2004. *How the Bible Became a Book: The Textualization of Ancient Israel*. Cambridge: Cambridge University Press.

Schnocks, J. 1996. Eine intertextuelle Verbindung zwischen Ezechiels Eifersuchtsbild und Sacharjas Frau im Efa. *BN* 84:59–63.

Schöttler, H.-G. 1987. *Gott inmitten seines Volkes: Die Neuordnung des Gottesvolkes nach Sacharja 1–6*. Trier: Paulinus-Verlag.

Schultz, R. L. 1999. *The Search for Quotation: Verbal Parallels in the Prophets*. JSOTSup 180. Sheffield: Sheffield Academic Press.

———. 2003. The Ties That Bind: Intertextuality, the Identification of Verbal Parallels, and Reading Strategies in the Book of the Twelve. Pages 27–45 in Redditt and Schart 2003.

Scott, R. B. Y. 1949. Secondary Meanings of *ʾaḥar*: After, Behind. *JTS* 50:178–79.

Segal, B.-Z., and G. Levi, eds. 1990. *The Ten Commandments in History and Tradition*. Jerusalem, Magnes/Hebrew University

Seitz, C. R. 1990. The Divine Council Temporal Transition and New Prophecy in the Book of Isaiah. *JBL* 109:229–47.

———. 1994. The Book of Isaiah 40–66. Pages 307–552 in vol. 4 of *NIB*.

Sellin, E. 1922. *Das Zwölfprophetenbuch*. Leipzig: A. Deichertsche.

———. 1931. Der Stein des Sacharja. *JBL* 50:242–49.

———. 1942/43. Noch Einmal der Stein des Sacharja. *ZAW* 59:59–77.

Seybold, K. 1974a. *Bilder zum Tempelbau: Die Visionen des Propheten Sacharja*. Stuttgart: KBW Verlag.

———. 1974b. Die Bildmotive in den Visionen des Propheten Sacharja. Pages 92–110 in *Studies on Prophecy*. Leiden: Brill.

Shead, A. G. 2002. *The Open Book and the Sealed Book: Jeremiah 32 in Its Hebrew and Greek Recensions*. JSOTSup 347. Sheffield: Sheffield Academic Press.

Siebeneck, R. T. 1957. Messianism of Aggeus and Proto-Zacharias. *CBQ* 19:312–28.

Siegert, F. 2004. Christus, der "Eckstein", und Sein Unterbau: Eine Entdeckung an 1 Petr 2.6f. *NTS* 50:139–46.

Sinclair, L. A. 1975. Redaction of Zechariah 1–8. *BR* 20:36–47.

Smith, M. 1987. *Palestinian Parties and Politics that Shaped the Old Testament*. 2d ed. London: SCM Press.

Smith, P. A. 1995. *Rhetoric and Redaction in Trito-Isaiah: The Structure, Growth, and Authorship of Isaiah 56–66*. Leiden: Brill.
Smith, R. L. 1984. *Micah–Malachi*. Waco, Tex.: Word.
Snaith, N. H., and H. M. Orlinsky. 1967. *Studies on the Second Part of the Book of Isaiah*. Leiden: Brill.
Snyman, G. 1996. Who Is Speaking? Intertextuality and Textual Influence. *Neotestamentica* 30, no. 2:427–49.
Soderlund, S. 1985. *The Greek Text of Jeremiah: A Revised Hypothesis*. JSOTSup 47. Sheffield: JSOT Press.
Soggin, J. A. 1989. *Introduction to the Old Testament: From Its Origins to the Closing of the Alexandrian Canon*. 3d ed. London: SCM Press.
Sommer, B. D. 1996a. Allusions and Illusions: The Unity of the Book of Isaiah in Light of Deutero-Isaiah's Use of the Prophetic Tradition. Pages 156–87 in *New Visions of Isaiah*. Edited by R. F. Melugin and M. A. Sweeney. JSOTSup 214. Sheffield: Sheffield Academic Press.
———. 1996b. Did Prophecy Cease? Evaluating a Reevaluation. *JBL* 115:31–47.
———. 1996c. Exegesis, Allusion and Intertextuality in the Hebrew Bible: A Response to Lyle Eslinger. *VT* 46:479–89.
———. 1998. *A Prophet Reads Scripture: Allusion in Isaiah 40–66*. Stanford: Stanford University Press.
Sperber, A. 1992. *The Bible in Aramaic*. 2d Impression. Leiden: Brill.
Stade, B. 1881. Deuterozacharja: Eine Kritische Studie. *ZAW* 1:1–96.
———. 1882a. Deuterozacharja: Eine Kritische Studie. *ZAW* 2:151–72.
———. 1882b. Deuterozacharja: Eine Kritische Studie. *ZAW* 2:275–309.
Stead, M. R. 2007. Zechariah and the "Former Prophets": An Intertextual Examination of the Re-use of the Prophetic Tradition in Zechariah 1–8. Ph.D. diss., University of Gloucestershire.
———. 2009. Sustained Allusion in Zechariah 1–2. Pages 144–70 in Boda and Floyd 2009.
Steck, O. H. 1991a. *Studien zu Tritojesaja*. Berlin: de Gruyter.
———. 1991b. Tritojesaja im Jesajabuch. Pages 3–45 in Steck 1991a.
———. 2000. *The Prophetic Books and Their Theological Witness*. St. Louis, Mo.: Chalice.
Stephenson, F. R. 1969. The Date of the Book of Joel. *VT* 19:224–29.
Strand, K. A. 1982. The Two Olive Trees of Zechariah 4 and Revelation 11. *AUSS* 20:257–61.
Strauss, H. 1999. (ה)שׁמן in den Traditionen des hebräischen Kanons. *ZAW* 111:256–58.
Stravrakopoulou, F. 2005. The Blackballing of Manasseh. Pages 248–63 in *Good Kings and Bad Kings*. Edited by L. L. Grabbe. LHBOTS 393. ESM 5. London: T&T Clark International.
Stuhlmueller, C. 1988. *Rebuilding with Hope: A Commentary on the Books of Haggai and Zechariah*. Grand Rapids: Eerdmans.
Sukenik, E. L. 1934. *Ancient Synagogues in Palestine and Greece*. London: Oxford University Press.
Süring, M. L. 1980. *The Horn-Motif in the Hebrew Bible and Related Near Eastern Literature and Iconography*. Berrien Springs, Mich.: Andrews University Press.
———. 1985. The Horn-Motifs of the Bible and the Ancient Near East. *AUSS* 22: 327–40.

Sweeney, M. A. 1996. *Isaiah 1–39: With an Introduction to Prophetic Literature*. FOTL. Grand Rapids: Eerdmans.

———. 2000. *The Twelve Prophets: Micah, Nahum, Habakkuk, Zephaniah, Haggai, Zechariah, Malachi*. Collegeville, Minn.: Liturgical.

———. 2003. The Place and Function of Joel in the Book of the Twelve. Pages 133–54 in Redditt and Schart 2003.

Sykes, S. 1997a. Time and Space in Haggai–Zechariah 1–8: A Bakhtinian Analysis of a Prophetic Chronicle. *JSOT* 76:97–124.

———. 1997b. Time and Space in Haggai–Zechariah 1–8: A Bakhtinian Analysis of a Prophetic Chronicle. Ph.D. diss., Union Theological Seminary.

Tai, N. H. F. 1996. *Prophetie als Schriftauslegung in Sacharja 9–14: Traditions- und Kompositionsgeschichtliche Studien*. Stuttgart: Calwer.

Talstra, E. 1991. Hebrew Syntax: Clause Types and Clause Hierarchy. Pages 180–93 in *Studies in Hebrew and Aramaic Syntax: Presented to Professor J. Hoftijzer on the Occasion of His Sixty-Fifth Birthday*. Edited by L. van Rompay, H. L. Murre-van den Berg and J. Hoftijzer. Leiden: Brill.

———. 1992. Text Grammar and Computer: The Balance of Interpretation and Calculation. Pages 135–49 in *Actes du troisième Colloque international Bible et informatique: Interprétation, herméneutique, competence informatique = Proceedings of the Third International Colloquium Bible and Computer: Interpretation, Hermeneutics, Expertise: Tübingen, 26–30 August 1991*. Association internationale Bible et informatique. Paris: Champion. Geneva: Slatkine.

———. 1995. Deuteronomy 9 and 10: Synchronic and Diachronic Observations. Pages 187–210 in de Moor 1995.

Tanner, B. L. 2001. *The Book of Psalms Through the Lens of Intertextuality*. New York: Peter Lang.

Thiel, W. 1973. *Die seuteronomistische Redaktion von Jeremia 1–25*. Neukirchen–Vluyn: Neukirchener Verlag.

———. 1981. *Die deuteronomistische Redaktion von Jeremia 26–45: Mit einer Gesamtbeurteilung der deuteronomistischen Redaktion des Buches Jeremia*. Neukirchen–Vluyn: Neukirchener Verlag.

Thiselton, A. C. 1992. *New Horizons in Hermeneutics: The Theory and Practice of Transforming Biblical Readings*. Grand Rapids: Zondervan.

Thompson, J. A. 1974. The Date of Joel. Pages 453–64 in *A Light Unto My Path: Old Testament Studies in Honor of Jacob M. Myers*. Edited by H. N. Bream, R. D. Heim and C. A. Moore. Philadelphia: Temple University Press.

Thompson, T. L. 1999. *The Bible in History: How Writers Create a Past*. London: Jonathan Cape.

Tidwell, N. L. A. 1975. Waʾomar (Zech 3:5) and the Genre of Zechariah's Fourth Vision. *JBL* 94:343–55.

Tiemeyer, L.-S. 2003. The Guilty Priesthood (Zech 3). Pages 1–19 in *The Book of Zechariah and Its Influence*. Edited by C. M. Tuckett. Aldershot: Ashgate.

———. 2004. Compelled by Honour—A New Interpretation of Zechariah ii 12a (8a). *VT* 54:352–72.

———. 2006a. A Busy Night at the Heavenly Court. *Svensk Exegetisk Årsbok* 71: 187–207.

———. 2006b. *Priestly Rites and Prophetic Rage: Post-Exilic Prophetic Critique of the Priesthood*. Tübingen: Mohr Siebeck.

Tigchelaar, E. J. C. 1996. *Prophets of Old and the Day of the End: Zechariah, the Book of Watchers and Apocalyptic*. Leiden: Brill.

Tollington, J. A. 1993. *Tradition and Innovation in Haggai and Zechariah 1–8*. JSOTSup 150. Sheffield: JSOT Press.

Torrey, C. C. 1930. *Pseudo-Ezekiel and the Original Prophecy*. New Haven: Yale University Press.

Tov, E. 1981. Aspects of the Textual and Literary History of the Book of Jeremiah. Pages 145–67 in *Le Livre de Jérémie*. Edited by P.-M. Bogaert. Leuven: Leuven University Press.

———. 1985. The Literary History of the Book of Jeremiah in the Light of Its Textual History. Pages 211–37 in *Empirical Models for Biblical Criticism*. Edited by J. H. Tigay. Philadelphia: University of Pennsylvania Press.

———. 1997. *The Text-Critical Use of the Septuagint in Biblical Research*. Jerusalem: Simor.

Tov, E. (with R. A. Kraft and P. J. Parsons). 1990. *The Greek Minor Prophets Scroll from Nahal Hever: 8 Hev XII gr*. Oxford: Oxford University Press. New York: Clarendon.

Treves, M. 1957. The Date of Joel. *VT* 7:149–56.

Tuell, S. S. 1992. *The Law of the Temple in Ezekiel 40–48*. Atlanta: Scholars Press.

Tull, P. K. 2000a. Intertextuality and the Hebrew Scriptures. *CurBS* 8:59–90.

———. 2000b. The Rhetoric of Recollection. Pages 71–78 in Lemaire and Sæbø 2000.

Uehlinger, C. 1994. Die Frau im Efa (Sach 5,5–11): Eine Programmvision von der Abschiebung der Gottin. *BK* 49:93–103.

Unterman, J. 1987. *From Repentance to Redemption: Jeremiah's Thought in Transition*. JSOTSup 54. Sheffield: JSOT Press.

Van Seters, J. 1997. The Chronicler's Account of Solomon's Temple Building. Pages 283–99 in Graham, Hoglund and McKenzie 1997.

VanderKam, J. C. 1991. Joshua the High Priest and the Interpretation of Zechariah 3. *CBQ* 53:553–70.

———. 2004. *From Joshua to Caiaphas: High Priests After the Exile*. Minneapolis: Fortress.

Vanhoozer, K. J. 2001. From Speech Acts to Scripture Acts. Pages 1–49 in *After Pentecost: Language and Biblical Interpretation*. Edited by C. G. Bartholomew, C. Greene and K. Möller. Carlisle: Paternoster.

Viberg, A. 2000. An Elusive Crown: An Analysis of the Performance of a Prophetic Symbolic Act (Zech 6:9–15). *Svensk Exegetisk Årsbok* 65:161–69.

Wallis, G. 1972. Erwagungen zu Sacharja VI 9–15. Pages 232–37 in *Congress Volume: Uppsala, 1971*. Leiden: Brill.

Waterman, L. 1954. The Camouflaged Purge of Three Messianic Conspirators. *JNES* 13:73–78.

Watts, J. D. W. 1972. Zechariah. Pages 308–65 in *Broadman Bible Commentary*. Vol. 7, *Hosea–Malachi*. Edited by C. J. Allen. Nashville: Broadman.

Webb, B. G. 1987. *The Book of the Judges: An Integrated Reading*. JSOTSup 46. Sheffield: JSOT Press.

———. 1990. Zion in Transformation: A Literary Approach to Isaiah. Pages 65–84 in *The Bible in Three Dimensions: Essays in Celebration of Forty Years of Biblical Studies in the University of Sheffield*. Edited by D. J. A. Clines, S. E. Fowl and S. E. Porter. JSOTSup 87. Sheffield: JSOT Press.

———. 2003. *The Message of Zechariah: Your Kingdom Come*. Leicester: Inter-Varsity.

Weinberg, J. P. 1992. *The Citizen-Temple Community*. JSOTSup 151. Sheffield: JSOT Press.

Weiss, M. 1990. Ten Commandments in History and Tradition. Pages 67–81 in Segal and Levi 1990.

Wellhausen, J. 1885. *Prolegomena to the History of Israel*. Edinburgh: Black.

———. 1903. Zechariah. Pages 5391–95 in *Encyclopaedia Biblica*. Edited by T. Cheyne. London: Black.

———. 1963. *Die kleinen Propheten übersetzt und erklärt*. Reprint of 3d ed. Berlin: de Gruyter.

Westermann, C. 1969. *Isaiah 40–66: A Commentary*. London: SCM Press.

Wevers, J. W. 1969. *Ezekiel*. NCBC. London: Nelson.

Whitley, C. F. 1954. The Term Seventy Years Captivity. *VT* 4:60–72.

Willey, P. T. 1997. *Remember the Former Things: The Recollection of Previous Texts in Second Isaiah*. Atlanta: Scholars Press.

Williamson, H. G. M. 1985. *Ezra, Nehemiah*. WBC 16. Waco, Tex.: Word.

———. 1988. The Governors of Judah under the Persians. *TynBul* 39:77–82.

Willi-Plein, I. 1974. *Prophetie am Ende: Untersuchungen zu Sacharja 9–14*. Bonner biblische Beitrage 42. Köln: P. Hanstein.

Winkle, R. E. 1987. Jeremiah's Seventy Years for Babylon: A Re-assessment: Part 2, The Historical Data. *AUSS* 25:289–99.

Wolff, H. W. 1977. *Joel and Amos: A Commentary on the Books of the Prophets Joel and Amos*. Philadelphia: Fortress.

Wolters, A. 2000. Word Play in Zechariah. Pages 223–30 in *Puns and Pundits*. Edited by S. B. Noegel. Bethesda, Md.: CDL.

———. 2009. The Whole Earth Remains at Peace" (Zech 1:11): The Problem and an Intertextual Clue. Pages 128–43 in Boda and Floyd 2009.

Worton, M., and J. Still. 1990. *Intertextuality: Theories and Practices*. Manchester: Manchester University Press. New York: St. Martin's.

Woude, A. S. van der. 1974. Die beiden Sohne des Ols (Sach 4:14): Messianische Gestalten. Pages 262–68 in *Travels in the World of the Old Testament*. Edited by M. S. H. G. Heerma van Voss, P. H. J. Houwink ten Cate and N. A. van Uchelen. Assen: Van Gorcum.

———. 1980. Seid nicht wie eure Vater! Bemerkungen zu Sacharja 1:5 und seinem Kontext. Pages 163–73 in *Prophecy*. Edited by J. A. Emerton. Berlin: de Gruyter.

———. 1988. Zion as Primeval Stone in Zechariah 3 and 4. Pages 237–48 in *Text and Context: Old Testament and Semitic Studies for F. C. Fensham*. Edited by W. Claassen. JSOTSup 48. Sheffield: JSOT Press.

Wright, D. P. 1987. *The Disposal of Impurity: Elimination Rites in the Bible and in Hittite and Mesopotamian Literature*. Atlanta: Scholars Press.

Wright, D. P., D. N. Freedman and A. Hurvitz, eds. 1995. *Pomegranates and Golden Bells: Studies in Biblical, Jewish, and Near Eastern Ritual, Law, and Literature in Honor of Jacob Milgrom*. Winona Lake, Ind.: Eisenbrauns.

Young, I., ed. 2003. *Biblical Hebrew: Studies in Chronology and Typology*. JSOTSup 369. London: T&T Clark International.

———. 2005. Biblical Texts Cannot Be Dated Linguistically. *HS* 46:341–51.

Zimmerli, W. 1979. *Ezekiel: A Commentary on the Book of the Prophet Ezekiel*. Philadelphia: Fortress.

———. 1983. *Ezekiel 2: A Commentary on the Book of the Prophet Ezekiel, Chapters 25–48*. Philadelphia: Fortress.

Zorn, J. R. 1993. Mesopotamian-Style Ceramic "Bathtub" Coffins from Tell En-Nasbeh. *TA* 20:216–24.

———. 1997. More on Mesopotamian Burial Practices in Ancient Israel. *IEJ* 47:214–19.

INDEXES

INDEX OF REFERENCES

Index of Authors